1001 QUESTIONS ANSWERED ABOUT FLOWERS

Norman Taylor

ILLUSTRATIONS BY
JAMES MACDONALD

DOVER PUBLICATIONS, INC.
New York

To

M. S. T.

who suggested questions I

might have ignored

Published in Canada by General Publishing Company, Ltd., 30 Lesmill Road, Don Mills, Toronto, Ontario.

Published in the United Kingdom by Constable and Company, Ltd., 3 The Lanchesters, 162-164 Fulham Palace Road, London W6 9ER.

Bibliographical Note

This Dover edition, first published in 1996, is a slightly altered republication of the work originally published by Dodd, Mead & Company, New York, in 1963. For the Dover edition the photographs, each of which appeared on a separate page in the original, have been reduced and printed two to a page. The Dover edition also includes some minor corrections to the text.

Library of Congress Cataloging-in-Publication Data

Taylor, Norman, 1883–

1001 questions answered about flowers / Norman Taylor ; illustrations by James MacDonald.

p.   cm.

Originally published: New York : Dodd, Mead, 1963. With slight modifications.

Includes index.

ISBN 0-486-29099-9 (pbk.)

1. Flowers—Miscellanea. 2. Plants—Miscellanea. 3. Flowers—United States—Miscellanea. 4. Plants—United States—Miscellanea. I. MacDonald, James. II. Title.

QK50.T39   1996

582.13—dc20   95–44998
                                                                    CIP

Manufactured in the United States of America
Dover Publications, Inc., 31 East 2nd Street, Mineola, N.Y. 11501

CONTENTS

PHOTOGRAPHS

I. FORM AND FUNCTION
OF FLOWERS

The form, function and structure of flowers are so fundamental that this first section is devoted to these subjects. Scarcely less important is the intimate relationship between insects and flowers for upon it the survival of most plants is utterly dependent. While many flowers set colorful and fragrant traps to lure their much-needed insect visitors, there are others which invite them with a more sinister result—the death of the insect. These insect-destroyers are often called carnivorous plants because, like an animal, they capture and eat their victims, not tiger-like in ferocity but just as deadly.

1. What is a flower? So simple a question would scarcely need an answer if flowers were only just as simple. Actually they are extremely complex and it would cater to the vanity of the sentimentalist if we could say that they were created only for our enjoyment—their alluring forms, their color and frequently their quite seductive odor. But such a concept is fantastically false. The true function of flowers is reproduction and nothing else, and upon the sex life of flowers our very existence depends. Without it there would be no wheat or rice, no coffee or chocolate, no timber or cotton, no quinine or digitalis, and in a few years the earth would return to something like its reputed condition in the first chapters of Genesis.

2. In what does the sex life of flowers consist? Basically it is very like the reproductive process in man or any other animal. Male and female must be brought together at the proper time in order that fertilization may be completed to perpetuate the race.

3. How do flowers accomplish this? While the sex organs of flowers are their most essential organs, they do not usually stand naked and their arrangement within the flower is neither an accident nor has nature left these delicate sex organs without proper protection. To understand their arrangement it is necessary to look at a typical flower rather carefully.

Just beneath the showy petals is a usually greenish envelope known as a *calyx* which is often divided into individual *sepals*. This calyx usually covers the flower while it is still in bud, and even after the flower opens is still the outer envelope of normal flowers. The next inner circle of organs comprise the *petals,* which are sometimes of separate segments, as in a pink, but are quite often united to form a cup-shaped *corolla,* as in the lily-of-the-valley.

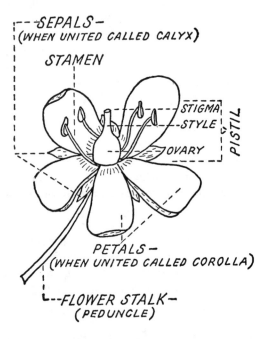

Within these outer envelopes of calyx and corolla are placed the sex organs. They consist, usually of a central female organ, including an *ovary,* clustered around which are the male organs or *stamens.* These produce the familiar yellow "dust," which is the male fertilizing pollen. This, at the proper time, must be deposited upon the prolongation of the ovary (known as the *style* and *stigma*). This usually happens when the stigma is slightly sticky. What is called *pollination* is then completed, and the stage is set for the *fertilization* of the ovules. It is these fertilized ovules (future seeds) within the ovary (the future fruit) that ensure the perpetuation of nearly all flowers.

4. Are the answers to Questions 2 and 3 an oversimplification of the facts? Most decidedly! There are perhaps 150,000 different kinds of flowering plants in the world of infinite variation in the shape and arrangement of the essential organs, in the number of their petals, in whether or not they have a united corolla or separate petals, whether the corolla is "regular," *i.e.* nearly symmetrical, like a wild rose, or "irregular," *i.e.* somewhat lopsided like a snapdragon or sweet pea. Then, too, nature appears to delight in creating exceptions. In some flowers there are no petals, in others both calyx and corolla are lacking. Some flowers bear only male organs, the female being borne on separate plants, which are then *dioecious,* as in the holly and pussy willow. In others the male and female organs are in separate flowers both borne on the same plant, as in the walnuts and oaks; these are said to be *monoecious.* It is obvious, then, that flowers are not so simple as they seem and that nature has left us with not only bewildering complexity but many exceptions to the "typical" flower outlined in Question 3. Some examples of these exceptions are noted in the next few questions.

5. What is an example of a common eastern wildflower that has no petals? The beautiful Mayflower (*Hepatica americana*), which blooms in early May has no petals. Lacking these, its sepals are colored

The Mayflower (*Hepatica americana*), which has no petals, is one of the earliest wild flowers to bloom.

like petals and serve the same function, *i.e.* to attract the insects that will pollinate it. The *Hepatica* is called by various other names in different sections of the country, as blue anemone, liverwort and kidneywort. Its leaves being liver-shaped it was named with the Greek word for liver (*Hepatica*). It is easily cultivated in a woodsy soil under partial shade.

6. Are any flowers pollinated by birds?   Yes, especially in the tropics. A common example is the silk tree (*Albizzia Julibrissin*), often incorrectly called mimosa. This handsome tree from the eastern Mediterranean, much cultivated in the South, has small pinkish flowers crowded into a cluster resembling a powder puff. In June and July hummingbirds hover, and in seeking the nectar drive their slender bills into the heart of the cluster. In doing this they unwittingly deposit the pollen on the stigma and pollination is completed. *Julibrissin* is the Persian vernacular for the tree.

7. Is any flower pollinated by a snail?   In nature self-fertilization of a flower appears to be very rare, judging by the elaborate devices that flowers produce to ensure cross-fertilization, *i.e.* the bringing to a flower the pollen from a similar but separate one, hence ensuring that it is never pollinated with its own pollen. Mostly this is accomplished by insects, especially bees and butterflies, which constantly flit from flower to flower, and inevitably carry a load of pollen. But sometimes flowers have such a stinking odor that no insect will go anywhere near it. The most remarkable of these flowers that are avoided by all insects is an East Indian arum, allied to our jack-in-the-pulpit. It produces a club-shaped flower cluster, comprising hundreds of tiny flowers, the male below and the female above. A snail which is native to the region would be a voracious eater of the foliage of this arum, but the plant has a diabolical trap. At the tip of the flowering column the plant secretes a sweetish, sticky substance, but only when the male flowers are ready. This delectable sweet is far more attractive to the snail than the foliage, and as it crawls up the flowering column, it scrapes off the pollen and deposits it on the receptive females just before it reaches its sugary goal. The denouement is tragic. The sweet substance is violently poisonous, and the snail quickly dies. The quite devilish arum thus destroys its foliage eater, but only after the victim has ensured pollination.

8. Is pollen light enough to be carried by the wind?   Most pollen is not, for it is generally sticky enough to cling to the body of a visiting insect. But some plants, perhaps because their flowers have no showy petals, have pollen of such a consistency that it is easily carried considerable distances by the wind. One sea captain collected pine pollen eighty miles out to sea from a pine forest. All the catkin-bearing trees—such as oaks, beech, birch, walnut, hickory, willow and poplar—depend entirely on the wind for cross-pollination. The same is true of all the grasses, including corn, wheat, rice and thousands of others. One of the most beautiful is the famous pampas grass (*Cortaderia Selloana*) of the Argentine. The showy terminal plumes are like "a waving sea of silver" and their pollen is completely wind-borne. Of course the wastage of wind-scattered pollen is enormous, as only if it lands on a receptive female can it be of any use.

9. Are any plants pollinated by water?   Many aquatics are. Among these is the the legendary eelgrass (*Vallisneria spiralis*), sometimes called tapegrass. This is so romantic that Maurice Maeterlinck in his *Intelligence of the Flowers* devoted a whole section of the book to its extraordinary nuptials. The plant is rooted in the mud and has long tape-like leaves that sway in every current of the water. Its flowers are very tiny, and the sexes are separate. The male flowers lie almost flat on the mud; the females grow on long coiling stems that just permit the flowers to float on the surface. By a marvellously timed operation the male flowers with their pollen become detached from their submerged stalks and are so bouyant that they float to the already receptive female flower. After pollination is completed, the male flowers float off to destruction. The female flowers slowly contract their coiling stalk and finally reaching the mud, mature the fruit of what Maeterlinck called "this heroic kiss."

10. Are there flowers that appear to be unfriendly to their insect visitors?   One of the unkindest is the Dutchman's pipe (*Aristolochia durior*) often called the pipe vine. It is a rampant native of eastern North America with large, handsome leaves useful for trellises. Its flower is of very peculiar structure; it has the form of a hollow tube bent from its stalk first downward and then upward, and ending in a three-lobed lip or doorway, through which insects enter, attracted by its vile odor. The insect finally reaches the bottom of the curved part of the flower. Above him there is only the entrance way, for in the other part of the flower are the stamens and stigma. (See Question 3.) The stigma matures some time before its own pollen is ripe so that self-fertilization is impossible. The visiting insect, always pollen-laden, pollinates the receptive stigma and naturally seeks its way out. But the Dutchman's pipe is not through with it. The insect tries flying out but is impeded by the angle of the entrance doorway and falls back exhausted to the bottom of the bent tube, whose sides are too smooth to permit crawling out. After frantic efforts to escape and stirring up a cloud of pollen, which matures before his final release, the now pollen-laden insect crawls out of his trap because the pipe vine has no further use for the insect. The vine provides a now wrinkled and nearly withered tube up which the exhausted insect easily crawls to freedom. Cross-fertilization is thus not only necessary but certain, even if it is a little tough on the visitor.

11. What is "mimosa"?   An incorrect but widely used name for the silk tree, which is pollinated by hummingbirds. (See Question 6.)

12. What is the blue anemone?   It is a local name for the May-flower or hepatica. (See Question 5.)

13. Are liverworts and kidneyworts the same?   Yes, both are local names for the Mayflower or hepatica. (See Question 5.)

14. What is tapegrass?   A submerged aquatic more often called eel-grass. (See Question 9.)

15. What is the pipe vine?   Another name for the Dutchman's pipe, whose flowers are quite unkind to visiting insects. (See Question 10.)

16. Are there any flowers that prevent cross-fertilization?   Yes, quite a few. Some of our native violets (*Viola*) accomplish this by bearing two sorts of flowers, the showy ones that everyone knows, and small, almost hidden ones, borne at ground level, which never open until the drama is completed. The showy upper violets are often functionless and produce little or no seed. But the basal ones, inconspicuous and without obvious petals, are so tightly closed that self-fertilization is imperative. The pod ultimately splits open and releases more seed than is ever produced by the showy flowers. These permanently closed flowers are technically called *cleistogamous* flowers, a word derived from Greek, meaning "closed marriage."

17. Is there a flower that taps an insect visitor hard enough to frighten it off?   The European barberry (*Berberis vulgaris*), often grown in American gardens is a shrub whose flowers provide a tapping device just strong enough to drive a bee out of its flower, but only when cross-fertilization has been guaranteed. The flower is so constructed that the six stamens, which are partly covered by the curved tips of the petals, each fits into a small socket. A bee visitor, laden with foreign pollen, must strike the receptive stigma *before* it reaches the nectar at the bottom of the flower and without touching the stamens. But at the moment it forces its proboscis into the nectar it cannot avoid hitting the broadened bases of the stamens. Instantaneously two pollen-laden stamens dart out of their sockets and give the bee two smart pollen-dusted taps. Scarcely any bee fails to take the hint. In other words he comes into the flower dusted with foreign pollen and leaves it with a fresh dose, to repeat the process of cross-fertilization. Many other plants have analogous mechanisms.

18. What flower provides a warm room for its insect visitors? Many flowers do this and one of the most interesting is the huge, white, waxy flower of our evergreen magnolia (*Magnolia grandiflora*) a native of the southeastern United States and often called the bull-bay. Its beautiful white flowers bloom in June when the nights are cool, and certain insects, laden with foreign pollen find a snug shelter under the three inner petals. These are arched over the already receptive stigma and the insects dust it with the foreign pollen, thus ensuring cross-fertilization. The insect cannot get out until hours or even days later, for the incurved petals trap it in what amounts to a heated chamber, the temporarily closed flower of the magnolia being appreciably warmer than the outside air. The insect, often a rose beetle, tries to get out after enjoying the warmth, but is not allowed to until the laggard stamens within the flower finally produce their pollen; then the insects are permitted to leave. Not so, however, before they have become dusted with pollen, when off they go to repeat the process. The premature ripening of the female absolutely prevents self-fertilization, and the laggard potency of the male completely ensures cross-fertilization. Few things in nature are so wonderfully timed.

19. What is foreign pollen? In cross-fertilization (the source of many garden hybrids) pollen from another flower of the same species is called foreign pollen because it ensures cross-fertilization. Self-fertilization involves the use of its own pollen, which is rather rare in the plant world. (See Question 16.) Foreign pollen *must* come from the same species, as all other pollens are completely inert if dusted on the stigma of the wrong flower.

20. Are flowers monogamous?   Absolutely so. Notwithstanding the enormous production of males (pollen) and the copious dusting of the females (the stigma), only a single pollen grain can ever fertilize the ovule. There are hence no liaisons, no premarital excursions, but only one final and solitary impregnation of the female by the male. This is the quintessence of monogamy.

21. Are some flowers more attractive at night than in the daytime? Many are, not only more attractive to us, but to certain night-flying moths. One such plant is the Italian honeysuckle (*Lonicera Caprifolium*), often called the fragrant woodbine in this country, where it has run wild. Its creamy white flower has a long tube too deep for bees to reach the daytime quota of nectar. But towards dusk the nectar rises in the flower tube to a point where night-flying moths can reach it. Not only does the flower produce this seductive sweetness, but at night its wonderfully rich fragrance is much stronger. Such lures can hardly be ignored and the insect, always laden with foreign pollen, finds a different set-up than usual. The stigma is far above the stamens, and in its hurry to reach the nectar the insect dusts the stigma *before* it reaches the level of the stamens, thus ensuring cross-fertilization. Heedless of this the busy insect, in its frantic digging for nectar, becomes dusted with pollen, but only after the honeysuckle has accomplished its apparent purpose.

22. What is the smallest flower in the world?   A duckweed (*Lemna*), often called duck's meat, is a minute aquatic which floats on the surface of ponds, sometimes the whole plant being less than one-twentieth of an inch in diameter. Its almost microscopic flowers are, of course, still smaller. *Lemna* is often a pest in quiet garden pools, for it is very prolific and may cover the water. Its flowers are so small and so fugitive that little is known of their sex life.

23. What is the largest flower in the world?   It is the flower of *Rafflesia arnoldi,* a native of the Indo-Malayan region which so far has no common name. It was first discovered in 1818, and was promptly named *Rafflesia* in honor of Sir Stamford Raffles. He not only found the plant but founded Singapore. The plant is completely parasitic on the bruised roots of a woody vine that is first cousin to the grape. *Rafflesia* has no stem or leaves. It often gets its hold on the roots with the help of an elephant. Their huge feet, mud-encased, easily crush the roots, and sometimes the mud contains the seeds of what one observer called "the greatest prodigy of the vegetable world." However planted, the seeds grow and ultimately produce this gigantic flower. It is whitish, measures eighteen to twenty inches across, and weighs fifteen pounds. No flower in the world is so large and so heavy, and as it is without any stem it lies prostrate on the forest floor. So putrid is its odor that only carrion-liking flies will help to pollinate it.

24. What is duck's-meat?   Another name for the duckweed, the smallest flower in the world. (See Question 22.)

25. What is the fragrant woodbine?   The American name for the Italian honeysuckle, a night-charmer of insects. (See Question 21.)

26. Some flowers digest dead insects. How is this done?   Nearly all plants are incapable of digesting such protein food as meat or a dead insect. But a few have this peculiar attribute, and they are scattered all over the world, never plentifully. The devices they use to capture and digest insects appear ruthless, and because some of them involve active movement they are often called carnivorous plants, but a better term is insectivorous plants. They often prepare their rather gruesome meal by secreting a chemical solvent which effectively promotes the absorption and digestion of the dead insect, which has been trapped for that purpose.

27. Is there an insectivorous plant on the Pacific Coast?   Yes, the extraordinary California pitcher plant, more often called cobra-plant, and named by science *Darlingtonia californica* in honor of William Darlington, an early American botanist. It is a bog plant with solitary yellowish-purple flowers, which are innocent of insect eating. But its leaves are formed into a tubular, water-holding structure twelve to thirty inches long, capped by an arched, white-spotted, hooded flap and a forked appendage. The inside of the tube is covered with downward-pointing hairs which permit the insect to crawl down but not up. Near the bottom of the tube is the lethal fluid in which it drowns and after suitable preparation is digested. In the East it is best grown in sphagnum moss, in a greenhouse, and should be kept moist.

28. Is there a pitcher plant in the East?   Yes, there are at least two, both drowning their prey and then digesting them. The more common is *Sarracenia purpurea,* variously called sidesaddle flower, huntsman's-cup and Indian pitcher. It bears pouchy, tubular, greenish-purple leaves in a rosette, and a rather showy purplish flower which is the

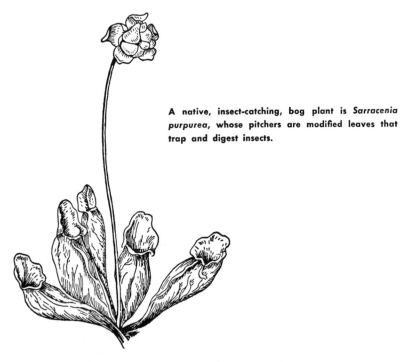

A native, insect-catching, bog plant is *Sarracenia purpurea,* whose pitchers are modified leaves that trap and digest insects.

floral emblem of Newfoundland. The other is *Sarracenia flava,* usually called yellow pitcher plant or trumpets. Its showy, trumpet-like pitchers (really modified leaves) are very handsome, being sometimes a yard long, greenish-yellow and with a crimson throat. Its yellow flowers are two to four inches wide, and the plant inhabits wet bogs from Virginia to Florida.

Both of these eastern pitcher plants were named for Dr. D. Sarrazin of Quebec, who first sent the plants to Europe in the seventeenth century.

29. Do pitcher-plants grow in other parts of the world? In the East Indies and in the Indo-Malayan region there are over forty species of *Nepenthes,* which are the most spectacular of all insectivorous plants. Many of them hang from trees in the hot steaming forests, and it is their leaves that kill the insects. Their usually rather indifferent flowers appear to play no part in the tragedy of *Nepenthes.* The leaves are usually somewhat oblong, with a curious prolongation of the midrib which may be twelve to twenty inches long and which hangs like a cord far below the main body of the plant. At the end of this hanging naked midrib is a gorgeously colored pitcher which is erect, often six inches long, and with a distinct flap acting like the hinged top of a coffee pot. The outside of the pitchers, of which there may be a dozen on a single plant, are red, yellow, and purple, often streaked and so showy that they attract many insects. Still more attractive are tiny honey glands which line the interior of the pitcher. But once inside the insect is doomed, for the upper part of the tube is lined with downward-pointing hairs so that there is no way for the insect to go but down. When he reaches the smooth, almost glazed surface of the lower third of the pitcher, he slips helplessly into the lethal liquid at the bottom. Drowning, decay and digestion are inevitable, for the plant benefits from this elaborate method of supplementing its diet.

These plants are often grown in greenhouses and sometimes may be seen in a florist's window.

30. What is a sundew? Perhaps the most "innocent" of all the insectivorous plants is our sundew (*Drosera*) which glistens in bogs, throughout most of the world. Always low plants (there are over eighty species), they have a rosette of small, usually colored leaves covered with very slender hairs, each of them bathed in a sticky mucus-like substance that glistens in the sun. These sticky almost microscopic tentacles mean inevitable death to any insect caught by even one of them. In its frantic fight for freedom, the insect touches a few more hairs and is hopelessly enmeshed. Death and digestion by the plant soon follow. The pretty, white flowers of the sundew are completely innocent, but the apparently innocent leaves are death traps.

31. What is the bog violet?   Merely another name for the butter-wort. (See Question 36.)

32. What is the cobra-plant?   A Pacific Coast insectivorous plant, so called from its assumed resemblance to a cobra. (See Question 27.)

33. Is the sidesaddle flower the same as our eastern pitcher plant? Yes. (See Question 28.)

34. What is the Indian pitcher?   A local name for the common pitcher plant of the East. It is also called huntsman's-cup. (See Question 28.)

35. In the South many peope call a plant trumpets. Is this a carnivorous plant?   Yes. (See Question 28.)

36. Is there a plant the leaves of which quietly smother their insect visitors?   The butterwort or bog violet (*Pinguicula vulgaris*) is the possessor of this refinement of destruction. It is a bog plant, scarcely over six inches high, with a basal rosette of ovalish leaves that are about two inches long. Its solitary, violet-blue flowers are small but attractive and have nothing to do with smothering. The leaves, however, are far more deadly. The upper side of each leaf is covered with a greasy, sticky secretion in which an insect visitor may be mired. Immediately the leaf margin begins rolling over the insect, smothers and crushes it so that final digestion is hastened. After this the apparently innocent leaf unrolls and serenely awaits another victim. Very few carnivorous plants are so actively destructive.

37. What is the Venus's-flytrap?   Perhaps the most actively destructive insectivorous plant in the world grows in bogs only in North and South Carolina. It was named many years ago *Dionaea muscipula,* as *Dionaea* was Greek name for Venus and *muscipula* is Latin for a flytrap. No plant is better named. It produces a basal rosette of flat stalked leaves, the blades of which are two hinged lobes, fringed with stiffish bristles. Above this basal rosette of leaves stands a pretty cluster of white flowers which have nothing to do with impending tragedy. But the hinged leaf blades are so sensitive to the smallest irritation that they immediately respond to the faint impact of a fly landing between them. Almost instantly the bristly lobes fold together, crush the insect, digest it, and resume their apparently innocent posture. Once caught in the trap-like jaws, there is no escape. The blades are so sensitive that they can easily be made to close by careful tickling with a toothpick.

II. THE ORCHIDS

The staggering complexity of flower forms and their often weird relationship to the insect world would fill a much bigger book than this. But there is still one whole family of flowers that far exceed any others in their color, and especially in their often grotesque deviation from a "typical" flower as outlined in Question 3.

These are the orchids, the largest family of plants in the world of which about twenty thousand different kinds are known—most of them tropical, although a few grow wild in the United States.

While the diversity of flower structure is bewildering, there are a few basic facts about all orchids that will help to identify them. The flower is always irregular (see Question 4) and has three outer segments, the sepals, which are often, but not always, similar and not particularly showy. The three inner segments, the petals, are of two kinds. A pair of these petals may be more or less alike but the third one never is. This third petal forms a lip or spur of such infinite variety of color and form that the identification of tropical orchids is only for the experts. It is the gorgeous color and form of these petals that make orchids so supreme.

A much simpler arrangement of the few orchids that can be included here is to divide them between those that are native to the United States and a few tropical sorts that most of us see only in florist shops.

1. Native orchids in the United States, all of them growing in the ground, often in bogs and woods, some of which can be cultivated with care. The few that can be included here comprise Questions 38–53.
2. Tropical orchids that can only be grown in the greenhouse, and all of which are to be found in the better florist shops. This is a minute fraction of the tropical species, many of which are tree-perchers (epiphytes). The tropical orchids are discussed in Questions 54–63.

38. Is the pink lady's-slipper difficult to grow? Very. It is often called moccasin flower (*Cypripedium acaule*), from its being shaped somewhat like a swollen slipper. It grows in sandy woods in a highly

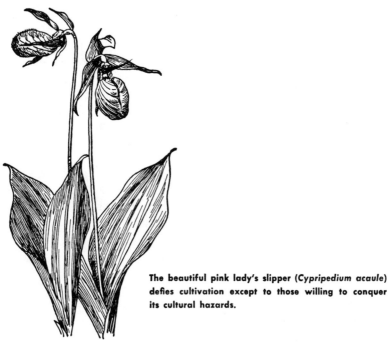

The beautiful pink lady's slipper (*Cypripedium acaule*) defies cultivation except to those willing to conquer its cultural hazards.

acid soil, has extremely brittle roots and is next to impossible to transplant successfully. The flower is always solitary, and stands at the summit of a scurfy stalk which arises from between the only two basal leaves. Perhaps the most useful method of trying to get it established in the wild garden is to dig out frozen clumps and plunge them in a prepared bed of three parts sand to two parts of acid peat. Even then failures are common. May-flowering.

39. Is the yellow lady's-slipper easy to grow?   Yes, it is one of the easiest of all the native orchids to establish in the wild garden. Named *Cypripedium calceolus pubescens* it grows in rich woods where the soil is not particularly acid. It is a showy orchid, ten to twenty-five inches high, the leafy stem clothed with ovalish leaves often six inches long. At the summit the solitary flower (rarely two) is yellow, often lined with purple, and very showy. Dug from the wild when dormant, it usually succeeds in the rich soil of a shady wild garden. May-flowering.

40. Which is the aristocrat of our native orchids? Many would vote for the showy lady's slipper (*Cypripedium reginae*), so named because it is perhaps the queen of native orchids. It is a leafy-stemmed plant, sometimes twenty to twenty-four inches high, crowned with one or two (rarely three) gorgeous, highly irregular flowers that are three inches wide. The sepals and petals are white, as is the much inflated lip, although splotched with crimson-magenta in front. It grows in swamps, bogs and wet woods and resents moving to the wild garden. June-flowering.

41. What is the showy orchis? Some enthusiasts would vote for this superb native orchid as our finest wildflower. Often called gray orchis (*Orchis spectabilis*), it is truly spectacular in its native woods in the eastern states. Not over twelve inches high it has two basal,

Many enthusiasts consider the showy orchis (*Orchis spectabilis*) to be our finest eastern wild flower.

shining leaves from which spring a small cluster of breath-taking flowers. The petals and sepals form a kind of purple-magenta hood, but the lip is white and violet-blotched. It is of reasonably easy culture in cool shady places in rich woods soil. Spring-flowering.

42. Are there two native bog orchids that have solitary flowers? Yes, but no one needs to confuse them. One is the snakemouth (*Pogonia ophioglossoides*) also called rose pogonia and the adder's-mouth. The other is the dragon's-mouth (*Arethusa bulbosa*), sometimes called the wild pink. Both have pinkish flowers, but at flowering time the snakemouth's solitary, flat leaf is conspicuous, while the fugitive, also solitary leaf of the dragon's-mouth may be lacking. Also, the snakemouth has a small leaf-like organ just beneath the flower, but this is lacking in the dragon's-mouth. Both of them are practically impossible to grow. *Pogonia* was derived from the Greek for a beard, as its flower has a minute yellow beard on the lip. The beard is lacking on the lip of *Arethusa,* which was named for the nymph. It is one of our choicest small wildflowers with its pinkish-purple fringed flowers. Both species flower in May or early June.

43. What is the moccasin flower? Merely another name for the pink lady's-slipper. (See Question 38.)

44. What is the gray orchis? A rather pedestrian name for the showy orchis. (See Question 41.)

45. What is the grass pink? A very beautiful native bog orchid named *Calopogon pulchellus. Calopogon* is from the Greek for "beautiful beard," and *pulchellus* is Latin for "beautiful," as though the christeners wanted to emphasize the beautifully fringed, yellowish-orange lip. The petals and sepals are pinkish, but the plant need never be confused with those in Question 42, because the grass pink has grass-like leaves, and its flowers are borne in small clusters—never solitary as in the dragon's-mouth and snakemouth. *Calopogon* is difficult to grow outside its native habitat which is in cool, acid bogs in eastern North America. June-flowering. Sometimes called swamp pink.

46. What are fringed orchids? Splendidly fringed flowers of several species of *Habenaria,* of which there are about twenty native in eastern North America. Two of the finest are the yellow-fringed orchis (*Habenaria ciliaris*), often called the rattlesnake master, and the purple-fringed orchis (*Habenaria psycodes*). Both grow in moist or wet places; their culture eludes most amateurs. The habenarias have the lip usually fringed or split into three segments, and there is usually a long spur to the flower. As the flowers are borne in a dense, terminal cluster the plants are extremely showy. Summer-flowering.

47. Is there a native orchid that lives on the dead remains of other plants? The coral-root (*Corallorhiza*) does exactly that. It is what the botanists call a *saprophyte, i.e.* a plant that, living on the decayed residue of dead plants, has no green coloring matter of its own and consequently looks a little ghostly. Our native ones are small plants, usually not over six to eight inches high, with sickly, yellowish-white stems that are leafless. The flowers are in a terminal, sparse cluster, usually white, and mostly downward pointing, never showy and quite small. The plants are of interest because of their method of getting their food. Many people mistake them for parasites. But parasites have no roots while the coral-root was named *Corallorhiza* from the Greek words for coral and root. This exactly fits the condition of the roots of the coral-root. Most of them are summer-flowering.

48. Is the wild pink really a pink?   No. It is actually another name for an orchid, the dragon's-mouth. (See Question 42.)

49. Are the dragon's mouth and the adder's-mouth the same?   No. The adder's-mouth is another name for the snakemouth, which is also called the rose pogonia. (See Question 42.)

50. What is the swamp pink?   It is the grass pink. (See Question 45.)

51. What is the rattlesnake master?   A beautiful yellow-fringed orchis. (See Question 46.)

52. Is there a native orchid that grows in meadows?   The ladies'-tresses (*Spiranthes cernua*) is one of several of these orchids that grow chiefly in meadows and grassy, moist places. They are a bit hard to find for they are small, with few or no narrow leaves. But the Greek name for them sets them apart from all other native orchids. *Spiranthes* means a coiled flower. Actually the flower is not coiled, but the flowering stalk is slightly twisted and the small, whitish, irregular flowers appear as if twisted because they are inserted upon the spirally twisted stalk. The specific name *cernua* fits them well, for the flowers are slightly nodding. As garden subjects they are too inconspicuous to be worth growing. August or September-flowering.

53. What is the rattlesnake plantain?   A native American orchid of dryish woodlands, unique among wild plants in having variegated leaves. It is often called adder's-violet. Its scientific name is *Goodyera pubescens,* which was to honor a British botanist, one John Goodyer, who flourished from 1592 to 1664. Our plant is exclusively American, being found from Maine to Florida and westward. It is scarcely over eight inches high, its chiefly basal leaves green, but blotched with white, especially on the veins. From the basal leaves arises a stiffish flowering stalk, crowned at the top by a spire-like cluster of small, irregular, whitish flowers each of them scarcely one-half of an inch long and summer-blooming. The plant is inconspicuous but of considerable interest for its naturally variegated leaves.

54. Is there an edible plant among the tropical orchids? Yes. The only orchid of economic importance is one first made known to us by Cortez in his conquest of Mexico. It is grown not for its flowers but for the long slender pods that follow. These are the vanilla beans. Vanilla was well known to the Aztecs who cultivated it for its delightfully flavored, aromatic pods. It is a vine-like orchid with greenish-yellow flowers, and the vanilla beans are seven to nine inches long and pencil-thick. Called by the scientists *Vanilla planifolia,* this Mexican orchid has gone all over the tropical world. Today most vanilla comes from Mexico, the islands in the Indian Ocean, and Tahiti. A mature plant in a vanilla plantation is a vine six to eight feet high, which clings to the bark of trees or fence posts and may yield forty to fifty vanilla beans annually for many years. In spite of synthetic vanillin, gourmet cooks still prefer the pod of this Mexican orchid.

55. What is the most popular orchid flower in America? It is what most people call *the* orchid, as if there were no other. So popular is it in all florists' windows that the public never bothered to invent a common name for it, as everyone calls it cattleya. Its correct name is *Cattleya labiata,* from William Cattley, a British patron of botany and a collector of rare plants, who died in 1832. Originally a Brazilian, tree-perching orchid it is now grown by the thousands in many commercial greenhouses. The plant has a thickish stem (pseudobulb) topped by a single leaf, five to seven inches long. But its great beauty is the flowers which are about six inches wide, the sepals and petals rose-lilac, and the petals much wider than the sepals. In the center is the gorgeous magenta-purple lip, its throat yellow, but orange-spotted, and crisped on the margin. So popular are cattleyas that over two hundred named forms have been bred by orchid fanciers, some of them finer florist's flowers than the typical *Cattleya labiata.*

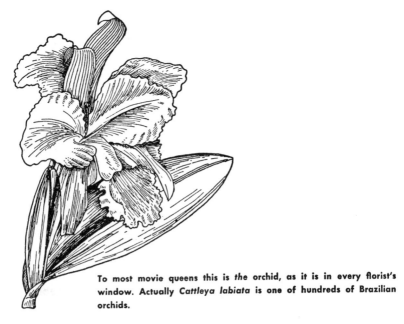

To most movie queens this is *the* orchid, as it is in every florist's window. Actually *Cattleya labiata* is one of hundreds of Brazilian orchids.

56. What orchid flower keeps best in the house? Two are out-standing, both tree-perching and from the Asiatic tropics. One of them, known only by its technical name of *Cymbidium insigne,* is a native of Siam. Its cut flower will last from eight to ten days if kept away from radiators and out of the wind. *Cymbidium* has a compressed stem (pseudobulb) which bears narrow leaves two to three feet long. The flower cluster (which often includes twenty blooms) is very showy; the individual flower is three to four inches wide, the sepals and petals whitish-rose. The lip is boat-shaped (hence *Cymbidium,* which is from the Greek for a boat), white, the front lobe maroon and crimson spotted.

The other long-keeping orchid flower is the beautiful moth orchid (*Phalaenopsis amabilis*) from the Philippines and Malaya. It is a little less durable than *Cymbidium,* but has very attractive flowers, three to five inches wide, generally dull white and yellow-blotched. The lip is usually, but sparsely, purple-spotted. Both these orchids are expensive for they require months of careful culture in the greenhouse.

57. Which tropical orchid is named for a British earl? The Earl Fitzwilliam, a British statesman, lived at Milton Manor in Northhamptonshire, and was at first called Viscount Milton. In honor of him a beautiful Colombian tree-perching orchid was named *Miltonia roezli,* because he was a patron of horticulture. It has never had a common name, although it is often cultivated in greenhouses. Its single, narrow leaf is about one foot long, and its flower is three to five inches wide, flattish, and white, with a purple blotch or band at the base of each petal. The lip is brownish. Its specific name also honors Benedikt Roezl, an Austrian collector in tropical America.

58. What is the butterfly orchid? One of a huge group of tropical American, tree-perching orchids, of which only this one, *Oncidium Papilio,* is in much cultivation. It has only a single leaf, but a beautifully arched flowering stalk upon which are borne many flowers with a faint resemblance to a butterfly. The individual flowers are solitary, about three inches wide, the narrow petals and sepals brown but yellow-spotted, the lip yellow with a brown margin. The flowers bloom in succession on the arching flowering stalk that may be a yard long. It blooms most of the year in the greenhouse. *Papilio* is Latin for "butterfly."

59. What is the most widely grown orchid from Nepal? The stunning *Coelogyne cristata,* is one of the easiest greenhouse orchids to cultivate, and is the pride of most amateur orchid growers. A native of Nepal, it has never had a common name, but is treasured for its several drooping clusters of very showy flowers. The leaves are nine to twelve inches long, the individual flowers three to four inches wide, and white. The orange-yellow throat of the lip is particularly handsome, and the middle lobe of the lip is slightly toothed (hence *cristata* for crested). A beautiful, free-flowering orchid easily grown in a moderately warm greenhouse, preferably in orchid peat.

60. Which is the Mexican orchid most commonly seen in the florist shops? Unquestionably it is *Laelia anceps,* so called because *anceps* means keeled, and one lobe of the lip is prominently yellow-keeled. Its thickened stem (pseudobulb) bears only one or two leaves, but the flowering stalk is frequently eighteen to thirty inches long and very showy. The flower is about four inches wide, generally pale rose-purple, but the lip is deeper purple, white-streaked, and one lobe has a yellow keel. This species is not difficult to grow in an amateur's greenhouse, as it is a tree-perching plant; it thrives best in orchid peat, in moderate heat.

61. What are the most popular Old World orchid flowers?   Next to *Cattleya* (see Question 55) the most widely grown Old World orchid is surely *Dendrobium.* There are over nine hundred species in the hot, steaming forests of the Indo-Malayan region. Of all these much the best known is *Dendrobium nobile,* a tree-perching orchid from the Himalayas with very short leaves and stunningly beautiful flowers, usually borne in clusters of two or three. They are two to

This Himalayan orchid, *Dendrobium nobile,* has no common name but is offered by most good florists.

three inches wide, white or rosy purple, with a white-edged lip and a dark, purple throat. So popular is *Dendrobium* with orchid fanciers that in addition to the many wild species, there are now innumerable hybrids, some of them even more showy than the one above. In spite of their popularity these plants have no common name.

62. Is there a tropical orchid that grows so high in the mountains that it can be cultivated only in a cool greenhouse? *Odontoglossum pulchellum* which grows in the high mountains of Mexico and Guatemala thrives when the night temperature in the greenhouse is no more than 50°F. It is a tree-perching orchid, with only two or three very narrow leaves, and with a flower cluster twelve to fifteen inches long and very showy. The flowers are white, but purple-dotted at the base of the yellow, crested lip; fragrant; and about one inch wide. It is winter-blooming in a cool greenhouse. It has no common name. *Odontoglossum* is from the Greek for "tooth" and "tongue," and refers to the crested lip.

63. What is the most spectacular orchid from Java? Many orchid growers would vote for *Vanda tricolor,* a tree-perching plant from hot, steaming forests. Unlike many orchids it has a stem two to three feet high, and many leaves, growing in two rows. The flowers measure two inches wide; the yellow petals and sepals are wavy-margined and brown-spotted. The lip is light purple, streaked with darker purple; the side lobes of the lip white. Since the flowers are borne in clusters of from eight to ten, this is one of the most showy of cultivated orchids. *Vanda* is a native name, and the plants need a greenhouse kept at 70°–80°F. during the day and not below 60° at night.

III. EASTERN WILDFLOWERS

64. While nature has apparently decreed that the form and function of flowers are dictated by the necessity of their survival, are there other features of the plant world that if not quite so important are still very much so? In other words, when we have seen the sex organs of flowers, their relations to the insect world, the capacity of some species to capture and digest their insect prey, and the wonderful intricacy of orchid flowers, have we glimpsed only a part of the whole?

What, in truth, is that whole concept of the plant world? Leaving out the flower features already outlined in Chapters I and II, what else about them is really significant? Many things; among them their distribution over the earth. For most of us that means how and why wildflowers are found from the Atlantic to the Pacific, in marshes, prairies, forests, mountains and deserts.

The answers to such questions lie far outside the scope of this book, but some basic facts help us to understand the main features of the distribution of flowers in the United States. It is dictated by two major controls: temperature and rainfall. Except for Florida, the Gulf Coast and the southwestern deserts, all of which verge on the subtropical, temperature is less important for wildflowers than it is for shrubs and trees. Wildflowers die down in the winter and are often snugly blanketed with snow. For them hardiness is far less important than it is for shrubs and trees, whose buds are exposed to wintry blasts.

It is quite otherwise with rainfall, which is a major factor in flower distribution, as it also is for trees and shrubs. Along the Atlantic seaboard there is an average annual rainfall of 35 to 48 inches. It is this adequacy that has produced the luxuriant forests that stretch from the Atlantic to the Appalachians, and even westward in locally favorable places. It makes gardens and lawns not only feasible but reasonably free from the necessity for irrigation.

But west of the Appalachians there is a distinct change. The farther west we go, even to the escarpment of the Rocky Mountains, there is a progressively diminishing rainfall, as anyone can see in driving from Pittsburgh to Denver. At first, as we go westward, there is the park-like landscape of western Indiana and Illinois, which is a tension zone between forest and prairie. Then we cross hundreds of miles of treeless prairie, or find only poor poplars in the river bottoms. This is the region where the rainfall is not over 20 inches annually, and is often less.

If it is much less, say 3 to 10 inches per year, we get the deserts of western Texas, New Mexico, Arizona and southern California, which are naturally treeless. Here keeping gardens and lawns healthy can only be done only by expensive irrigation. The semi-desert or dry region also extends from the western side of the Rocky Mountains to the slopes of the Sierra Nevada and Cascades of California, Washington and Oregon. This is the dry, bleak, treeless, sagebrush country, more sparsely populated, but occasionally punctuated by well patronized spots like Reno or Las Vegas.

West of the Sierras and Cascades there is an entirely different distribution of rainfall. In northern coastal California, and in Oregon and Washington the rainfall varies from 60 to 150 inches a year, making it gardenwise as luxuriant as England, and watering the finest evergreen forests on earth. South of Monterey the rainfall decreases markedly and San Diego, except for irrigation would be a desert.

65. Are climatic factors the only ones that govern the distribution of wildflowers?   By no means. Quite apart from major climatic zones (based on temperature and rainfall) there is the equally important factor of what sort of environment the flower chooses to thrive in —in other words its habitat. The latter dictates its site locally while the climatic factors are equally dictatorial as to its distribution over the country. Some flowers grow in pools and streams, others in bogs or marshes, still others on sandy dunes, some in rich cool woods and a few on rocky outcrops. All of these are the habitat of flowers, as are the roadside thickets and fields where most of our introduced wildflowers are found.

66. Is it possible to sort our eastern wildflowers into significant categories?   Yes, and such a scheme is outlined in Question 70.

67. Many of our eastern wildflowers have been chosen by school children or the state legislature as the floral emblem of the state. Are there floral emblems for all the fifty states?   Yes and the list follows:

STATE FLOWERS

Alabama	Goldenrod
Alaska	Forget-me-not
Arizona	Giant cactus
California	California poppy
Colorado	Columbine
Connecticut	Mountain laurel
Delaware	Peach blossom
Florida	Orange blossom
Georgia	Cherokee rose
Hawaii	Hibiscus
Idaho	Mock orange
Illinois	Violet
Indiana	Zinnia
Iowa	Wild rose
Kansas	Sunflower
Kentucky	Goldenrod
Louisiana	Magnolia
Maine	White pine
Maryland	Black-eyed Susan
Massachusetts	Trailing arbutus
Michigan	Apple blossom
Minnesota	Showy lady's-slipper
Mississippi	Magnolia
Missouri	Hawthorn
Montana	Bitter-root
Nebraska	Goldenrod
Nevada	Sagebrush
New Hampshire	Lilac
New Jersey	Violet
New Mexico	Spanish bayonet
New York	Rose
North Carolina	Flowering dogwood
North Dakota	Wild rose
Ohio	Carnation
Oklahoma	Mistletoe
Oregon	Oregon grape
Pennsylvania	Mountain laurel
Rhode Island	Violet
South Carolina	Carolina jasmine

South Dakota	Pasqueflower
Tennessee	Iris
Texas	Bluebonnet
Utah	Globe tulip
Vermont	Red clover
Virginia	Flowering dogwood
Washington	*Rhododendron macrophyllum*
West Virginia	Great laurel
Wisconsin	Violet
Wyoming	Painted-cup

68. Is there a national flower for the United States? No. Many attempts have been made to choose one but all have failed. Current suggestions include flowering dogwood, mountain laurel and columbine, none of which has countrywide distribution. One flower that is countrywide in its distribution, at least in some of its forms, is the goldenrod, and this is also a candidate for our national flower. But many consider it not much more than a roadside weed, which it is in some of its more rampant forms.

69. Do many other countries have national flowers? Yes, and the list follows:

NATIONAL FLOWERS

Argentina	Ceibo
Australia	Wattle
Belgium	Poppy
Bolivia	*Cantua buxifolia*
Brazil	Cattleya
Canada	Sugar maple
Chile	Chilean bellflower
China	Narcissus
Costa Rica	Cattleya
Denmark	Clover
Ecuador	Cinchona
Egypt	Lotus (water lily)
England	Rose
France	Fleur-de-lis
Germany	Cornflower
Greece	Violet

NATIONAL FLOWERS (*Continued*)

Holland	Tulip
Honduras	Rose
India	Lotus (*Zizyphus*)
Ireland	Shamrock
Italy	Lily
Japan	Chrysanthemum
Mexico	Prickly pear
Newfoundland	Pitcher plant
New Zealand	Silver fern
Norway	Heather
Persia	Rose
Poland	Poppy
Russia	Sunflower
Scotland	Thistle
South Africa	*Protea cynaroides*
Spain	Pomegranate
Sweden	Twinflower
Switzerland	Edelweiss
Wales	Leek

70. Into what habitats may eastern wildflowers be classified?
How could a nature tramper or flower lover sort out Eastern wildflowers into significant categories? The luxuriance and diversity of
our eastern wildflowers is so great that only the broadest outline of
their different habitats would be very helpful. And in a book like this
only a selection of our eastern wildflowers is possible. Arranged by
habitats they might be sorted thus:

1. Flowers that grow in the water or in swamps, marshes or bogs.
   These begin at Question 71.
2. Flowers that grow in moist places, rarely in water, swamps,
   marshes or bogs. These begin at Question 96.
3. Flowers that grow in the forest, whether the cool forests of the
   north or the warmer woods in the south. These begin at Question 126.
4. Shrubs and trees whose flowers are sufficiently showy to be gathered as wildflowers. These begin at Question 174.
5. Flowers that grow in open places that are not especially dry.
   These begin at Question 186.

6. Flowers that grow usually only in dry, often sandy open places. These begin at Question 208.
7. Wildflowers that are not native to America, but which since their introduction have run wild. These begin at Question 224.

Not all the plants assigned to their preferred habitat necessarily always grow there. Aquatics are sometimes swamp plants, and a plant that grows in open woods may also spread to a thicket or even to a roadside. In other words, the scheme is only a guide to preferences and usual habitats, not a hard and fast rule.

Also, as every professional knows, there is a much more accurate method of sorting our eastern flora into far more definite categories. But being based wholly on technical characters and involving a technical familiarity with plant families, it is omitted from this book.

FLOWERS FOUND GROWING IN SWAMPS, BOGS OR IN WATER

71. What beautiful aquatic flower has become a pest? In the St. John's River in Florida and elsewhere, navigation is often impeded by millions of plants of a spectacularly showy floating aquatic. It is the water hyacinth (*Eichhornia crassipes*) which was introduced into Florida before anyone knew it would become a pest and cost thousands of dollars to control. But a river or lake covered with it is a stunning sight when the plant is in bloom. The flower is violet, with the upper part blue-patched and yellow-spotted. Crowded in a dense spike and standing well above the water, the water hyacinth may be a pest but is a gorgeous one. The flowering spikes are held aloft by the rosette of spongy leaves that have sufficient air chambers in their interior to float the plant on the water. It never roots in the mud.

72. What northern aquatic flower is sometimes mistaken for the water hyacinth? This is the pickerelweed (*Pontederia cordata*), sometimes called the alligator wampee. It lines the shallow shores of many fresh-water streams and, rooting in the mud, it often invades neighboring marshes. The plant is eighteen to thirty inches high, with a single, arrowhead-shaped, dark green leaf and a showy spike of flowers. The petals are violet-blue, with a distinct yellow-green spot. The individual flower is generally funnel-shaped. Because the plants usually occur in great abundance, they make many pond-edges a blue

In midsummer the pickerelweed (*Pontederia cordata*) blue-lines the edge of many ponds and streams.

delight in summer. They were named in honor of Giuglio Pontedera, the professor of botany at Padua (1688–1757).

73. What is the most fragrant aquatic flower in our eastern flora?
The beautiful and surpassingly fragrant white water lily (*Nymphaea odorata*) often rather inappropriately called the toad lily and, with much more aptness, the water nymph. It grows in shallow pools, always rooting in the mud. Its floating, roundish leaves are pinkish beneath, and deeply cleft at the base. The flowers are white, with many sharp-pointed petals, generally opening in the morning but closing or closed by noon. They are usually four to five inches wide. It was named, of course, for the Greek nymph.

74. Is there a yellow pond lily?   Yes, the spatter-dock (*Nuphar advena*), often called the yellow pond lily or cow lily. It is a rather coarse aquatic, always rooting in the mud of shallow ponds. Leaves ovalish, nearly a foot long; some are submerged, some floating and a few rise on erect stalks above the surface. The yellow flowers, never quite open, are globe-shaped, without odor, and are about two and a half inches thick and far less attractive than the closely related white water lily. Its flowers always stand above the water surface, and it frequently grows with its more attractive relative—the white water lily.

75. Is there an American lotus?   Of the two species of lotus known in the world, one is the famed lotus of the Nile and Asia (which is not the plant of the lotus-eaters) and the other is the American lotus (*Nelumbo lutea*), often called water chinquapin. This is an immense aquatic, growing from one to two feet above the water surface, its leaves cup-shaped and one to two feet wide. The pale yellow flowers measure from eight to ten inches wide, and they may stand even higher out of the water than the leaves. The flower closes at night. It is followed by a pod, its top with many holes (when ripe) like a pepper-shaker, through which the seeds are released. The American lotus, never very common, is inclined to be spotty in its distribution, but it is abundant along the Illinois River. *Nelumbo* is a name for the Asiatic species in Ceylon.

76. What is the water arum?   An aquatic or bog plant known to science as *Calla palustris,* often called wild calla and confused by many with the true calla lily. This latter is tropical and belongs to the group properly known as *Zantedeschia*. Our native water arum has long-stalked, thick, coarse leaves that are ovalish and about three inches long. The flowers are yellowish, very minute, crowded on a finger-thick stalk (spadix) about one inch long, which is not entirely covered by a white leaf-like structure that is green on the outside. *Calla* is the ancient classical name for this plant, which also grows in Europe and Asia.

77. Does the cattail have flowers?   The cattail, which covers miles of marshy or wet land is often called the great reed mace and was named by Linnaeus *Typha latifolia*. It is an immensely rampant plant, its long narrow leaves about three-fourths of an inch wide but five to nine feet high, nearly as tall is the brownish spike, which is flower-bearing. This is five to six inches long, cylindric, about thumb-thick and on it are crowded hundreds of nearly microscopic flowers without petals or sepals. The cattail is one of the most primitive of all plants, but it does bear flowers, although they are inconspicuous. The brownish fruiting spike is popular as a winter decoration. The plant is also found almost throughout the world, and there is a narrower leaved kind known as *Typha angustifolia.*

78. What is the alligator wampee?   The pickerelweed. (See Question 72.)

79. Are the toad lily and the water nymph the same?   Yes, but they are both local names for the white water lily. (See Question 73.)

80. Does the spatterdock have any other names?   Yellow pond lily and cow lily are both local names for it. (See Question 74.)

81. What is the water chinquapin?   The American lotus. (See Question 75.)

82. Has the flower of the wild calla anything to do with the true calla lily?   No. (See Question 76.)

83. What is the great reed mace?   The cattail. (See Question 77.)

84. Will the rose mallow grow in ordinary garden soil?   This is a question asked by many gardeners, because it is one of the most handsome of all the native plants in our salt marshes. The rose mallow (*Hibiscus Moscheutos*) should not be confused with the marsh mallow, a European plant naturalized in our salt marshes. Our native plant, first cousin to the hollyhock, is a stout perennial, three to six feet high, often called the sea hollyhock. Its ovalish, sometimes angled leaves are white and felty beneath; and its bell-shaped flowers are four to seven inches wide, white or pink, and generally blooming in August. While its natural habitat is in saline marshes, it will grow in fresh marshes and has many times been transferred to ordinary garden soil—of course when it is dormant. *Hibiscus* was Vergil's name for some mallow, but not this one.

85. What is the sweet flag?   This is a reed-like perennial of swamps and fresh-water marshes, of interest not for its flowers, which are microscopic, but because its underground stems yield calamus (not calomel), a home remedy for colic. It grows about two feet high, from a long thick underground, aromatic stem (or rhizome). Among the sword-shaped leaves and looking like them is a flower-bearing stalk that produces from about its middle a short spike-like organ crowded with minute greenish flowers. The plant was named by Linnaeus *Acorus Calamus, Acorus* being the classical name of the sweet flag, which is also found in Europe and Asia. The pulverized rootstocks are sometimes used in sachets.

86. What is the habitat of the golden club?   It grows in water and in swamps, but usually in the water where its leaves may be six to twelve inches long, depending on the depth of the water. It is also called floating arum and water dock, but its technical name is *Orontium aquaticum*. Its leaves are ovalish, long-stalked, and from among them arises a tall, slender, spike-like organ, the upper part of which is crowded with almost microscopic, golden flowers. These have no petals, but the slender, golden, flower-bearing organ is quite striking in April or May.

87. Are the bogbean, the marsh trefoil and the bog myrtle all the same?   They are widely used names for the buckbean. (See Question 93.)

88. What is the sea hollyhock?   The rose mallow. (See Question 84.)

89. What is grass-of-Parnassus?   A very beautiful, white-flowered bog or wet-meadow plant, the flowers usually green veined or green tinged. There are at least two forms of it, our eastern one, *Parnassia glauca,* and another found in the mountains of California, *Parnassia fimbriata* which has beautifully fringed petals. Our eastern species has basal, ovalish, long-stalked leaves that may be only one to two inches long. From among them rises a long, slender flowering stalk, clothed by a stalkless leaf and topped by a white, wax-like flower with five petals, which are faintly green-veined. The plant is easily cultivated in a cool, wet, shady place.

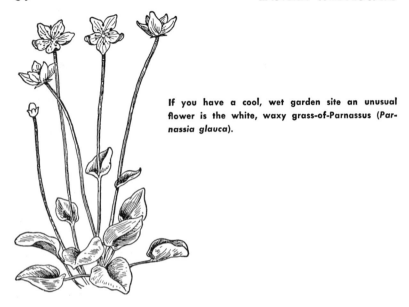

If you have a cool, wet garden site an unusual flower is the white, waxy grass-of-Parnassus (*Parnassia glauca*).

90. Is the marsh marigold really a marigold?   No, and neither is it a cowslip, but rather a distant relative of the buttercup that the botanists call *Caltha palustris*.

It is a swamp or marsh perennial that covers wet places with a sheen of golden-yellow bloom in April or early May. It grows about four to six inches high, is hollow-stemmed and bears round or kidney-shaped leaves, mostly basal, but with one or more just beneath the flowering cluster. The flowers are about three-fourths of an inch wide, buttercup-like, with five to nine petal-like sepals, as it has no petals. *Caltha* is the old Latin name for the true marigold and was applied to the marsh marigold because it had golden yellow flowers, as has the cowslip, an equally incorrect name for our native plant.

91. How did the common names of flowers originate?   The vernacular or common names of flowers are often incorrect, sometimes inappropriate, but as persistent in the language as death and taxes. They vary geographically, with the sophistication of the public who coin them, and generally have little to do with the true identity of the plant. Some we inherited from Old English, some are French, Spanish or Creole, and many are just made up to the confusion of all but their coiners. What, for instance, are the correct or most accepted names of the following vernaculars?

> Floating arum = Golden club. (See Question 86.)
> Water dock = Golden club. (See Question 86.)
> Water willow = Swamp loosestrife. (See Question 92.)
> Wild oleander = Swamp loosestrife. (See Question 92.)

92. Is the swamp loosestrife a useful garden flower? Yes and no. It will not grow in dry places, but in moist or wet ones it thrives, sometimes too rampantly. Its rooting at the tips of its arching branches often makes it invasive, and if left alone, hard to control. It is, however, one of the showiest of our swamp plants. It is often called water willow (which it is not) or wild oleander (which is absurd). Its correct name is *Decodon verticillatus*. It is a woody perennial, three to eight feet high and as wide, with leaves often in opposite pairs. Towards the tips of the branches, and at the leaf joints, there is a dense, stalkless cluster of showy, pink-purple flowers that are produced profusely. Few wild swamp plants are so easy to grow in moist garden sites.

93. Is there a long-blooming bog flower suited for cultivation? One of the best is the buckbean (*Menyanthes trifoliata*), variously called bog myrtle, bogbean, and marsh trefoil. It grows in cool bogs and can easily be cultivated in the bog garden if it is not too sunny and hot. The plant is a little fleshy, is inclined to sprawl and bears long-stalked compound leaves with three leaflets (hence *trifoliata*). The white flowers, in terminal, ten-to-twenty-flowered clusters, bloom from May to July. The individual flower is about one-half of an inch long, shortly funnel-shaped and bearded on the inside.

94. Does the cranberry bear flowers? This native American, sprawling, vine-like bog plant certainly does flower from June to early August. It has slender, wire-thin stems and nearly stalkless evergreen leaves, scarcely one-half of an inch long. The pink flowers are borne singly on a thread-thin stalk that arises at the lower leaf joints. The corolla is scarcely one-half of an inch wide, followed in the fall by the familiar cranberry. The cultivation of the cranberry (*Vaccinium* *macrocarpon*) is recommended only for the experts, in a cranberry bog where the water level can be controlled.

95. Is there another swamp pink besides the one mentioned in Question 45?   Yes, the name in Question 45 is that of an orchid better called the grass pink. But the true swamp pink (*Helonias bullata*) is a bog perennial of the lily family, found wild from Staten Island, New York, to Georgia. It has basal, nearly evergreen leaves that are six to fifteen inches long. At the center rises a hollow flower stalk, twelve to twenty inches high, crowned with a dense cluster of twenty to thirty small, pink flowers that are scarcely one-half of an inch wide. It is showy in April or early May. *Helonias* is from the Greek for "swamp" and *bullata* means "blistered" or "puckered," and is of unknown application here as the plant is smooth.

Flowers Growing in Moist Places

96. What is the earliest-blooming of our wildflowers?   On Washington's birthday it is often possible to scrape away the snow to uncover our earliest and most stinking wildflower. This is, of course, our skunk cabbage (*Symplocarpus foetidus*), also known as swamp cabbage, and quite appropriately as polecat-weed. Long before the large, deep green, cabbage-like leaves develop, the skunk-cabbage has set the stage for its carrion-scented nuptials. These take place in a hooded, partially closed, beautifully colored organ, within which are the male and female flowers, both very tiny and crowded on a club-shaped organ. Only carrion-loving insects can pollinate the plant, even if the snow has gone. Its foliage, which is handsome, is equally malodorous. The plant likes cool, moist or wet woods, and is not worth cultivating.

97. Is there a native spirea that grows in moist places?   The meadowsweet (*Spiraea alba*) grows in just such places throughout much of the East and westward to South Dakota. It is a slender shrub, three to six feet high, with brownish twigs and a sparse terminal cluster of many, small, white flowers that bloom from June to August. Closely related to it is the hardhack (*Spiraea tomentosa*) a lower shrub, its leaves prominently rusty-felty beneath, and with a spire-like, terminal, and showy cluster of rose-pink, very small flowers, which bloom from July to September. It grows westward to Arkansas, mostly in moist places.

98. What is the sheep laurel? It is a low evergreen shrub, called also lambkill and dwarf laurel. Its poisonous juice is injurious to animals and man. Its technical name of *Kalmia angustifolia,* was given to it in 1753 by Linnaeus in honor of his friend Peter Kalm, a Swedish botanist, who discovered the sheep laurel on his three-year travels in eastern North America from 1748–1751. It has small, opposite leaves, and lavender-rose flowers in small, lateral clusters, mostly in June. Sheep laurel grows in moist, acid places and is difficult to cultivate and nearly impossible out of the bog garden.

99. What is Labrador tea? This is an upright bog shrub, scarcely three feet high, found from Greenland to Pennsylvania and westward. Its small, evergreen, alternate leaves are rusty and hairy beneath, and the margins are rolled. Its small white flowers, gathered in a ball-shaped terminal cluster, bloom in May or June, with five spreading oblong petals. The flowers are not showy but are interesting because while belonging to the heath family, unlike most of them they do not have a bell-shaped or funnel-like corolla. Its technical name of *Ledum groenlandicum* emphasizes the fact that it is found chiefly in the cool north. It can be grown only in cool bogs.

100. Are swamp-cabbage and the polecat-weed the same? Yes, both these, and several other names, have been applied to the skunk-cabbage. (See Question 96.)

101. Is there a gentian whose flowers are never open except by force? The closed or bottle gentian (*Gentiana andrewsi*) is the commonest gentian of the eastern states, usually growing mostly in moist shady places. It is twelve to eighteen inches high with clustered, oblongish leaves that are without marginal teeth and are one to two inches long. At the leaf-clusters, and in a terminal one, the stalkless, very handsome blue flowers are crowded. They are almost unique in having the incurving tip of the corolla so tightly closed that most insect visitors are excluded and self-pollination appears assured. But bumblebees not infrequently force open the corolla and cross-fertilization is then accomplished. The plant is the easiest to grow of any of

The blue flower of the closed gentian (*Gentiana andrewsi*)
only opens when forced to by a bumblebee.

the gentians, and while American, was named for Henry C. Andrews,
an English botanical artist.

102. Is the fringed gentian difficult to grow?   Next to impossible,
as the plant lives only two years, blooms in the autumn of the second
year, and then dies. It is the finest of all our native gentians. It is
named *Gentiana crinita,* but this specific name which means "long-
haired" scarcely suggests the beautifully fringed, deep blue, terminal
and solitary corolla. The flower is nearly two inches long, very showy
and seldom blooms before October. Attempts to dig it from the wild
are almost always fatal. The rather elaborate technique of cultivating
it is beyond the patience of most gardeners. Its lengthy procedure is
described in Taylor's *Wild Flower Gardening,* issued by Van Nostrand
in 1955.

**103. Are there any native lobelias worth growing in the wild gar-
den?**   There are two, both preferring some shade and a moist site.
The finest is the cardinal flower (*Lobelia Cardinalis*), often called the
scarlet lobelia. This is an erect, somewhat stiff perennial, two and a
half to five feet high, its nearly stalkless, coarsely toothed leaves three
to five inches long. From among the upper ones, and in a terminal
cluster, the gorgeously scarlet, irregular flowers bloom from July to
September.

The other lobelia is not quite so spectacular and is known as the blue or great lobelia, with the technical name of *Lobelia siphilitica,* as it was once thought to be a remedy for syphilis. It is a perennial, two to three feet high, its oblongish leaves three to five inches long. The deep blue flowers are rarely over one inch long and appear in rather sparse terminal clusters, with a few among the upper leaves, blooming in August or September. Both plants were named *Lobelia* in honor of Matthias de L'Obel, a Belgian botanist (1538–1616) who went to England and helped found the first private "botanic garden."

104. What wildflower was named for an Englishman who came to Virginia in 1705?   One of our most fragile wildflowers, variously called spring beauty, Mayflower, grass-flower and good-morning spring, was named *Claytonia virginica* in honor of John Clayton, one of our earliest botanical explorers. It is a shy little plant, four to six inches high, which almost completely dies down by midsummer, well after its early spring bloom. The leaves are narrowly lance-shaped, two to five inches long. The flowers are about five-eighths of an inch wide, white, but often tinged or streaked with pink. They are quite fleeting and wilt at once if picked. This is scarcely a garden plant as, while a perennial, its seasonal growth is ephemeral.

105. What is the bottle gentian?   The closed gentian. (See Question 101.)

106. Are the dwarf laurel and the lambkill the same?   Yes, they are both alternative common names for the sheep laurel. (See Question 98.)

107. What wildflower was named for the gardener of Charles I? The spiderwort (*Tradescantia virginiana*) was so christened by Linnaeus in honor of a Dutch plantsman, John Tradescant, who left Holland to become head gardener to Charles I. Also called snake grass or widow's tears, this is perhaps the most fleeting of our native flowers. The plant is a brittle, weak-stemmed, watery-juiced perennial, scarcely fit for cultivation unless in a moist place in the shade. It grows two to three feet high, and its usually channelled leaves are twelve to fifteen inches long. The flowers are bluish or violet purple, with only three petals, and are ephemeral and useless as cut flowers. The plant is a close relative of the Wandering Jew (*Tradescantia fluminensis*), a variegated form of which is popular for window boxes.

108. Is there a wildflower named for a director of the Amsterdam botanical garden? When Linnaeus named the common dayflower *Commelina communis* he wanted to honor Johann Commelin, a Dutch botanist, who was the director of the Amsterdam botanical garden, and also his nephew Caspar. Such distinguished sponsorship seems scarcely necessary for this little annual weedy dayflower which few would notice if it were not for its brilliant blue flower. It is a diffuse, weak-stemmed plant, growing generally in the shade. The flower is terminal, usually solitary, with a boat-shaped structure beneath it, and with only three petals which are fragile and fleeting.

109. What are bluets? Delightful, wispy little meadow plants named *Houstonia caerulea* in honor of William Houston, a botanical collector in Mexico and the West Indies. Many know them as Quaker ladies or innocence, as they suggest both in their simplicity and primness. Scarcely six inches high, the small leaves are chiefly basal, and from them arises the thread-thin stalk with a solitary flower at the top. The flower is less than one-half of an inch wide, mostly pale blue, rarely white or violet, but with a yellow eye and blooming in May. It is difficult to grow unless in soil through which cool water trickles.

110. Is the Virginia cowslip really a cowslip? No, this is an unfortunate common name for *Mertensia virginica,* a beautiful native perennial of moist places, often called American lungwort or Roanoke bells. It has nothing to do with the true cowslip. The plant is an easily grown parennial, preferably on a moist site, in partial shade. It is usually not over eighteen inches high and is a profuse bloomer. It has pale green, long-stalked oblongish leaves, three to seven inches long. The flower is purplish at first but turns blue as it expands, is not over one inch long, drooping, and is borne in a somewhat one-sided terminal cluster. It was named by Linnaeus in honor of Carl Franz Mertens, a German botanist.

111. Does the sea pink grow only in salt marshes? Not quite, for it also grows along saline shores, and is one of our finest pink, fall-flowering plants. Named by Linnaeus *Sabatia dodecandra* in honor of L. Sabbati, an Italian botanist, it grows wild along the coast from Connecticut to Louisiana. Many call it the rose pink. It is a rather weak-stemmed, forked perennial, with small, stalkless, opposite leaves and a loosely branched, open cluster of flowers. These are about three-fourths of an inch wide and apparently have eight to twelve narrow petals (actually eight to twelve lobes of the corolia). *Dodecandra* means having twelve stamens. (See Question 3.)

112. Are the snake grass and the widow's tears the same as the spiderwort? Yes. (See Question 107.)

113. What is the preferred name for the flowers frequently called Quaker ladies and innocence? Bluets. (See Question 109.)

114. What is the turtlehead? This is a name for several perennial wildflowers, properly called *Chelone glabra* or *Chelone lyoni* which is the red turtlehead. The first is a white-flowered perennial of moist places, with opposite, toothed leaves. It grows from Newfoundland to Georgia. Its stalkless, irregular two-lipped flowers are borne in a compact, terminal cluster, only one or two flowering simultaneously. As a garden flower the much finer red turtlehead is preferred, its flowers being rose-purple. Both are summer blooming. *Chelone* is from the Greek for a turtle's head, in allusion to the shape of the flowers.

115. Is the touch-me-not also known as jewelweed? Yes, both names are applied to a group of plants that have the singularly appropriate name of *Impatiens,* which is Latin for impatience in allusion to the explosive bursting of its pods; whence also touch-me-not. These watery-juiced plants also glisten a little, thus jewelweed. Their stems are nearly translucent. Both our local species have irregular, spurred, yellow or golden-yellow flowers, but apart from the beauty of these the following fruit is the most interesting feature of the touch-me-not. The fruit is an elastically explosive capsule when mature, discharging the seeds for a considerable distance, especially if touched. Neither is suited to the garden as their tissue is fragile. Both are summer-bloomers.

116. What are monkey flowers? A group of mostly perennial plants, the flowers of which are two-lipped and spotted, giving the appearance of a face. Christened *Mimulus,* which is Latin for a little mimic, *i.e.* the grinning face, they are much more common in the West, but the eastern *Mimulus ringens* is a rather plentiful perennial, one to four feet high, with a four-angled stem, opposite somewhat oblong leaves and violet flowers. It can easily be cultivated in a partially shaded moist site.

117. Are meadow beauty and handsome Harry the same? Yes, but both are local names for a beautiful, summer-blooming flower also called dear grass, or *Rhexia virginica.* The plants of this family are mostly gorgeous tropical shrubs and trees, so that this delicate native wildflower is not only attractive in itself but a lonely outpost of an immense tropical family. It grows in acid wet or moist places in eastern North America, is nine to fifteen inches high, and has an angled stem, with opposite, stalkless leaves, their margins hairy-fringed. The flowers about one and a half inches wide, in few-flowered clusters, the four slightly oblique petals, purple and showy. Difficult to cultivate outside an acid bog.

118. What are the American lungwort and the Roanoke bells? Both are local names for the Virginia cowslip. (See Question 110.)

119. What is the rose pink? The sea pink. (See Question 111.)

120. Are Joe-pye weed and the purple boneset the same? Both are common valid names for a tall, rather coarse perennial, better known as *Eupatorium purpureum,* which is almost weedy in moist places. It is found throughout eastern North America, often growing in dense colonies. It stands seven to nine feet high and has somewhat oblong, coarsely toothed leaves borne in clusters of five or six. The flower heads are purple, in a round, much branched, showy cluster that may be six to nine inches wide in late summer. The plant is so rank-growing that it is scarcely worth cultivating, although it is quite showy when in bloom.

121. What is the queen-of-the-meadow? A feathery, spirea-like perennial, three to five feet high, suggesting a real *Spiraea* and often called meadowsweet. Its correct Latin name is *Filipendula Ulmaria.* Not only is it easy to grow; it is widely cultivated in ordinary garden soil throughout the eastern states, mostly in moist places. The leaves are once-compound, the leaflets white-felty beneath. The flowers are small, white, and are borne in a lax, open, terminal cluster. The queen-of-the-meadow originally came from Europe and Asia, but often appears as if a native American wildflower. (For a related plant see Question 171.)

122. How many different buttercups are there in the eastern states?
There are at least thirty-five species and may be more, all of them belonging to the group called *Ranunculus,* which was the Latin name for the buttercup, but means a little frog, in allusion to the semi-aquatic habitat of some species. Many varieties are called "crowfoot." Some of our commonest buttercups have come from Europe, and are plentiful on lawns and pastures, often as troublesome weeds. Nearly all of them have an acrid juice, divided or compound leaves, and practically always yellow flowers with five petals. None of these is to be confused with the florist's ranunculus, which is really the Persian buttercup (*Ranunculus asiaticus*) and can be grown only in a greenhouse in the eastern states. It is far more showy than any of our wild buttercups, being mostly double-flowered and deep yellow or orange.

123. What is the blue flag? A native iris, commonly called blue flag because its beautiful blue petals stand out flag-like. It is the most common of the native irises of the northeastern states, and was named by Linnaeus *Iris versicolor* which means "variously colored." The plant grows in moist or wet places, rises about twelve to thirty inches in height and has sword-shaped leaves. The terminal flowers bloom one by one from a sheath-like, papery organ. The three main divisions of the flower have very showy petals that are blue, but violet-veined, and touched with yellow at the base, thus *versicolor*. As a garden flower it does not compare with the tall-bearded (German) irises, or with the Japanese iris.

124. What is the starflower? In moist, thin woods or sometimes in open moist places, one can often find in May or June a small white flower with five pointed petals. The flowers look so star-like that starflower seems a more appropriate name for it than chickweed wintergreen, or its technical name of *Trientalis borealis,* which literally means "northern" and "a third of a foot," which is the approximate

height of the plant. It is curious in having a very thin, wiry stem, and
is crowned with a cluster of five to nine pointed leaves three to four
inches long. From the center of this terminal leaf-cluster arise one or
two thread-thin stalks, each with its star-like white flower. The plant is
scarcely worth cultivation.

**125. When our grandmothers had weepy eyes, what wildflower
did they turn to for a remedy?** To the goldthread, often called
yellowroot and canker-root, but known to science as *Coptis trifolia*.
This is a tiny perennial, never more than six inches high, with golden-

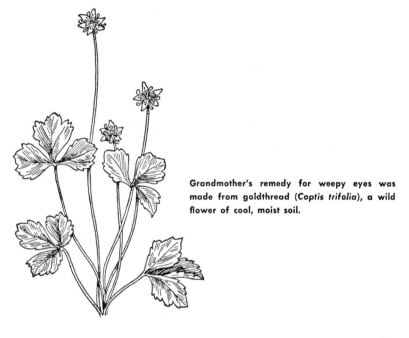

Grandmother's remedy for weepy eyes was
made from goldthread (*Coptis trifolia*), a wild
flower of cool, moist soil.

yellow, thread-like roots, an infusion of which was used to treat weepy
eyes. The small, evergreen, leaves are compound, with three wedge-
shaped, toothed leaflets. There is a solitary, long-stalked white flower,
with five to seven sepals colored like the much smaller petals. It grows
only in cool, moist places, mostly in the North, and is sometimes cultivated more for its interest than its beauty.

Woodland Flowers

All of the flowers noted in Questions 96–125 grow in moist places, sometimes in or along the edges of the woods, in bogs, marshes or wet meadows. The following wildflowers are definitely wood-lovers, and grew in the manificent forests that once stretched from the Atlantic to the crest of the Appalachian Mountains. Huge tracts of the eastern states are still covered by such forests, and it is in the shade of these, and in the rich soil of the forest floor that nearly all of the wildflowers in the following section will be found.

These forests are of three or four different types. In the far north they are predominately coniferous trees such as the fir, spruce, larch, hemlock and pine—cool evergreen forests. A little farther south these evergreens are replaced by thousands of square miles of non-evergreen forest composed largely of beech, birch, sugar maple, elm, tulip-trees and others, all of which drop their leaves in the fall.

Still further south the forests are more open. Here there is a much less dense canopy, and the chief components are what the foresters call the oak-hickory type, with several different kinds of oak, the hickories, sweet gum, sassafras, sycamore, and other trees, none of which is evergreen. The forest floor is not so rich, and more light filters down through the canopy.

Finally there are the huge pine forests of the coastal plain, stretching from southern Maryland to the Gulf of Mexico, the chief components of which are the loblolly, the long-leaf and other pines. The wildflowers in such places are very different from those of the North.

In the relatively high altitudes of the Appalachian Range, many northern wildflowers are found far south of their greatest frequency; this is particularly true in the Great Smoky National Park in North Carolina.

The wildflowers in the following questions are arranged according to their occurrence in the forest types mentioned above.

126. Who was Peter Collinson, and what wildflower was named for him? He was a Quaker merchant in London (1694–1768) who collected, or had collected for him, rare plants from all over the world, so that his garden at Mill Hill became famous. One of his importations from America was a not very showy perennial known as horse balm or richweed, which Linnaeus named *Collinsonia canadensis* in honor of this erudite Quaker merchant. It is a strong-smelling, smooth herb, two to four feet high, with a square stem and opposite, somewhat oval leaves, four to eight inches long. Because of its lemon-scented flowers, some people call it citronella (no relative of true citronella). The corollas are irregular and borne in a long, often branched, terminal cluster. It is summer-blooming, and inhabits rich woods.

127. Are the twinflower and twinberry the same?   No, but they have a superficial resemblance and are often confused. Both are low, creeping plants with evergreen, opposite, roundish short-stalked leaves. The twinflower, named *Linnaea borealis* after the immortal Linnaeus, has its twin flowers borne at the end of thread-thin stalks that are about three-fourths of an inch long. The flowers are nodding. The corolla is bell-shaped, about one-half of an inch wide, white, tinged with pink, and has five distinct if small lobes. The fruit is dry. Found in cool, rich woods in the North.

128. What is the partridgeberry?   This is the preferred name for the twinberry (see Question 127) and is also known as squawberry and teaberry. It was named by Linnaeus *Mitchella repens* to honor his friend John Mitchell, of Virginia, who sent it to Linnaeus before 1753. It is a trailing, prostrate, evergreen plant whose small rounded leaves are often blotched or margined with white. Toward the tip of the stem are borne the twin flowers, in an essentially stalkless cluster. The corolla is white, small, and has four, small, but distinct lobes (not five as in the twinflower) followed by handsome, red berries that are joined, hence twinberry. The partridgeberry is a favorite for the indoor terrarium. It grows in the woods, but much farther south than the twinflower.

129. In several questions it has been necessary to mention Linnaeus and to refer to him as immortal. Why is this?   To all flower lovers, botanists, pharmacists and foresters he *is* immortal, for to him we owe our system of naming all plants with a *generic* name, like *Viola* (for all the violets) and a specific name like *odorata* (which designates only one of many species, as the sweet violet). Before the time of Linnaeus the naming of new plants was in considerable confusion.

This Swedish botanist was born in 1707 and died in 1778. To him explorers from all over the world sent thousands of specimens, many of which he grew in his world-famous garden in Upsala. His real name was Karl Von Linne, and in 1753 he published his *Species Plantarum* in Latin. It named and described all the plants known to him at that time, many of them American. Ever since, it has been the Bible for all flower lovers, who unite in calling him the most famous botanist in the world.

130. What is the richweed? A rather widely used common name for the horse balm. (See Question 126.)

131. Who was Dr. Short and how did one of our most rare wildflowers come to be named for him? In 1788 Michaux, one of the early botanical explorers, found in the mountains of North Carolina a

This rarest of wild flowers, named *Shortis galacifolia*, was lost and not re-discovered for ninety years.

plant that no one had ever seen before. He took the specimen to Paris. As it was only in fruit, the plant was not christened, and for ninety years no one could find it again, although many tried. Thus its flowers were completely unknown until it was re-discovered in 1877 by Asa Gray who named it *Shortia galacifolia* in honor of Dr. Charles W. Short of Kentucky, a friend of Gray, a collector of plants, a physician and a wealthy patron of botany. Ever since it has been one of our rarest wildflowers, shy and difficult to cultivate, although now available from dealers. It is a small plant, with galax-like basal, evergreen leaves (hence *galacifolia*) and beautiful, white, wax-like flowers, one at the end of a stalk not over five to six inches high. The five petals are rounded and faintly notched. This rare and interesting plant has tempted many to grow it, but this can be done only in deep shade, and the woodsy soil must be full of humus. It will not stand heat, drought or wind. Although known for nearly a hundred years simply as *Shortia,* the modern attempt to call it "Oconee Bells" ignores its somewhat romantic history.

132. What is galax?   A plant closely allied to *Shortia* (see Question 131), and also growing in southern mountains is the much better known and far commoner *Galax aphylla,* locally called beetleweed. It is a stemless, evergreen plant, with leaves which are nearly round, about three and a half inches wide, and green at first but bronzy with age. It is found in practically all florist shops, because its foliage is universally used for funeral wreaths. Its flowers are arranged in a spike-like cluster, the five petals white and not so showy as *Shortia.* *Galax* is from the Greek for "milk," probably in allusion to the white flowers.

133. Has any wildflower been named for Thomas Jefferson?   Yes, the twin-leaf or rheumatism root (*Jeffersonia diphylla*) was so named in 1793 by B. S. Smith, a Pennsylvania doctor and naturalist. It is an erect perennial, six to eight inches high, with long-stalked, solitary leaves, cleft so nearly to the middle as to superficially resemble two leaves (hence *diphylla*). The solitary, long-stalked, eight-petalled flowers are white, about one inch wide, and bloom in May. The plant is found only in rich woods, especially in the mountains of the eastern United States.

134. Did a half-mad genius dedicate a wildflower to a governor of New York?   Constantine Rafinesque, an erratic and brilliant French naturalist, dedicated our cowtongue or bluebead to De Witt Clinton by naming one of our most beautiful northern wildflowers *Clintonia borealis.* The plant, sometimes called the yellow bead-lily, is a perennial of cool forests, with two or three basal, oblong or ovalish leaves that are finely hairy on the margin. The flowers grow in a terminal cluster of three or four, are drooping, nearly an inch long, greenish-yellow, and bloom in May–June. The blue, football-shaped berries are quite striking and grow about one-half an inch long. The *Clintonia* is of easy culture in the shady wild garden, but only in cool regions.

135. Is the Indian turnip the same as the Jack-in-the-pulpit?   Yes; it acquired the name "Indian turnip," because the natives in the eastern states actually used the bitter, acrid, half-poisonous root as food. They found that by heating the root they could drive off the acrid juice, just as the South American Indians treat the poisonous root of the cassava (mandioca). The plant, familiar to nearly everyone as *Arisaema triphyllum,* is a deep-rooted, stout perennial with only two compound leaves, divided into three leaflets. The flowering stalk is fleshy, twelve to eighteen inches long and crowned with a beautifully furrowed, greenish "pulpit," rising about two inches and with a terminal arching flap. Within the "pulpit" is the "Jack," a stiff club-shaped organ upon which are crowded hundreds of almost microscopic flowers. The plant is of easy culture in cool, moist woods, but languishes in the sun and does not like wind.

136. What is the dragonroot?   This is a close relative of the Jack-in-the-pulpit (see Question 135), but with an irregularly divided, solitary leaf made up of seven to eleven pointed segments. Its technical name, *Arisaema Dracontium,* and its other common name of green dragon, remind us that it was once thought to yield the famous dragon's-blood of the Canary Islands. Of course it does nothing of the kind, but its juice is acrid and half-poisonous. Unlike the Jack-in-the-pulpit, the dragonroot has no "pulpit," but the long, flower-bearing "Jack" protrudes far beyond the tapering leaf-like organ that replaces the "pulpit" in this species. It blooms in April or May and is found mostly in cool, rich and moist woods.

137. Is the trailing arbutus the same as one of our Mayflowers?
Yes, and this delightfully fragrant, spring-blooming evergreen plant is also called ground laurel. Linnaeus named it *Epigaea repens* when it reached him from America, *Epigaea* being from the Gerek for "on the earth" and *repens* meaning "creeping," which exactly describes it. Its leaves are ovalish, about two inches long and minutely hairy on

the margin. They stay green all winter, but are replaced by new leaves after the plant blooms, usually in April. The flowers are small, bell-shaped, about one-half of an inch long, white or pinkish, and are very fragrant; they are followed by a tiny capsule, sometimes, but not always, full of extremely minute seeds. The trailing arbutus is not easy to grow, and digging out wild plants invites almost certain failure. Small potted plants from a dealer who carries native plants are less likely to fail, but they must be planted in a sandy, quite acid earth in dryish woods. Ordinary garden culture is useless.

138. Has synthetic wintergreen replaced the real thing? Almost entirely, for the active principle in the leaves of our common wintergreen has been produced synthetically, and is not only chemically and therapeutically identical but indistinguishable by taste, odor or texture. Nevertheless, many die-hard cognoscenti prefer the real thing, which is a small evergreen plant with its stems half underground, its oval-shaped leaves about one and a half inches long, toothed and a little bristly on the margin. The usually white or pinkish, nodding flowers are scarcely one-fourth of an inch long and bloom in June–July, followed by a pea-size scarlet berry. So fragrant is the juice of this plant (smelling like birch bark) that a number of its common names are quite appropriate, *i.e.* spiceberry, checkerberry and teaberry. It was named scientifically for a Dr. Jean-Francois Gaultier, a court physician at Quebec for whom Linnaeus called it *Gaultheria procumbens*. As an ornamental, the plant is scarcely worth growing, and its culture or collection for its methyl salicylate (its active principle) has been practically eliminated by the synthetic product.

139. Why was the pepper turnip so called? The name was applied to the bitter, acrid root of the Jack-in-the-pulpit. (See Question 135.)

140. Are there variegated leaves among any of our wildflowers? The blotching or streaking with white or yellow of otherwise green leaves is so common among cultivated plants that many people wonder why it is so rare among wildflowers. Whatever the cause or utility of variegated leaves, they are certainly rare among wild plants. One of them is the partridgeberry (see Question 128); another is the dragon's-tongue or spotted wintergreen (*Chimaphila maculata*), also

(Roehrs)

This Asiatic orchid, *Cymbidium insigne*, is one of the showiest and long-lasting, when cut, of all the huge orchid tribe. (Question 56)

(Roehrs)

This Mexican orchid is grown all over the tropical world; not for its greenish-yellow flowers but for the pods that follow it. They are the only source of vanilla. (Question 54)

(Roehrs)

Also long-keeping when cut are the white flowers of this orchid, *Phalaenopsis amabilis*, which comes from the Philippines and

(Roehrs)

Laelia anceps, a Mexican orchid with rose-purple flowers, is in every florist's shop and is easily grown in an amateur green-

called rheumatism root. Its evergreen leaves are lance-shaped, pointed, one to three inches long, dark green but mottled along some of the veins with white. The flowers are white, nodding, in a sparse terminal cluster, with the five concave petals more or less waxy. The plant is less than six inches high, and difficult to transplant from the rich woods in which it grows. It is summer-blooming and a beautiful, variegated-leaved wildflower, well named, since *maculata* means spotted.

141. Have we a true geranium among our wildflowers? Yes, and it *is* a true geranium, while our common garden variety belongs to a group known as *Pelargonium* which are South African in origin. Our native species in the East is the wild geranium or cranesbill, properly assigned to *Geranium maculatum,* and also called the alumroot. It is a woodland perennial, twelve to twenty inches high, its five to nine inch leaves parted nearly to the middle. The flowers are about one inch wide, and are not so showy as the garden geranium. The five rounded petals are rose-purple, and are followed by an elastically splitting, beaked pod. April–May blooming and of easy culture in partial shade in a woodsy soil.

142. What is the ground holly? Merely another name for the wintergreen. (See Question 138.)

143. Do some people call the trailing arbutus the winter pink? Yes, because its flowers are among the first to bloom in early spring. (See Question 137.)

144. Is there a wild columbine in the eastern states? Of all the sixty species of columbine, many of them superb garden plants, the only real native in the East is *Aquilegia canadensis,* the wild columbine so common in rocky woods. It is a perennial, fifteen to twenty-four inches high, with twice or thrice compound leaves, the leaflets lobed. The flowers are terminal, yellow and red, and the five petals prolonged into five hollow spurs that are knobbed at the end. The showy flowers bloom in April or May. Some forms may, rarely, be all yellow or all white. It grows easily in the wild garden and sometimes in ordinary garden soil if the site is shady.

145. Are there any wildflowers that derive their food from other plants?   Two species, closely related, without green coloring matter in their leafless stems are true parasites and steal their food from other plants to which they are attached. The first is the Indian pipe or corpse-plant (*Monotropa uniflora*), sometimes called pipe-plant. It is four to six inches high, and its ghostly white stem is leafless but clothed rather sparingly with white, pointed scales. At the summit is a single, nod-ding, white flower which is very rarely pinkish-salmon. The other is the pinesap (*Monotropa Hypopitys*), which has several flowers in the cluster, the petals red or touched with yellow. Neither, of course, can ever be cultivated for they are parasites on the roots of other plants or on fungi and have no true roots of their own.

146. Are there two eastern wild flowers known as alumroot?
Yes; one of them is the wild geranium. (See Question 141.) The other is the American sanicle (*Heuchera americana*), a close relative of a fine garden plant known as coral bells which comes from the southwestern states. Our local species is a woodland plant, its flowering stalk eighteen to twenty-four inches high, its leaves mostly basal, nearly round and with roundish marginal teeth, the leaf blade mottled in youth and ultimately green. The flowers are rather small, and are borne in a sparse, terminal cluster, greenish-white and with protruding stamens. (See Question 3.) It is a plant of open woods named by Linnaeus in honor of Johan Heinrich von Heucher, a German botanist.

147. What wildflower closely resembles the American sanicle?
The foam flower or coolwort (*Tiarella cordifolia*), often called the false mitrewort, does have a superficial resemblance to the American san-icle, but it is only about half as tall and has pointed instead of roundish leaves. Also the flowers are pure white and more profuse. In cool, moist woods the plant often occurs in extensive patches, which in May or June carpet the ground with a white, very attractive, foam-like sheen. Some of that sheen is due to the fact that the foam flower has twice as many stamens as the American sanicle.

148. What is the mitrewort?   This is a close relative of the foam flower and the American sanicle, but differs from both in having a pair of stalkless, opposite leaves inserted about halfway up the stem, which may be eight to sixteen inches high. The mitrewort (*Mitella* *diphylla*), also called bishop's-cap, was so named because its fruit resembles a bishop's mitre. It blooms in May, and its five white petals are beautifully fringed. It is found in rich woods and is not difficult to grow in the wild garden if shaded from the sun and wind.

149. Why is the Solomon's-seal so called?   The underground stem (rhizome) of this plant, when detached, leaves a scar that somewhat resembles a seal, whether Solomon's or not! There are several species, most of them having arched stems ten to thirty-six inches high, with pointed, opposite pairs of leaves at intervals along the stem. At each pair of leaves, and sometimes a few at the end, are borne two (or rarely more) greenish flowers followed by a bluish-black fruit not unlike a grape. All of them grow in the woods and are of easy culture in the wild garden, blooming in May-July. *Polygonatum* is from the Greek for many "knees," in allusion to the jointed underground stems.

150. What is the false Solomon's-seal?   This is a close relative of the true one, and is called wild spikenard and, in Latin, *Smilacina racemosa*. It differs from the true Solomon's-seal, in having its oval-shaped leaves alternately arranged on the stem. Its small white flowers are all in a terminal, plume-like cluster that may be four inches long. It is a woodland plant, fifteen to thirty inches high, and the flowers are followed by a pinkish-red berry, often called "treacleberry." *Smilacina* is a diminutive of *Smilax* to which the false Solomon's-seal is related. The plant is easy to grow in a wild garden and flowers in May.

151. Is there a wild lily-of-the-valley?   A plant so called is common in moist woods from Labrador to North Carolina, but it is nothing like so attractive as the true one which is isolated in the mountains of the Carolinas and is mostly a garden plant. The wild lily-of-the-valley is often called Mayflower, perhaps because its Latin name, *Maianthemum,* means literally a flower of May. It was named *canadense* by Linnaeus in 1753, because to him, at that date, nearly everything that grew north of Virginia was Canadian. The plant is only three to six inches high, and bears on its stem two or three somewhat oval, practically stalkless leaves that are heart-shaped at the base. The very small white flowers, borne in a terminal cluster in May or June, are followed by a few, yellowish-white, brown-spotted berries which ultimately turn pale red, hence its other common name of bead-ruby.

The flowers are not fragrant and the plant scarcely warrants a place in the wild garden. (For the true lily-of-the-valley see Question 519.)

152. What is the fairy-cap?   The mitrewort. (See Question 148.)

153. What is the treacleberry?   The false Solomon's-seal. (See Question 150.)

154. What is a bellwort?   Several plants are so called, all closely related and all belonging to the group known as *Uvularia,* natives of the woodlands from Quebec to Florida. The most common is *Uvularia grandiflora,* called variously bellwort, strawflower, cornflower and wood daffodil, nearly all of these inappropriate common names, because each has been applied to better known plants. The bellwort is a slender, rather beautiful perennial, eight to twenty inches high, with a forking stem and only two or three nearly stalkless, long-pointed leaves at or near the fork, their under side finely white-hairy. The flower is solitary, terminal, drooping, and about one and a half inches long; it is pale yellow and mostly May-flowering. (For the garden strawflower see Question 679.)

155. What is the baneberry?   There are two native woodland plants so called, both belonging to the group known as *Actaea.* They are perennials, one to two feet high, with twice- or thrice-compound leaves, the ultimate leaflets deeply cleft and toothed. The flowers are numerous, white, small, and are crowded in thick terminal clusters that stand well above the leaves. It is by their distinctive fruits that the baneberries can be most easily distinguished. The white sort has china-white, glistening berries with a conspicuous, blackish-purple eye. The berry of the red baneberry is coral colored. The berries of both are poisonous.

156. Are the trout lily and the yellow adder's-tongue the same?
Yes, both are local names for what most people call the dogtooth violet (*Erythronium americanum*), a common, spring-blooming plant of moist woods, usually growing in colonies. It has only two basal, brown-mottled leaves, four to six inches long, and pointed at the tip. The solitary, nodding, lily-like flower is at the tip of a stalk six to ten inches high. The petals and sepals are both yellow, sometimes tinged

on the outside with brown-purple. The plant is of easy culture in the wild garden if the site is moist and shady.

157. What is the best native violet for the garden? By all odds the finest and most easily grown is the Confederate violet (*Viola priceana*). Although thought by some to be a variety of the common blue violet, it is very different in color and habit. The Confederate violet is native from Kentucky to Georgia and westward, and is so vigorous in growth that it tends to spread rather rampantly, particularly in the shade. It has the typical, heart-shaped leaves of most violets, but its flowers are more showy than any other native violet. Its flowers stand well above the foliage (six to eight inches high) and are whitish or pale blue, streaked with much deeper blue. It may be nearly three-fourths of an inch wide, and as they are numerous, the plant is very showy in early May.

158. Are there many violets among our Eastern flora? There are at least fifty different species, besides many varieties and hybrids, so that their identification is quite difficult. A good many are stemless and bear two sorts of flowers; the familiar showy ones and those that never open and grow at ground level. (See Question 16.) Other violets have stems that bear leaves. Violets grow in a variety of places from wet swamps to dry, sandy, open sites. One of the best-known is the meadow or blue violet (*Viola papilionacea*) which resembles the Confederate violet (see Question 157) but is not so handsome and has mostly violet-colored flowers, without the striking veining of deep blue found in the larger flower of the Confederate violet. The common blue violet was named *papilionacea,* because that word means "like a pea flower," but it only faintly resembles a pea.

159. What is the wood daffodil? The bellwort. (See Question 154.)

160. Is the bead-ruby the same as the wild lily-of-the-valley? Yes. (See Question 151.)

161. What is the wild bleeding heart? A shy, woodland beauty not over one to two feet high, found in the forests, mostly in the mountains, from New York to Georgia and Tennesee. It is closely related to the common bleeding heart of our gardens, which comes from Japan.

Our local plant has very fragile, basal leaves that are much divided, and nodding, pink flowers that are spurred, and borne in a loose, terminal, arched cluster. The wild bleeding heart was named *Dicentra eximia;* the first word means two-spurred, and *eximia* implies out of the common run, which it certainly is. It blooms in June or July; and if cultivated, should be put in a shady part of the rock garden.

162. Is the Dutchman's-breeches closely related to the wild bleeding heart? Yes, they are so closely related that both belong to the *Dicentra.* (See Question 161). The Dutchman's-breeches was named *Dicentra Cucullaria,* but it is more frequently known as white eardrops or colic-weed. It is a very fragile, delicate plant with much dissected leaves that are pale beneath. The flowering stalk, never much above six inches high, is crowned with a few, two-spurred white flowers, the tips of the spurs yellowish, in April or May. The plant is so fragile that cultivation is possible only in the shadiest, most wind-free part of the wild garden.

163. What eastern wildflower blossom resembles the flowering dogwood? In the cool woods of the north there grows the beautiful, low plant known as bunchberry (*Cornus canadensis*) or crackerberry or dwarf cornel, which is first cousin to the flowering dogwood. And like that tree its "flower" is not a flower at all. The bunchberry is a woody plant, not over six inches high, with a cluster of basal, ovalish leaves about one and one half inches long. Among them is a collection of tiny green flowers, immediately beneath which are four showy, greenish-white organs that look like petals, but are not. They are bracts, and as in the dogwood, they are commonly, but incorrectly called the "flower." The fruit is a red berry, much like that of the dogwood. The plant is difficult to cultivate, except in the northern wild garden.

164. Is the trinity lily the best of all the wakerobins for the wild garden? By far; most gardeners call it the great white trillium (*Trillium grandiflorum*). It is easily grown in partial shade, preferably in woodsy soil. A strong-growing plant, twelve to eighteen inches high, whose stem is topped by a cluster of three somewhat oval leaves, four to six inches long, crowned in May by a stunning, white, waxy flower that may be three and a half inches across. The flowers often fade to

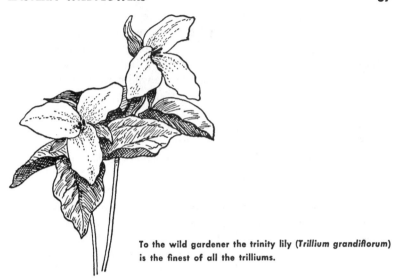

To the wild gardener the trinity lily (*Trillium grandiflorum*) is the finest of all the trilliums.

pink. The plant is easily dug from the wild (when dormant), and is also carried by most dealers in native plants.

165. How many different trilliums are there in the eastern states?
There are at least a dozen species, besides a number of forms and varieties, all of them often called wakerobin. One of the finest is the painted trillium (*Trillium undulatum*), also called the smiling wake-robin. It grows twelve to eighteen inches high, and at the end of the stem is a cluster of three ovalish, tapering leaves. From them arises an erect flower stalk about two inches long, topped by a beautiful white flower, nearly three inches across, each petal marked with a crimson **V**. It is one of the most beautiful of our wildflowers and blooms in May. *Trillium* is from the Latin for "three," in allusion to the leaves being in threes, as are the petals also.

166. Is there a wild blue phlox sometimes called sweet William?
Yes, and its profusion of handsome flowers covers acres in some deep forests. It is usually called the blue phlox, as it is a true phlox and not really a sweet William, which is a European pink. The native plant (*Phlox divaricata*) is a bushy perennial, twelve to eighteen inches high, with creeping stems which root, thus increasing the size

of the plant. The leaves are broadly lance-shaped and two inches long. The flowers appear in a profuse cluster. The corolla is about one inch wide, and the color ranges from blue to purple or mauve. The plant is more common in Michigan and Illinois than in the East, and is easily grown in the half-shade of the wild garden.

167. Are Indian lettuce and canker lettuce the same? Both common names refer to the shinleaf. (See Question 172.)

168. What is the gay-wings? Another name for the flowering wintergreen. (See Question 173.)

169. Is there a wildflower whose leaves "go to sleep"? Many tropical trees fold up their leaflets at night or in cloudy weather, and there is one native wood sorrel (*Oxalis violacea*) which always does the same. It is a perennial plant, not more than six inches high, with compound leaves composed of three slightly notched leaflets. These droop and fold together at nightfall and on cloudy days, apparently "going to sleep." The flower stalk bears from three to six flowers, the petals of which are light magenta or (rarely) white and bloom in May or June. It is of fairly easy culture in the shady wild garden. *Oxalis,* from the Greek for "sour" is in allusion to the acid juice of nearly all the sorrels.

170. What is the rue anemone? One of the frailest and most delicate of all eastern wildflowers, so fragile and fleeting that it is hardly worth cultivating. It is called *Anemonella thalictroides. Anemonella* is a diminutive of *Anemone,* to which the plant is closely related, and *thalictroides* means "like a meadow rue" of which the rue anemone is a tiny replica. It is about six to eight inches high with leaves thrice compound, the ultimate segments three-lobed. The flowers are white, very fragile, on weak, thin stalks, usually two or three in a cluster, without petals, with the six petal-like sepals replacing true petals.

171. What is the goatsbeard? A stout spirea-like perennial, related to the queen-of-the-meadow (see Question 121), but differing from it in having thrice-compound leaves. The goatsbeard (*Aruncus dioicus*) also has the male and female flowers on separate plants, so that cross fertilization is essential. It is three to six feet high, the thrice compound leaves with many leaflets. The flowers are in tight, finger-thick clusters, of which there may be from eight to eleven on the upper part of the general flowering stalk. The petals are very small, yellowish-white and usually June-blooming. The goatsbeard is of the easiest culture almost anywhere. It does best if there is some shade.

172. Are the shinleaf and consumption-weed the same? Yes. The plant is also called Indian lettuce and canker lettuce, but its scientific name is *Pyrola americana*. It is an evergreen plant with basal, round-ish, dark green leaves, the stalks of which are longer than the leaf blades. The flowers are fragrant, white, waxy, and quite numerous in a loose terminal cluster, the individual flowers nodding. August blooming, and uncertain as a cultivated plant, and suited only for rich woods soil in the wild garden.

173. What is gay-wings? A delicate, extremely beautiful woodland wildflower, commonly called flowering wintergreen (*Polygala pauci-folia*), but also known as fringed milkwort. Its oval bright green leaves survive the winter, but turn bronzy. The flowers are about one inch wide, showy, crimson-magenta, the wings handsomely fringed. Besides these showy flowers, the plant bears, underground, very small flowers, that never open but produce a small capsule. They are cleistogamous, as are some violet flowers. (See Question 16.)

SHRUBS AND TREES

A wildflower traditionally is one borne upon an herbaceous plant; the flowers on trees and shrubs are not usually called wildflowers at all. But the early explorers of America, like Michaux, Pursh, Bartram, Nuttall and Dr. Short of Kentucky were quite impressed by the beauty and variety of the flowers found on our native shrubs and trees. Perhaps nowhere else in the world, except in China and Japan, are there so many different kinds of superlative flowering trees and shrubs as in our eastern states. Many of these have been rescued from the forest and are now much appreciated garden plants. Hence it seems appropriate to answer a few questions about them, even if they are not technically considered as typical wildflowers.

But the answering of such questions can hardly begin until a more basic query is disposed of.

174. Do all trees and shrubs have flowers?   They do or otherwise their survival would be impossible, as without flowers there would be no seed. (See Question 3.) But many of our finest native shade trees and shrubs bear such inconspicuous flowers that they excited the wonder of neither the early American explorers nor of us today. For some of these flowers have no petals, others are green and small, a few are almost microscopic, and a good many either bloom so early, or their flowers are so hidden by foliage, that most people would say they have no flowers. That is completely incorrect, but we should be quite right in saying that these are not *flowering* trees, in the garden sense of that term.

Among native trees and shrubs that many people (incorrectly) suppose to have no flowers, because these are inconspicuous or hard to see are:

Willow	Birch	Chestnut
Poplar	Alder	Elm
Beech	Bayberry	Mulberry
Oak	Walnut	Paper mulberry

There are several other trees, such as most species of ash and, of course, all the coniferous evergreens such as pine, spruce, fir, etc., which bear only naked ovules in what is scarcely a *flower* at all, *i.e.* a cone, between the scales of which the naked ovule awaits its fertilization by the pollen of the male.

175. What native tree in the eastern states bears the largest flower? The cucumber tree (*Magnolia macrophylla*) of the southeastern states has a huge, white, fragrant flower, ten to twelve inches wide, that blooms in May or June after the leaves expand. It is a round-headed tree, never much more than fifty feet high, which bears enormous leaves that are twelve to thirty-six inches long, oblong, and softly hairy on the under side. The six petals may be slightly purplish at the base. This is a magnificent lawn tree, which, like all magnolias, must be transplanted with care. For a related, and still finer tree see Question 18.

176. What is the flame azalea?   Many people would consider it our most magnificent native shrub. Found in the mountains from Pennsylvania to Georgia, and christened *Azalea calendulacea,* it is not over twelve feet high, usually less, and has elliptic leaves two to three inches long. Its irregular flowers are borne in clusters of eight to twelve which bloom after the leaves expand. The corolla is sticky on the outside, orange or scarlet or both, about two inches wide with handsome protruding stamens. There are several native varieties and these have been crossed with Asiatic species to produce scores of horticultural varieties. The culture of the flame azalea is easy if it is given partial shade, acid humus, is never allowed to dry out and is free from wind.

177. What native azalea flowers before the leaves expand? The pinkster flower (*Azalea nudiflora*) always does, usually in late April or May. It is a handsome shrub, two to five feet high, its alternate leaves oblongish, two to four inches long. The flowers grow eight to ten in a cluster, about one and one-half inches wide, pink or pinkish-white, the showy stamens far protruding. There are several varieties as the shrub is popular as a garden plant. Its culture is the same as for the flame azalea. (See Question 176.)

178. The flowers of what native shrub are preferred by many women to commercial sachet? In the southeastern states there grows a densely hairy shrub called the Carolina allspice or sweet-scented shrub, known to science as *Calycanthus floridus,* and called in some states merely sweet-shrub or strawberry-shrub. With so many common names denoting fragrance, it is little wonder that the dark, nearly chocolate-brown flowers have a spicy, haunting and quite lasting odor, even when dry; hence their feminine popularity. The flowers are nearly two inches wide, not showy, and are not borne in clusters. The plant is of easy culture in any ordinary garden soil.

179. What is the fastest growing native flowering tree? The catalpa, which was the Indian name for the tree in the central states where it is native from Indiana to Arkansas. It is a medium-sized tree, christened *Catalpa speciosa,* and often called Indian bean from its long slender pod. The leaves are ovalish, and nearly twelve inches long, opposite, and hairy beneath. The flowers are very showy, the irregular corolla white but yellow-striped and conspicuously purple-spotted, about two inches wide. They are arranged in a branching cluster nearly seven inches long, and in late May or June the tree is very handsome. Seedling catalpas make an astonishing growth in a single season—often several feet—but the wood is soft and the tree is relatively short-lived. A close relative (*Catalpa bignonioides*) occurs in the southeastern states, and is variously called the bean-tree or cigar-tree because of its long, slender pods. *Catalpa speciosa* is the taller tree and is much grown as a lawn specimen.

180. What native flowering tree produces blooms on naked twigs? While still apparently dormant, and before the leaves expand, the redbud (*Cercis canadensis*), often called the Judas-tree, is a welcome harbinger of spring. Relatively common, this small tree or large shrub, splashes the bare forests from New York to Florida with brilliant color. It is so lovely in early spring that the redbud and a Chinese relative are quite often cultivated. It has broadly oval leaves, and the small, pea-like, rosy-pink flowers, so numerous that they nearly cover the bare twigs, are followed by a pea-like pod that is about three inches long. The culture of the redbud is easy, preferably in an open sandy soil, as it does not like heavy moist places.

181. Was the flowering dogwood ever linked with the Crucifixion? Many trees have reputedly furnished the timber for the Cross, most of them purely conjectural. But the most fantastic error was a pamphlet issued by an ardent but botanically naive missionary who claimed that the Cross was made of our flowering dogwood! This tree was not discovered until the sixteenth century in the eastern United States, and was called by Linnaeus *Cornus florida*. For some unexplained reason in the deep South, it is also called boxwood, which it is not. It is one of our most beautiful flowering trees, growing naturally in the under-canopy of the forest, and not usually over thirty feet high. The leaves are ovalish, and three to five inches long. The flowers are small, green, rather inconspicuous, but beneath the stalkless cluster are four, showy, brilliantly white and notched organs, often wrongly called "petals." Actually they are bracts, and it is to them that the flowering dogwood owes its spectacular beauty, usually in the first week in May. Its bright red berries are attractive in the fall. (For a related plant see Question 163.)

182. What flowering tree produces the rarest honey? The native sourwood, in spite of its name, is the eager target of thousands of bees when it is in full bloom. From its nectar they make a honey that epicures crave, and which is rare or wanting in the usual shops, as most of it is locally consumed. This predominately southern tree, called sourwood or sorrel from its bitter juice, was scientifically called *Oxydendrum arboreum,* because this quite literally means "sour tree." It is medium-sized, with alternate, longish, toothed leaves that are almost shining yellow-green. From mid-June into July it produces sparse, arching clusters of small, bell-shaped, white flowers, that suggest those of the lily-of-the-valley, and the tree is hence often called the lily-of-the-valley tree. The flower clusters are so numerous that the tree is a midsummer garden treasure, but it is slow-growing and certainly hardy only from Boston southward.

183. What beautiful native shrub produces poisonous honey? The dangerously poisonous honey of our great laurel (*Rhododendron maximum*) is discarded by all careful bee-keepers because it may be fatal. This strikingly fine evergreen shrub, the only rhododendron of the northeastern states, is often called the rosebay because of its rose-pink flowers. In the north it rarely grows above ten feet, but in the Carolina mountains it may reach twenty feet, although it is not really a tree. The leaves are oblong, seven to ten inches long, densely hairy beneath. The flowers are bell-shaped, about one and a half inches wide, and are grouped in a tightish cluster, but these showy blooms are partly hidden by the foliage. It should only be grown in partial shade, in an acid soil. It will not stand wind or heat.

184. Are the strawberry-shrub and the sweet-shrub the same? Yes, both are local names for the Carolina allspice. (See Question 178.)

185. Who was Peter Kalm, and what native shrub was named for him? He was a brilliant pupil of Linnaeus who induced him to go to America. He landed in Philadelphia in 1748 and spent the next three years in collecting plants in Pennsylvania, New York and Canada. From there he sent specimens of the beautiful mountain laurel, and the father of botany named it *Kalmia latifolia* in his honor. It is a splendid evergreen shrub, with pink and white flowers, and Kalm considered it one of his best finds. Because of its flower color it is often called calico-bush, and it is easier to grow than its close relative, the rhododendron. It thrives in partial shade and in an acid soil, preferably protected from strong winds. (For a related plant see Question 98.)

While it is perfectly true that the states east of the mountains comprised a huge forest area, these woodlands did not cover all of it. Even before settlement had cleared thousands of square miles for agriculture, there were open places. Such areas were, and are, quite unsuitable for the flowers whose existence depends upon the coolness, shade, and wind-free environment of the forest, not to speak for the moment of the rich forest humus in which they grow. Such conditions never exist in the open—in other words the ecological conditions dictate the sort of flowers that grow in the water, in forests and in the open. So true is this that a proper understanding of the distribution of our hundreds of eastern wildflowers can only be attained by answering, at least in part, the next question.

186. What is ecology?   Basically, without descending to textbook verbosity, its definition is very simply indicated by the Greek origin of the term: the knowledge of home, *i.e.* habitat. Ecology is thus a study of the habitat or environment. Every successful gardener, farmer and forester is an ecologist, even if he never heard the term, because the concept of ecology is as old as the Greeks, although the word ecology is of reasonably recent coinage. Today there exists a huge literature about it and there are ecological societies here, in England, Germany, Sweden and many other countries.

If the term is easily defined, its implications are exceedingly complex. It involves a study of light; humidity; the evaporating power of the air; the composition, acidity and moisture-holding capacity of the soil; the competition between plants for food and light; the tolerance of darkness by some plants and the intolerance by other plants of reduced light. None of these factors operates individually, and it is the totality of their impact, plus a few more factors that we can leave to the experts, which dictates the occurrence of any flower in what we must assume is its preferred habitat. All of these matters have been studied statistically, instrumentally and chemically, but again, we can leave such complexities to the experts and answer our much simpler next question.

187. How has ecology dictated the distribution of our wildflowers?
Fundamentally it is absolute in its working. The amount of light filter-

ing down through the canopy of the woods to the forest floor, controls all light-demanding species from growing there. Furthermore, within the different types of forest, there exists a sharp difference in the composition of the upper layer of soil. In some evergreen spruce, fir and pine forests, that upper layer is so acid that only certain types of wildflowers will tolerate it. Again, the forests that shed their leaves in the fall have a very different type of humus. And, before their leaves expand in the spring, the amount of light reaching the forest floor dictates the coming into bloom of many spring-blooming wildflowers. Such a spring profusion of light never occurs in evergreen forests.

But at the edges of the forest, in the open places and the clearings that came with agriculture and in what we call thickets, none of these forest factors is significant. For the flowers that usually grow in open places are light-demanding; they often grow in mineral soil; their humus demands are usually slight; and they tend to be as widely distributed as their exceedingly common environments.

Perhaps the only difference between these wildflowers of the open places, and it is not a very stringent one, is that some of them, while growing in the open, do not usually grow in dry sandy sites, while others are generally confined to such places. For the convenience of those interested in their possible cultivation we can separate these plants of the open thus:

1. Growing in open, but not usually dry places. (See Questions 188–207.)
2. Growing in open, but generally dry and often sandy places. (See Questions 208–223.)

FLOWERS GROWING IN OPEN, BUT NOT USUALLY DRY PLACES

188. Is the painted cup a parasite? Most varieties are, and the eastern *Castilleja coccinea* has so far resisted all attempts to grow it, for it is partially parasitic on the roots of other plants. Growing twelve to twenty inches high, its stem is rusty-hairy, and its leaves, towards the summit, are a gorgeous scarlet and are usually mistaken for the flowers. The real flowers, found among these floral leaves, are small, inconspicuous and yellowish-green. The dramatic floral spike blooms in midsummer, and the plant grows in open places from New Hampshire to Florida and westward.

189. What is the fireweed?   A ubiquitous plant that follows forest fires throughout the north temperate zone, and also grows in many open thickets. Sometimes it is called giant willow-herb because of its willow-like leaves, but was christened *Epilobium angustifolium,* and is so common that it also picked up the quite inappropriate names of French willow and blooming Sally. It is a wand-like plant, three to four feet high, whose four-petalled flowers grow in a showy terminal rose-purple cluster. Its four-sided, slender pod has seeds with a tuft of silky hairs at one end. The flowers are so liked by bees that the plant is cultivated by California bee-keepers.

190. Is there a native lupine in the eastern states?   The wild lupine or Quaker bonnets (*Lupinus perennis*) is one of the most beautiful eastern wildflowers, although most gardeners prefer the much more showy hybrids. The plant is one to two feet high, its compound leaves

In open sandy places our wild lupine (*Lupinus perennis*) often called Quaker bonnets, is a profuse June flower.

with usually eight leaflets arranged in a cluster. The flowers are pea-like, blue when fully open (pinkish in bud), in a showy terminal cluster in May-June. The plant is difficult to dig from the wild. *Lupinus* is from the Latin for "wolf," from an ancient notion that lupines impoverished the soil! Lupines often grow in open places where the soil is none too rich. That Quaker bonnets have anything to do with its impoverishment remains unproved.

191. How many different goldenrods are there in our eastern flora?　Over sixty are known, all belonging to the group called *Solidago,* and practically all of these have minute yellow flowers in showy clusters. While many of them are almost weed-like in thickets or along roadsides, their profusion of fall bloom makes the goldenrods very handsome plants. So much so that they are cultivated in England, where there is only one wild species. Ours are perennials, with alternate leaves. The flowers are crowded in very small heads that are numerous in their leafy branched clusters.

192. What native asters were involved in the creation of the Michaelmas daisies?　Many years ago the English imported from here two native, showy asters, and by crossing them with each other and with other species, produced finer garden plants than either of the presumptive parents. These are the New England aster and the New York aster, both named by Linnaeus who never suspected that a hundred and fifty years later they would contribute to what the English called Michaelmas daisies—the finest fall flowering perennial, next to the chrysanthemum. (See Question 826.)

　The New York aster (*Aster novi-belgi*) is a perennial with long, narrow, stalkless leaves, and usually lilac or bluish-violet flower heads in a loose, open cluster. The flower heads have twenty to thirty-five rays, rarely a few more, most of them about one-half of an inch long. It is found in open, often moist places. The New England aster (*Aster Novae-angliae*) has pinkish or purple flower heads which contain about twice as many rays as the New York aster. Its leaves are almost stem-clasping. It, too, prefers open, usually moist sites. Neither of these native asters has anything to do with the garden aster, which is a *Callistephus* from China, hence often called the China aster.

193. Is there a native passion-flower in the eastern states?　This predominately tropical group, which often has gorgeous flowers, is rare in temperate regions, but one of them, the Maypops (*Passiflora incarnata*) is found wild from Maryland to Florida, and is a hairy vine often fifteen to twenty feet long; usually called wild passion-flower. It has deeply three-lobed leaves, and solitary, long-stalked flowers. These were ultimately named passion-flower because devout Italians called them *fior della passione,* seeing in them the crown of thorns of the Crucifixion. The white flower has five sepals, crowned with a double or triple fringe of hairs which are purple or pink. The five petals are also white. Summer-blooming, and followed by a yellow, football-shaped, fleshy, edible fruit.

194. What is Oswego tea?   Nicholas Monardes, a celebrated physician of Seville, published a book late in the sixteenth century, entitled (in English) "Joyful newes out of the newefound world." To honor this Spanish doctor, Linnaeus, nearly two hundred years later, named Oswego tea *Monarda didyma*. It is also called bee balm or red balm. The plant is an aromatic perennial with a square stem, and opposite, oval, pointed leaves. The brilliant, scarlet flowers are in a close cluster that may be two inches wide, beneath which is a ring of leaf-like, red-tinged organs (bracts), making the whole cluster very handsome. It is summer-flowering. During the Revolution a not very enticing tea was made from the plant in northern New York State.

195. Is there a flowering moss that is not a moss?   Yes, one of our rarest wildflowers is persistently and incorrectly called "flowering moss" in spite of the fact that mosses bear no flowers, as that word is rightly understood. A much better name for this "flowering moss" is pyxie or better yet *Pyxidanthera barbulata*. It is a low, moss-like, evergreen plant, with hundreds of tiny, crowded, moss-like leaves. Among them, and quite profusely, are borne tiny, bell-shaped white or pinkish flowers in mid-April or early May. Its cushion-like, prostrate growth should make it a valuable ground cover, but its natural habitat in moist, acid places in the pine barrens of New Jersey makes its garden culture quite hazardous. It occurs as far south as South Carolina.

196. Why is the cup-plant so called?   The coarse sunflower-like cup-plant (*Silphium perfoliatum*) has its upper leaves joined at the base, and so surrounding the stem that they make a distinct water-holding, cup-like depression; hence the other name of Indian cup. It is a stout perennial, three to seven feet high, the smooth stem four-sided. The lower stalkless leaves are four to ten inches long. The flower heads are nearly three inches wide, yellow, and are grouped in an open, terminal cluster, blooming summer and early fall. The plant is found at the edges of the woods and in thickets, westward to the prairies.

197. What is the sneezeweed? A rather coarse, sunflower-like, perennial plant of open places in the eastern states, more valuable for its derivatives than for itself. Its Latin name of *Helenium autumnale* is in honor of Helen of Troy, although all the sneezeweeds are American. The eastern species, often called yellow star or false sunflower, grows four to six feet high, and can be ignored as a cultivated plant because of its coarseness and rampant invasiveness. The leaves are alternate, lance-shaped, three to five inches long. The flower heads are about two inches wide, yellow, and borne in a flat-topped, rather profuse cluster. From this rather weedy plant have been derived several much finer garden varieties; one with lower stature; another with red flowers; and a third, known as Riverton Gem, with red and gold flower heads.

198. Are there two different plants called hardhack in the East? Yes, one is a *Spiraea* (see Question 97); the other is a very different plant called shrubby cinquefoil (*Potentilla fructicosa*), and also prairie-weed, since it grows westward into the prairie region. It is a small shrub, twelve to thirty-six inches high, with compound leaves composed of from three to seven lance-shaped leaflets, about three-fourths of an inch long and silky-hairy. The many, small yellow flowers grow in small clusters, which are decidedly showy and are summer-blooming. While the plant is native in the United States, it is also found in Europe and Asia. It is often cultivated, especially in some of its fine horticultural forms. It prefers a neutral or slightly alkaline soil.

199. The root of what wildflower was once used as a cure for the "worms"? In the olden days, and even now in some primitive areas, people used the root of worm-grass or pinkroot (*Spigelia marilandica*) for ridding themselves of the "worms." Since then it has been supplanted by more reliable drugs. Some people call it Indian pink, perhaps because of its bright red flowers. The plant is a perennial, twelve to twenty inches high, with a four-sided stem and opposite leaves that are ovalish, smooth and about three and a half inches long. Its scarlet flowers are yellow inside, and are borne on a sparse, one-sided cluster; blooming in May or June. It is not found wild north of Maryland.

200. Why is the Indian cucumber-root so called?   In open, usually moist places in the east, one often finds a rather inconspicuous herb with two, widely separated tiers of leaves and a nodding cluster of greenish flowers. Its underground tuber looks and tastes a little like a small cucumber, and was used as food by the Indians. The plant is about two feet high, and the leaves are three to five inches long and about half as wide. It sometimes grows in the woods. Its Latin name (*Medeola*) was derived from Medea, the sorceress, who was much more deadly than the tuber of this innocuous wildflower.

201. What showy wildflower is called false dragonhead?   The name is usually applied to *Dracocephalum virginianum,* which is also called obedient plant. It grows three to four feet high, on a wand-like, four-sided stem. Its opposite leaves are oblongish, three to five inches long and toothed on the margin. The flowers are purple-red, rose-pink or even lilac, irregular (see Question 4) and are arranged in a terminal, showy, spire-like cluster. There are several garden varieties, for they are popular as cultivated plants; of easy culture in any ordinary garden soil and are summer-blooming. In some books the false dragon-head is called *Physostegia virginiana,* and nurserymen are apt to use this name.

202. Is there a phlox called "flowering moss"?   Yes, and the name is just as inappropriate as the other plant so called. (See Question 195.) The plant called flowering moss is prostrate, forms moss-like patches, but produces a profusion of bloom, which no real moss can. It is inappropriately called ground pink. This in spite of being incorrect, is the nearly universal common name. It is a true phlox (*Phlox subulata*), and one of our most showy ground covers. The plant is only an inch or two high. Its small leaves are moss-like, and among them are found a profusion of pinkish, magenta or white flowers with five notched petals, very showy because of the profusion of flowers, mostly in April and May. It is of the easiest culture, in full sun, in any ordinary garden soil.

203. What eastern wildflower is known as the burnet? A rather strong-growing perennial, five to six feet high, with showy white flower spikes is so called and named technically *Sanguisorba canadensis,* as Linnaeus thought its reputed ability to stop bleeding was true. *Sanguisorba* is from *sanguis,* blood, and *sorbere,* to drink or dry up. The plant has compound leaves, its opposite, stalked leaflets oblongish and toothed on the margin. The flowers are very small, white, and are crowded in dense, finger-thick spikes three to six inches long. These terminal clusters are so numerous that the burnet is showy in midsummer. Its leaves are sometimes used for flavoring.

204. What golden-flowered plant did the Indians use to heal wounds? The golden ragwort (*Senecio aureus*), which may be poisonous, contains an active ingredient used by the Indians to heal wounds, and by the early settlers to promote menstruation. It is a showy herb of open, usually moist places, twelve to thirty inches high, its basal leaves violet-like, the stem leaves oblongish, stalkless and very jagged. The terminal, open, profuse flower cluster is showy in May or June and is composed of several flower heads that are about one inch wide. The heads have from eight to ten golden yellow rays (not petals as many think).

205. Which of our wildflowers was named for one of England's greatest herbalists? Amid the splendor of the court of Henry VIII and Queen Elizabeth I, there came the greatest development of gardens and palaces than has ever happened since. At one of them John Gerard, the famous herbalist, was superintendent for twenty years. In 1597 he issued his "Herball or Generall Historie of Plantes," which has become an English classic. A hundred and fifty years later, Linnaeus was so much impressed by this Englishman's learning that he designated one of our most beautiful wildflowers *Gerardia purpurea,* and ever since the plant has been so called for it has no common name. It is an annual plant, six to fifteen inches high, with thin, stiff, wiry, forked stems which have opposite, very small leaves that are scarcely one inch long. Towards the top of the stem, usually in pairs, are borne the cup-shaped, purple flowers, the lobes of which are flaring and about three-fourths of an inch wide. August–September blooming.

206. What is the star-bloom? Another name for the worm-grass. (See Question 199.)

207. Are moss pink and moss phlox the same?   Both are local names for the flowering moss or ground pink. (See Question 202.)

Flowers Growing in Open, but Generally Dry Places

Many gardeners, hampered by dry banks or sandy soil, wish there were plants that would stand such unhappy sites. Fortunately among the eastern wildflowers there are a few that thrive only in the open, in full sun, in sandy or otherwise poor, gritty soil and are hence a boon to the distracted gardener cursed with such sites. From among such plants only a few can be admitted here and they might well begin with our first question.

208. Is there a native cactus in the eastern states?   The only native cactus in the eastern states is the prickly pear (*Opuntia compressa*), which grows in pure sand. Like many cacti, it has fleeting or no leaves, and these are replaced by thick, water-storing, ovalish joints, three to five inches long, usually spiny and untouchable also because of the minute barbed bristles that are found on the flat joints. The flowers are yellow, showy, and solitary, borne at the tip of the joint, about two and a half inches wide, and are followed by a pulpy, greenish-purple, edible fruit. The plant hugs the ground and is useful for hot, dry, sandy places. Years ago it was introduced into northern Africa and is known there as the Barbary fig.

209. Is there a native century plant in the eastern states?   Not quite but nearly so. The century plants are tropical American succulent plants, with thick, woody stems, crowned with a rosette of thick, spiny-margined leaves. The local plant belongs to the same group and is technically known as *Agave virginica*. It has no stem but a basal rosette of thickish, unarmed leaves eighteen to twenty-four inches long, sometimes with fine marginal teeth. The flower stalk, arising from the rosette, is three to five feet high, bearing greenish-yellow tubular flowers about 2 inches long, that are night-fragrant. The plant, variously called false aloe, American aloe (it is, of course, not a true aloe) and rattlesnake master, is native in dry open places as far north as Virginia, and, as a cultivated plant, not safely hardy farther north.

210. What is the Spanish bayonet? This is a superlatively useful garden plant for open, dry, sandy places and is native from Delaware southward. It is commonly called, also, Adam's-needle and bear grass (*Yucca filamentosa*). It is a stemless plant, with an essentially basal cluster of partially erect leaves, about two feet long and an inch wide, the margins thready. The midsummer-flowering stem is eight to twelve feet high, with white or cream-white flowers in a showy, branched cluster. The plant is hardy as far north as Boston.

211. Is there any native flower that grows on sand dunes? The beach pea (*Lathyrus maritimus*), a relative of the sweet pea, is common along the dunes of the Atlantic coast, and a similar plant, also called beach pea (*Lathyrus littoralis*), is found along the Pacific coast. Our eastern one is a sprawling perennial, growing in salt-impregnated sand, and is usually not over two feet high. It bears compound leaves, the end of the leaf stalk ending in a slender, coiling tendril. The pea-like flowers, about one inch wide, are borne in clusters of from six to eight, are violet-purple and showy in midsummer. It is an ideal plant for open sandy places but not for ordinary garden soil.

212. What is the bearberry? This is, perhaps, the finest and most difficult to grow of all our native ground-covers. It is a prostrate vine, the stems often rooting at the joints and hence making large patches of handsome, evergreen foliage that turns bronzy in the winter. The leaves are about one inch long and very numerous. The bell-shaped flowers are white or pinkish-white, and not over one-third of an inch long, and followed by a reddish, mealy, insipid berry. The bearberry (*Arctostaphylos Uva-ursi*), often called the hog cranberry and mealberry, is common in pure sandy places, and also along railroad embankments and on rocky slabs. It is impossible to grow it by digging fresh clumps. One relatively safe way is to cut frozen sods of the plant and plunge them in a specially prepared bed eighteen inches deep, filled with a mixture of six parts clean sand and four parts of acid humus (peat). Do not water the thawed-out clumps with tap water, which is often alkaline. Use rain water until the plants get established, after which rainfall should be sufficient. It is sometimes called barren myrtle.

213. Are the orange milkweed and pleurisy-root the same? These are different names for what many people call butterfly-weed—*Asclepias tuberosa*—a native plant of dry, open, often sandy places and by far the most showy of the eastern milkweeds. It is the only one of the milkweeds that does not have a milky juice, and is a deep-rooted perennial, one to two feet high, and is difficult to dig out. The leaves are oblongish, nearly stalkless, opposite, two to six inches long, and hairy on the under side. The flowers are orange, growing in a branched, flat-topped terminal cluster which is very showy in mid-summer and is followed by erect, ridged pods. The seeds have a fine silky tuft. It is easy to grow, in open, sandy places if one has the patience to dig out the deep root, of course, when the plant is dormant. The root, which is probably poisonous, was once widely used as the source of a drug for pleurisy.

214. What yellow-flowered plant turns black when dry? No one knows why the foliage of the clover broom (*Baptisia tinctoria*) turns black when dry. Its root contains an active ingredient that was once used as a cure for fevers, but is now supplanted by much better drugs. It is a stiffish, much branched, dome-shaped plant, eighteen to thirty inches high, often called shoofly. The compound leaves have three wedge-shaped leaflets. The flowers are very numerous, pea-like, yellow and bloom in midsummer. The plant grows in hot, dry, often sandy places, but is not easy to transplant. Its wild relative, the blue-flowered false indigo (*Baptisia australis*) is offered by dealers in native plants as easier to grow than the clover broom.

215. What is the golden aster? An odorous, sticky and hairy summer blooming plant of dry sandy places, from New Jersey southward, where it becomes quite common, almost weedy. It is technically called *Heterotheca subaxillaris*. The alternate leaves are clasping towards the top of the stem which is ten to twenty-four inches high. The flower heads grow in a sparse, branching cluster, yellow, the heads about one inch wide and not particularly showy. As the plant is an annual or biennial it is scarcely worth growing.

216. The root of what wildflower was used as an antidote to the poison of a rattlesnake? Throughout the region where rattlesnakes thrive there grows a showy perennial, one to three feet high, usually known as gay-feather or rattlesnake master (*Liatris scariosa*), and, among gardeners as blue blazing-star. It has numerous narrow leaves, and towards the top an interrupted cluster of flower heads. These are button-like, about three-fourths of an inch thick, and beautifully colored with magenta-purple or violet and showy in the late summer. This and several other species of *Liatris,* are valuable garden plants for open dry places, and are of easy culture. (See Question 794.)

217. The root of what wildflower is called the Indian potato? On Long Island, New York, there is a seaside village which was once called Goodground, until the realtors thought Hampton Bays more stylish. It was called Goodground because of its plentiful supply of the groundnut or Indian potato (*Apios americana*), also called potato bean or wild bean. Upon the root of this usually prostrate vine the Shinnecock Indians depended for part of their food. It sometimes sprawls over bushes, and has compound leaves with from three to nine somewhat oval, pointed leaflets. The flowers are pea-like, in small clusters mostly at the leaf joints, and are velvety, reddish or brown-lilac and moderately showy in late summer. The pea-like pods are straight, rather thick and many-seeded. *Apios* is from the Greek for "pear," in allusion to the pear-shaped, edible root.

218. Are the mealberry and the barren myrtle the same? Yes, but both of them are local names for what is better called the bearberry. (See Question 212.)

219. Is the flowering spurge worth cultivating? If you have a sandy, dry, almost impossible garden site, the flowering spurge or milk purslane (*Euphorbia corollata*) is emphatically worth growing, for it thrives naturally in just such places from Ontario to Florida and westward. It reaches fifteen to twenty-five inches high and has from twenty-five to perhaps eighty stalkless leaves on each stem. At the summit is a three-to-seven-forked cluster, which is again two-to-five-forked, so that the final effect is showy, not because of the flowers, but for the ring of white, conspicuous appendages below them. The flowering spurge is of easy culture in sandy but not in heavy soil.

220. What is the wild pink? A sand-inhabiting perennial, scarcely eight inches high, known as *Silene caroliniana,* and very sticky just beneath the flower. The leaves are mostly basal and clustered; a few on the stem are smaller and opposite and nearly stem-clasping. The flowers, sparse at the summit, are reddish-pink, about three-fourths of an inch wide, the five petals wedge-shaped. They bloom in May or June. The plant is scarcely known in cultivation, but is worth it in dry, sandy, open places.

221. What is a catchfly?   A general term for plants belonging to the group known as *Silene,* which is from the Greek for "saliva," in reference to the sticky stem of some species. One that is not so sticky is the beautiful fire pink (*Silene virginica*), also known as Indian pink, which grows in open thickets, or even in thin woods from Ontario to Georgia and westward. This catchfly has opposite, toothless and essentially stalkless leaves and produces a rather meager cluster of brilliantly scarlet flowers in midsummer. There are five notched petals. It is often grown in the wild garden, rarely exceeds ten inches in height, and is of easy culture.

222. What is the difference between the trumpet-flower and the trumpet-creeper?   Both are rather rampant native vines, with very beautiful flowers. The trumpet-creeper threatens to become a showy but weedy nuisance along roadsides and on farms. The trumpet-creeper (*Campsis radicans*), also known as trumpet-vine, has compound leaves with from five to thirteen toothed leaflets, and small clusters of brilliantly orange-red, tubular flowers in midsummer. The closely related trumpet-flower, better known as the cross-vine (*Bignonia capreolata*), has only two leaflets in its compound leaf, but these are terminated by a branched, coiling tendril, which the trumpet-creeper never has. The flowers are tubular, showy, and yellowish, and bloom in May or June. The plant is called the cross-vine because a cross section of the stem has a cross-like pattern.

223. What is the wild bean?   The groundnut. (See Question 217.)

Introduced Flowers

All the eastern wildflowers that begin with Question 71 and end with Question 223, are truly native American plants. But in the eastern United States there are over one thousand different flowers that are not native to the New World, although they are now so widely distributed and so common that they are usually called weeds. Such plants hardly ever grow in the woods.

These newcomers are extremely common along roadsides, in fields, and often in gardens, where nobody wants them, for some, like the dandelion and dock, are persistent and obnoxious weeds. But some, like the common white daisy, the Queen Anne's lace or the butter-and-eggs, have such beautiful flowers that they can hardly be ignored in a book like this. Obviously a few of these introduced flowers must be included here, since many have asked where they came from and how.

Most of them came from Europe or Asia, generally unknown to their introducers. In the early days of the settlement of the country there was a large importation of the seed of food, forage and ornamental plants. Such seed was hardly ever free of impurities, any more than modern grass seed is absolutely weed-free. It was the impurities in these colonial seed importations that resulted in one-fifth of our flowering plants being of foreign origin. Not all of these newcomers are weeds, for some of them, like the elecampane and purple loosestrife, are so handsome that they are even cultivated. If all introduced flowers are not weeds, perhaps it is better to ask our next question.

224. What is a weed?   The lamented L. H. Bailey defines a weed as a plant that is not wanted. The late Professor Fernald of Harvard says "A troublesome or aggressive plant which intrudes where not wanted." Webster's *New International Dictionary* (second edition) defines a weed as "any plant growing in ground that is or has been in cultivation, usually to the detriment of the crop. . . . An economically useless plant." None of these definitions except the first is completely satisfactory, for most of them ignore the fact that the same plant may be a weed in one place and not in another. Perhaps the safest definition is the oldest, in Dr. Bailey's *Cyclopedia of Horticulture* (1913), that a weed is "a plant that is not wanted." We have many such, and a few questions about them will be answered below.

225. Where did the dandelion come from?   This pernicious weed was once called by an imaginative botanist "the tramp with the golden crown." Its many-rayed flower head would repay breeding, for many respectable garden flowers are not so showy. The date when it came from Europe to the New World is quite unknown, but the dandelion

(*Taraxacum officinale*) is now ubiquitous to the distress of all gardeners. Its extremely deep taproot makes eradication difficult. Perhaps it is no longer a weed when a large-leaved form of it is cultivated for its bitter-juiced foliage, gathered each spring as "greens." Lowell's "Ode to a Dandelion" scarcely damned it as all gardeners do.

226. What is the scarlet pimpernel?   A European weed often called there the poor-man's-weatherglass (*Anagallis arvensis*), because its flowers are open in sunshine but close when rain threatens, and at night. The plant is scarcely six inches high, and has opposite, practically stalkless leaves. From the joints of the leaves there appears a solitary, thin-stalked flower, with apparently five separate petals which are usually scarlet, but sometimes whitish or purplish. The plant is common in fields and roadsides, and sometimes in gardens; but since it is an annual, eradiction is easy by never letting it sow its seed.

227. Is there legislation against one of our showiest weeds?   Many counties, especially in the North, have stringent laws for the eradication of the devil's-paintbrush (*Hieracium aurantiacum*), commonly called orange hawkweed, perhaps one of the most handsome European weeds ever to get a start here. Left to itself it would cover square miles of pastures, for its seed is like the dandelion's in floating on the wind. The plant is a perennial, seven to fifteen inches high, with basal, hairy, nearly stalkless leaves. The flowering stalk is densely hairy, and is crowned with a few gorgeous orange flower heads, very beautiful, especially in late afternoon sunshine. It is, however, one of the worst weeds in the country.

228. Is Queen Anne's lace related to the carrot?   Sometime, over two thousand years ago, the carrot was unknown as a vegetable, but its wild ancestor was all over Europe and came here with the early settlers. People call it the wild carrot; some prefer Queen Anne's lace, and still others call it the bird's nest. Linnaeus named it *Daucus Carota,* and it has become one of our most persistent weeds. Its finely cut leaf has almost thread-like segments, and both the foliage and the eighteen-inch, wiry stems are tough, and harsh or rough to the touch. The flowers are white, exceedingly small, perhaps a hundred in a flat-topped cluster that may be three inches wide, blooming any time

from June to September. As the flower cluster withers it curls up something like a bird's nest. In spite of its beautiful lacy flowers, the weed
is so hard to eradicate that some people call it the devil's-plague.

229. Why is the star-of-Bethlehem considered a pest? This very
handsome little Mediterranean plant with its white star-like flowers
is an invasive weed, infesting our gardens and lawns. It is a bulbous
herb, the bulbs so prolific that it spreads rapidly. The plant, which is
first cousin to the South African chinkerichee, is scarcely six inches

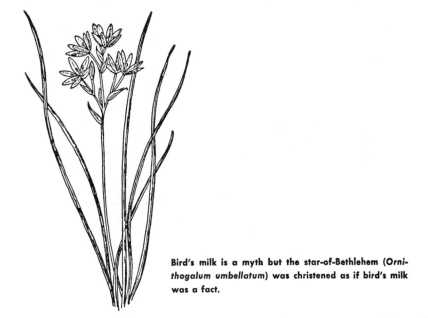

Bird's milk is a myth but the star-of-Bethlehem (*Ornithogalum umbellatum*) was christened as if bird's milk
was a fact.

high, has narrow, thickish, almost grass-like leaves, and in May produces a terminal cluster of flowers. These have six spreading petals,
some of which have a green stripe on the back. Often called the summer snowflake and Sleepy Dick, it was originally named *Ornithogalum
umbellatum,* as *Ornithogalum* means "bird's milk," perhaps an allusion to the white flowers.

230. What is our most night-fragrant weed? An Asiatic import
that lives literally on the wrong side of the tracks is bouncing Bet

(*Saponaria officinalis*), sometimes called soapwort, because the leaves when bruised form a lather in water. It grows in waste places, even on cindery railway embankments, and is despised by those who do not know its night fragrance. The plant is a perennial, one to two and a half feet high, with opposite, toothless leaves that may be up to three inches long. At the top of the stalk is a cluster of pinkish-white flowers, about one inch long, with five petals (or more in double-flowered forms). The plant is sometimes called London pride, and at night its wonderfully spicy carnation-like odor is quite ravishing. Some of its close relatives are garden plants.

231. What is the moneywort?   This is a low, prostrate perennial that roots at the joints and is often called creeping Charlie or creeping Jenny. A European import, it just misses being a weed, as it is a fairly good summer ground-cover. Named *Lysimachia Nummularia,* its creeping stems are ten to twenty inches long, clothed with small, opposite, roundish, short-stalked leaves about three-fourths of an inch wide. At the leaf joints there is a pair of stalked yellow flowers in midsummer; which have five ovalish but pointed petals. It is frequently cultivated as a ground cover, but sometimes escapes to become a minor weed.

232. Is one of our commonest weeds a chrysanthemum?   Yes and no, for our common white daisy or oxeye daisy was christened *Chrysanthemum leucanthemum,* which is technically correct, but that hardly makes it the equal of the gorgeous garden chrysanthemums. It is closely related to the Shasta daisy, one of our most useful garden plants, but few would care to cultivate the common white daisy, which came from Eurasia, as it is one of our most persistent weeds. It is a perennial twelve to eighteen inches high, with cut or divided leaves, and solitary, white flower heads that are about one and a half inches wide, with many rays that are commonly mistaken for petals. Dishonest dealers in pyrethrum, an insecticide, often adulterate true pyrethrum flowers with the dried flowers of this daisy. (For the Shasta daisy see Question 749.)

233. Do we have a weed that is first cousin to the snapdragon?
The beautiful toadflax or butter-and-eggs (*Linaria vulgaris*) belongs to the same family as the snapdragon and came here from Europe and

Asia to become a not very troublesome weed. It is not quite a foot high and has many very narrow leaves about two inches long. At the tip of the stem is a compact cluster of highly irregular flowers. (See Question 4). These are about one inch long, yellow and orange, with one of the petals a slightly curved spur. The plant was once called ransted, after a Welshman of that name who is supposed to have introduced it into America.

234. What is sweet clover? Any of several tall, sometimes weedy plants, all from Europe or Asia and valued by many farmers as an indication of good soil. They have compound leaves with three essentially stalkless leaflets. The plants are from three to six feet high, belong to the group known as *Melilotus,* which is from the Greek for "honey" and "lotus," in allusion to the clean fresh odor of the crushed foliage, and perhaps to the fondness of insects for its small, sweet-smelling, pea-like flowers. These are yellow or white in the three species of melilot that are common weeds along roadsides and in pastures. Its dried foliage was once thought to have medicinal value. Both the dried foliage and the flowers contain coumarin and have the pleasant odor of tonka beans.

235. Where did the Canada thistle come from? It was introduced into America from Europe, not from Canada, where it is nothing like such a pest as it has become here. In fact, the hardy Scots made it their national floral emblem and venerate it for the very reason most people here detest it. The thistle (*Cirsium arvense*) is a very spiny perennial, two to three feet high, its leaves large, deeply lobed, and the lobes tipped with vicious prickles. The terminal flowers are extremely handsome, crowded into a tight head about one and a half inches across and of a gorgeous lilac or magenta, or rarely white, color. Beneath the flowering heads is a row of prickly miniature leaves. The prickly nature of the thistle so impressed the Scotch that one of their national mottoes reads "Touch me who dares."

236. What European weed is called the candlewick? The mullein or velvet plant (*Verbascum Thapsus*) is often so called. It is a stout European plant that lives only two years. The first year it has a basal rosette of large, densely woolly leaves that are velvety, oblongish and eight to fifteen inches long. The next and last year it sends up a stout stalk, also velvety, often four to five feet tall, its summit crowned with a tight, spike-like cluster of yellow flowers, mostly in midsummer. Our forefathers smoked the dried leaves of mullein to relieve the congestion of the common cold, but modern drugs have supplanted its reputed value. The velvety coating of the plant prompted some people to call it Adam's-flannel.

237. What is the devil's-plague? A colorful name for the beautiful but nearly ineradicable Queen Anne's lace. (See Question 228.)

238. Is the black nightshade poisonous? This European annual weed has not only conquered America, but much of the rest of the world, in spite of its reputed toxicity. There is no doubt that its wilted foliage and unripe berries are dangerously, even fatally poisonous. However, a garden variety of the same plant bears berries that are safe if cooked, and some Pacific islanders use the boiled leaves like spinach. It is an erect or scrambling plant, one to two feet high, with alternate, long-stalked lobed leaves three to five inches long. The flowers are white, about one half of an inch wide, in drooping clusters in midsummer; they are not showy. The fruit is a black berry, certainly poisonous when young and suspect when ripe, especially in the wild form. The plant has given rise to the sunberry and wonderberry, both edible and safe.

239. Is the winter cress related to watercress? No, the winter cress (*Barbarea vulgaris*) is an erect, European weed in fields and along roadsides and does not grow in the water. Because of its bitter, but non-poisonous juice it is often called bitter winter cress. It grows twelve to eighteen inches high, with its leaves cut into one to four lobes, or even compound. The not particularly showy, yellow four-petalled flowers appear in a branched, terminal cluster, quite early in the spring. It is not a very invasive weed, appears to like moist, open places and is one of the earliest of our weeds to flower. It is used as cress by those who do not mind its bitter juice, and is often called yellow rocket.

240. What is the coughwort? The name was applied to this European weed long ago, when it was supposed to be of some use in pulmonary complaints. Even the father of botany believed it had a virtue

(J. Horace McFarland Company)

The white, fragrant flowers of the cucumber tree (*Magnolia macrophylla*) may be ten or even twelve inches wide. (Question 175)

(J. Horace McFarland Company)

The profusion of small pink flowers on the naked twigs of the redbud (*Cercis canadensis*) make it a showy harbinger of spring. (Question 180)

(J. Horace McFarland Company)

The tiny white flowers of the sourwood (Oxydendrum arboreum) bloom in midsummer and from them bees produce a superlative

(J. Horace McFarland Company)

One of the best native broad-leaved evergreens is the mountain laurel (Kalmia latifolia) whose flowers bloom in late May or

for coughs, as Linnaeus christened it *Tussilago Farfara,* the first name meaning *cough* and *go,* while *Farfara* was the classical name for the coltsfoot, which is what most people call it. Early in April or late March it sends up a single, scaly flowering stalk, twelve to eighteen inches high, crowned with a solitary yellow flower head, about three-fourths of an inch across, with many rays. Later on, the leaves appear. They are basal, long-stalked, angular, cobwebby on the upper surface, and covered on the underside with long, white-woolly hairs. It is not a very invasive pest, and some know it only as clayweed.

241. Why was one if our pernicious weeds called heal-all? Long ago superstition and old wives' remedies dominated the simple, and no "remedy" clung on so persistently as the heal-all or self-heal (*Prunella vulgaris*). The plant is in no modern pharmacopoeia, but some still consider it good for hemorrhages or diarrhea. Actually it is a Eurasian, aromatic, perennial weed, six to twelve inches high, now common throughout most of North America. It has a square stem and opposite, lance-shaped leaves, three to four inches long. The flowers are small, violet, and crowded in dense clusters, some terminal, others at the leaf joints; all are midsummer-blooming. *Prunella* is supposed to be from a German word for quinsy, for which the plant was a reputed remedy.

242. What is Adam's-flannel? The name for a very woolly plant better known as mullein. (See Question 236.)

243. What is Morden's pink? In the agricultural experiment station at Morden in western Canada there was developed a fine garden flower from the common purple loosestrife (*Lythrum Salicaria*), and this has ever since been known as Morden's pink. The original purple or wand loosestrife is a Eurasian perennial that has become common in the marshes of North America. It is a wand-like plant, two to three and a half feet high, with willow-like leaves and a showy, terminal spike of bright purple flowers. It is easily grown in ordinary garden soil as is its derivative Morden's pink, which has larger, more showy pink flowers.

244. What Eurasian weed has the purest blue flowers? Although blue as a flower color is fairly common, the true blue of the gentians

and of some campanulas is actually quite rare. One introduced weed
that certainly qualifies in this category is the summer-blooming blueweed or Viper's bugloss (*Echium vulgare*), sometimes called the
blue thistle—because of its densely hairy stem, or the blue devil because it is sometimes considered a troublesome weed. It lives only
two years, is eighteen to thirty inches high; its stems and small leaves
bristly-hairy. The brilliantly blue flowers are borne in a lateral cluster,
the corolla with slightly uneven lobes.

245. What is a Saint Johns-wort?   Many plants are so called, but the
commonest in the eastern states is a European plant known as *Hypericum perforatum*. This is a usually much-branched perennial, one to
two feet high and a little woody at the base. The leaves are very numerous, stalkless, narrow and not over two inches long, and more or
less resinous-dotted. The flowers are yellow, in small clusters at the
ends of the branches, but showy because of their profusion in midsummer. There are many native St. Johns-worts but this introduced
one is by far the commonest, especially along roadsides and in fields.

246. What blue-flowered European weed yields chicory?   The bitter root of the blueweed or chicory (*Cichorium Intybus*) has been
used for years as a not very pleasant adulterant or adjunct of coffee,
hence its other name of coffeeweed. It is a tough-stemmed perennial,
one to three feet high, its basal leaves dandelion-like, while the stem
leaves lance-shaped and remotely toothed. The flower heads are blue
or violet-blue, rarely white, and resemble the flowers of the dandelion
so much that the plant is often called the blue dandelion. It opens only
in sunshine. Chicory is much more common in the northeastern states
and Canada than farther south.

**247. What Eurasian weed had an exaggerated reputation as a
medicine?**   Many have had, but the elecampane (*Inula Helenium*)
above all. It was used by the ancients to cure the diseases of women,
catarrh, skin affections and tuberculosis—in all of which diseases it
was probably of no service, according to modern experts. It was even
thought once to be useful for horses; hence its other name of horse-
heal. It is a stout perennial, four to six feet high, the rough oblong
leaves nearly two feet long. The flower heads somewhat resemble a

small sunflower, are yellow, about two and a half inches wide, and have many, slender rays.

248. Are the blue thistle and the blue devil the same? Yes, both are local names for the blueweed. (See Question 244.)

249. What is the flower color of coffeeweed? Blue; the name is a local one for chicory. (See Question 246.)

250. In many books about the introduced plants treated in Questions 224–249, there are terms like *naturalized*, *adventive* and *endemic*. What do these mean? A naturalized foreigner, like the dandelion, is one that has become so thoroughly established that most people think it is native. An adventive plant is also a foreigner, but one that may escape from a garden, but scarcely ever becomes really established, as the hyacinth sometimes does. Endemic means native and restricted in its distribution, like the trailing arbutus, which, of course, no introduced foreign plant can ever be.

IV. WESTERN WILDFLOWERS

THE PRAIRIES AND THE GREAT PLAINS

As one leaves the forested areas of the East, which trickle over the Appalachian Range into Ohio and Indiana, we come in western Illinois to the beginning of that vast grassland that stretches from the Mississippi to the Rocky Mountains—the prairies and the Great Plains.

There is a difference between the two, based upon the amount of rainfall. From the Mississippi to about the 100th meridian was the so-called tall-grass prairie. West of that and up to the Rockies, where rainfall would not support the tall grass, occurred the short-grass prairie—properly called the Great Plains. Here the scanty rainfall never penetrated much over two feet, while in the tall-grass prairies the rainfall was enough to penetrate four to six feet below the surface.

In both regions the soil below the penetration point of rainfall was more or less permanently dry—hence the lack of trees, although some experts think the annual burning of the prairies by the Indians contributed to the treeless expanses of the Middle West. When protected from fire, cultivated trees *do* grow in the tall-grass country, but there were none when the first pioneers trekked westward.

They were astonished to see the great profusion of wildflowers in these trackless wastes. None of those flowers would tolerate shade, but they could stand bitter winters, and a few of them have since become valuable garden plants, like our annual phlox (*Phlox drummondi*). And the ease of cultivating these very superior soils, compared to the huge effort of clearing land of trees, has resulted in making this region the largest crop-producing area in the country.

So much is this true that the natural conditions that supported the prairie wildflowers have been largely destroyed. Consequently many of the wildflowers once found in profusion will now be found only along fencerows, railway embankments, roadsides, and in the few square miles that were never touched by the plow. All the flowers mentioned in Questions 251–288 will be found in these great grasslands, but not as commonly as they once were.

251. What is the prairie willow?   This is one of the smallest of all the willows, usually two and a half to four feet high, and unlike most native willows, growing in dry, open prairies, as well as eastward. The prairie willow (*Salix humilis*) has oblong leaves, pointed at both ends, the margins rolled, the underside of the leaf very rough. They are one and a half to four inches long. The very early catkins, much smaller than those of the familiar pussy willow, may bloom in March, or even in late February.

252. Is there a wild rose on the prairies?   There are several, but one of the most common is the prairie rose, (*Rosa setigera*), which is a scrambling, vinelike plant, not usually over six to nine feet long. Its leaves are compound, with three (rarely five) leaflets that are nearly stalkless. The terminal leaflet is long-stalked. The flowers are pink, about one and a half inches wide, and quite numerous. In spite of the name *satigera,* which means "bristly," the prairie rose has few or sometimes no prickles.

253. Is there a mesquite on the prairie?   The true mesquite, which grows farther west, is represented on the grasslands by the prairie mesquite (*Prosopis glandulosa*). It is not a tree like the true mesquite, but a very prickly shrub, three to five feet high, with twice compound leaves. The ultimate leaflets are stalkless, very narrow and arranged in from nine to eleven pairs, with a terminal leaflet scarcely one and a half inches long. The flowers are very small, and are arranged in a finger-thick spike two to five inches long. They are greenish-yellow, fragrant, and bloom in midsummer.

254. What is the prairie acacia?   Unlike most acacias, the prairie acacia (*Acacia angustissima*) is not a spiny shrub or tree, but an un-armed herbaceous plant, never over three feet high, that grows in the dry, open prairies of the Middle West. It has twice-compound leaves, the ultimate divisions comprising from twenty to thirty pairs of very small leaflets. The flowers are very small and are crowded in a dense, ball-like, stalked cluster that may be one and a half inches thick. They flower in midsummer and are yellow or salmon-yellow.

255. Are the prairie sage and the prairie sagewort the same? Not quite the same, but they are closely related. Both have aromatic foliage, and both grow on open dry prairies. The prairie sage (*Arte-misia ludoviciana*), called also the white sage, is a widely variable plant, more or less erect, but not over three feet high. It has narrow usually uncut leaves which are crowded and white-felty beneath. The flowers very numerous, crowded in tiny heads which are grouped in loose, open clusters. The prairie sagewort (*Artemisia frigida*) is a low, mat-forming perennial, with many silvery leaves, divided into several segments. The flower heads stand well above the prostrate mass of foliage, and are scarcely one-third of an inch wide. Neither plant is particularly showy, but interesting as the prairie relatives of the sage-brush, which grows farther west.

256. Did the black-eyed Susan come East from the prairies? Al-most certainly, for it was once a native plant on the prairies, and spreading east as a pernicious weed, it not only captured waste places and roadsides but invaded fields and was finally made the state flower of Maryland. The black-eyed Susan (*Rudbeckia hirta*) usually lives only two years, but is sometimes a short-lived perennial growing eight to fifteen inches high and bristly-hairy throughout. Leaves are chiefly basal, but a few appear on the stem, which is crowned by one or more flower heads. These are about two inches across, the many rays golden-yellow, the center dark purple-brown. Its eradication (by plowing under) is obligatory in some counties.

257. What is the Texas star? It is an annual, somewhat weedy plant, also called star-of-Texas (*Xanthium texanum*), that once cov-ered acres of dry, open prairies, but is now often cultivated in gardens where there are poorish soils. It grows two to four feet high, the stem wand-like, the alternate leaves narrow, and about two inches long. The long-stalked flower heads are mostly solitary, about two and a half inches across, its eighteen to twenty yellow rays showy. It is summer-blooming. In the garden it will stand both great heat and poor soil.

258. What prairie mallow has become a valued garden plant? The poppy mallow, *Callirhoë involucrata,* an extremely hairy perennial from the prairies of the Middle West, is now very popular as a garden plant for hot, dry sites. It is not over two feet high, and is inclined to sprawl. The leaves are maple-like, nearly round in general outline but cut into pointed lobes. The flowers are solitary, long-stalked, reddish-purple, and about two inches wide, with the five petals faintly notched. It is found on the prairies and plains from Missouri to Wyoming and southward.

259. What is the prairie potato?   When some of our ancestors were travelling across the prairies to the apparently limitless West, they were very thankful for the edible root of the prairie potato (*Psoralea esculenta*), often called the prairie turnip, and, by the Indians, the breadroot. It has a turnip-like root, and its densely hairy, much-branched stem may be eight to twenty inches high. The leaves are compound, the five leaflets all arising at the same point. The flowers are blue, pea-like, about one inch long, and are crowded in dense, leafy, terminal, spire-like clusters in May or June. (For a related plant, used similarly by the Indians in the East, see Question 217.)

260. Is there a larkspur that grows on the prairies?   Yes, although it is far less showy than our garden hybrids. The prairie larkspur (*Delphinium virescens*) is a densely hairy perennial twelve to thirty inches high, with its chiefly basal leaves much dissected into narrow segments. The flowering stalk is wand-like, crowned with a terminal spike of nearly stalkless flowers. These are irregular, about one-half of an inch long, white or greenish- or bluish-white and not particularly showy. It was named *virescens* which means "greenish," as some of the flowers have a greenish tinge.

261. What prairie garden flower has a poisonous juice?   The juice of all species of the group known as *Euphorbia* is more or less poisonous, with some of them violently so. Over the prairies there once grew what was called ghostweed, and what gardeners know as the familiar snow-on-the-mountain (*Euphorbia marginata*). This is an annual, bushy plant, eight to fifteen inches high, much branched. Its oblongish leaves are one to three inches long. The lower leaves are green; the upper are white-margined. The flowers are inconspicuous, without petals. Beneath the flowers is a collection of brilliantly white, leafy structures (bracts) which make this very showy annual a popular garden plant. Its culture is easy in any ordinary garden soil. (For a related plant see Question 629.)

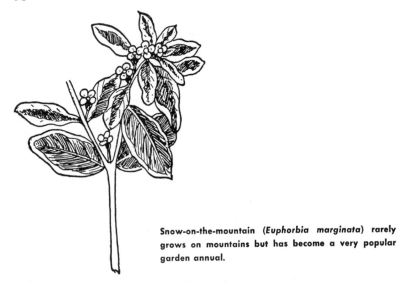

Snow-on-the-mountain (*Euphorbia marginata*) rarely grows on mountains but has become a very popular garden annual.

262. What garden flower is called the bluebell in Texas and the Canada pest farther north?   Neither name seems particularly appropriate for this prairie annual which has purple flowers and which no gardener would call a pest. It is common from Nebraska to Texas, grows about two feet high and has opposite, bluish-gray, somewhat oval leaves two to three inches long. The flowers are nearly bell-shaped, but flaring, nearly two inches long, pale purple, but darker blotched at the base, arranged in a showy, branched cluster. It is also called prairie gentian. The correct name is *Eustoma russellianum.*

263. What prairie flower was named for Easter?   The French settlers who came to the northern part of the prairie region noticed and named the pasqueflower (*Anemone patens*) because of its beauty and spring-blooming. Today it is often called prairie anemone and is a silky-hairy perennial, four to six inches high, the flowering stalk higher. The leaves have three main divisions, each of which is divided into many segments. The flowers are bluish-purple, blooming before the leaves develop, are about two inches wide and very showy. They are followed by a copious collection of long, plumy, silky fruits. When there are many plants growing together these slender, brownish fruits suggest a smoky haze over the ground, hence the rather common name of prairie smoke. The plant is of easy culture in ordinary garden soil, and was chosen the state flower of South Dakota. (For the pasque-flower of Europe see Question 563.)

264. Besides the pasqueflower is there another flower called prairie smoke? Yes, the plumy fruits of *Geum triflorum* are so called, as is the plant itself, which is a hairy perennial, eight to fifteen inches high, common on the prairies from Minnesota to New Mexico and west-ward. It has compound leaves with seven to seventeen leaflets which increase in size upward. The flowers are purplish, followed by long, plumy silky fruits.

265. Are there two flowers called prairie lily? Yes, and they are so different that many people wonder why they should ever have been called a lily at all, for neither of them is. The commonest prairie lily is often called gumbo lily (*Mentzelia decapetala*) and is sometimes called evening star. It lives only two years, is twelve to eighteen inches high, and has much-cut leaves. The flowers are three to five inches wide, white or yellow; opening towards sunset, and bewitchingly night-fragrant. It is often cultivated for its showy and fragrant flowers, and is easy to grow from seed planted one-fourth of an inch deep.

The other so-called prairie lily (*Cooperia drummondi*), also called the rain lily, is found from Texas into Mexico, and is a bulbous plant, about twelve inches high, with many basal, grass-like leaves. The flowers are solitary on a hollow stalk, tubular, three to five inches long, white but tinged red, night-blooming, and freely flowering after rains. Its culture in the North is difficult, as it will not stand slushy winters.

266. What is the prairie clover? A beautiful prairie perennial also called the red tassel-flower, although its flowers are actually violet or purple. It grows two to three feet high and has much-divided leaves, the leaflets narrow and about three-fourths of an inch long. The flowers are extremely small, crowded in a solitary, long-stalked, clover-like head that may be as much as two inches long and are rather showy in summer blooming. Some people call it thimble-weed, and its technical name is *Petalostemum purpureum*.

267. Is there a prairie flower called the thistle poppy? Yes, but it is perhaps better called prickly poppy (*Argemone intermedia*) and by some it is called devil's fig. It is a spiny-leaved and spiny-flowered annual with yellow juice. It grows three to four feet high, and its spiny-margined leaves are bluish-gray. At the end of each stalk there is a solitary, stalkless, white flower (rarely tinged pink) three to five inches wide and showy. *Argemone* is the Greek for a "poppy-like" plant, the juice of which was an eye remedy. The juice was once also popular as a remedy for warts.

268. What is the prairie pointer?   Not a dog, but a most charming wildflower that creeps westward to Pennsylvania and the District of Columbia. It is known in the East and to gardeners as the shooting star (*Dodecatheon Meadia*), sometimes called pride-of-Ohio. It is a small perennial, eight to ten inches high, its mostly basal, oblongish leaves often tinged with red at the base. The flower stalks are naked, crowned by a sparse cluster of nodding, white or lilac flowers that are about three-fourths of an inch long, the five apparently separate petals so bent backward that the center of the flower appears to point; hence the name prairie pointer. It is easily grown in the wild garden, in partial shade and a moist site.

269. Is the queen-of-the-prairie related to the queen-of-the-meadow?   Yes, and for the latter see Question 121. The prairie plant, *Filipendula rubra,* is a graceful perennial, four to seven feet high, its compound leaves with seven to nine lobed leaflets. The flowers are very small, pink, but very numerous, in a terminal, much branched, more or less flat-topped and showy cluster. It is summer blooming, is often cultivated and is easy to grow in any ordinary garden soil.

270. What is the state flower of Texas?   In May the roadsides of Texas are so covered by the flowers of the bluebonnet that it was natural for Texans to adopt it as the state flower. It is an annual lupine, *Lupinus subcarnosus,* about six to eight inches high, its foliage silky-hairy. The leaves are compound, the usually five leaflets rather fleshy. The flowers are pea-like, blue with a cream-white spot, scattered in showy clusters that are about three inches long. It is rare in cultivation, as the garden hybrid lupines are much finer plants.

271. In Question 262 there is a plant sometimes called prairie gentian. Is there another by the same name?   Yes, and this prairie gentian is a true gentian, not just a relative of it. This plant, called by no other name than prairie gentian is *Gentiana affinis* and grows about twelve inches high. It is a perennial, with many pairs of opposite, narrow, pointed and fleshy leaves about three-fourths of an inch long. The flowers are blue, about one inch long in sparse terminal clusters or a few scattered at the leaf insertions. Its corolla is fringed and quite handsome, but not as showy as the eastern fringed gentian. (See Question 102.)

272. Is there a prairie flower that should suggest Rockefeller Center? Many years ago Asa Gray named the prairie trefoil *Hosackia americana* in honor of Dr. David Hosack of New York, who founded the first botanical garden in that city. He ultimately gave the land to Columbia University. They still own it, but on that land Rockefeller Center now stands. Modern botanists have decided, however, that the correct name of the prairie trefoil is *Lotus americanus*. It is an annual plant, five to fifteen inches high, with compound leaves consisting of three narrow, stalkless leaflets. The flowers are small, solitary, pink, scarcely one-fourth of an inch long, and are summer-blooming. The plant has nothing to do with the lotus of the lotus-eaters, which is an Asiatic shrub.

273. What prairie flower is called thimble-weed? It is a local name for the prairie clover. (See Question 266.)

274. Is there an orchid that grows on the prairies? Yes, the prairie orchis (*Habenaria leucophaea*) is a showy fringed species found on wet prairies and also rare in the East. It grows fifteen to thirty inches high and has lance-shaped, rather blunt leaves five to ten inches long, but much diminished toward the showy terminal flower cluster. This is spike-like, four to ten inches long and composed of beautifully fringed petals, one of them deeply three-lobed, the spur long, slender and curved. The specific name of *leucophaea* well designates the color; *i.e.* dusky white, or white tinged with green. It is difficult to grow.

275. What is the locoweed? Cattle-raisers in the West are plagued by dangerously poisonous plants that cause the blind staggers and often death to cattle and sheep. One of the worst locoweeds is *Oxytropis lamberti,* a deep-rooted perennial of the Great Plains, eight to fifteen inches high, its compound leaves with seven to fourteen pairs of silky leaflets. The flowers are pea-like, on leafless stalks, twice the height of the foliage, crowded in dense, short spikes, either purple or violet. It is supposed, but not proved, that locoweeds absorb selenium from the soil, which most plants reject, and that it is this chemical that stupefies cattle and sheep. There are many other locoweeds.

276. What garden flower came from the southern prairies? The annual phlox (*Phlox dummondi*), often called Texan pride, originated as a wild plant in eastern Texas and perhaps in adjacent states. It has since gone all over the temperate world as it is a valuable, prolific and easily grown annual phlox. It is a bushy, many-stemmed plant, twelve to eighteen inches high, with lance-shaped leaves that are up to three inches long. The flowers in the wild form are white, but there are many colors in several horticultural varieties. One of these has fringed petals; another bears a star-like flower. All are of the easiest cultivation in full sun in any ordinary garden soil.

277. Most of these prairie flowers are relatively low plants; is there a tall one? The prairie burdock (*Silphium terebinthaceum*) grows seven to nine feet high from a coarse, woody taproot, and has essentially naked stems. Its mostly basal leaves are long-stalked, oblongish, eight to fifteen inches long, turpentine-scented when crushed, hence its other name of rosin-plant. The flower heads are few or many, in rather sparse clusters, yellow, somewhat sunflower-like. The plant is summer-blooming, but too coarse to be worth cultivating.

278. What is the pride-of-Ohio? A local name for the shooting star. (See Question 268.)

279. Is there a prairie flower that is sometimes too exuberant in the garden? Yes, the showy primrose (*Oenothera speciosa*) often becomes too rampant in the garden if it is not rigidly curtailed. It is a fine, day-blooming perennial, one to three feet high, its leaves lance-shaped or narrower. The flowers are showy, white, changing to pink, and are nearly three inches wide. Sometimes, because of its showy flowers, it is rather inappropriately called the prairie poppy. It is a handsome garden plant, if kept under control. It has, of course, in spite of its common name, nothing to do with a true primrose. Some of its relatives are called evening primrose, hence the error of calling this a showy "primrose."

280. What is the prairie cornflower? A branching, several-stemmed perennial, one to three feet high, remarkable for its foliage being covered with matted hairs. Its technical name of *Ratibida columnifera* is unexplained, but the central, erect, cone-like structure in the flower head, often standing above the rays as much as one inch and a half, is prominent enough to be called *columnifera, i.e.* column-bearing. The rays of the head are bent downward, not very showy, usually yellow, or sometimes purplish. The central, brownish cone of the flower head is so prominent that the plants are often called simply coneflower.

281. Is there a prairie flower which yields a dye? The prairie indigo (*Baptisia leucantha*) has foliage that turns black when dry, but like several other species of *Baptisia* it was used by the early settlers as a source of a fairly poor blue dye. It is a much-branched, stiff perennial, twenty to forty inches high, its compound leaf with only three short-stalked, wedge-shaped leaflets. The flowers are pea-like, white or sometimes purple-tinged, arranged in a spire-like, terminal cluster that may be as much as a foot long, but is usually less. Its oblongish pods are black when ripe. (For related plants see Question 214.)

282. What is the devil's-fig? A prairie plant usually called the thistle poppy. (See Question 267.)

283. Is there a prairie trillium? Yes, but it also occurs east of the Appalachian range although its common name is prairie wakerobin (*Trillium recurvatum*). It is about nine inches high, and its terminal three leaves are stalked, ovalish, often purple-mottled and two to four inches long. It has practically stalkless, solitary flowers with recurved segments which are brown-purple. While it grows on open prairies, it does better in a partially shady corner of the wild garden.

284. What weedy prairie mallow has become a popular garden flower? All over the prairies there grows a showy and quite weedy plant often called scarlet mallow (*Sphaeralcea coccinea*) and some-times called red false mallow. It really is a false mallow for it does not belong to the same group as our fine garden mallows. It is a peren-nial, eight to twelves inches high, its narrow segmented leaves silvery-hairy. The flowers are brick-red, showy, about three-fourths of an inch wide, in a terminal, floriferous spire-like cluster. Its culture in the garden is very simple as it thrives in poor or even sandy soil, but it should not be grown in a wet or very moist place.

285. Is the prairie parsley edible?   This is not advised as many of its close relatives are dangerously poisonous, like the European hemlock used to kill Socrates. The prairie parsley (*Polytaenia nut-talli*) was named for its discoverer, Thomas Nuttall, an English nat-uralist who came here in 1808 and ultimately became the curator of the botanical garden at Harvard University. The prairie parsley is a perennial, eight to ten inches high, with mostly long-stalked basal leaves, considerably cut into narrow segments. Its tiny, yellow spring-blooming flowers are arranged in a flat-topped cluster.

286. Is the prairie iris a true iris?   No, but very close to it for it belongs to a group only technically different from true *Iris*. The prairie iris (*Nemastylis geminiflora*) is a bulbous prairie herb, with three or four very narrow leaves and a stem six to twelve inches high. At the summit are one or two bluish-violet flowers which open for only a few hours before noon. With its segments somewhat rounded, its flowers are completely regular, *i.e.* symmetrical, and bloom in May or June. Some call the prairie iris a celestial lily, which it is not!

287. Does the prairie flax yield fiber?   Not commercially, although it is closely related to true flax, which is widely cultivated in the north-ern prairie states. *Linum lewisi* was named for its discoverer, Meri-wether Lewis, of Lewis and Clark fame. This prairie flax is closely related to the European flax, which is the source of linen from its stems and of linseed oil from its seeds. The prairie flax is a blue-flowered perennial while the commercial flax plant is an annual. The prairie flax is a leafy-stemmed plant with blue five-petalled flowers in one-sided clusters.

288. What is the red false mallow?   A popular prairie plant much cultivated. (See Question 284.)

THE ROCKY MOUNTAINS

No one who approaches the stupendous massif of the Rocky Mountains can ever forget the shattering impact of that escarpment as he leaves the endless monotony of the prairies and the Great Plains. Gone are the stark treeless wastes, the blinding sunlight and the parched land. The mountains beckon—their wonderful evergreen forests, the mountain meadows, the snow-clad peaks (in the spring and winter) and the rushing torrents that will ultimately feed the Missouri and Mississippi rivers to the east, and the great Colorado River to the south and west.

But quite apart from the emotional appeal of this dramatic contrast between the sea of grassland and the vegetative luxuriance of the mountains, there is a basic ecologic reason for the difference. Elevation, coolness and moisture permit the growth of thousands of plants that could not survive on either the prairies or on the Great Plains, which extend roughly between the 100th meridian and the mountains.

Here there are forests of spruce, pine, the Douglas fir, with other firs and evergreens. Beneath them grow hundreds of what are, perhaps, the finest wildflowers in America, if we exclude the Cascades and the Sierras, which rise about 1,000 miles still farther west. In a book like this it is obvious that only a fraction of this floral wealth can possibly be described. So it must be understood that the following questions reflect only a selection of them. For those who want more details than are possible here, the following books are suggested:

M. Armstrong: Field book of western wild flowers (1915)
F. E. and E. S. Clements: Rocky Mountain Flowers (1928)
P. A. Rydberg: Flora of Colorado (technical; 1906)

289. What is the bitterweed? A high mountain, aromatic and resinous plant (*Actinea grandiflora*), not over one foot tall. Its foliage is densely woolly, the lower leaves much dissected, the upper ones undivided. The flower heads are usually solitary, yellow, and nearly three inches wide, showy, its rays with three teeth. A related bitterweed, also found in Colorado, yields a kind of rubber from its milky juice. *Actinea* is often grown in the garden, but it does not like winter slush at its roots.

290. What is the state flower of Colorado?   This is the Rocky Mountain columbine (*Aquilegia caerulea*), which has become one of our most beautiful garden columbines. It does not like the low elevations in Colorado (5,000 feet), and thrives best between 8,000 and 10,000 feet, preferably in partial shade. It grows two to three feet

Many columbines grow in the Rockies, but one of the finest is the State Flower of Colorado, *Aquilegia caerulea*.

high, has compound leaves, and produces extremely showy bluish-purple flowers in May or June. The highly irregular flower may be two inches wide, with long straight spurs knobbed at the tip. In spite of its preference for cool mountains, it is easy to grow in eastern gardens, in any ordinary garden soil.

291. Is the sagebrush found in the Rocky Mountains?   Yes, but only in the more open and drier parts of the mountains, and especially west of them in the Great Basin. The sagebrush (*Artemisia tridentata*) is the state flower of Nevada. It is an extremely aromatic shrub, from four to eight feet high, its small, wedge-shaped, silvery-coated leaves with three to seven teeth towards the blunt tip. The flower heads are scarcely one-eighth of an inch wide, but are very numerous in a cluster from twelve to eighteen inches across, but not showy since the flower heads are a dusky greenish-yellow.

292. Is there a mahogany in the Rocky Mountains? No, but a common misnomer in that region is the mountain mahogany, which is not a mahogany but a shrub (*Cercocarpus montanus*) not over five feet high. It has alternate, evergreen leaves, that are coarsely toothed and one to two and a half inches long. The flowers are rather small, greenish-white, followed by a long-plumed, silky fruit that is more attractive than the flowers themselves. *Cercocarpus* is from the Greek for "tailed fruit."

293. What Rocky Mountain flower yields edible seeds? The Indians in the mountains, and beyond, valued both the roots and the seeds of the balsamroot (*Balsamorrhiza sagittata*). It is a low, turpentine-scented perennial with thick edible roots and mostly basal, long-stalked leaves that are white-woolly on both sides. The flower head is solitary, very showy, nearly three inches wide, pale yellow, with ten to twelve rays narrow and pointed. The seeds which follow the flowers were cooked and eaten by the Indians. It is one of our most showy western flowers, usually not over fifteen to eighteen inches high, often less, and blooms in April.

294. What is the Rocky Mountain bee-plant? In the mountains, and even out on the Great Plains there grows the stinking clover (*Cleome serrulata*), which, in spite of its scent, draws bees like a magnet. It is an erect annual, two to three feet high, its compound leaves with three very narrow leaflets. The flowers are pink or white from two to three inches long and wide, its four petals narrowed towards the base. The flowers are numerous in a showy, terminal cluster. The Rocky Mountain bee-plant is so valuable for honey that it is widely grown in California by bee-keepers. (For a related plant see Question 620.)

295. What mountain flower was named for a wood nymph? In the Rockies, and also in the mountains of Europe and Asia, there grows a white-flowered, prostrate plant called mountain avens (*Dryas octopetala*). *Dryas* is from the Greek for "wood nymph," especially one that haunts oak trees. The mountain avens is scarcely over four inches high and has somewhat oblong leaves about one inch long. The flowers solitary, erect, white, and about one and a half inches wide, and are followed by plume-like, feathery fruits about one inch long. It blooms in May and can be cultivated in the rock garden.

296. Is the wallflower of the west anything like the wallflower of our gardens? No, although they are closely related. The western wallflower (*Erysimum asperum*) is an erect plant, two to three feet high, its foliage bluish- or grayish-green. The leaves are alternate, oblongish, with a few shallow teeth or none, and are about three inches long. The flowers are yellow, with four petals in a showy terminal cluster, followed by erect, thin pods. The western wallflower grows from Ohio to the Pacific, and is common in the Rocky Mountains. Sometimes it is called the Siberian wallflower and the prairie rocket.

297. What are "little elephants"? This is a fanciful, but most descriptive name for the flowers of *Pedicularis groenlandica,* an erect perennial of the Rocky Mountains, eight to twelve inches high. Its stem is well clothed with somewhat cut leaves, and at the top is an extremely showy spike, four to six inches long, of fantastically shaped red or purple flowers. These are highly irregular (see Question 4), the upper lip prolonged into a cylindric tube, one-half to three-fourths of an inch long, so bent upward and outward that it inevitably suggests an elephant's trunk. This is one of the most remarkable and showy flowers of the Yellowstone and Grand Teton national parks.

298. Is there a wild clematis in the Rocky Mountains? Over much of Colorado, Wyoming and northern New Mexico, there grows a scrambling slender vine known as hill clematis (*Clematis ligusticifolia*), sometimes called the western virgin's-bower. It has compound leaves with five to seven somewhat oval leaflets that are one to three and a half inches long. Unlike most of the group this clematis has the male flowers on one plant and the female on another. (Dioecious. See Question 4.) There are no petals, but the four sepals are petal-like, white and usually mistaken for petals. As the flowers are borne in wide clusters the plant is showy in midsummer.

299. What is the Yellowstone Park's official flower? The western fringed gentian (*Gentiana thermalis*), which closely resembles the fringed gentian of the East (see Question 102) although its flowers are deeper blue. All over the Rockies, especially in the alpine meadows there are many different kinds of gentian—far too many to enumerate here. One, called the Rocky Mountain fringed gentian (*Gentiana elegans*), has blue flowers often tinged with lighter streaks or patches. It also bears far more flowers than the western fringed gentian, but some think it is only a variety of *Gentiana thermalis*.

300. Is the prairie rocket found in the Rockies?   Yes, but it is better known as the western wallflower. (See Question 296.)

301. What is the skyrocket?   A dazzlingly spectacular western flower (*Gilia aggregata*), found from the Pacific Coast east into the Rocky Mountains. It is closely related to the common garden perennial, *Gilia rubra*, but is more showy, although as a biennial it is much less cultivated. In its native habitat it literally sets the countryside ablaze with color. It is about two feet high, its finely dissected leaves have thread-like segments. In summer its gorgeous, long clusters of funnel-shaped red (or rarely white) flowers are well named skyrocket. *Gilia* was named to honor P. Salvador Gil, an eighteenth-century Spanish botanist.

302. Are the skunkweed and the sky pilot the same?   Not quite, but very nearly so, in spite of the incongruity of their common names. Both are found in the upper reaches of the Rockies, on flat ledges or clinging to cliffs, and both belong to the group known as *Polemonium* which is in the phlox family. The sky pilot (*Polemonium eximium*) is hardly eight inches high, has a dense mass of foliage, from which arises a short-stemmed, close cluster of sky-blue, fragrant, tubular flowers that are about three-fourths of an inch long. Where there are many of these, the effect, in full sunlight, suggests the blue Colorado sky. The skunkweed (*Polemonium confertum*), which is first cousin to the sky pilot, has denser foliage, and blue flowers that are nearly twice the size of those in the sky pilot. Both are extraordinarily showy mountaineers.

303. What edible Rocky Mountain plant was named for Captain Meriwether Lewis, of Lewis and Clark fame?   This is an extraordinary, stemless plant called bitter-root (*Lewisia rediviva*) which has a root much used by the Indians as food in the spring, but becoming bitter by midsummer. It has a cushion of tiny, fleshy leaves, scarcely an inch long, and the flowering stalk is equally short. The rose-pink, or (rarely) white flowers appear to hug the ground, and when they fade the whole plant becomes very inconspicuous. *Rediviva* means

The bitter-root (*Lewisia rediviva*) was once the favorite food of western Indians. Its root becomes bitter by midsummer.

literally "restored to life," in allusion to the plant's long period of dormancy and quick revival in the spring.

304. What are "languid ladies"? The droopy pale blue flowers of a perennial in western mountains closely allied to the eastern Virginia cowslip (see Question 110). The Rocky Mountain plant, also called mountain bluebell (*Mertensia oblongifolia*), is not over nine inches high, with spoon-shaped leaves not over two inches long. The flowers are purple below, fading to blue at their tips. They are arranged in a somewhat one-sided, close, cluster, each flower nodding like any languid lady. *Mertensia* was named for Francis Karl Mertens, a professor of botany at Bremen (1764–1831).

305. What Rocky Mountain shrub was named for a botanist who never visited there? The antelope-brush (*Purshia tridentata*) was named for F. T. Pursh, a German botanist who came to the northeastern states in 1799, was made curator of the botanical garden at Baltimore and went to England in 1812. He never saw living plants of the antelope-brush, which is four to six feet high and has silvery foliage, its leaves not over one-half of an inch long and three-toothed at the tip. The flowers are yellow, solitary, not over one-half of an inch wide and are not showy. The plant extends westward to the Pacific Coast.

306. Are there many species of blazing star? There are quite a few in the West, one of the showiest being *Mentzelia laevicaulis,* which grows from the Rocky Mountains to the Pacific coast. It is a stout perennial, two to three and a half feet high, its leaves narrow, two to eight inches long and wavy-margined. The flowers are three to four inches wide, borne in clusters of two or three at the ends of the branches, and are bright yellow, the stamens (see Question 3) very numerous and adding much to the beauty of the flower.

307. What is the sidesaddle goldenrod? A western goldenrod (*Solidago ciliosa*) found from Colorado to the Pacific Coast, with a leaning grayish-green stem that ultimately bends upward, but never more than eight inches high. The leaves are narrow, their margins fringed with short hairs. The flower heads are clustered at the summit and are not particularly showy, but the yellow rays are longer than in the eastern goldenrods. The plant is also called Rocky Mountain goldenrod.

THE SOUTHWESTERN DESERTS

After the high coolness of the mountains, the southbound traveller in the West is rather suddenly faced with intense heat, scanty rainfall and a sparse population. He has reached what we loosely call the desert, although it is not really one. A true desert, of which there are very few in the world, does not support any vegetation.

But our southwestern deserts support a good many of what one imaginative botanist called the Fantastic Clan, the cacti; as well as many other plants that store water or have ingenious devices to conserve it over long, intensely hot, rainless periods.

Besides the quite obvious water storage in the fleshy stems of the cacti, desert plants have various protective leaf coverings to reduce water loss. Some have thick, felty hairs; others look as though varnished, while still others shed their leaves during the drought and are as leafless as most cacti for months or weeks until the rains bring a brief emergence of foliage. Such plants exist at the very fringe of possible existence, surviving inadequate rainfall, rocky or sandy soil, no shade and scorching heat.

Our southwestern deserts comprise southern California and Nevada, much of Arizona and New Mexico, western Texas and quite a slice of southern Colorado. Throughout this huge area the rainfall is usually between three and ten inches a year, often locally less, but hardly ever much more. Under such conditions the wonder is not that plants exist, but that so many of them have such brilliantly colored flowers. Nowhere in North America can one see such spectacular color—never sheets of it as one often finds on the prairies, but in scattered plants that blaze with it. In the questions that follow, some of these dramatic denizens of our deserts will come as a surprise to those who have never been there, and, it is hoped, as a pleasant reminder to those who have.

A considerable number of these desert flowers are borne on the stems of cacti or among the prickly twigs of shrubs or small trees. Perhaps such should not be classed as wildflowers at all, but to omit them would impoverish this book as much as their omission from the landscape would impoverish the desert.

No one who has driven across the Mohave Desert or through the fantastically grotesque growth of the giant cactus near Tucson, can help feeling that here nature, at the very limit of possible vegetation, has produced some of our weirdest examples of it.

308. What is the largest cactus in the world? This is the giant cactus (*Carnegiea gigantea*), named for Andrew Carnegie, who once set up a laboratory to study desert vegetation at Tucson. Commonly called suwarro or saguaro, the giant cactus may be forty to sixty feet high, its barrel-like, ribbed trunk nearly two feet thick. Old plants

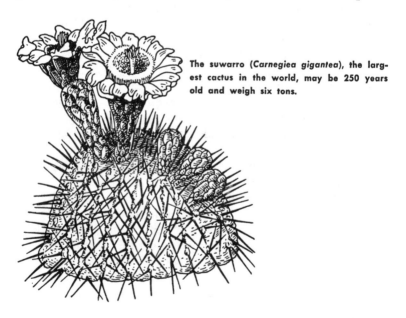

The suwarro (*Carnegiea gigantea*), the largest cactus in the world, may be 250 years old and weigh six tons.

may have three or four huge candelabra-like branches that ultimately point upward. These leafless branches, or the main stem, produce at their tips, white flowers that may be four inches long and half as wide, followed by a red, egg-shaped fruit, widely used for sweetmeats. A full-grown plant of this vegetable giant may weigh 6 tons and be 250 years old. They are endemic (see Question 250) only to southern California and Arizona and to adjacent Mexico.

309. What is the sotol?   A coarse, tough woody plant of the desert, usually called bear grass (*Dasylirion texanum*) with half its short trunk buried in the ground. At the top of its usually four-foot trunk there is a large cluster of bright green leaves two to three feet long and one-half of an inch wide, the margins armed with yellowish-brown prickles. The base of the leaves are spoon-shaped and these are often sold in florists' shops as "spoonflowers." From the crown of leaves there springs a flowering stalk twelve to fifteen feet high, crowned with a huge, branching cluster of small, innumerable, white, lily-like flowers.

310. Are the gold poppy and the desert poppy the same?   No, but they are both in the poppy family, although neither of them is a true poppy. The gold poppy (*Eschscholtzia mexicana*) is related to the California poppy, and like it is an annual which covers the Arizona deserts with its golden yellow flowers. If there is a winter rain, it will bloom in February. Its leaves are very small, much divided and rather inconspicuous in comparison with the showy flowers. The desert poppy (*Arctomecon merriami*) grows about a foot high and has mostly basal, fan-like leaves covered with long brown hairs. Its solitary white flower has four to six petals that soon wither. The flower is one and a half to two inches wide and is borne on a naked stalk.

311. Does the desert willow have flowers like our pussy willow?   Not in the least, for in spite of its common names of desert willow and flowering willow (*Chilopsis linearis*) is not a willow at all. Perhaps the Mexican and New Mexican name of *mimbre* would fit this small desert shrub or tree which is never over fifteen feet high, and is usually less. The leaves are willow-like, from three to five inches long. The flowers are showy, lilac, about one and one-half inches long, with a pair of yellow stripes inside, followed by a slender, many-seeded pod that may be a foot long. It prefers the moister sites in the desert.

312. Is the cliff rose really a rose?   No, for while it is in the rose family, it is not related to the rose and was named *Cowania stansburiana* for John Cowan, a London merchant who long ago imported desert plants into England. It is an aromatic, evergreen shrub, four to six feet high, its stiff branches sticky. The leaves are about one half an inch long, three to five lobed, sticky above but white-hairy beneath and very bitter. The flowers are solitary but profuse, about three-fourths of an inch wide, the five petals white or pale yellow. The Indians once used its silky inner bark for making sandals, string and cloth.

313. Is there a desert plant called wild licorice?   Yes, and it is closely related to the Spanish licorice from which comes all commercial licorice. The American plant, often called desertweed (*Glycyrrhiza lepidota*), is a perennial, from two to three feet high, its compound leaves with fifteen to nineteen, oblongish, scaly leaves which have prominent dots beneath. The flowers are pea-like, small, white, and crowded in stalked spikes that are shorter than the leaves. Its roots do not yield licorice.

314. What is the largest desert flower?   In the East there is a dangerously poisonous plant known as jimsonweed with very showy flowers that are about six inches long. In the southwestern deserts this is replaced by the desert trumpet flower (*Datura meteloides*), a stout perennial sometimes called the sacred datura because its narcotic root and leaves were used by the Indians to induce visions. Its leaves are unequally oval shaped, about two inches long, the upper ones in pairs. The flowers are fluted, trumpet-shaped, fragrant, bluish or white, six to eight inches long and very handsome. For a related plant see Question 453.

315. What desert plant looks like an old buggy whip?   The ocotillo (*Fouquieria splendens*) is enough like one to have been named coach whip, but is also called the vine cactus although it is neither a vine nor a cactus. It is a tall, very slender, prickly plant, usually with six to eight stems that are from eight to twenty feet tall and generally leafless, except after the meager rains. The flowers are scarlet, tubular, and about one inch long, but produced in such profusion that the ocotillo is one of the showiest desert plants, often used for a prickly

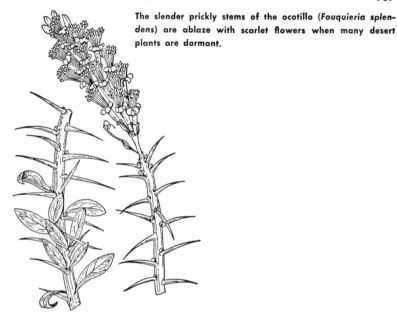

The slender prickly stems of the ocotillo (*Fouquieria splendens*) are ablaze with scarlet flowers when many desert plants are dormant.

hedge. Its bark yields wax, hence another name of candlewood. It is also, but more rarely, called Jacob's staff.

316. What is the desert dandelion? An annual (*Malacothrix californica*) which is found from the deserts of southern California to Colorado. It is showy enough to be cultivated, but needs a sandy soil. The plant is taller than our common dandelion, being about one foot high. Its basal rosette of much divided leaves is woolly in youth. The flowers are solitary but profuse, so that in its native habitat it is quite showy, mostly in March. Cultivated plants bloom later than this. The flower head may be one and three-fourths inches wide, somewhat dandelion-like, but not a true dandelion.

317. The wood of what yellow-flowered desert shrub is almost inflammable? The extremely resinous wood of the greasewood or creosote bush (*Larrea tridentata*) will so easily ignite that it is commonly used to start camp fires. It is a particularly evil-smelling shrub, much-branched and usually about five to eight feet high, its two tiny leaflets about one-third of an inch long. The flowers are solitary, but very profuse, yellow, only about one-half of an inch wide. It grows in the most impossibly dry places, and is perhaps the most drought-resistant shrub on the desert.

318. Is there a desert snapdragon?   Closely related to the true snap-dragon is a desert replica, christened *Mohavea confertiflora* after the desert in which it grows; it is found also in Nevada and Arizona. It is an annual, with a sticky-hairy stem, not usually over one foot high. Its flowers are irregular (see Question 4), crowded in a dense, ter-minal, leafy cluster, the snapdragon-like corolla pale yellow, but streaked with tiny purplish dots in lines.

319. Is there an exception to the rule that desert flowers bloom after spring rains or in midsummer?   Yes; unlike most of the sages the autumn sage (*Salvia greggi*) blooms when the desert is mostly bare of flowers. It is a woody or almost shrubby perennial and grows from two to three feet high and has opposite leaves, without marginal teeth, about three-fourths of an inch long and dotted with aromatic glands. The flowers are very showy, about one inch long, scarlet or red, crowded in a six to eight flowered terminal cluster. Culture is difficult or impossible in the North without a greenhouse.

320. Are the desert plume and the prince's plume the same?   Yes; both names are common in the California deserts (and sometimes outside them) for a stiffish perennial known as *Stanleya pinnata,* and named for Edward Stanley, the Earl of Derby. This is a bluish-green plant, three to five feet high, its sparse foliage comprising small, pointed leaves that are divided into narrow segments. The flowers are golden-yellow, about one inch wide, with only four petals, and borne in midsummer in a long, terminal and showy cluster. The plant is often cultivated in eastern gardens and is easy to grow in most or-dinary garden soils.

321. What is the most fantastic plant on the desert?   Fantastic or not, Captain John C. Frémont, the first to see it called the Joshua-tree (*Yucca brevifolia*) "the most repulsive tree in the vegetable kingdom." But some Mormons en route from California to Salt Lake City in 1857 thought these fantastic trees of the Mohave Desert guided them on their route as Joshua guided the Jews, and promptly called them

Joshua-trees. To anyone who sees them for the first time they look grotesquely unreal; their thick, woody stems may be from thirty to forty feet high and are branched at such erratic angles that they seem to have been put there by some wildly perverse gnome. At the ends of the thick branches there is a dense tuft of narrow, leathery leaves, from six to nine inches long and toothed on the margin. The flowers are white or greenish-white, about two inches long, are lily-like and followed by an egg-sized fruit. So valuable is this grotesque tree that in 1936 the government set aside an area of 1,344 square miles as the Joshua-tree National Monument, about 100 miles east of San Bernadino and only a few miles northeast of Indio, California.

322. What does palo-verde mean?   It is the Spanish name, used throughout our southwestern deserts, meaning green tree, although it is very infrequently green from its leaves, for it has none for most of the year. It is often called the green-barked acacia and was named *Cercidium torreyanum*. Its most distinctive feature is the smooth green bark, perhaps Nature's compensation for its usually leafless condition. Of course it does sometimes have leaves; these are twice compound, the ultimate leaflets very small and all lasting about one month before they fall. The flowers not pea-like, are nearly regular, about three-fourths of an inch wide, and rather showy because of the profusion of bloom. The plant is a large shrub or small tree, with many spreading branches.

323. What is the brittlebush?   This is a shrubby or woody perennial, very common in the desert and forming mound-like clumps from two to three feet high. Its foliage is strong-smelling; the leaves alternate and often silvery. The plant is inconspicuous except when it is in bloom, which comes mostly in April or May. The flower heads are yellow, about one inch wide, in profuse and branched clusters. The plant is often called *incienso* and was christened *Encelia farinosa,* in honor of Christopher Encel who wrote about oak galls in 1577.

324. What desert shrub is often called candlewood?   The ocotillo. (See Question 315.)

325. What lily-like desert plant grows in pure sand?   The desert lily (*Hesperocallis undulata*), sometimes called the California daylily, grows in just such places and can be found among dune ripples in southern California. Its basal, keeled, rather thick leaves are white-margined. The flowering stalk is one to two feet high, and crowned with a terminal cluster of four to eighteen white, fragrant flowers, the segments green-streaked on the back. It flowers in February or March, and its cultivation outdoors in the East is difficult or all but impossible without a greenhouse.

326. What is a beard-tongue?   This is a general name for a variety of very showy flowers found in the western states, on the prairies, in the mountains and on the deserts. All belong to a group of nearly 300 different kinds, called *Pentstemon.* This name is from the Greek meaning five stamens, which these flowers have, although one of them is functionless and usually bearded, like a bearded tongue. This, and the two-lipped flower make the beard-tongues among our most showy western plants.

327. Where does the fire beard-tongue grow?   Only from southern Utah to New Mexico and into California, mostly in canyons and on mountain slopes. The fire beard-tongue (*Pentstemon eatoni*) is a gray-ish-green perennial, one to two feet high. The flowers are fiery crimson-scarlet, growing in terminal, branched clusters, the corolla barely two-lipped. The plant has opposite leaves, at least the upper ones are and almost stem-clasping.

328. What is the desert beard-tongue?   A localized species (*Pentstemon parryi*) found only in southern Arizona and adjacent Mexico. It is a smooth perennial, one to two feet high, its extremely showy, almost symmetrical flowers rose-magenta and found in very floriferous, terminal clusters. Its opposite leaves have no marginal teeth.

329. Are the globe tulip and the Mariposa lily the same?   Yes, and the latter is the preferred common name of the very charming far-western, bulbous plants found in the group known as *Calochortus,* which are especially common in California. They have erect stems, narrow, grass-like, but rather fleshy leaves. The flowers are solitary or in sparse clusters, tulip-like, and very showy, with six segments, the three inner more showy than the outer segments. *Calochortus* is

Greek for beautiful grass, in allusion to their grass-like leaves. They are also called butterfly-tulip.

330. What Mariposa lily is called the golden bowl?　This is a showy perennial from southern California, called the golden bowl because its tulip-like, golden-yellow flowers are like a small open bowl. Named *Calochortus clavatus,* the plant has a somewhat zigzag stem, from two to three feet high, its opposite leaves without marginal teeth. Its flowers are borne singly or in sparse clusters and are from two to three inches wide, the petals brown-lined.

331. What is the desert Mariposa lily?　A red bulbous perennial of the desert, also called the red Mariposa lily (*Calochortus kennedyi*), almost unique among the group in having red flowers. It grows about two feet high and has opposite leaves without marginal teeth. The flowers are borne singly on each flower stalk, or in sparse clusters; they are about two inches wide, are smoky-red, terra-cotta or orange, and hence often called the orange Mariposa lily. The plant is found on dry hills in the deserts of Arizona, Nevada and southern California.

332. Are the Jacob's staff and the candlewood the same?　Yes, both are local names for the ocotillo. (See Question 315.)

333. Are all cactus flowers confined to the Americas?　All the native ones are, for this purely American family of fleshy succulents extends from the United States to the Argentine, overwhelmingly confined to the deserts, especially in the mountains in Mexico, Peru, Bolivia and parts of Brazil. There are scores of species of cacti in the United States, varying from giants like the suwarro (see Question 308) to small trailing kinds with thin cylindrical stems. Most of them are extremely spiny. A very few non-American species are reputedly native in western Africa.

Because of their wide use as hedges in tropical countries, our native cacti are now running wild along the Mediterranean, in India and especially in Australia, where one of our prickly pears is their chief botanical pest. The government has even imported an American insect enemy of the cacti to try to control this most unwelcome immigrant.

While few cacti bear leaves, or only ephemeral ones, practically all of them have large, fleshy stems that are green and function as leaves. Some of these stems are enormous and hold much water, which, in rainless years, carries these greatest of all desert plants through droughts that would kill most other plants.

While the cacti are mostly leafless, they make up for this in having the most spectacular, sometimes bizarre, and usually showy flowers. These may range from the eerie, ethereal white of the night-blooming cereus, its huge corolla stealing into perfect bloom only towards midnight, to the passionate reds and pale yellows of other cacti.

A few of these weird denizens of our southwestern deserts have prompted the next few questions.

334. What is the strawberry-cactus?   A low, clump-forming leafless plant with cylindrical, erect stems that have eleven to fourteen distinct ribs, the stems not over one foot long. The plant is very spiny, usually with five or six central, curved spines, surrounded by ten straight ones—all yellowish-brown. The flowers are strawberry-red, or purple, from two to three inches long and wider than this when expanded. They are so numerous on the clump that these are showy. The plant was named *Echinocereus engelmanni,* in honor of Dr. George Engelmann, a St. Louis physician who spent much time on western botany.

335. What desert cactus is called the claret cup?   A very showy, clump-forming cactus bearing the somewhat formidable name of *Echinocereus triglochidiatus,* which means having three barbed bristles. It has cylindric, stout stems, not over twelve inches high with five to eight ribs and three to eight spreading spines about one inch long. The flowers are scarlet, about one and one-half inches wide, so numerous that the plant is very handsome when in bloom.

336. What is the calico-cactus?   An extremely spiny, barrel-shaped cactus (*Echinocereus viridiflorus*) scarcely four inches high, its eleven to thirteen ribs practically hidden by the plentiful spines. These are arranged in clusters, the central spine of the cluster much larger than the others. The flowers are not so showy as in the last two (see Questions 334 and 335), are greenish-yellow, about one and one-half inches wide, sometimes pink-tinged. The long central spine in each cluster is brownish-red. These spines are so ferocious that it is practically impossible to handle the plant without stout gloves.

337. What desert cactus flowers bloom in the evening and wither by morning? The sinita (*Lophocereus schotti*) does this but it is not the real night-blooming cereus, which is tropical. The sinita is so striking that a National Monument has been set aside for its preservation. It is a mostly unbranched columnar cactus, four to six feet high, its stout, thick stems about four inches in diameter, with only a few shallow ribs and comparatively few spines. There is a tuft of white hairs at the summit of the columnar stems. The flowers are small, red, about an inch across, and scattered singly at the spine clusters. These spines are short and thick.

338. What color are the flowers of the most famous narcotic cactus? The peyote (or peyoti), often called "mescal buttons," *Lophophora williamsi,* has rather inconspicuous pinkish-white flowers, but few Indians and no pharmacologists are interested in them. It is a low, half-

Volumes have been written about the peyote (*Lophophora williamsi*) a miniature narcotic cactus yielding mescaline.

buried cactus with five to thirteen low ribs, and its root and buried plant body has become famous as it yields mescaline which induces narcotic, and now forbidden, visions. It was much discussed by Aldous Huxley in his *Doors of Perception* and in a book by the writer entitled *Narcotics: nature's dangerous gifts*. It grows in the deserts of Texas and adjacent Mexico.

339. Why is one of our desert cacti called "cream cactus"? The cream cactus (*Mammillaria applanata*) was so named because its sap looks like watery cream. The plant body is so small that when not in bloom it looks rather like gray rounded stones. But the tubercled body is so plentifully provided with sharp spines that it, and its relatives are thus often called "pincushion cactus." The flowers, which are cream-yellow, have the tips of the petals whitish so that the flower is darker at the center than at the edges.

340. What is the fish-hook cactus?   A very small pincushion cactus (*Mammillaria microcarpa*), so called because in addition to the straight spines, of which there may be fifteen to thirty, there are one or more central hooked spines, all very sharp and damaging to the touch. The plant body is nearly globular, or sometimes partly cylindric, never more than six inches high and tubercled. The flowers are very showy, pale purple, about one and a half inches wide and bloom in midsummer in spite of infernal heat.

341. What cacti are called prickly pears?   There is a very large group of cacti so called all belonging to the genus *Opuntia*. They stretch from the United States to the Argentine. Some, like our eastern representative (see Question 208) are prostrate; but others, mostly in the tropics, are tree-like. All have flat or somewhat cylindrical joints and few or no leaves, and practically all are spiny. But unlike most all other cacti, they have tiny cushions of minute, barbed hairs which, while not poisonous, are extremely irritating to the skin. Consequently all the plants mentioned at the next few questions should be handled only with thick, impervious gloves, as the almost microscopic barbed hairs are next to impossible to extract from the skin.

The flowers of the prickly pears are generally showy, and solitary, (*i.e.* never in clusters), growing directly on the edges or tips of the green joints. In some of them the flowers are followed by a juicy, sometimes edible fruit, as in the tuna, which are commonly sold at desert markets. But the fruits are provided with the same cushion-like tufts of barbed hairs, and these must be removed or choking will inevitably result. This applies to all the prickly pears that immediately follow.

342. What is the tuna?   In our southwest there is a prickly pear called tuna (*Opuntia megacantha*) which is tree-like, ten to fifteen feet high with ovalish or broader, flat joints fourteen to twenty four inches long, the one to five spines white. It is actually a native of Mexico, but was cultivated in the mission gardens and has now run wild, but not widely. It is grown for its pear-shaped, red, edible fruit (but see Question 341) which is about three inches long. The flowers are yellow or orange, nearly three inches wide. It is not the tuna of tropical America which is a prostrate prickly pear known as *Opuntia Tuna*.

343. What is the "Teddy bear"?   A tremendously spiny prickly pear, one of a group known as *cholla* (*Opuntia bigelovi*), its spines so formidable that the plant can scarcely be touched. It has cylindrical, tubercled joints and hardly exceeds four feet in height. The flowers are scarlet or paler, but not particularly showy. It is common from southern California to Utah and Arizona and into Mexico.

344. Is our southwestern nopal the cochineal plant?   No; the true nopal, upon which the cochineal insect lived and produced the once-famous cochineal dye, is a tropical plant. Our nopal, or cacanapa, as it is often called, is *Opuntia lindheimeri* and a tree-like, flat-jointed cactus, eight to twelve feet high. Joints ovalish or broader, sometimes nearly circular, bluish-green and eight to ten inches wide. The spines have only one to six in each cluster. The flowers are showy, about three inches wide, yellow or red. The plant grows from southern Louisiana to Texas and into Mexico.

345. What is the "beavertail"?   A flat-jointed prickly pear (*Opuntia basilaris*), never more than four feet high and often scrambling or even prostrate. The joints are flat, slightly tubercled, usually without spines, but plentifully supplied with the tiny barbed hairs mentioned in Question 341. The joints are broadly oval, six to nine inches long. The flowers are very showy, nearly three inches wide, purple or rarely white.

THE PACIFIC COAST

346. Why are Pacific Coast flowers different from those found elsewhere in the United States?   Because the plants that bear them are often found nowhere else. This is probably due to the geological history of the region, a striking example of which is the isolation of the big-tree (*Sequoia gigantea*) in the Sierras, and the redwood (*Sequoia sempervirens*) along the northern coast of California. Both trees are found nowhere else in the world, although the fossil remains of both of them show wide distribution of *Sequoia* in past epochs. So it is with many Pacific Coast flowers.

The southern part of that coast is arid, and its desert flowers are found from southern California to western Texas, as we can see by reading again Questions 308–345. Such plants have every protective device to conserve moisture.

But the rest of California, Oregon, Washington and British Columbia have vastly different conditions. There is a progressive increase of rainfall as one goes northward along the coast, ranging from about 40 inches per year near Monterey to 80 to 100 inches in northern California and adjacent Oregon. While the interior valleys are hot and dry, the coastal region not only has more than adequate rainfall but is benefited by daily cool fogs from the Pacific. The result makes the region from northern California to Vancouver the greatest evergreen forest on earth, with a magnificent accompaniment of wildflowers.

Traversing the area, also, are two great mountain chains, the Sierra Nevada and the Cascades, both catching much rainfall from the Pacific that is never caught by the low, arid interior valleys. Such mountains have some of the finest evergreens at their lower elevations (4,000–8,500 feet), while higher up are mountain meadows ablaze with wildflowers. Still higher, on Mounts Whitney, Hood, Baker, Shasta and notably on Mount Rainier, there are alpine fell-fields where another group of wildflowers grows in the icy substratum, watered by the glaciers.

Nowhere else in the United States is there such diversity of climate and elevation, and nowhere else, except in the subtropical regions (Florida and the Gulf Coast) is there such diversity in the wild flora. So handsome are some of these Pacific Coast wildflowers that they are now cultivated as prized garden flowers, wherever the climate suits them. Many of them do not like the conditions in the East, and nearly all of them fail to thrive in the prairie region. Many of them grow better in England where they find a climate quite similar to northern California, Oregon and Washington.

The Pacific Coast is thus endowed with a unique diversity of climate, topography and geological history. No wonder that this is reflected in an aggregation of wildflowers that perhaps only eastern Asia can rival. Of the several thousand species of trees, shrubs and wildflowers found in this region, only a few can possibly be included here, together with some notes on their cultivation where this is possible.

Not all Pacific Coast wildflowers, however, are found in gardens, and some of them appear to resent cultivation. For the convenience of the garden-minded, all the wildflowers included here may be separated as follows:

1. Pacific Coast wildflowers not usually cultivated: See Questions 347–359.
2. Flowers grown from bulbs: See Questions 360–380.
3. Flowers with ordinary roots—not bulbous: See Questions 381–423.
4. Flowers borne on shrubs or trees: See Questions 424–443.

347. Does the California rose grow in that state?   The California rose is an unfortunate misnomer well embalmed in botanical literature, for it is not a rose and does not come from California. Actually it is a weedy, prostrate Japanese relative of the morning-glory and is known as *Convolvulus japonicus*. It has arrow-shaped leaves and double flowers that are pink or white. It has become a pestiferous weed in the eastern states, although many Californians say it is unknown in that state!

348. Is the sand strawberry edible?   It certainly is for the plant, which grows from Alaska to Patagonia, was taken from Chile to France in 1712 and became one of the parents of our cultivated strawberries. Along our Pacific Coast it is a prostrate, vine-like perennial, named *Fragaria chiloense,* because it was supposed to be confined to that country. It has compound leaves with three wedge-shaped leaflets that are bluish-green beneath. The flowers are white, about three-fourths of an inch wide, and are inclined to droop beneath the foliage. The fruit is large, dark red and firm.

349. Are there two flowers known as the California pea?   Yes, but one of them is better known as the beach pea and will be found in Question 211. The true California pea is a perennial, six to eight feet high, its compound leaves made up of from six to eight pairs of small, light-green leaflets, the leaf ending in a tendril. The flowers are extremely showy, pea-like, about two-thirds of an inch long, bluish-violet but streaked with darker lines, borne in handsome clusters of from ten to fourteen blooms on each stalk. Its technical name is *Lathyrus violaceus* and it is first cousin to the sweet pea, which is an Italian annual.

350. What is the ruff gentian?   A very beautiful species (*Gentiana calycosa*) which is found in mountain meadows from Washington south to California, and in high meadows in Montana and Wyoming. It is an alpine plant, never more than twelve inches high, usually less, and has opposite leaves without teeth. The flowers are solitary or in sparse clusters, about one and a half inches long, blue, but streaked with bands of paler blue. It is autumn-blooming.

351. Is the redwood ivy the same as the inside-out flower?   Both are common names for *Vancouveria parviflora,* an evergreen ground-cover named for Captain George Vancouver, who landed at Vancouver in 1791. It is not over twelve inches high, has compound leaves,

A beautiful ground-cover in the redwood forests of California is the inside-out flower (*Vancouveria parviflora*).

the leaflets with thickened margins and not over two inches long, usually considerably less. Flowers white or tinged with lavender, quite small, but borne in many-flowered clusters on a naked stalk. The flower segments are reflexed, hence the name "inside-out flower." The plant grows in deep evergreen woods and generally resists cultivation in the East.

352. What is the stinging lupine?   This is a Californian annual plant, one to two feet high, called *Lupinus hirsutissimus.* Its foliage is covered with nettle-like stinging hairs. It has long-stalked, compound leaves with from five to seven leaflets. The flowers are pea-like, about three-fourths of an inch long, purple, crowded in a dense, rather showy terminal cluster. It is summer-blooming.

353. What is the snow plant?   A spectacularly striking plant of the high Sierras (*Sarcodes sanguinea*), impossible to cultivate because it lives on the dead remains of other plants, has no green coloring matter and hence is a true saprophyte (see Question 47). It also grows on mountains in Oregon and western Nevada and in the latter state picking it is forbidden. The plant is from six to fifteen inches high. It has no green leaves, but its fleshy, scaly stem is crowded with the brilliant, scarlet flowers. As the whole plant is scarlet, it makes intensely dramatic contrasts against the snow from among patches of which it grows with astonishing speed, early in the spring.

354. Are there two different plants called the California poppy?
Yes, and while one of them is scarcely ever grown as a garden plant, the other is cultivated nearly throughout the world. The wildflower that is almost unknown in gardens is *Papaver californicum,* an annual from twelve to twenty-four inches high, its leaves two to three inches long and divided or parted. The flowers are about two inches across, borne on a long, hairy stalk; the five petals are red, but green or

The ever-popular California poppy (*Eschscholtzia californica*) is a perennial but blooms from seed the first summer.

blackish-green at the base.

The ever-popular California poppy (*Eschscholtzia californica*) of our gardens is also a wild plant from eight to twelve inches high and is a perennial. But as it blooms from seed in one season, it is usually grown as an annual. It has finely-dissected, bluish-green leaves, and a long-stalked, solitary, very showy flower, three to four inches wide, blooming from July to October. The four petals are orange-yellow, each with a deep orange spot at the base. Because it is difficult to transplant, the seed should be sown in May in a sunny place, preferably in sandy loam. Thin out the plants so that they are eight to ten inches apart. Sometimes persisting over the winter in the South.

355. What did Californian settlers use for tea?   Before the gold rush the dried foliage of *Psoralea physodes* was used as a substitute for tea, and so came to be called California tea. It is an erect perennial, one to two feet high, with compound leaves composed of from three to five leaflets. The flowers are small, pea-like, and greenish-purple in a not very showy cluster. (For a related plant see Question 259.)

356. What is the Columbia windflower?   A very beautiful anemone (*Anemone deltoides*), growing only in deep evergreen forests of Washington, Oregon and northern California. It has a vigorous underground rootstock from which arises a compound leaf with three toothed leaflets. The flower stalk is thin, arising from a trio of upper leaves. The flower is white, waxy, solitary, and about one and a half inches across, the five petals rounded. It is difficult or impossible to grow it in the East.

357. What is the giant trillium?   In deep woods of the Pacific Northwest there grows a trillium (*Trillium chloropetalum*), that may be two feet high and hence is called the giant trillium as there is no other species that size in the area. It has three very large leaves just below its stalkless, showy flower. The three petals are oblong, about two inches long, and are brown-purple, rarely greenish or white. This is one of the western trilliums that can be grown in shady wild gardens in the East.

358. Are the California pink and the Indian pink the same?   Yes; but the name Indian pink has also been applied to two different plants in the East (see Questions 199 and 221). The California pink or, as westerners often call it, the Indian pink (*Silene californica*), is really a catchfly. It usually grows ten to fifteen inches high, but its sticky stem sometimes scrambles onto bushes up to twice that height. The flowers are crimson, about one inch across, the five petals deeply four-cleft. It is a showy spring-bloomer.

359. What is the showiest coneflower in California? The California coneflower (*Rudbeckia californica*) has very large solitary lemon-yellow flower heads, five to six inches wide. The plant is a rather coarse, hairy, unbranched perennial, three to six feet high, its ovalish leaves often two-cleft. The flower heads have seven to nine rays that may be as much as two inches across; they bloom in summer and autumn.

360. What romantic story clings to the floral firecracker? In the stagecoach era of California's history a stagecoach driver, with his daughter Ida-May, first brought to the attention of botanists the showy bulbous plant that came to be called the floral firecracker or firecracker plant. It was named *Brevoortia Ida-Maia* to honor F. C. Brevoort, an American naturalist, not forgetting the daughter of the stagecoach driver. It is a bulbous plant with narrow, basal leaves, and a flower stalk two to three feet high, topped with a profuse cluster of flowers. These are tubular, about one and a half inches long, nodding, scarlet but tipped with green, and very handsome. Its outdoor culture in the East is difficult and next to impossible north of Washington, D.C., without a greenhouse.

361. What are the triplet lilies? These are very showy, mostly Californian bulbous plants belonging to the group known as *Brodiaea*, of which there are many species on the Pacific Coast. Only three of them can be noted in the next three questions. They are closely related to the floral firecracker (see Question 360) and all of them have crocus-like bulbs (actually corms), narrow, basal, grass-like leaves and funnel-shaped flowers with six petals of various colors. (See Questions 362–364.) Few of them are successful garden plants in the East.

362. What triplet lily is called pretty-face? The very showy Californian bulbous plant known as *Brodiaea ixioides*. It is from ten to eighteen inches high, its flowers salmon or salmon-yellow, streaked with purple and about one-half to three-fourths of an inch long.

363. Is there a wild hyacinth on the Pacific Coast? The plant so called, which is not a true hyacinth, is a triplet lily, known as *Brodiaea lactea*. It is found from British Columbia to California and is ten to eighteen inches high. The flowers are lilac or white, not over one-half inch long.

364. What is the snake lily? A California triplet lily, unlike all others in having a twining stem three to eight feet high. The snake lily (*Brodiaea volubilis*) has rose-red or pink flowers, one-half to three-fourths of an inch long, but as there are fifteen to thirty flowers in the cluster, the plant is showy in midsummer.

365. What Mariposa lily is called the cat's-ear? A beautiful bulbous plant that is native in woodlands from British Columbia and Washington to Montana and Utah is called the cat's-ear because of the densely hairy petals. It was named *Calochortus elegans,* and its sword-shaped leaves are far higher than the flowers, which are borne near the ground. The flowers are greenish-white, often purple-tinged, followed by a narrow pod about two inches long. It does not take kindly to cultivation in the East. (For related species see Questions 329–331.)

366. The bulb of what Pacific Coast flower was the source of Indian food and a kind of molasses? Long before the region was settled by white men, Indian women would collect the bulbs of the camas (*Camassia Quamash*), often called the quamash or bear grass and sometimes known as blue camas. The bulbs are highly nutritious and when boiled yield a kind of molasses. The plant has basal, sword-shaped leaves and a showy terminal flower cluster often twelve to fifteen inches long. The flowers are blue, or rarely white, not tubular but with six separate petals. Its culture in the East is not difficult if the bulbs are planted in the fall like tulips and left undisturbed.

367. The bulb of what California flower was used by the Indians to make a lather? The California soapwort (*Chlorogalum pomeridi-*

anum), which is also called the amole, was once used by the Indians as a kind of soap. Its onion-like bulb produces long, wavy-margined, mostly basal leaves and a many-branched flowering stalk three to five feet high. The flowers, are white, but purple-veined, and so fragrant that the plant is a favorite among California bee-keepers. It is closely related to the camas and can be grown in the East under similar conditions. (See Question 366.)

368. What is blue dicks? A Californian bulbous plant (*Dichelostemma capitatum*) with onion-like leaves, but without the onion odor. The leaves are six to eight inches long, and are mostly basal. The flower stalk is taller than the leaves and bears rather close clusters of from four to ten blue flowers, below which are four leaf-like structures (bracts, see Question 163). These are metallic or purplish and add much to the showy flower cluster. The plant is closely related to the Mariposa lilies and just as difficult to grow in eastern gardens.

369. The East has only one common dogtooth violet; are there more in the far West? Many more, all belonging to the group known as *Erythronium,* some of which are so handsome that they are cultivated in gardens, often precariously. They are plants of deep, mostly moist woods, and the next three questions are about the most desirable ones. (For the eastern species see Question 156.)

370. What is the avalanche lily? A dogtooth violet (*Erythronium montanum*) which grows at the snow-edge on the highest mountains in Washington and Oregon. Its cultivation in the East is practically impossible unless one's wild garden is far north or high up on a mountain above the tree-line. Unlike most of its relatives, its broadly lance-shaped leaves are not mottled. The flowers are very showy, several in a cluster, pale lavender or whitish, the outer petals recurved. The plant never grows higher than six to eight inches.

371. Will the fawn lily grow in eastern gardens? Yes; this is one of the most satisfactory of all the western dogtooth violets for eastern wild gardens. It needs cool shade and a soil rich in humus. The fawn lily (*Erythronium californicum*) is nearly twelve inches high and has decidedly brown- or white-mottled leaves. The flowers are showy, nearly one and a half inches long, and cream-white.

372. What is the chamise lily?   A western dogtooth violet (*Erythronium grandiflorum*) commonly called "Adam and Eve" and sometimes "Easter bells." It is much taller than its relatives, often reaching a height of twenty-four inches, and its leaves are not mottled. The flowers are bright yellow, about two inches high, the outer petals strongly recurved. The plant is relatively easy to grow in eastern wild gardens in cool shade and in good humus soil.

373. Are the Pacific Coast fritillaries suited to eastern gardens? Generally not, but they are extremely handsome bulbous plants, all belonging to the group *Fritillaria,* which also contains the old garden favorite called the crown imperial, which is Persian. Our western sorts are mostly unbranched plants, often with clustered leaves, and lily-like, usually nodding flowers with six similar segments. Of the many species found in the West only three can be considered here. None of them takes kindly to cultivation in the East, although they all do well in California gardens.

374. What is the checkered lily?   A beautiful bulbous plant, growing from British Columbia to California, so called because of its handsome, mottled flowers. Named *Fritillaria lanceolata,* it grows about eighteen to twenty-four inches high, its six to fourteen narrow leaves scattered on the stem. The flowers are about one and a half inches long, dark purple but mottled greenish-yellow. It is not suitable for eastern gardens.

375. How high does the yellow fritillary grow?   It is lower than most of its cousins, rarely exceeding nine inches in height. It was named *Fritillaria pudica* as *pudica* means bashful or retiring, and this suits its few-flowered clusters and low stature. The leaves are narrow, but broader towards the tip. The flowers are only one to three in a cluster, about three-fourths of an inch long, orange-yellow and purple-tinged. It is quite unsuited to eastern gardens.

376. Where does the scarlet fritillary grow?   Only in southern Oregon and northern California. This, one of the showiest of all the group, has a stout stem, fifteen to thirty inches high, its leaves narrowly lance-shaped. The flowers are nearly one and a half inches long, are brilliantly scarlet but checkered with yellow. Christened *Fritillaria recurva,* this striking plant is not for eastern gardens.

377. Are the blue camas and the quamash the same? Yes, they are both local California names for the camas or bear grass. (See Question 366.)

378. What is the chaparral lily? This, one of the tallest of all the Pacific Coast lilies, found from Oregon to southern California, grows six feet high. The chaparral lily, *Lilium rubescens,* is exceeded in its flowers by many others, as they are only about two inches long. They are at first pale lilac, but ultimately rose-purple and fragrant. The plant has clustered leaves.

379. Are the Oregon lily and the Columbia lily the same? Both names are applied to a lily, *Lilium columbianum,* which grows from British Columbia to California. It is two to four feet high and has scattered or clustered, shining leaves. The flowers are orange-red, numerous, and nodding, about two inches long, and copiously dusted with dark spots. Its petals are strikingly bent downwards.

380. What are Easter bells? Another name for "Adam and Eve" or the chamise lily. (See Question 372.)

All of the above Pacific Coast flowers are bulbous plants, grown from planted bulbs. (See Questions 360–380.) None of the following flowers has bulbs, but ordinary roots. Some are annuals of which the seed must be sown every year. But most of them are perennials that should, with proper care, persist for several or many years.

For the convenience of the garden-minded the annuals and perennials are separated thus:

Annuals: Questions 381–403.
Perennials: Questions 404–423.

381. What are "red maids"? The name is given in California to a rock purslane (*Calandrinia ciliata menziesi*), which is a sprawling annual, seldom over twelve inches high, with narrow, somewhat fleshy leaves about two inches long. The flowers are rather profuse in branched clusters, red or rose and about one-half of an inch long. The plant is little grown in the East.

382. What are "Chinese houses"? The name in California and among most gardeners is applied to a beautiful annual, *Collinsia bi-*

Chinese houses (*Collinsia bicolor*) was so named in California because its tiered flowers look a little like Chinese tenements.

color, native to California, but grown as one of the finest garden annuals. The plant is not over twenty-four inches high and has oblongish, toothed leaves one to two inches long. The flowers are very irregular (see Question 4), two-lipped, purple and white, arranged in leafy, tiered terminal clusters. The plant blooms profusely in the spring, but does not like intense summer heat.

383. What are "blue-lips"?   This is the name on the Pacific Coast for an attractive annual, *Collinsia grandiflora,* eight to fifteen inches high, its narrow leaves about one inch long and toothed on the margin. Flowers, showy, about three-fourths of an inch long, very irregular (see Question 4), the upper lip purple or white, the three-lobed lower lip blue or violet. The plant was named in honor of Zaccheus Collins, a Philadelphia botanist.

384. What Australian annual has run wild along the rocky coast of California?   The ice-plant (*Mesembryanthemum crystallinum*) is so plentiful along that coast that most people think it is a native there. It is a low, prostrate annual, often called the sea fig or sea marigold, with alternate, flat, fleshy, leaves, clasping at the base and plentifully sprinkled with glistening dots—hence the name ice plant. The flowers are nearly stalkless, very profuse, about three-fourths of an inch wide, pale pink or white, with so many petals that the flower looks daisy-like. The plant is much grown in gardens, but needs plenty of heat and a sandy soil.

385. Why were some beautiful western flowers named *Nemophila*? That word is from the Greek roots for "grove" and "love," because most nemophilas are best grown in at least partial shade. So popular have they become as garden plants that names like "fiesta-flower," "five-spot," and "baby blue-eyes" have been attached to those in Questions 386–388. All these are annuals with hairy stems and much cut or divided leaves. The flowers are showy, in clusters at the tips of the branches, mostly bell-shaped.

386. What California nemophila grows the tallest? The fiesta-flower, *Nemophila aurita,* which grows from the Sacramento valley southwards, mostly in low, shady woods, is of a scrambling habit, climbing by the prickles on its stem to a height of three to six feet. The leaves are deeply cut, and stem-clasping. The flowers are about one inch wide, violet, but lighter on the outside.

387. Why was a California nemophila called the "five-spot"? The flower of the five-spot, *Nemophila maculata,* has white flowers, the base of each five segments with a purple spot. The plant is about four to six inches high with lyre-shaped, much cut leaves, and is moderately popular as a garden flower.

388. What is the garden favorite among the nemophilas? The baby blue-eyes, *Nemophila menziesi,* is one of the most favorite of all garden annuals, growing wild in California, but cultivated almost throughout the world. It is only about six inches high, often less, its leaves cut into from seven to nine segments. The flowers are broadly bell-shaped, about three-fourths of an inch wide, brilliantly blue but with a white or pale blue center, borne singly but numerous and very handsome. The plant is often used as an attractive edging. Sow seeds where wanted.

389. What California flower was named for an explorer? The associate of Captain Lewis on the epoch-making trip to the Pacific in

1804–5 was Captain William Clark of Virginia. For him a California annual, *Clarkia elegans,* was christened and it has since become a very popular garden flower. It has an erect, reddish stem, eighteen to thirty-six inches high, its leaves ovalish and remotely toothed. Its rose-colored or purple flower is nearly three inches wide, has only four petals and is borne either singly or in sparse clusters. Sow seeds where wanted as it is difficult to transplant. (See also Question 619.)

390. What are "fairy fans"? A charming little California annual, *Eucharidium breweri,* scarcely nine inches high and closely related to *Clarkia* (see Question 389). It has narrow leaves and showy flowers in terminal clusters. These flowers are fragrant, deep pink, the four petals fan-shaped, with one lobe longer than the other two. It is a hardy annual, the seeds of which should be sown where wanted, as it resents transplanting.

391. Are "red ribbons" closely related to "fairy fans"? Yes; but the plant is twice as high as in fairy fans (see Question 390). Also red ribbons, *Eucharidium concinnum,* has somewhat oblong or oval leaves, and its rose-purple flowers have petals in which the lobes of the petal are nearly equal. It is a hardy annual, the seeds of which should be sown where wanted.

392. What are "yellow or golden bells"? A rather showy annual found from California to Mexico, called also the California golden bells or whispering bells from its persistent flowers. Christened *Emmenanthe penduliflora,* it was well named, for the first term is from the Greek meaning an "abiding flower," and the second signifies a "flower that hangs." It is a sticky-foliaged, branching plant, twelve to eighteen inches high, its leaves cut into fine segments. The flowers grow in a loose, branched cluster, cream-yellow, about one-half of an inch long and suggest the lily-of-the-valley, hanging by a longish, slender stalk and very persistent. Its culture is easy as a hardy annual.

393. Is "farewell-to-spring" well named? Yes, for it never begins to bloom before the end of June and stays in flower until October. It is a very popular tender annual, is wild from British Columbia to California, and grows twelve to thirty inches high. It was christened *Godetia amoena,* the second name signifying "pleasing," which it certainly is, as the hybridizers have created several horticultural forms, which, as garden plants, are superior to the wild species. The leaves are narrow, one to two inches long, often with associated smaller ones. The flowers are showy, one to two inches wide, the four petals lilac-crimson or reddish-pink. The flower cluster is leafy and terminal. Treat this plant as a tender annual (see Question 608) and do not thin out too much as it blooms more freely when a bit crowded.

394. Are the satin-flower and farewell-to-spring closely related?
Yes; but the satin-flower, *Godetia grandiflora,* is only half as high and has oblongish leaves that taper at both ends. Its flowers are more showy, being three to five inches wide, each of the four satiny petals red, but with a deeper red blotch at the base of each petal. It is a frequently cultivated California annual and some of the garden forms are white, crimson or carmine.

395. What is the sea marigold?   A name in California for the ice-plant. (See Question 384.)

396. What are "tidy-tips"?   This is a very popular annual, *Layia elegans,* which grows wild in California. It has a hairy stem, one to two feet high and branched. The leaves are narrow, one to one and two-thirds inches long, without marginal teeth. The flower head is solitary, composed of eight to twenty yellow rays (often mistaken for petals), the tips of which are white; hence the common name. It is of easy culture if treated as a hardy annual.

397. Is the white daisy of the Pacific Coast the same as the one in the East?   No; they are not even very closely related. (For the white daisy of the East, see Question 232.) The white daisy, *Layia glandulosa* of the West is a sticky-hairy annual found from British Columbia to Idaho. It has a mostly unbranched stem, one to two feet high, with narrow leaves about one inch long. The flower head solitary, about one and a half inches wide, its rays white or rarely pinkish. It is not as popular a garden plant as the closely related tidy-tips.

398. Are there two blazing stars on the Pacific Coast?   Yes; one is a perennial that grows from the Rocky Mountains to the coast (see Question 306); the other is an annual known as *Mentzelia lindleyi.*

This is one to four feet high, its leaves two to three inches long, coarsely toothed or even cleft into segments. The flowers are one and a half to two and a half inches wide, nocturnal and closing in the morning, and very night-fragrant. This Californian annual is easily grown in the East from seed sown where wanted.

399. What is the escobita? A California annual, often called the owl's-clover, *Orthocarpus purpurascens,* which is scarcely twelve inches high and has its leaves much cut into thread-thin segments, the upper ones much reduced in size, colored like the flowers and found just below them. The flowers are very showy, in a terminal spike that may be four inches long. The individual flower is very irregular (see Question 4), with two lips, about one inch long, purple or crimson, the lower lip white but streaked with yellow or purple. This is a handsome annual and is easily grown from seed in the East.

400. What is the California bluebell? Of the several plants that are so called, especially in southern California, two of the best known are annuals, *Phacelia campanularia* and *Phacelia Whitlavia.* The first grows about six to eight inches high, has velvety and wrinkled leaves with a reddish leaf stalk and deep blue, bell-shaped flowers that are white-marked. *Phacelia Whitlavia* grows up to eighteen inches high, its stem loosely branching and hairy. The leaves are ovalish and toothed on the margin. The flowers are bell-shaped, about one inch long, blue or purple. Both the California bluebells bear their flowers in one-sided clusters and are important bee plants, easily cultivated in the East as annuals.

401. Is the "bird's-eyes" related to the skyrocket? Yes; but not too closely as the skyrocket is a plant common also in the Rocky Mountains (see Question 301) while bird's-eye (*Gilia tricolor*) is an annual, confined to California. It grows eighteen to twenty-four inches high, its leaves finely dissected into narrow segments. The flowers are fragrant, in loose clusters, more or less bell-shaped, violet or lilac but the yellow tube purple-streaked. It is widely grown as a hardy annual.

402. What are "cream-cups"? This is an attractive California annual, *Platystemon californicus,* which covers acres of the landscape with cream-white flowers in early summer. It is an erect plant, six

Acres of California landscapes are covered with the white flowers of cream-cups (*Platystemon californicus*), and it is also a garden annual.

to twelve inches high, its narrow leaves about two inches long and stem-clasping. The flowers are poppy-like, but only about one inch wide, cream-white or sometimes yellowish-white. It is a rather popular flower garden annual, the seeds of which should not be sown until the arrival of settled warm weather.

403. Are whispering bells and California golden bells the same? Yes, both are local names for a plant usually called yellow bells or golden bells. (See Question 392.)

The Pacific Coast perennials that follow are all cultivated in that area, and some of them are also grown in the East, but not all. Many perennials that are wild from central California to British Columbia do not take kindly to the eastern climate, especially to summer heat and deficient rainfall. The next questions are concerned with these Pacific Coast perennials.

404. Is the "California fuchsia" a true *Fuchsia*? No; the garden fuchsia is a shrub while the California fuchsia is a perennial, often called "hummingbird's-trumpet" (*Zauschneria californica*). It is a sprawling or partly erect plant, eight to fifteen inches high, its densely hairy leaves oblongish and about three-fourths of an inch long. The flowers are brilliant scarlet, fuchsia-like, very showy in branched clusters, and late flowering. It is not suited to eastern gardens.

405. What is the California tree mallow?   A quick-growing perennial, *Lavatera assurgentiflora,* found wild only on the islands off the
southern coast, but grown in southern California as a quick-growing
temporary hedge. It is six to twelve feet high, and may bloom the
first season from seed. The leaves are alternate, maple-like, three to
six inches wide, with five to seven coarsely toothed lobes. The flowers
appear one to four at each leaf joint, are about two inches wide,
purple, the petals with a tuft of hairs. It is quite unsuited to culture
in the East.

**406. Is the California bleeding heart the same as the wild bleeding
heart of the East?**   Not quite, but the western one is often considered as only a form of the eastern plant (see Question 161). But the
Pacific Coast plant has rose-purple flowers, and has been christened
Dicentra formosa. It will grow in the East in shady, cool, moist sites.

407. What are "golden eardrops"?   This is a huge California
bleeding-heart, *Dicentra chrysantha,* its stout, leafy stem three to five
feet high, the bluish-green, much divided leaves rather handsome. The
flowers are yellow, in a branched, showy cluster, the twin spurs of the
flowers very short, quite unlike the garden bleeding-heart. It is almost
impossible to grow in the East.

408. What is elk grass?   From British Columbia to California there
grows an attractive plant of the lily family, also known as the fire lily,
Xerophyllum tenax, the latter term meaning strong, which the plant
certainly is. It is a stout perennial, its flowering stalk four to five feet
high, with basal, grass-like but wiry leaves nearly two feet long and
one-sixth of an inch wide. The flowers are borne on a showy terminal
cluster nearly twenty inches long, the individual flowers small, white
or greenish-white but with protruding violet stamens (see Question 3). The plant cannot be grown in eastern gardens, and in the
west is often known as bear grass or pine lily.

409. What is the "grass pansy" of California?   This is a winter-
blooming violet, often called the golden violet, *Viola pedunculata.*
Still another name for it is the yellow pansy. It is not a true pansy
but a violet that is dormant in the summer and produces its leaves
and flowers in the late fall and winter; hence it is impossible to grow

in the East. Its stem is six to twelve inches high; the leaves are more or less ovalish or triangular, about two inches wide. The flowers, somewhat pansy-like, are nearly one inch long, showy, yellow but brown-streaked.

410. Can the sea dahlia be grown in the East? This seaside perennial found along the coast of southern California into Mexico, is not a true dahlia, but a peculiar tickseed, *Coreopsis maritima,* with a hollow stem nearly three feet high and leafy. The leaves are much-divided into narrow segments. The flower heads are showy, yellow, about three inches wide and solitary. Because it will not stand slushy winters it cannot be grown in the East. For related plants, see Questions 621 and 789.

411. What is the seaside daisy? A seaside perennial of the Pacific Coast often called beach aster, *Erigeron glaucus,* although it is actually a fleabane. It has a clammy stem six to twelve inches high, and its basal leaves have winged stalks and no marginal teeth. The flower heads are solitary, purplish-violet, about one and a half inches wide and are summer-blooming. It is not suited to eastern gardens.

412. Is there a lady's-slipper in the far West? Yes; it is a very showy orchid, closely allied to the eastern species (see Questions 38–40) and found from Alaska to California and eastward to Montana and Wyoming, growing mostly in cool, moist forests. It is about two feet high, with a leafy stem, the leaves lance-shaped, hairy, nearly six inches long and three inches wide. The flowers are extremely showy, nearly four inches wide, the "slipper" white, but the hanging, narrow, pointed segments of the flower chocolate-red. It is a very handsome perennial quite unsuited to eastern gardens, and is usually called mountain lady's-slipper (*Cypripedium montanum*).

413. What spectacular flower of the Pacific Coast was named for a British nurseryman? John Fraser, a nurseryman of Chelsea, England, made long trips in western North America early in the latter part of the eighteenth century and was honored by having the deer's-tongue or columbo (*Frasera speciosa*) named for him. It is a short-lived perennial, three to five feet high, its chiefly basal leaves nearly twelve inches long, with nine to thirteen rather prominent veins or ribs. The flowers are greenish-white, purple-spotted and grouped in a floriferous branching cluster that may be two feet long. This is an extremely handsome plant, growing from Oregon to California, and eastward to Montana. It is often cultivated west of the Rockies, but is hazardous in the East.

414. What is the "gum" plant?   It has nothing to do with the gum trees so common in California, as the gum plant, often called the tarweed (*Grindelia robusta*) is a sticky, gummy, Californian perennial, not over two feet high. It has toothed, clasping, ovalish leaves, one to two inches long. The flower heads are solitary, about one and a half inches wide, gummy, yellow and not especially showy. The gummy exudate of some related species, and perhaps of this one, has a medicinal value in treating asthma; the chief source of the drug is California.

415. What are "witches' teeth"?   This is a low perennial found wild from Washington to California and named for the New York physician who founded the first botanical garden there, now the site of Rockefeller Center (see Question 272). The witch's-teeth (*Hosackia gracilis*) does not grow above twelve inches high and is a weak-stemmed plant with compound leaves having three to seven leaflets. The flowers are pea-like, about three-fourths of an inch long, borne in close, small clusters at the leaf joints, the corolla rose-pink, but the upper petal yellow. It is scarcely worth cultivating.

416. What is the "mist maiden"?   This is a delightful little perennial found wild on the highest mountains from Alaska to California and eastward to Montana. Unlike many Pacific Coast plants, it does well in the East, especially as a low edging plant. Christened *Romanzoffia sitchensis,* it is scarcely six inches high and has heart-shaped or angled, mostly basal leaves. The flowers are delicate, broadly bell-shaped, white, and not over one-half of an inch wide, their stalks very slender and arising directly from the ground.

417. What is the most evil-smelling of Pacific Coast flowers?   The yellow skunk-cabbage (*Lysichitum americanum*) shares this odium with our eastern species (see Question 96), and is quite like it in evil odor, but has a yellow sheath to the microscopic flowers that are crowded on the club-shaped organ within the sheath. It blooms very early in the year like the eastern one. No one would dream of cultivating either of them!

418. Bear grass and pine lily are common names for what Pacific Coast flower?   Both apply to what is usually called elk grass. (See Question 408.)

419. What Pacific Coast flower is useful as a bee plant?   Beekeepers in California often cultivate the sulphur-flower (*Eriogonum umbellatum*) for that purpose, although it is not worth growing for ornament. It is a perennial, about one foot high, its chiefly basal, ovalish leaves about two inches long and conspicuously white-woolly on the under side. The flowers are rather small, inconspicuous and golden-yellow, in a close, ball-like cluster, much frequented by bees.

420. Is there a relative of the bluebead of the East on the Pacific Coast?   Yes; they are closely related, but the one from the West grows only in the mountains from Alaska to California. It is there called the queen cup or bride's bonnet, (*Clintonia uniflora*), and unlike the eastern species it has only a solitary, lily-like, white flower. The berries of both sorts are blue. For the eastern plant see Question 134.

421. Is the prickly phlox related to the skyrocket?   Yes; the prickly phlox, which is not a true phlox, is really *Gilia californica*. It is a woody-stemmed perennial, two to three feet high, and could almost be called a shrub. Its leaves are divided into from five to nine rigid, stiff segments that are only one-half of an inch long. The leaves are so numerous and stiff that the plant appears spiny, but bears no true spines. The flowers are rose-pink or lilac, about one and a half inches wide, borne in few-flowered clusters. For related plants see Questions 301 and 401.

422. What Pacific Coast wildflower has a leaf stalk two to three feet long?   An extraordinary saxifrage, perhaps the biggest in North America, grows on wet banks in Oregon and California and is locally called the umbrella plant (*Peltiphyllum peltatum*). It is a perennial, three to four feet high, with very large, basal, and long-stalked leaves that look like miniature storm-shredded umbrellas, as the leaves are cut into from nine to fifteen toothed lobes. The flowers are small, pinkish, and very numerous in a showy, much-branched cluster. This unique saxifrage can be grown only in the East in moist, cool, shady places, preferably in slightly acid humus.

423. What is the yellow pansy?   A name in California for the golden violet. (See Question 409.)

While, as in most other regions, most of the native flowers are borne by annual or perennial plants, many very fine and showy flowers decorate shrubs and trees. As in the East, it is doubtful that the flowers of these woody plants should be classed as wildflowers at all, but some of them are so showy or the trees and shrubs that bear them are so interesting that it is certainly justified, and it may prove helpful to answer a few questions about them.

Much of the magnificent evergreen forests of the Pacific Coast bear no flowers, or none in the garden sense of that term, as their technical flowers have no petals and consequently must be excluded here. But among the forest trees and in other parts of the region, there are flowering shrubs and trees noted at the next few questions. One of the handsomest is the first.

424. What is the state flower of Washington?   The California rose-bay (*Rhododendron macrophyllum*) is a magnificent broad-leaved evergreen shrub, from six to ten feet high, found from British Columbia to California. Its evergreen leaves are four to six inches long. The flowers are numerous, nearly two and a half inches across, rose-purple, but brown-spotted and in bloom in May or early June. In the East the plant prefers cool, moist woodlands and should not be subjected to heat, drought or strong winds. (For a related plant see Question 183.)

425. Is the mountain laurel of the Pacific states the same as the one in the East?   No, for the eastern mountain laurel is usually a shrub (see Question 185) whereas the Pacific Coast plant is a tree usually called California laurel (*Umbellularia californica*). Because of its aromatic foliage it is often called "spice tree" and in Oregon it is called "myrtlewood," because it yields a beautifully grained, brownish-green wood widely used for bowls, utensils, etc. The tree is medium-sized, usually under thirty feet high, with alternate, short-stalked, evergreen leaves three to five inches long and without marginal teeth. The flowers are small, yellowish-green, which, soon falling, are crowded in dense ball-like clusters and bloom from January to May, depending on elevation. It is hardy in the East only as far north as Norfolk, Virginia.

426. What is the California buckeye? This is an extremely showy tree (*Aesculus californica*), not over forty feet high and round-headed. The leaves are compound, the five to seven narrowly oblong leaflets two to five inches long and pointed. The flowers are quite showy, about one inch long, white, but rose-tinted, fragrant, in an erect, stiff cluster that may be six to eight inches long and about half as thick. Unlike the horse-chestnut, the California buckeye blooms in midsummer.

427. Is the California barberry the same as the Oregon grape? Not quite, but they are certainly first cousins and both belong to the group known as *Mahonia*. Much the most widely cultivated is the Oregon grape (*Mahonia Aquifolium*), which, of course, is not a grape, but a handsome evergreen shrub, three to ten feet high, its compound leaves having from five to nine shining, spiny-margined, holly-like leaflets. The flowers are fragrant, yellow, in dense, erect clusters in April or May. The tree grows from British Columbia to Oregon, is widely cultivated in the East and is hardy nearly everywhere. Its closest relative, which some think is only a variety of it, is the California barberry (*Mahonia pinnata*) which is somewhat higher than the Oregon grape, has from seven to thirteen leaflets, and, in the East, is hardy only from Washington, D.C. southward. It grows from California into New Mexico and Mexico.

428. Who discovered the most spectacular poppy in California? The Reverend T. Romney Robinson (1792–1882), an Irish astronomer, discovered what many consider the finest wildflower on the Pacific Coast, if not in all America. It is the Matilija poppy (*Romneya coulteri*), often called the California tree poppy or giant poppy. It is really not a shrub but a woody perennial, from six to eight feet high, with branching stems and stalked, lance-shaped, deeply lobed leaves borne in pairs. The flowers are solitary at the ends of the twigs, nearly six inches wide, the petals waxy. The plant is impossible to grow in

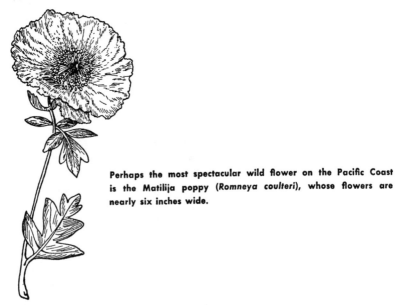

Perhaps the most spectacular wild flower on the Pacific Coast is the Matilija poppy (*Romneya coulteri*), whose flowers are nearly six inches wide.

the East outside a greenhouse and not easy inside, for it has very brittle roots that are easily broken.

429. What is the toyon?   A splendid evergreen shrub, called also the Christmas berry (*Heteromeles arbutifolia*) from its wide use as holiday decoration in California, where it is native and often called the redberry or California holly. It is an important bee plant, and a fine shrub, from ten to fifteen feet high, with alternate, leathery, oblong leaves that are sharply toothed and pointed at the tip. The flowers are about one-fourth of an inch wide, borne in dense very floriferous clusters, to be followed by a bright red, showy berry, which persists through the winter. The shrub is not hardy in the East above Charleston, South Carolina.

430. Are the myrtlewood and the spice tree the same?   Yes; they are both local names for the California laurel. (See Question 425.)

431. Are laurelwood and myrtlewood the same?   No; myrtlewood is the name in Oregon for the California laurel (see Question 425). But laurelwood, better known as madroña (*Arbutus menziesi*) is a tree up to one hundred feet high, found wild from British Columbia to California. The leaves are evergreen, alternate, somewhat oblong, about four inches long, and lacking marginal teeth. The flowers are urn-shaped, white, about one-third of an inch long, borne in loose, terminal clusters, followed by an orange-red fruit. It is not hardy in the East above Norfolk, Virginia.

432. What is the California lilac? This is a quite wonderful shrub or vine commonly called the blue blossom or blue myrtle (*Ceanothus thyrsiflorus*), and often trained on walls from Oregon to California. It is not hardy in the East much above Norfolk, Virginia. The leaves are evergreen, obviously three-veined, oblong, one to two and a half inches long and more or less shiny. The flowers are blue, extremely numerous, in lateral clusters, and when in full bloom present a strikingly beautiful plant that is much cultivated in England, but does not thrive in the eastern states.

433. For what hero of California was a fine flowering shrub named? In the turmoil of separating California from Mexico, Captain John C. Fremont played a leading part. But he was also an explorer and found there a shrub since named flannel-bush, and christened in his honor *Fremontia californica*. It became so popular that it has acquired various other common names like leatherwood, mountain leatherwood, and even slippery elm, which it is not. It is an evergreen shrub, from six to ten feet high, the lobed leaves about one inch long and felty beneath. The flowers are solitary at the leaf joints, about two inches wide and bright yellow. The shrub is hardy in the East only from Norfolk, Virginia, southward.

434. What is the giant poppy? The Matilija poppy. (See Question 428.)

435. What is the tree poppy? Several Pacific Coast plants have *poppy* as part of their name, notably the Matilija poppy (see Question 428), and the California poppy (see Question 354). Most of them are not true poppies (*Papaver*), nor is the tree poppy (*Dendromecon rigidum*), often called bush poppy. It is an evergreen shrub two to eight feet high, stiff and rigid, its lance-shaped leaves leathery, one to two inches long, without marginal teeth, and sometimes falling in dry seasons. The flowers are solitary, one to three inches wide, golden or smoky yellow, its four petals rounded and slightly eroded at the tip. Winter slush and alternate freezing and thawing make its cultivation in the East next to impossible.

436. What is the bladderpod?   A disagreeable-smelling shrub, locally called "burro fat" (*Isomeris arborea*), found only in southern California and adjacent Mexico, with all but unbelievable flowers. It has alternate, compound leaves, the three leaflets bluish-green and about three-fourths of an inch long and scarcely one-fourth of an inch wide. The flowers have four minute, yellow petals from which protrude six long stamens, and an even longer style (see Question 3). As the flowers are arranged in a leafy cluster up to six inches long, and the inflated, pear-shaped, long-stalked fruit are often found at the same time the effect is rather weird. It is a shrub three to ten feet high, usually nearer the lower figure.

437. What flowering shrub is misnamed slippery elm in California?   The flannel-bush. (See Question 433.)

438. What is the mountain heather?   A heather-like, nearly prostrate evergreen shrub (*Cassiope mertensiana*) growing in alpine fell-fields from Alaska to the highest mountains of California and hence unsuited to ordinary gardens in the East. It is not over eight inches high, and its very small, scale-like leaves are loosely pressed against the twigs. The flowers are almost perfectly bell-shaped, white, nodding, and solitary but profuse, and about one-fourth of an inch long.

439. Is there a Pacific Coast flower that is closely related to the eastern wintergreen?   Yes; but the western species is more of an erect shrub than the eastern wintergreen (see Question 138). The Pacific Coast plant is the salal (*Gaultheria Shallon*), and is an aromatic shrub twelve to eighteen inches high, with roundish or oval evergreen leaves three to five inches long. The flowers are almost perfectly urn-shaped, about one-half of an inch long, pink or white, and arranged in a terminal cluster two to five inches long. The fruit is berry-like and purplish-black.

440. What is the Oregon box?   It has nothing to do with boxwood, but is a low evergreen with stiff branches, christened *Pachistima*

Myrsinites. The latter name means "myrtle-like" and the foliage of the Oregon box suggests a miniature edition of the true myrtle of the Mediterranean region. The Pacific Coast plant, however, is never more than two feet high and has a spreading habit. The leaves are opposite, oblongish, one-half to one and a half inches long, toothed toward the tip, the margins slightly rolled under. The flowers are white to reddish, very small and borne at the leaf joints. The tree is grown in the East, mostly in the rock gardens in partial shade and in peaty, sandy soil.

441. Are the redberry and California holly the same? Both are local names for a plant much used for Christmas decorations on the Pacific Coast. (See Toyon, in Question 429.)

442. What is the tree lupine? There are many lupines in the Middle West and along the Pacific Coast (see Questions 190, 270 and 352) but all of them are herbaceous plants without a true woody stem. The tree lupine (*Lupinus arboreus*) from California is shrubby and from four to eight feet high. Its compound leaves, hairy both sides, have their finger-shaped leaflets arranged in a circle at the top of a common stalk. The flowers are pea-like, sulphur-yellow, in loose clusters at the ends of the branches. Culture is not easy in the East.

443. What is the Oregon laurel? The madroña. (See Question 431.)

V. OLDER CULTIVATED FLOWERS

444. What is the difference between wildflowers and cultivated flowers? There is a vital one. All wildflowers must survive the intense competition for food, light and the hazards of a natural environment. That they do survive these is the measure of their adaptability. No garden flower is ever in such a predicament, for every good gardener seeks to protect them from the bitter conditions for survival that all natural vegetation must conquer. The failure to do so would mean the extinction of any wildflower. But garden or cultivated flowers, which we often strive to make secure in the purely artificial conditions of a garden, are free from that struggle. Just by virtue of being cared for they are in the enviable position of not needing to conquer the hazards of their native habitat. That is the fundamental difference between wildflowers and the cultivated ones. But there are other, and historically, perhaps more important differences of which a major one is where the ancestors of our garden flowers originated.

445. Where do most garden flowers come from? Historically minded botanists have long since determined that there were two main centers in which most cultivated plants originated. One is in the New World and the other is the vast area between the Near East and the Pacific Ocean, especially in the Himalayas, China and Japan. The New World area is much smaller, including the uplands of Mexico and Central America, and a fairly narrow belt in the Andes, stretching from Ecuador to Chile.

From these two centers most of our cultivated garden flowers have come, those from the Old World having been cultivated for centuries before the discovery of America. All the species originating in the New World have a fairly recent history so far as garden flowers are concerned. As an example, the chrysanthemum, the national flower of Japan, which came originally from China, has been extensively cultivated and hybridized for over two thousand years. But the dahlia, which is still wild in the uplands of Mexico and Guatemala, was introduced into cultivation only after 1789, when the first plants were sent from Mexico to the botanic garden at Madrid.

Both Europe and the United States have been far more deficient in the origination of cultivated flowers than Asia and tropical America, but there are a few from both sources that are significant. In America, for instance, some of our wildflowers have become garden flowers of importance as was noted in the section on prairie flowers, the Pacific Coast annuals, and, more rarely, the wildflowers of the eastern United States.

There is still a third area that was the home of several important garden flowers—South Africa. From it came many species of heath, the gladiolus and the garden geranium. If we omit Europe and the temperate part of North America, which are numerically less significant, it will give the gardener some idea of the relative importance of the three main areas to list some of the flowers that came from each.

Asia	*Tropical America*	*South Africa*
Chrysanthemum	Dahlia	Geranium
Japanese anemone	Cosmos	Mesembryanthemum
Japanese flowering cherries	Tuberose	Freesia
Japanese iris	Marigold	Gladiolus
Most peonies	Poinsettia	Ixia
Kerria japonica	Nasturtium	Cape cowslip
Forsythia	Zinnia	Montbretia
Pachysandra terminalis	Century plants	Cape marigold
Japanese flowering quince	Cacti	African daisy
Fleece-vine	Peruvian lily	
Chinese sacred lily	Mexican ivy	
Narcissus	Chilean bellflower	
Hollyhock	Lantana	
Crape myrtle		
Gardenia		
China aster		
Chinese forget-me-not		
Camellia		
Foxglove		

Such a list, which is very far from complete, illustrates the relative importance of the three main areas that appear to be the most prolific in the origination of garden flowers.

The climatic and other natural conditions in these three regions dictate how the plants that come from them must be grown. The directions for culture of garden flowers reflect these conditions without it being necessary to detail them here. They are highly necessary, however, as failure to follow them invites more or less certain failure to grow the plant.

These garden flowers that were once rescued from the wild have been vastly changed by selection, hybridizing and the occasional throwing off of "sports" or mutants as they are technically called. Such a "sport" will be suddenly thrown off from a population of normal plants, for no apparent reason, and will exhibit a quite different aspect from its progenitors. These sports, often showing difference of height, color or form, have been of great value to those who isolate and protect them. The navel orange was such a sport in a Brazilian monastery years ago.

Without going into the technicalities of hybridizing, selection, etc., there are terms now becoming common in non-technical magazines and even in seedsmen's catalogs that may puzzle the amateur flower lover. One of them is the subject of the next question.

446. What is a tetraploid?   This term is fairly common in catalogs and its significance is sometimes exaggerated. It is one of a group of terms, fundamental to geneticists and of more than passing interest to flower lovers. The chromosome comprises the rod-like, microscopically visible bodies in which the hereditary units, called genes, are located. The chromosome is usually definite in number for any given species, and these chromosome numbers have been determined for many garden flowers. Usually the chromosomes exist in pairs, and are thus called *"diploid."* But sometimes the diploid set is doubled; it is then called a *"tetraploid."* The assumption that tetraploid plants are superior to ordinary ones is not always true, but sometimes it is, notably in the tetraploid strains of tobacco, cotton, marigold and snapdragons. In other words a tetraploid may or may not imply a superior flower, and merely tagging a flower as a tetraploid does not tell the amateur quite enough.

Quite often a tetraploid or, more often a sport, will have a different flower color from other plants in the population, and this quite naturally brings us to the next question.

447. What are the most usual colors found in flowers?   No reliable statistics exist for the prevailing colors in the wild flora of the earth, including shrubs, vines, trees and herbaceous plants. Most estimates indicate that white is the commonest, but definite percentages are elusive. There are hundreds of thousands of flowers and some of them are inconspicuous, a few have no petals and many trees bear flowers so small as almost to escape detection.

A recent survey of flower color in several hundred garden plants may bear some relation to the total flora, but it is somewhat doubtful Among these garden flowers the percentage of the total population for each color is as follows:

white	28%	blue	16%
yellow	19%	pink	13%
red or purplish	17%	orange	4%
	lavender and violet 3%		

Such estimates, based on a very small fraction of the whole, may not be very significant and, among cultivated flowers there is the well-known tendency for a *variety* of a certain species to have a quite different color from its parent. Such variation is common in many groups, often to the confusion of the amateur and incidentally making the above tabulation somewhat suspect.

Flower color, too, may vary from a totally different cause, which is the length of the time the plant is exposed to light.

448. What are long-day and short-day flowers? In 1920 two scientists discovered that plants, and especially their flowers, are peculiarly responsive to the length of the day. This varies from about twelve hours at the equator (a short-day region) to almost twenty-four hours at the Arctic Circle during their brief summer (a long-day region). Such astronomical data has, of course, been known for centuries, but Doctors Garner and Allard were the first to point out its significance to plants and their flowers. For instance, a short-day plant brought into a long-day region increased tremendously in vigor. Sometimes it changed its flower color, and most of all it changed its time of blooming. And this striking effect of the length of the day on flowers has already been commercially recognized. Florists, by darkening the greenhouses for retardation of bloom, or by electric illumination to speed it up, can now deliver flowers with far greater precision than before. This process was given its rather repulsive name of photoperiodism by its authors. It was a major discovery in the plant world.

449. Who first grew cultivated flowers and for what purpose?
Historically the cultivation of flowers was not esthetic but utilitarian.
For during the eras of the Greeks and Romans and all through the
Dark Ages, the cultivation of many of our finest garden flowers was
undertaken only for what they called their virtues, *i.e.,* their real or
reputed medicinal value. This was the age of simples, which were
usually decoctions of various plants, sometimes mixed with such
therapeutically effective ingredients as a lizard's eyes, a frog's tongue
or the essence of boiled adder.

Such bizarre remedies have long since gone, but the flowers that
produced them have become garden favorites. A few of these flowers
persist in this country and elsewhere, and some cultivated plants yield
remedies of proven value. Many of these medicinal plants, if used in
improper doses, are violent poisons.

After the era of simples, and before the discovery of the Spice
Islands, largely by the Dutch, the people of Europe, and of course
here, had no pepper, no spices and relied for flavoring upon another
group of flowers that were aromatic or pungent. This was the great
era of herb gardeners, a revival of which is quite popular in England
and here—mostly by ladies who deplore commercial adulterants of
flavorful herbs. Among them also are some of our most fragrant garden flowers.

But still the emphasis was on utility rather than the sheer beauty
of flowers. It was not until the time of Shakespeare that England went
mad over flower color, and sent many species here as soon as colonial gardens were made ready for them. Shakespeare knew so many
flowers and wrote plays and sonnets so full of references to them that
there are now Shakespeare gardens both here and in England.

We come finally to the garden flowers that are grown only for
beauty, without a tinge of utility. To recapitulate this brief outline of
flower history, it may be summarized thus:

A. Flowers grown chiefly because their foliage or roots were supposed to be medicinal. Quite a few of these are remedies discovered by early settlers of America, or by the Indians. Question 450–488.
B. Flowers grown chiefly because their foliage, roots, flowers or
   seeds are aromatic and often fragrant. Questions 489–548.

C. Flowers mentioned by Shakespeare or grown at his time; the dawn of the esthetic appeal of flowers. Questions 549–603.

Flowers Grown Chiefly Because Their Foliage or Roots Were Supposed to Be, and Sometimes Are, of Medicinal Value, Either Here or in England

450. What is wild ginger?   A native woodland plant of the eastern United States, the roots of which the Indians taught our early settlers to like. Before refrigeration, when meat and fish were often a bit high, wild ginger helped to mask the flavor. The wild ginger (*Asarum canadense*) is a low perennial with kidney-shaped leaves and curious, chocolate-red flowers borne at ground level and usually hidden by the foliage. Wild ginger is an interesting plant for the wild garden, and will grow in partial shade and in woodsy, not too acid soil.

451. What summer-flowering wildflower was once widely used as a medicine?   Years ago the most widely used cathartic came from Culver's-root (*Veronicastrum virginicum*), often called the black-root. It is a tall wildflower of the eastern states, its stem three to seven feet high, with clusters of lance-shaped leaves and a terminal cluster of small white flowers that bloom in midsummer. Its fresh root is a violent cathartic, often called extract of leptandra. It may be grown in the wild garden, in partial shade, not so much for its beauty as for a link to the days of simple remedies.

452. Is our common white hellebore as dangerous as the true hellebore?   Very nearly, although the handsome white hellebore (*Veratrum viride*) was once used in medicine. Often called the Indian poke or green hellebore, its roots are violently poisonous, inducing explosive vomiting and even death if too much is eaten. The plant is rather striking and thrives in wet woods, being a stout perennial, three to six feet high, its stem hairy and faintly ridged. The basal leaves are broadly lance-shaped, six to eight inches long or even more, stem-clasping, and reduced in size toward the summit. The flowers are quite small, greenish-yellow, but the large, much-branched cluster is quite showy in midsummer.

453. What is stramonium?   This is an extremely dangerous poison contained in the juice of one of our most striking weeds (*Datura Stramonium*), well known as Jimsonweed and often called the thorn-apple from its prickly pods. Originally a native of Asia, it first appeared as a weed at Jamestown, Virginia, in early colonial days—whence its name of Jamestown weed, now shortened to Jimsonweed. It has a rank odor, is from three to six feet high, and its leaves are nearly triangular, irregularly wavy-margined, toothed and from five to

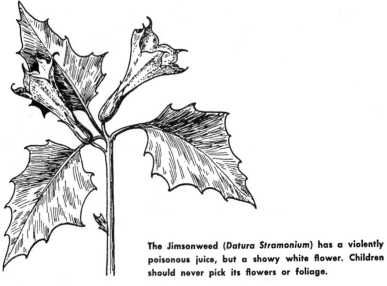

The Jimsonweed (*Datura Stramonium*) has a violently poisonous juice, but a showy white flower. Children should never pick its flowers or foliage.

six inches long. Its long-tubed, funnel-shaped flower is white, very showy, sometimes violet-streaked and nearly six inches long. It is an annual, should never be cultivated and children should be warned against experimental nibbling as its juice is often fatal. Several valuable drugs have been extracted from its foliage. (For a related plant see Question 314.)

454. What is the mayapple?   The early settlers were often plagued with constipation and learned from the Indians of a mild cathartic found in the roots of the Mayapple (*Podophyllum peltatum*), variously called Indian apple, Mayflower and also mandrake—which it certainly is not. It is one of our most showy wildflowers in the eastern states, grows about ten inches high, its naked stem forked at the top and bearing two stalked, five to seven lobed leaves that are nearly twelve inches wide. From that fork arises a stalked, nodding white flower, about two inches wide, followed by a yellow, juicy fruit which is eaten by some, when it is fully ripe, although the unripe fruit is poisonous as are the leaves if eaten. An attractive and easily grown May-flowering perennial for the shady wild garden. (For the true mandrake, see Question 828.)

455. The Cherokee Indians first told the early settlers about goldenseal. Why? Long before America was discovered the Indians used goldenseal (*Hydrastis canadensis*) which later became so popular that it was variously named Indian dye, orangeroot and also turmeric-root—which it could not be for turmeric comes from the Far East. The plant is a rather inconspicuous, perennial wildflower, now so hard to find that it is cultivated for its medicinal properties, which were also known to the Indians, although its chief value to them was the yellow dye in the roots. It grows about eight inches high, has only two leaves that are five to seven lobed, and a solitary greenish-white flower. The growing of goldenseal is not difficult in a cool, moist, shady wild garden in rich woods soil that is not too acid. It is impossible to grow it in ordinary garden soil.

456. What wildflower was used by the Indians to make red dye? Our early settlers found the Indians in the East painting their faces and dyeing their clothes red with the root of the bloodroot, appropriately christened by Linnaeus *Sanguinaria canadensis,* as the first name means *blood.* The juice is so red that this beautiful woodland perennial was subsequently called redroot, Indian paint and tetterwort, the latter name reflecting its use as an ointment for ulcers. At the summit of the stem are the seven to nine-lobed leaves that enclose the flower until its opening expands the leaves, usually in May. The flower is white, about two inches wide, its usually eight petals concave and waxy. This is a beautiful wildflower easily grown in shady, moist places in a woodsy soil.

457. What is Indian tobacco? Although the Indians had plenty of smoking tobacco, they also used the dried tops of so-called wild tobacco (*Lobelia inflata*) for a very different purpose. This annual, not very showy wildflower came to be called Indian tobacco, because the Indians chewed it, causing a profuse promotion of saliva that ultimately made the spitoon a bit of early Americana. But scientists found that Indian tobacco promoted vomiting, and it was of use in asthma, hence its other names of puke-weed, asthma-weed and eyebright. In overdoses it is extremely poisonous. It is scarcely worth cultivating. (For related and much more handsome plants, see Question 103.)

458. What native wildflower was used by the Indians to ease the pains of childbirth? A plant which appropriately came to be called the squawroot or papooseroot was so used by the Indians, and later was investigated by early American doctors, with rather uncertain verdicts. It is the blue cohosh, an erect perennial, two to two and a half feet high. Just beneath the large, terminal cluster of greenish-yellow flowers, there is a thrice compound leaf, with two to three-lobed leaflets. This is a fine plant, May-blooming, for the shady wild garden. Its technical name is *Caulophyllum thalictroides*.

459. What Mayflower is incorrectly called the mandrake? Both are unfortunate but widely used names for the mayapple. (See Question 454.)

460. What showy wildflower was mistakenly thought to be valuable as a medicine? A large, rather striking perennial, known as boneset (*Eupatorium perfoliatum*), was for years so used, and acquired its other common names of Indian sage and feverwort. In spite of its very wide early use for a variety of ills, the modern pharmacologists say "there is no reason for its official recognition." But wild gardeners with moist open places think its three to six foot stem crowned with a huge flat-topped cluster of tiny white flower heads makes it a fine plant for informal decoration. The stem passes through the much wrinkled, grayish-green leaves. (For a related plant, see Question 120.)

461. What is the orangeroot?   Another name for goldenseal. (See Question 455.)

462. Is the pokeweed or poke poisonous?   The American Indians used a decoction of the perennial root of the poke (*Phytolacca decandra*), hence often called Indian poke, to promote vomiting, and fatal cases of poisoning are known from eating the root. But some people insist that the ripe black berries are good in pies. The plant is three to eight feet high, rather coarse, and one of the few native plants to be classed as a weed. Sometimes called the pinkberry, it has usually purplish stems, ovalish leaves without marginal teeth, and small, greenish-white flowers in long clusters, followed by the blackish berry. So far from cultivating it, most gardeners consider it a pest.

463. What medicinal native wildflower is mistakenly called turmeric-root?   The goldenseal. (See Question 455.)

464. What autumn-flowering shrub furnishes witch hazel?   An otherwise scarcely noted shrub (*Hamamelis virginiana*) is the source of this worldwide remedy which is distilled from the leaves of this shrub. It grows nearly everywhere in moist places and may be six to ten feet high and has somewhat oblique leaves from four to six inches long. In October or November, often after leaf-fall, the golden-yellow, four-petalled flowers appear on naked twigs, followed a year hence by the explosive discharge of two black seeds from the fruit. Of garden value only for its very late bloom and of the easiest culture.

465. What is the Virginia snakeroot?   A rather weak-stemmed perennial, eight to eighteen inches high, its roots once thought to be a valued medicine but now in disfavor. Christened *Aristolochia Serpentaria* because the first name implies its use in childbirth, it is now far more interesting because of the extraordinary method of ensuring cross-fertilization of its somewhat inconspicuous flowers (see Question 10). The plant has little appeal to the wild gardener for its mid-summer bloom is not at all showy, and its medicinal value is slight.

466. What is the tetterwort?   The name for a plant used by the Indians to cure ulcers, better known as bloodroot. (See Question 456.)

467. What flower was called asthma-weed? The Indian tobacco, which was once used for that disease. (See Question 457.)

468. What is black cohosh? A native perennial of the eastern states, often called the black snakeroot (*Cimicifuga racemosa*) long thought to be a remedy for certain ills, but now largely discredited. It grows three to six feet high and has thrice-compound leaves, the ultimate leaflets thin, tapering at both ends, toothed or even deeply cut, and about three inches long. The flowers are small, white, in finger-like clusters, these long stalked, standing well above the foliage. Its long, wand-like showy flower cluster, blooming in July and August, make it a welcome midsummer feature of the wild garden. Its culture is easy in any half-shady site.

469. What is Indian paint? The name for the bloodroot which the Indians used as a dye. (See Question 456.)

470. What is puke-weed? A not very elegant colonialism for Indian tobacco. (See Question 457.)

471. Is the Carolina jasmine poisonous? This beautiful southern vine, also called the yellow jasmine (or jessamine to the romantic) is not the true jasmine and was christened *Gelsemium sempervirens*. It is a handsome, porch-climbing vine, ten to twenty feet high with opposite, evergreen leaves that are oblongish and about three inches long. At the leaf joints there are dense clusters of yellow, very fragrant flowers that are funnel-shaped and about one inch long. It is easily grown anywhere south of Norfolk, Virginia, but its juice is dangerously poisonous. From it a drug has been extracted used, with care, by physicians for certain nervous disorders.

472. What Indians used the root of a wildflower for promoting nausea? The Seneca Indians found that the root of Seneca snakeroot (*Polygala Senega*) could be used for this purpose, and the drug derived from that root is now known as senega. The plant is eight to eighteen inches high, its upper leaves alternate, oblong-lance-shaped and practically stalkless, the lower ones smaller and scale-like. The flowers are greenish-white, small in a narrow, terminal spire-like cluster in May or June. The plant is not very showy and few grow

The beautiful porch-climbing Carolina jasmine (*Gelsemium sempervirens*) is native in the South and has a poisonous juice.

it in the wild garden—mostly those interested in Indian lore. (For a related plant, see Question 173.)

473. What is eyebright?   A rather fanciful name for the Indian tobacco. (See Question 457.)

All of the wildflowers whose roots or foliage yield medicines or poisons that are noted in Questions 450–473 are natives chiefly of the eastern states. There were, of course, many others known by the Indians and often utilized by the early settlers, for doctors were scarce and remedies, whether efficacious or not, were eagerly gathered from the wild, when drugs were scarce and expensive.

Much more certain in their life-saving capacity are the following, often very showy plants, that besides their handsome flowers are the source of such standard remedies as digitalis, belladonna, licorice, morphine and scopolamine. Naturally plants that contain such strong active constituents are often dangerously poisonous if eaten by the careless. In other words reckless nibbling of their foliage may be very dangerous, and all children should be warned that handsome garden flowers like the foxglove, for instance, may be picked and admired, *but not eaten.* None of these flowers or their foliage is poisonous by contact, as in the poison ivy. Not one of these flowers is native in the New World.

474. An English farm woman in Shropshire became famous for what garden flower grown in her barnyard?   In 1775 a doctor William Withering in talking to this otherwise unknown woman, heard that foxglove was "good for dropsy." The doctor was interested, tried the powdered leaves on a patient and from these early experiments have come digitalis, one of the lifesaving drugs in certain types of heart disease.

No garden flower yields such a valuable drug as the foxglove (*Digitalis purpurea*) the only source of a widely used heart remedy.

The foxglove, a native of Europe, is now cultivated nearly all over the temperate world as an extremely handsome garden flower. Sometimes called the fairyglove or thimbles (*Digitalis purpurea*) the plant lives only two years. The second year it may be three to six feet high, its stem having large, oval shaped leaves, eight to twelve inches long, with a winged leaf stalk. The flowers are extremely showy, slightly irregular but generally tubular, purple on the outside but dark-dotted on a white background on the inside, the mouth of the flower with a tuft of long hairs. The flowers are a little nodding and crowded in a dense, terminal cluster.

The culture of foxglove is troublesome for since it lives only two years there must be regular sowing of seed in August or September. Winter the seedlings in a cold frame, from which they may be planted out the next spring. Put them two to three feet apart, in good rich garden soil, preferably in partial shade. The foxglove does not like heat and dryness; as a result the finest plants are found along the coast of New England and in Washington and Oregon. Its cultivation for the extraction of the drug is only for the experts.

475. Is the autumn crocus a true crocus?   No; but from its beautiful fall-blooming crocus-like flowers it came to be called autumn crocus or meadow saffron (*Colchicum autumnale*), and its bulbs contain a violent poison, which is also a valuable drug known as *colchicine*. This is much used in gout, but is so dangerous that doctors are warned against over-dosing. As a garden flower the plant is superb. The bulbs should be planted three inches deep in July or August and they will soon send up practically stemless, crocus-like flowers, although much larger. These are variously colored but generally purplish. The next spring the rather coarse leaves appear, which may be eight to ten inches long and wither down by midsummer. There are many garden hybrids of the autumn crocus, usually more showy than the typical form.

476. Why is the deadly nightshade so called?   Because the juices of its foliage, its roots and berries are fatal in even small doses. But from belladonna, which is its usual name, is extracted the valuable drug atropine. This is used in many prescriptions, but with extreme care as it, too, is potentially dangerous. The plant is a Eurasian perennial, from two to three feet high, with alternate, oval shaped leaves that are three and a half to five inches long. The flowers are usually in pairs, nodding, reddish-purple, about one inch long, followed by a black and extremely dangerous berry against which all children should be warned. Its culture for the extraction of atropine is only for the experts, and growing the plant otherwise is not advised. *Atropa* is most appropriately named for Atropos, that one of the three fates who cut the thread of life.

477. Is there a relative of the deadly nightshade in the United States?   Yes, it is scattered as a potentially dangerous weed nearly throughout the country although it is native in Europe and Asia, where it is called bittersweet (*Solanum Dulcamara*). Here it is usually called climbing nightshade or withywind, and is a scrambling, vine-like plant often six feet long. The leaves are alternate, ovalish from two to four inches long, sometimes lobed at the base. The flowers are in loose clusters, violet, but green-spotted and with prominent yellow stamens (see Question 3). The berries are bright red and fatally poisonous, as are the wilted leaves of this plant which should never be cultivated, and should be destroyed if it grows wild. (For a related plant, see Question 238.)

478. What is the color of the flower of the plant which furnishes bitter aloes?   The yellow flowers of aloe (*Aloe vera*) are about one inch long and are plentiful in a nodding cluster. This erect plant is practically stemless, being made up of a basal rosette of very thick, stalkless leaves one to two feet long. The margins and tip are spiny, and the juices of the fleshy leaves furnish bitter aloes, a valuable drug known since the days of Alexander the Great (333 B.C.). This species comes from North Africa and so cannot be grown outdoors except in southern California or the drier parts of the Gulf Coast. Over half a million pounds of bitter aloes are imported annually, as it is an ingredient of many cathartics.

479. What was the white-flowered plant that killed Socrates?   When Socrates was condemned to death, his Greek judges ruled that he must drink the hemlock. Today many suppose this meant the evergreen tree, but actually it was a decoction of the poison hemlock (*Conium maculatum*), which first deadens the nerves and soon kills. It is a rather inconspicuous plant, two to four feet high, with twice-compound leaves, the ultimate leaflets toothed or cut into segments. The flowers are very small, white, and are arranged in flat-topped clusters not unlike Queen Anne's lace. These are followed by tiny ribbed fruit which contains the poison in highest concentration, although all parts of the plant are dangerous. Because it looks something like parsley, the poison hemlock is also called "fool's-parsley." It is a Eurasian plant but has become naturalized here, and all children should be warned against it.

480. What color are the flowers of the plant that yields licorice?   In Question 313 there is noted a wild licorice of the Southwest which produces no licorice. The true licorice (*Glycyrrhiza glabra*) is a Eurasian relative of this, whose roots furnish the licorice of commerce. Very little of it goes into the licorice candy of our youth, a little more into medicine, but the twenty to thirty million pounds of the roots go to flavor tobacco and some candies. The plant is a perennial, three to four feet high, its compound leaves having four to eight pairs of leaflets that are clammy beneath. The flowers are pea-like, in long-stalked clusters from the leaf joints, and are violet-lavender or blue. The plant is difficult to grow here outside California, and even there it does not produce licorice commercially.

481. Is the Christmas rose a dangerous plant? This most popular European perennial, widely grown as a winter-blooming plant, is potentially poisonous, especially the roots. If these are pressed against the skin, they will produce painful inflammation. The juice of the root is hellebore, a dangerous poison. The Christmas rose (*Helleborus niger*), often called the winter rose or black hellebore, is an evergreen plant with a single leaf cut into seven or more segments. The flowers are white or pinkish-green, about two and a half inches wide, often blooming at year's-end, sometimes before, and quite often under the snow. The plant is of easy culture in moist garden soil, preferably in partial shade, but everyone should know that its juice is poisonous.

482. What yellow-flowered weed yields scopolamine? The henbane (*Hyoscyamus niger*), which is a European weed that has become established here, contains in its foliage and seeds the drug scopolamine. This is so dangerous that only very small doses, such as 1/100 of a grain, are considered safe. Its use for inducing "twilight sleep" in pregnancy was once very popular. It has since become an extremely valuable drug in many cases of hysteria, seasickness, and in mitigating the horrible withdrawal symptoms of narcotic addicts under treatment. Such a lifesaving drug is derived from a rather unimpressive plant, eighteen to thirty inches high, its alternate, oblongish leaves five to seven inches long, stem-clasping, clammy and of unpleasant smell. The flowers are yellow, funnel-shaped, nearly stalkless at the leaf joints, the tube often blackish or purplish veined. No one should grow it and children should be warned against it.

483. Does the oleander produce a poison or a drug? This showy-flowered shrub (*Nerium Oleander*) from the Mediterranean region is

in every garden in the South and is hardy about as far north as Norfolk, Virginia. It grows from ten to twenty feet high, and has evergreen, lance-shaped leaves, usually borne in two's or three's. At the
summit there is a splended cluster of white or pink flowers, each of
which appear to be slightly twisted. Later on, a cylindric fruit is
formed. All parts of the shrub are poisonous and children have been
killed by eating the fruit. The active constituent in the juice has some
uses in medicine. So popular is this very ornamental shrub that there
are several fine horticultural varieties offered by dealers. It is easily
grown in the South.

484. Is the garden poppy the source of opium?   No; the opium
poppy (*Papaver somniferum*) is nothing like so fine and showy a
plant. It is native in the Far East, annual, three to four feet high, with
gray-green angled leaves and a white, pink, purple or red flower two
to three inches wide. Following the flower is a greenish pod full of
seeds, familiar as the poppy seed sprinkled on buns. From the milky
juice of this unripe pod, opium is produced, from which morphine,
one of the most valuable drugs in the world, is extracted. Opium also
contains heroin, an absolutely forbidden drug, even for doctors. The
cultivation of this plant for the extraction of opium is quite properly
forbidden in this country. (See Question 552.)

485. What is the castor-oil plant?   A huge, tree-like herb, which in
the tropics is a shrub or tree, but here used mostly as a striking bedding
plant. It has a greenish or purplish, hollow stem four to nine feet
high, and is usually branched. The leaves are nearly three feet wide,
the stalk attached to the middle of the blade which is split almost to
the middle into several lobes. The flowers are small, without petals,
in a dense, branched cluster that may be ten to fifteen inches high,
followed by beautifully marbled seeds that are enclosed in a three-
sided, spiny pod. The seeds, which are highly poisonous, furnish
castor oil after proper processing. As grown here for ornament, and
it is strikingly handsome, the castor-oil plant (*Ricinus communis*) is
a tender annual, which will stand no frost. It needs rich soil, full sun
and adequate rainfall.

486. Is the garden heliotrope grown for anything except its flowers?
Yes; especially in Japan the garden heliotrope (*Valeriana officinalis*)

is widely grown for its roots which yield a medicine once used in certain nervous troubles. Here it is a spicily fragrant garden perennial, from two to five feet high, its leaves finely dissected. The flowers are small, pink or white, rarely lavender, in dense, head-like, long-stalked clusters, and showy in June or July. The drug is extracted from its roots which have an unpleasant odor. The plant culture is easy in any ordinary garden soil, but it tends to die out after three or four years, and should be replaced then with new plants.

487. Where does the medicinal squill come from? The name "squill" is a little confusing to the gardener, for there are two different plants so called. The common garden squill is a small, bulbous plant with tiny hyacinth-like, often blue flowers. But the medicinal squill (*Urginea maritima*), often called the sea onion or sea squill is a much taller plant from the Mediterranean region, quite commonly grown in gardens for ornament. Its bulb is four to six inches thick, and from it arise fleshy, lance-shaped leaves nearly eighteen inches long and four inches wide, and a flowering stalk up to five feet high. The flowers are small and whitish. *Urginea* was named for an Arabian tribe in Algeria, known as Ben Urgin. Its bulb contains a constituent widely used in certain types of heart trouble.

488. What is the black hellebore? Another name for the Christmas rose, or the hellebore derived from it. (See Question 481.)

Flowers Grown Chiefly Because They Are Fragrant or Because Their Seeds, Foliage or Roots Are Aromatic

489. What is a garden herb? The term is confusing, for technically an herb is any plant with a fleshy stem that dies down to the ground every winter, leaving no flower or leaf buds exposed to the winter cold—as shrubs and trees must do. But to the herb gardener the term has a much more restricted meaning. To them an herb is a plant that furnishes fragrance from its foliage, flowers, roots or seeds, and is mostly used as seasoning.

490. Are such herbs medicinal plants? Not usually, in the sense that the plants mentioned in Questions 450–488, which are the

source of real drugs or of poisons. Those that follow have been cultivated for centuries because, in addition to their often showy flowers,
they provide flavors and essences that no chemist can match. Some
of them, besides their flowers, have highly aromatic oils in their
foilage, as, for instance, mint, sage, coriander, anise, etc.

Still others are grown only for the quite marvelous fragrance of their
flowers, such as the carnation, tuberose, lily-of-the-valley, evening
stock, etc. Such flower fragrance appears to be of value in attracting
certain insects upon which the flower depends for cross-fertilization
(see Questions 3 and 7). But the aromatic oils and resins found in the
foliage of some of the culinary herbs are more difficult of explanation
as no technical reason has been found for their occurrence and it is
doubtful that they are of any value to the plant. The assumption that
such aromatic oils prevent grazing animals from nibbling such plants
is extremely doubtful, so that the very thing for which we value these
plants may be of no value to them.

For the garden-minded it may be helpful to separate the plants in
this section into two categories:

Plants grown chiefly for their flower fragrance. See Questions 491–
526.
Plants grown chiefly for their aromatic odors. See Questions 527–
548.

491. How can these fragrant flowers be grown by the amateur?
Some of these outstandingly fragrant flowers are borne on plants that
are perennials, which means that once established, they should persist
for years. (See Question 610.) Two of them, however, are biennials,
which live only two years and then die out. Such plants must be re-
sown every other year, but they occasionally are self-sown and thus
persist for a time. However it is not safe to rely on self-sown seed.
(See Question 609.)

Still a third group of these fragrant flowers are borne on annual
plants, the seed of which must be sown every spring as soon as warm
weather is assured (see Question 607). Of these annuals a few are what
are called tender annuals, usually tropical in origin. The seed of these
should be sown in boxes or pans in the house about six to eight weeks
before their transfer outdoors, which should not be until warm weather
has arrived. (See Question 608.)

A final group comprise plants raised from bulbs, some of which can be left in the ground for years. Other bulbous plants, however, must have the bulbs stored over the winter in a frost-free place and re-planted in the spring (see Question 611).

For the convenience of the gardener these categories can be summarized as follows:

> Perennial fragrant flowers: Questions 492–501
> Biennial fragrant flowers: Questions 502–503
> Annual fragrant flowers: Questions 504–510
> Tender annual fragrant flowers: Questions 511–515
> Bulbous fragrant flowers: Questions 516–526.

492. Can the sweet violet of the florist be grown outdoors? Not generally as it needs protection from frost which can be assured only in a hotbed or cool greenhouse. In frost-free regions, where the summer heat is not too intense, it can survive. The sweet violet (*Viola odorata*) of the florists is a native perennial from the cooler parts of Europe, Africa and Asia, with basal, heart-shaped leaves and beautifully scented, deep violet flowers. There are horticultural varieties that can be grown outdoors, but they mostly lack the enticing odor of the sweet violet. (See Question 549.)

493. What evening primrose is night-fragrant? An essentially stemless perennial from the central United States was christened *Oenothera caespitosa,* the second name meaning forming dense, turf-like mats, which this plant does. Its leaves are hairy, narrow, and sometimes cut into segments, the margins wavy. The flowers are very showy, about three inches wide, the four petals broad, white or pink. Its fragrance at night is quite entrancing, and it is easily grown in any ordinary garden soil.

494. What is the musk mallow? A hairy European perennial, one to two feet high, its leaves five-parted, the divisions cut into narrow segments. The plant is also called the musk rose (*Malva moschata*), and it occasionally escapes to roadsides in the eastern United States. The flowers are about two inches wide, mostly borne at the upper leaf joints, the five petals notched. It has a delightful, musk-like odor, and is easily grown in any garden.

495. What is the red valerian?   An easily grown and popular Eurasian perennial often called jupiter's-beard (*Centranthus ruber*), one to three feet high and with opposite, practically stalkless and almost stem-clasping leaves, three to four inches long. The flowers are almost scarlet—hence its other name of scarlet lightning—tubular, but with a short, straight spur at the base, and clustered in a showy, terminal cluster. Sometimes the flowers may be crimson or even white, but they are always fragrant. The plant can be grown in any ordinary garden soil, in full sun. It blooms from June to frost.

496. What fragrant flower is almost inflammable?   The gas plant (*Dictamnus albus*), an aromatic Eurasian perennial often called "burning bush" for its remarkable ability to create a gas which, on a windless summer evening, can be ignited by a lighted match. The

The almost inflammable gas plant (*Dictamnus albus*) is an old and quite permanent garden favorite, persisting for years.

foliage, but especially the flowers possess this unique quality. The plant is two to three feet high, and has compound leaves with nine to eleven leathery leaflets. The flowers are fragrant, white and not especially showy. The plant is easy to grow, but it does not like to be moved. If let alone, it is one of the most permanent plants in the garden. It is summer-blooming, and is also called fraxinella and dittany.

497. What is the difference between the carnation and the clove pink? There is very little because both are derived from the plant that Linnaeus christened *Dianthus Caryophyllus,* the second name referring to the clove. They have a spicy fragrance unique in the florists' carnation and in the hardy carnation. The clove pink is a rather rare variety here, but common enough in England where Galsworthy used it as the motif of "The Dark Flower." Florists' carnations can be grown only in the greenhouse, but the hardy carnation will often bloom from seed in a single season. South of Washington, it persists as a perennial. It is a Eurasian plant, one to three feet high, with narrow, opposite leaves that are smooth, without marginal teeth, and grayish or bluish-green. The flowers are solitary, of many colors but never green (St. Patrick's Day carnations are dyed!), consisting of many petals, and always fragrant, especially in the florist's carnation. If grown as an annual in the north, it is best treated as a tender annual. (See Question 491.)

498. What is the Cheddar pink? A low, mat-forming, European perennial closely related to the carnation and known to science as *Dianthus gratianopolitanus,* the latter rather formidable name meaning "from Grenoble, France." It is not over nine inches high, usually less, and is almost prostrate. It has very handsome, rather small, solitary flowers with rose-colored, beautifully fringed, very fragrant petals. The plant is easily grown in any ordinary garden soil, and is spring-blooming.

499. Is the grass pink different from the Cheddar pink? Yes, but they are closely related. The grass pink (*Dianthus plumarius*) is also mat-forming, but its usually forked flowering stem may be ten to fifteen inches high. The foliage is bluish-green, and the delicate, fragrant flowers have beautifully fringed petals. It blooms from May to August and is often called Scotch pink. The plant is of easy culture in any reasonably good garden soil.

500. What is scarlet lightning? A colorful name for a plant usually called red valerian. (See Question 495.)

501. Are dittany and fraxinella the same? Yes, both are alternative names for the remarkable gas-plant. (See Question 496.)

502. Is there a night-fragrant weed worth cultivating? The evening campion (*Lychnis alba*), a European plant, has run wild in the eastern states, where it has escaped from gardens. Often called white campion it rarely lives more than two years (see Question 491), but is popular as a garden flower because it blooms at night and is deliciously fragrant. It has opposite leaves and white flowers in a sparse terminal cluster, the flower opening towards evening and about three-fourths of an inch wide.

503. What is the dame's rocket? A beautifully night-fragrant Eurasian plant called also the dame's violet or garden rocket (*Hesperis matronalis*). It is really a perennial but so likely to die out that it is best grown as a biennial. (See Question 609.) It grows two to three feet high, is much branched, and has nearly stalkless leaves two to four inches long. The flowers are purple or violet-purple, delightfully night-fragrant, the individual flower with four petals. The flower cluster is terminal and rather showy, but the plant's chief attraction is its night-fragrance, for which it is often called the night rocket.

504. What night-fragrant flower was named after Jean Nicot? One of the most commonly grown garden flowers and most fragrant at night is *Nicotiana alata grandiflora,* named for Jean Nicot, who is generally credited with the introduction of tobacco to Europe. The plant, which is first cousin to tobacco, and, from its fragrance is often called jasmine tobacco, is best treated as an annual, although quite often it becomes permanent from self-sown seeds. It is three to four feet high, has alternate, oval shaped sticky leaves three to four inches long and a beautiful, funnel-shaped white flower, which opens on cloudy days and at night, when its quite marvelous fragrance is at its best. It needs a good rich soil and must not be allowed to get dry.

505. What is the night-scented stock? Probably *the* most fragrant annual, called also "evening stock," (*Mathiola bicornis*), was named for Pierandrea Mattioli (1501–1577), a famous Italian botanist who lived at Sienna. It is an annual, or best grown as such, not over nine inches high, flowering at midsummer, and has rather undistinguished, brown-purple flowers. Few would grow it except for its astonishing fragrance, which does not begin until nightfall. It is a Eurasian plant, with narrow leaves, one to one and two-thirds inches long, the flowers borne in a somewhat sparse, terminal cluster. Its fragrance is so ravishing that a single spray of it will scent up a room for a whole evening —some think disturbingly so. It is easily grown as an annual in any ordinary garden soil. (For the ten-weeks stock see Question 683.)

506. Why are so many night-fragrant flowers white? In the early part of this book (see Questions 3 and 7) it was pointed out that survival of many plants depends upon insect visitors to ensure fertilization. The odor and color of flowers are the chief attraction for insects and often it is a combination of both that lures the insect visitors. These night-fragrant flowers are apt to be white for that is most apparent as dusk gives way to darkness. Tennyson well knew this when he wrote: "Now sleeps the crimson petal, now the white."

Certain night-flying insects, especially moths, are inevitably lured to those white flowers, their ghostly whiteness standing out by moonlight. When, as in many of these denizens of darkness there is the added ravishment of perfume, it is no wonder that insects flit among such flowers, even as romantic lovers are prone to do. (For some night-fragrant flowers see Questions 230, 493, 502, 503, 504, 505, 511, 512 and 516.)

507. What is the sweet sultan? An annual from the Orient, and almost as popular as its related species, the cornflower. Sweet sultan (*Centaurea moschata*) is a smooth-stemmed plant, one to two feet high, its leaves toothed or cut into segments. The flower heads are solitary, about two inches wide, red, purple, pink or white in its many horticultural forms, all of them with a musky fragrance. The plant is easily grown in any ordinary garden soil; do not thin out the seedlings as it appears to flower more freely when a bit crowded.

508. What is the garden rocket? Another name for the dame's rocket. (See Question 503.)

509. What common garden flower was named for a city in Mexico? Many years ago, the four-o'clock (*Mirabilis Jalapa*) was given the second name because it was supposed to be the source of the drug jalap, which also was called after the Mexican city. To further complicate its naming, it is often called "marvel of Peru," although it may not be native there. The four-o'clock is an annual, or best grown as such from fourteen to thirty inches high and a quick grower. The leaves are ovalish and smooth. The flowers are fragrant, opening in the late afternoon, red, yellow, lavender or white, tubular, about one inch wide. The plant seeds so freely that it quite often maintains itself, but is sometimes an invasive nuisance.

510. Is the sweet alyssum the same as the snowdrift?   Yes, both names are applied to *Lobularia maritima,* a very popular garden annual from the Mediterranean region, widely used for edging paths or borders. It is a low, rather compact plant, often not over eight inches high, its small leaves lance-shaped, about one inch long. The flowers are pungently scented, small, white in the typical form, but lilac or purple in some hybrids, crowded in a dense, globe-like cluster and summer-blooming. Sow seeds in any ordinary garden soil and thin to six inches apart. The plant is of easy culture.

511. What is the night phlox?   A stunningly night-fragrant, South African plant that is best grown as a tender annual. (See Question 491.) It is not a true phlox, and was christened *Zaluzianskya villosa* for a Polish doctor named Adam Zaluziansky von Zalusian. It has a hairy stem, usually less than twelve inches high, with somewhat oval leaves that are about one inch long. The flowers are white or pale lilac inside, purple outside, tubular, borne in terminal, spire-like clusters. It must be grown as a tender annual (see Question 491), and is an attractive garden plant.

512. What popular, night-fragrant flower has no common name?   An almond-scented annual from Chile, *Schizopetalon walkeri,* is now a widely grown garden flower, less than twelve inches high. It has never acquired a valid common name, has alternate, ovalish leaves four to five inches long, and is rough to the touch and cut into many segments. The flowers have four fringed petals, are white, arranged in a long, terminal, spire-like, leafy cluster; a summer-blooming plant, it must be grown as a tender annual. (See Question 491.)

513. What is the pincushion?   A general name for the group that contains the sweet scabious (*Scabiosa atropurpurea*), often called mourning bride. This is a European annual, from two to three feet high, with opposite leaves, the basal ones broadly lance-shaped and cut into lyre-like lobes. Flower heads are nearly two inches wide, aster-like, blue, pink or lavender, and fragrant but not strongly so. The plant is rather bushy and should be planted ten to fifteen inches apart. It must be grown as a tender annual. (See Question 491.)

514. What is the sand verbena? A delicate, rather weak or almost prostrate annual (*Abronia umbellata*) from the Pacific Coast, its flowers suggesting a verbena. The leaves are opposite, slightly inequilateral, long-stalked and oval. The flowers are tubular, pink, about one-half of an inch long, the ten to fifteen blooms crowded in a dense cluster, below which are a row of colored, small leaves (bracts: see Question 163). The flowers are pleasantly fragrant, and the plant must be grown as a tender annual. (See Question 491.)

515. What is the night rocket? A name for the beautifully night-fragrant dame's rocket. (See Question 503.)

516. Is there a night-fragrant gladiolus? Yes; this is a very fine, small edition of the usually scentless gladioli. *Gladiolus tristis* from South Africa, is not over two feet high and has only three ribbed leaves about eighteen inches long and round in cross section. Flowers are about two inches long, tubular, white or yellowish-white, and are streaked with purple and very night-fragrant. Plant the bulbs (really corms) about four to five inches deep in good garden soil, but only after warm weather is certain. In the fall the bulbs must be dug out and stored in a cool, frost-free place until the following spring. South of Washington, D.C., they may safely be left in the ground all winter.

517. What is the correct pronounciation of gladiolus? Until recently there was little question that the preferred pronunciation was glad-i-ō′lus. But most of the experts and many amateurs prefer the probably more correct gla-dye′-o-lus, while some, almost certainly incorrect, insist on gla-de′e-o-lus.

518. Is there a fragrant garden crocus? Yes; the saffron crocus (*Crocus sativus*) has fragrant, autumn-blooming, white or lilac flowers that are borne at ground level. It has grass-like, short leaves that appear with or after the flowers. The plant does not take too kindly to cultivation; it is better to re-plant with new bulbs from time to time.

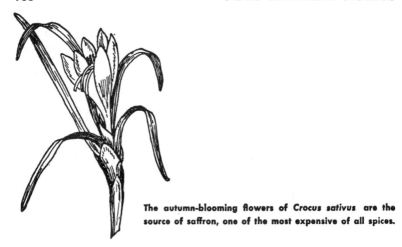

The autumn-blooming flowers of *Crocus sativus* are the source of saffron, one of the most expensive of all spices.

Plant the bulbs three to four inches deep, in good soil, in July or August for bloom six to eight weeks hence. The golden stigmas (see Question 3) are the source of saffron in Asia Minor, its ancestral home, and the plant is thus often called "vegetable gold."

519. Is the lily-of-the-valley a native flower? It is not quite certainly so, although its American home is deep woods in the mountains from Virginia to South Carolina. But its wide-spread occurrence in temperate Europe and Asia make it doubtful as an exclusively American contribution to fragrance in the garden. The plant is stemless, its two leaves arising directly from the ground. The flowers are white, nodding, urn-shaped, very fragrant, and are grouped in a somewhat one-sided cluster. A May-blooming plant, christened *Convallaria majalis,* the lily-of-the-valley is of easy culture under the shade of trees, less so in the open. It needs a rich woodsy soil and repays a top-dressing of manure every other year. (See Question 582.)

520. What is the pincushion? A general term for flowers that belong to the group containing the sweet scabious. (See Question 513.)

521. Is the winter daffodil a true daffodil? No; it does not even belong to the same group as the true daffodils. The winter daffodil (*Sternbergia lutea*) has another misleading common name of the lily-of-the-field, which it certainly is not, for the lily-of-the-field in the Bible is quite surely an anemone. The winter daffodil comes from Asia Minor and adjacent Europe, and is a crocus-like, bulbous plant blooming in the fall. The leaves are basal, eight to ten inches long and scarcely one fourth of an inch wide, appearing with or after the flowers and persisting over the winter. The flower is solitary, yellow, fragrant, about two inches long, and is fall-blooming. Plant bulbs three inches deep, in August, for bloom late in September or later.

522. The fragrance of what flower is almost overpowering? The fragrance of the tuberose (*Polianthes tuberosa*) has been variously described as ravishing, seductive, alluring and by a few other terms implying sexual enticement. It is a tuberous-rooted Mexican plant, all its basal leaves twelve to eighteen inches long, about one-half of an inch wide, and bright green, but often reddish at the base. The upper leaves are stem-clasping and smaller. The flowers are white, about one and a half inches long, in a short, terminal cluster, of such surpassing fragrance that the plant is widely cultivated in France for the perfumers. In the United States it is tender, and the tuberous roots should be planted in May in good soil, about four inches deep and grown through the first season, which usually will produce no flowers. Dig the tubers up before frost, store them in a cool, dark, frost-free place, and re-plant the following spring about five to six inches deep. They will flower the following October.

523. Where did our garden hyacinth come from? The original plant from which the garden hyacinth (*Hyacinthus orientalis*) has been developed was, and still is, a native of Greece and Asia Minor. It is a bulbous plant, its leaves nearly twelve inches long and about three-fourths of an inch wide. The flowers are very fragrant, some think cloyingly so, grouped in a tight, terminal cluster that may be five to seven inches long and half as thick; they are spring-blooming. The individual flower is small, urn-shaped and, according to variety, may be white, blue, pink or even yellow. Plant bulbs five to seven inches deep in a fine, rich garden soil and do not disturb them, unless they get too crowded. The Roman hyacinth is a variety with smaller flowers, but with several flowering stalks to each plant, while the garden hyacinth has a single flower stalk. All prefer an especially rich soil and hence respond to a winter mulch of manure.

524. What is the jonquil? A very fragrant bulbous plant from southern Europe and North Africa, cultivated for centuries for its prevailingly yellow flowers, which are spring-blooming. The leaves are rush-like, nearly eighteen inches long, the flowering stalk about the same height. The flowers are almost star-like, with a short central crown or cup, very fragrant, and borne in a sparse, terminal cluster. Plant bulbs in October, about five inches deep, and do not use manure. If plant food is needed, add about a cupful of commercial fertilizer to each square foot of soil surface. The large trumpet narcissus, usually called daffodil, has little or no odor (see Question 585).

525. What is the poet's narcissus? An extremely fragrant bulbous plant (*Narcissus poeticus*) from southern Europe, often called pheasant's-eye narcissus, with narrow grass-like leaves up to eighteen inches long. The flowers are white, the central crown or cup quite short, usually red or red-margined, while the pointed petals are white. It is spring flowering. Its culture is the same as for the jonquil. (See Question 524.)

526. Can the Chinese sacred lily be grown outdoors? Only in California and similar climates. In the East the plant (*Narcissus Tazetta orientalis*) is tender, winter-blooming and impossible outdoors. Perhaps the most fragrant of all the narcissi, it is often called the joss flower, and is usually grown in a bowl with pebbles and water. Plant the bulb about half covered with pebbles, fill the container nearly full of water and put it in a dark place until plenty of roots have developed. Then place it in a sunny window, and in an astonishingly short time it will send up leaves and its fragrant white or yellowish-white flowers. It is best to plant the bulbs around the first of the year.

In Question 449, it was pointed out that our ancestors in Elizabethan England began to appreciate the beauty of flowers, but there were still many gardens at the time that followed the monkish practice of growing herbs only for seasoning or flavoring. These highly aromatic plants are still with us for their popularity does not wane before the onslaughts of the synthetic substitutes. It is impossible to include here all these aromatic essences, but some are so common that most gardeners like to have a few of them, preferably close to the kitchen door.

For the convenience of the garden-minded they are separated thus:

Annuals, or best treated as such. See Questions 527–534.
Perennials, likely to persist for years. See Questions 535–548.

527. What flower did Keats immortalize in an exquisite poem?
Keat's poem "Isabella or The Pot of Basil" would certainly not have
been written if only the flowers of basil (*Ocimum basilicum*) had been
chiefly in his mind. For the outstanding feature of sweet basil, as it is
frequently called, is not the flowers but the aromatic odor of its foliage,
which is an intoxicating mixture of anise and licorice, with a dash of
spice and lemon. It is an annual from the tropical Old World, one to
two feet high, with purplish, opposite, ovalish leaves one to two inches
long. The flowers, scarcely one half of an inch long, are white or
tinged with purple, and are grouped in not very showy clusters in
summer. It is easily grown as a hardy annual, and its dried foliage re-
tains its odor for a long time if kept in well-sealed bottles. (See
Question 554.)

**528. The seeds of what flower were once used to offset the in-
sipidity of tiresome sermons?**   Long ago some of our feminine ancestors put a couple of seeds under the tongue, the pungent flavor of
which helped the captive audience to keep awake. They were the
seeds of dill (*Anethum graveolens*), an annual from the Mediterranean region, which grows three to four feet high, is rather coarse,
and has finely divided leaves and a cluster of small, yellow flowers.
These are followed in late summer by the highly aromatic seeds. Dill,
of course, is mostly used now to flavor dill pickles, where not only the
seeds but the aromatic leaves and fruiting cluster are utilized. It is
easily grown as an annual, its seeds planted only after warm weather
arrives.

**529. What yellow flower head was once used "to comfort the
brain"?**   In 1606 William Ram wrote that camomile would not only
do this, but he added the injunction to "eat sage, wash measurably,
sleep reasonably and delight to hear melody and singing." Such an
efficacious plant may have been the true camomile, but the German
camomile (*Matricaria Chamomilla*) has the same aromatic quality
and is an annual. It grows one to two feet high, is often called sweet
false camomile, and like the true camomile, which is a perennial, it is
only the small, yellow flower heads that are aromatic and used by

some to make camomile tea. It is an easily grown annual, but most
gardeners prefer the true camomile. (See Question 561.)

530. What very small flower is the source of caraway?   The seeds
of caraway (*Carum Carvi*) follow a tiny white flower scarcely one-
tenth of an inch long. The plant is actually a biennial (see Question
491) but is often grown as an annual. It is a Eurasian plant, one to
two feet high, its leaves dissected into thread-thin segments. The
flowers grow in clusters, are never showy, and are followed by highly
aromatic seeds used to flavor kümmel, sauerkraut, and much more
widely are used to sprinkle on cakes, buns and rolls.

531. What is the rose geranium?   An extremely fragrant South
African plant (*Pelargonium graveolens*), perennial in its native
country, but here grown outdoors only in summer as it will stand no
frost. Bring outdoor plants into the house, or better yet into a greenhouse for the winter. It is a somewhat woody plant, three to four feet
high, with its roundish, five to seven-lobed leaves so aromatic that the
oil from them is used to perfume soaps, tooth powders, and as an
adulterant of attar-of-roses. The flowers are rose-pink, in five to ten-
flowered clusters. The crushed, fresh foliage of the rose geranium will
scent up a room for hours.

532. Is borage a useful herb and how is it used?   This beautifully
flowered annual from the Mediterranean region (*Borago officinalis*)
acquired the second name since *officinalis* means "producing a medicine" and an Arab botanist of the thirteenth century thought that
the leaves and flowers of borage in wine "made one jolly." Today it
is little grown except for its striking blue flowers that are about three-
fourths of an inch long, with long-protruding stamens. The plant is
an easily cultivated, hardy annual, one or two feet high, its rough-
hairy oblongish leaves with a winged stalk. The plant is also, somewhat rarely, called cool tankard.

533. What flowering plant yields anise?   This is a European annual, so highly aromatic that its seeds dragged over the ground leave
a scent followed by the hounds of "fox-hunters." Anise (*Pimpinella
Anisum*) has been used since Roman times to flavor cakes and to
mask the flavor of some medicines that children loathe. It grows about

two feet high, has divided and toothed leaves and small, yellowish-white flowers in midsummer. Its highly aromatic seeds are often used to flavor cheese. Its foliage is also so aromatic that it must be used with care in salads.

534. Is sweet marjoram the same as marjoram? No; they are entirely separate plants, sweet marjoram (*Majorana hortensis*) being an annual, while marjoram (see Question 535) is a perennial, and is often called pot marjoram. Sweet marjoram would be a perennial, too, in warm regions, but is best and most usefully treated as an annual. It comes from the Mediterranean region, and grows one to two feet high, its opposite leaves stalked and about one half of an inch long and toothless. It is these that most herb gardeners harvest as a superb ingredient of salads, not waiting for its small, purplish-white flowers that are crowded in dense clusters. Besides its use in salads, the leaves enter many tasty recipes. Its culture as an annual is easy. If used regularly in salads, many plants are necessary.

535. What did Shakespeare say about marjoram? He makes the clown say in *All's Well That Ends Well:*

> Indeed, Sir, she was the sweet marjoram, of the
> salad, or rather the herb of Grace.

No one knows today whether he was writing about the sweet marjoram (see Question 534) or about the true marjoram (*Origanum vulgare*) which is a perennial plant of Europe, one to two feet high, with opposite, oval leaves about one inch long and faintly toothed on the margin. The flowers are small, purplish, borne in terminal, spire-like clusters. Its flowering tops and foliage are very aromatic, and are used to flavor many cooked dishes. The foliage and flowering tops can be harvested several times if the plant is cut back. It is sometimes called wild marjoram, and, because it lasts through the winter in mild climates, its other name is winter-sweet.

536. What is the mint geranium? It is neither a mint nor a geranium, but evidently picked up the misnomer because of its highly aromatic foliage, which is so strong that only a single leaf is enough to flavor a meat dish. One feminine suggestion to use a leaf to flavor an old-fashioned cocktail merely provokes masculine derision. This powerful plant is actually the costmary (*Chrysanthemum Balsamita*), an Asiatic perennial, two to three feet high, its alternate leaves toothed and highly aromatic. The flower heads are very small, white, the whole flower head scarcely one-eighth of an inch wide, and of little value to the herb gardener, who grows the plant only for its foliage.

537. What is mugwort?　　An herbalist in 1539 wrote that "If this herbe be within a house there shall no wycked Spyryte abide," and another claimed that if a footman "put it into his shoes . . . he may go forty miles before noon and not be weary." Today few grow mugwort (*Artemisia vulgaris*), although its foliage is very aromatic and it is first cousin to the still more aromatic wormwood (see Question 538) and to tarragon. It is a stout Eurasian perennial, three to four feet high, its stems purplish. The leaves oblong shaped, white-hairy beneath and are aromatic. The flower heads are small, yellow and are borne in spire-like clusters. Some still make mugwort tea from its flowers.

538. What flower is the chief ingredient in absinthe?　　The oil extracted from the young flower heads is not only very bitter but extremely dangerous, hence its name of wormwood (*Artemisia Absinthium*), often called absinthe in Europe. So dangerous is this oil that the French, who invented the liqueur, have now made absinthe a forbidden pleasure, well knowing that prolonged use can lead to fits, trembling, nausea and death. For centuries the plant has been notorious and one of the Crusaders upon his return to England, wrote with better insight than spelling: "Water of wormwoode is gode. Great lords among the Saracenys usen to drinke hitt." In proper doses it has been used as a stomach tonic ever since Roman days. It is a European, white-woolly, woody perennial, three to four feet high, with innumerable, tiny greenish flower heads. It is only from these that the oil is extracted, as neither the flower heads nor foliage has any value in cookery. People grow the plant because of its relatively fabulous associations with Roman orgies, the Crusades and the illicit trade in the absinthe liqueur. The plant is a fairly rare weed in the eastern states where it has escaped from cultivation. Since only the oil is dangerous, anyone can grow it safely, as the extraction of the oil is a complicated chemical process. It was once called wermuth, hence our word vermouth, a drink which contains minute fractions of this very bitter oil. (See Question 564.)

539. What is the lemon verbena?   A beautifully fragrant shrub from the Argentine, the lemon verbena (*Lippia citriodora*) is difficult to grow unless one has a greenhouse or can manage to bring it into the house as a tubbed specimen, and even then it is not too certain to survive the winter. It is a woody shrub six to eight feet high, with grayish-green, angular, lemon-scented leaves, two to three inches long. Sometimes called citronalis, the plant bears small white flowers in branched clusters. South of Norfolk, Virginia, it may be grown outdoors all winter. Northward it must be protected from frost. Sometimes it will survive in a gas-free and frost-free cellar.

540. Is wild marjoram the same as sweet marjoram?   No, wild marjoram is merely another name for the true marjoram. (See Question 535.)

541. Is the hyssop of the Bible the same as ours?   Almost certainly not, for the hyssop of the Bible is thought to be any one of several different plants, none of them our hyssop (*Hyssopus officinalis*), which is a Eurasian perennial twelve to eighteen inches high, its partly woody stem furnished with many narrow leaves, one to two inches long, which contain a somewhat bitter oil, with the scent of camphor and a dash of sage as well as an aromatic resin. Its showy blue flowers are borne in a terminal, one-sided, spire-like cluster. It thrives in fairly poor soil, and so does not need to be coddled. (See Question 574.)

542. Why grow catnip?   The Greeks and Romans grew catnip (*Nepeta Cataria*) because they liked to please their cats and that is now the chief reason for growing this Eurasian perennial that is quite common as a weed in the eastern states. It has a stiff, square stem, two or three feet high. The leaves are heart-shaped, grayish-green and hairy. The flowers are pale lilac or white, small, and crowded in clusters towards the tip of the branches. The fragrant oil in its foliage is what attracts cats, and this can be kept for winter use by drying the foliage before storing. The plant grows easily in poorish soils. (For a related plant, also attractive to cats, see Question 738.)

543. What plant yields horehound?   Who, as a child, did not love horehound drops, whether they were good for a cold or not. Today the drops are often flavored with a synthetic substitute, but die-hard perfectionists still prefer the real thing, which is a Eurasian perennial called horehound (*Marrubium vulgare*), sometimes called hound's-bane. Its square stem is hairy and its ovalish, opposite leaves, one-half to one and a half inches long, are white-woolly and rich in an aromatic oil. The flowers are small, white, in profuse but small clusters, mostly at the leaf joints. Only the fresh leaves are of any use as the dried foliage is practically useless. The plant is a fairly common escape from gardens over a good part of this country.

544. What flower makes the best homemade sachet?   The dried flowers of lavender (*Lavandula spica*) retain their delicious odor due to a slow-drying, aromatic oil that is more plentiful in the flowers and a little less so in the foliage. The plant is an ashy-gray perennial from the Mediterranean region, inclined to be woody at the base, one ᵣ three feet high, its wand-like stem plentifully supplied with sɳ ₄,

The dried flowers of lavender (*Lavandula spica*) make one of the best of all homemade sachets.

narrow, ashy-gray leaves. The flowers are small, and in interrupted, terminal, more or less one-sided clusters. They are blue and are extremely fragrant. If cut when fresh, these make most fragrant sachets, lasting for months. They should be dried quickly, in a shady, wind-free place. The plant prefers stony or indifferent sites and should not be planted in rich garden soil if it is to produce its finest odor. (See Question 559.)

545. What plant furnishes the most widely used seasoning in America?   As we import over two million pounds annually of the dried leaves of sage (*Salvia officinalis*), that distinction goes easily to this somewhat woody perennial from the Mediterranean region. It is one to three feet high, its lance-shaped, wrinkled, opposite leaves, two to four inches long, toothed and hairy on the under side. The flowers are blue, about one-half of an inch long and are borne in dense, close clusters, mostly in June. The aromatic oil in the foliage may be indigestible if used too freely. Because of the frequent adulteration of commercial sage, most herb gardeners prefer to grow their own.

546. What are "bitter buttons"?   The name is applied to the small, yellow flower heads of tansy (*Tanacetum vulgare*) which has a long and fabulous history. From the highly aromatic foliage of this rather weedy, European herb, the ancients made tansy tea, puddings, pancakes and apple tansy. Today some people still make tansy pudding, a confection of controversial flavor. Perhaps the feminine faithful hark back to Jherom Brunswyke, who wrote in 1527:

> I have heard that if maids will take wild
> Tansy and lay it to soake in buttermilk . . .
> and wash their faces there with it will make
> them look very faire.

Tansy, which is a weedy plant two to three feet high, has finely dissected leaves and small, button-like heads of golden-yellow flowers. It is fairly common as a weed over much of the eastern states, and is often grown in herb gardens, since its culture is easy.

547. What is the winter-sweet?   Another name for marjoram. (See Question 535.)

548. Are peppermint and spearmint the same? No, but they are closely allied. The experts, confronted with only the leaves of both plants, insist that chewing peppermint will leave a cool sensation in the mouth, while spearmint will not. The peppermint (*Mentha piperita*) is a European perennial, one to three feet high, its foliage full of the oil that yields peppermint, which is widely used to flavor candy and certain drinks—hence its other name of brandy mint. The leaves are about three inches long, narrow and with marginal teeth. The flowers are purple or rarely white in terminal clusters nearly three inches long. The plant is of very easy culture and is inclined to be rampant. (For spearmint see Question 566.)

FLOWERS MENTIONED BY SHAKESPEARE OR GROWN DURING HIS TIME, AND THE DAWN OF THE ESTHETIC APPEAL OF FLOWERS

Today it is almost impossible to reconstruct the history of gardening in England during its greatest flowering, which coincided with the productive life of Shakespeare and with the reigns of Queen Elizabeth I and James I. The East India companies of England and Holland were bringing new flowers into Europe, and the people of England went mad over these importations, as they also did over the flowers of the New World, mostly imported into Spain and England.

Not only were new flowers arriving, but English and Dutch gardeners began crossing old ones. We read about hundreds of varieties of tulips and carnations, most of which have since disappeared. Thomas Fairchild, a London nurseryman, was not quite happy about the practice of taking pollen from one flower and using it on another. He is reported to "have blushed for his work, believing it be unnatural and immoral"!

This was also the period when magnificent castles, manor houses and gardens were built upon a scale so lavish that it has never since been duplicated. Pleasure grounds, terraces, vistas, knot gardens, bowers, and a dozen other enticements were scattered all over England, but chiefly in and near London.

Shakespeare went to many such houses, and his plays are full of references to gardens and flowers. From that wealth of material and from the accounts of contemporary gardeners, we get a picture of the extraordinary development of the art of gardening, as well as lists of the flowers known to Shakespeare or commonly cultivated them. Only a fraction of these flowers can be included here and for the convenience of modern gardeners they are separated thus:

> Annuals: Questions 549–557.
> Perennials: Questions 558–578.
> Bulbous plants: Questions 579–592.
> Shrubs and trees: Questions 593–603.

549. What did Shakespeare think of the sweet violet? He mentions it in a couple of plays, notably in *A Midsummer Night's Dream,* where he notes Titania's special fondness for "a bank where the wild thyme blows, where oxlips and the nodding violet grows." For a description of the plant and its culture, see Question 492.

550. Where did the nasturtium come from? Soon after the nasturtium arrived in England from upland Peru, it was christened in proper Latin *Tropaeolum majus.* Because its young flower buds and fruits have a pleasant tang, the plant is called Indian cress. It is an easily grown annual, three to twelve feet high, and a natural climber on trellises or trees. The leaves are rounded, with the stalk arising in the middle of the leaf blade. The flowers are highly irregular, long-spurred, yellow or of other colors in several different horticultural varieties. There is also a dwarf form, scarcely over fifteen inches high. Both are of the easiest culture, in any ordinary garden soil, if treated as hardy annuals. (See Question 607.)

551. Was the summer savory known to Shakespeare? Both the winter and summer kinds are mentioned by Perdita in *The Winter's Tale.* It is no wonder, for the annual summer savory (*Satureia hortensis*), is one of the best of all leaves to add to salads. Savory is a European plant, nine to eighteen inches high, with opposite, lance-shaped leaves one to one and a half inches long, which are very fragrant and are usually harvested as wanted, often to the detriment of the small pink, lavender or white flowers. The plant is of the easiest culture as a hardy annual. (See Question 491.)

552. In *Othello* Shakespeare mentions a "drowsy syrup"; did he know of the opium poppy? In all probability he did, for the sleep-producing qualities of the plant were known for many centuries before his time. Opium was the *nepenthe* of Homer. (See Question 484.)

553. Was the pot marigold known to Shakespeare?   Very much so for he mentions it with affection in several plays, notably when Perdita in Act IV of *The Winter's Tale,* says:

> The marigold that goes to bed with the sun
> And with him rises, weeping.

The pot marigold (*Calendula officinalis*) should not be confused with the strong-scented African marigold, which is really Mexican. The former is a Europan annual, twelve to twenty inches high, with undivided, oblongish and scentless leaves two to three inches long and more or less stem-clasping. The flower heads are solitary, one to two inches wide, yellow or orange, the rays closing at night. The plant is easily grown as a tender annual. (See Question 608. For the African marigold see Question 692.)

554. Was basil known at the time of Queen Elizabeth?   Very well. It had been a common plant in monastery gardens and was even known to the Romans. (For its description and culture see Question 527.)

555. In *Love's Labour's Lost*, Act V, there is a delightful spring-song to what flower?   It is what we call the English daisy (*Bellis perennis*) but to Shakespeare this pert little plant "showed like an April daisy on the grass." Actually this daisy of literature and the poets is a European perennial, but is best treated here as an annual bedding plant, not over six inches high, with basal leaves. The flower head is solitary, borne on a naked stalk, is nearly two inches wide and is typically white, but pink and red forms are not uncommon. The plant will not survive northern winters here, but it runs wild over lawns in England, where perfectionists consider it a nuisance. Here plants must be raised in a hotbed or greenhouse to be ready for outdoor planting when warm weather arrives. Quite often it is also called the bachelor's button.

556. How many different kinds of carnations were known at the beginning of the seventeenth century?   Nearly a hundred named forms were enumerated in a catalog issued about 1603. Today only a handful are in culture, including the florist's carnation and a few hardy kinds that do not have quite the fine aromatic odor of the present-day florist's carnation. (See Question 497.)

557. Were hollyhocks known in the days of Shakespeare? Yes, and for many years before. We read of "hollyhocks, single and double" in Parkinson's *Paradisi in Sole* (1629), a classic of Tudor gardening. The hollyhock (*Althaea rosea*), originally a Chinese perennial, came from China to England in 1573. But in our climate and after centuries of cultivation, it is either an annual, which often seeds itself, or a biennial (see Question 491). It is a stiff, erect plant, five to nine feet high, the stem leafy, spire-like and hairy. The leaves are rounded, long-stalked, often five-to-seven-lobed. The flowers, almost stalkless, are borne in long, stiff, and wand-like clusters, the individual flower usually single. Some horticultural forms are double-flowered; white, pink, red or even yellow. The plant is of the easiest culture, either as an annual or as a tender annual. (See Question 661.)

558. Is the larkspur derived from a wild plant? Almost certainly not, for while we read of the wild larkspurs of Queen Elizabeth's time, they were nothing like so fine as our modern sorts. The garden larkspur comprises the progeny of a confused ancestry of European and Siberian perennials, all belonging to the group known as *Delphinium,* and so much hybridized that it is virtually impossible to attach a valid name to the modern larkspur. This is a cool-country plant, three to eight feet high, its leaves cut into broad segments. The flowers were originally blue, but may now be yellow, white or pink, according to the variety. They are irregular and twin-spurred, and are crowded in dense terminal spikes that may be two feet long and very showy. The plant needs a rich, deep soil, and does poorly or fails in hot, dry regions. In New England and along the coasts of northern California, Oregon and Washington they are superb garden plants. (For an annual larkspur see Question 625.)

559. The dried flowers of what plant were used to "dry up the moisture of a cold brain"? In 1629 Parkinson thought lavendar would do this, plus a lot of other more aromatic pleasantries. Modern women have not forgotten this. (See Question 544.)

560. Was the columbine of Shakespeare the same as our eastern North American one?   No, the European columbine (*Aquilegia vulgaris*) is more like the columbine of the Rocky Mountains (see Question 290). It is a better garden plant than any of the American species, and often grows up to two feet high. The flowers are one and a half to two inches wide and nodding, with spurs that are incurved and knobbed at the tip. The flowers are generally blue, but may be white or purple in some varieties; a few are even double-flowered. Of easy culture, this is a most satisfactory perennial.

561. Of what flower did Shakespeare say that it "riseth best when trodden most upon"?   He also said, "the camomile shall teach thee patience." Camomile (*Athemis nobilis*) has such a penetrating odor, especially when trodden upon, that many palace walks were edged with it. The plant is a European perennial, never over twelve inches high and often nearly prostrate. Its finely dissected leaves are very strong smelling, but its white flower heads are small and not showy. Its ability to be walked upon, and its resistance to drought have made it useful where grass turf is climactically impossible, as camomile can be mown. (For the German camomile see Question 529.)

562. What flower did Shakespeare think as dangerous as gunpowder?   The flower of the monkshood (*Aconitum Napellus*), but especially the juice of its root have been notorious as a deadly poison ever since the days of the Romans. Today, under scientific control, this aconite is still such a dangerous drug that few doctors use it. To the gardener the plant, often called the wolfsbane, is a European perennial, two to four feet high, its leaves divided into narrow segments. The flowers are blue, very showy, irregular, its broad helmet with a beak-like visor. In the garden it prefers partly shady places, a cool atmosphere, and a slightly acid soil. (For a better garden aconite see Question 831.)

563. Is the pasqueflower of Elizabethan gardens the same as our American species?   No, but they are closely related. The pasqueflower (*Anemone Pulsatilla*) of Eurasia is a better garden flower. It is a perennial, often called the Easter flower from its early bloom, growing nearly twelve inches high, its leaves divided and unfolding with the flowers. These flowers are extremely showy, bell-shaped, about two inches wide, blue or reddish-purple. They are followed by a hand-some plumy fruit. The plant is of easy culture in rich garden soil, and prefers partial shade. (For the American pasqueflower see Question 263.)

564. What plant did Shakespeare's audience think would drive away fleas?   The wormwood, a very aromatic herb about which a seventeenth century ditty directed housewives:

> Whose chamber is swept and wormwood is thrown
> No flea for his life dare abide to be known.

(For the description and culture of wormwood see Question 538.)

565. When did the garden peony reach England?   It is almost im-possible to say. The Chinese were growing it two thousand years ago, and a Buddhist monastery in 1073 claimed that they were growing thirty thousand plants. It reached England long after that, but was well known to Shakespeare. The peony (*Paeonia*) has been grown for so many centuries and hybridized so much that its original Siberian or Chinese ancestor is conjectural. As we know it today, the plant is a stout perennial, eighteen to thirty inches high, with divided leaves and immense, globe-shaped, long-stalked flowers. There are scores of varieties to choose from in white, pink, red and double-flowered forms. The peony is not easy to establish. It needs a good, rich garden soil, at least two feet deep, and is a gross feeder, so that a winter mulch of manure is helpful. Even with the best of care the plants are slow to get established and are rather shy of bloom for a year or two, and, of course, should not be moved. Plant only in the fall and see that the "eyes" of the root are at least two inches below ground level. The roots are fragile and should be handled carefully.

566. Shakespeare is full of mentions of mint: which one was it?   There were several varieties known then, one of which he called spear-mint. This is the mint (*Mentha spicata*) of today and even of the Romans, for Pliny said, "The smell of mint doth stir up the mind and taste to a greedy desire of meat." The spearmint is a Eurasian peren-nial, sometimes called green mint, one to two feet high, and so easy to grow that it can become a rampant but delightful nuisance. The flowers are small, growing in interrupted terminal clusters, and are purplish or white. (For the closely related peppermint see Question 548.)

567. In *The Merry Wives of Windsor* Shakespeare warns that the chairs should be scoured with what fragrant juice? It was balm (*Melissa officinalis*) known for centuries as a wonderfully fragrant plant, so beloved by bees that it is often called bee balm or sweet balm. It is a perennial from the Mediterranean region, its foliage so redolent of lemon that it is often called lemon balm. It is a bushy plant, one to two feet high, with a square stem and crinkly leaves. The small, white flowers are arranged in close clusters at the leaf joints. The plant is of easy culture and seeds so freely that it can become a rampant invader of other sites.

568. In *King Lear* Cordelia speaks of rank "furrow weeds," among them the cuckoo-flowers. What were they? The flowers of what many people call ragged robin because of its deeply lacerated petals. It is a catchfly (*Lychnis Flos-cuculi*), a rather weedy perennial, quite naturally scorned by Cordelia, and by many today, for it is sometimes a waif here as it escapes from gardens. It is a native of Eurasia, grows twelve to twenty inches high and has a sticky stem. The leaves are narrow, the upper ones smaller and stalkless. The flowers are rather showy, red or pink, and about one inch wide, with five petals all cut into four segments. (For a related plant see Question 502.)

569. What did Shakespeare mean by marjoram? It is difficult to say today, but it must have been one of two plants, both very fragrant. There are references to it in *The Winter's Tale,* in *All's Well That Ends Well* and in his beautiful sonnet Number 99. It seems most likely that he meant the pot marjoram (see Question 535), but it may also be the sweet marjoram (see Question 534).

570. What was the fleur-de-lis of France and of Shakespeare? It was certainly an iris, and probably what some botanists call *Iris florentina*, the Florentine iris, for at Florence they still grow it for the extraction of orris root, which is used to flavor tooth powders. The flower was adopted by Louis VII as the emblem of the King of France in 1137. It was then called the fleur-de-Louis—later shortened to fleur-de-lys, then to fleur-de-lis, and finally by Shakespeare and the

English to flower-de-luce. If all this seems historically correct, there is still the question of what was the species of *Iris,* which has had such a well-attested vernacular name since 1137. The real difficulty is that *Iris florentina* may be nothing but a white or albino form of what everyone knows as the German or tall bearded iris. If this is true, and the technical evidence is pretty convincing, the fleur-de-lis of French heraldry and Shakespeare's plays is almost certainly a very common garden iris. He and the French often called the fleur-de-lis a "lily."

571. What did Falstaff take as a relish for cucumber? In *King Henry IV* and in *Hamlet* Shakespeare mentions fennel (*Foeniculum vulgare*) with evident pleasure, and Pliny sang its praises 1,600 years before. This is a European perennial, three to five feet high, often grown as an annual. It has a bluish-green stem and leaves cut into thread-like segments. The small, yellow flowers form a much branched cluster, followed by tiny, highly aromatic seeds. The leaves, especially of the variety called by the Italians finochio, have swollen bases which are eaten when blanched. The latter is often called Florence fennel.

572. What is sweet balm? The balm. (See Question 567.)

573. What is the primrose of history and the poets? What we call the English primrose (*Primula vulgaris*) is the true primrose of which Shakespeare, Milton and a dozen lesser lights have sung. It is a low European perennial, scarcely six inches high, with a rosette of mostly basal, crinkly, practically stalkless leaves, and with solitary flowers borne at the end of a naked, usually frail flower stalk. The flowers are

The English primrose (*Primula vulgaris*) has been a garden favorite since the days of Shakespeare, but only for cool moist sites.

prevailingly yellow, with a darker center. Some horticultural forms may be of several other colors, or even may be double-flowered, but few of these have the delicate odor of the wild primrose, which is difficult to grow here. It needs partial shade, rich woodsy soil, plenty of moisture and coolness—a combination that it can best get only in the Pacific Northwest.

Two close relatives of the primrose are the cowslip (*Primula veris*) and the oxlip (*Primula elatior*). The first has deep yellow, fragrant flowers, while the oxlip has sulphur-yellow, nodding flowers. Neither is much grown here.

574. How was hyssop used in the gardens at the beginning of the seventeenth century?   Because of its fragrance it was often grown in pots to stand on stately balustrades. But, more often, because it will bear shearing, it was used as an edging for fragrant garden paths. (For description and culture see Question 541.)

575. What virtue had rue in the eyes of Shakespeare?   He mentions it frequently in *Richard II, All's Well That Ends Well* and *Hamlet,* always as a remedy for real or imagined ills. The Elizabethans admired rue so much they also called it herb of grace because it was associated with repentance. It is an evergreen, woody perennial from southern Europe, two to three feet high, with an extremely bitter juice. Its leaves are twice-compound, the leaflets small. The flowers are dull yellow, about one-half of an inch wide, in a terminal cluster. The moist foliage irritates the skin of some people, especially in hot weather. This is due to a bitter oil found in the hairs on the leaf surface. It is much less cultivated than it was in Shakespeare's time. It is named *Ruta graveolens.*

576. What flowering plant covered the bank where Titania was wont to sleep?   Shakespeare would not let his Queen of the Fairies in *A Midsummer Night's Dream* sleep on any less fragrant bed than thyme (*Thymus vulgaris*). But it had a multitude of more practical uses, mostly in cookery, which is its chief use today. The plant is an erect, somewhat woody perennial, six to eight inches high, a native of southern Europe. The highly aromatic leaves are small and nearly stalkless, with margins rolled. The flowers are very small, lilac or purplish. Thyme is easily grown as a culinary herb, which it has been ever since the days of the Greeks—one of whom wrote, "A cook is fully as useful as a poet."

577. What is lemon balm? Another name for balm, on account of its delicate lemon odor. (See Question 567.)

578. Did Shakespeare know the pansy? Pansies as we know them today did not originate until near the middle of the nineteenth century, mostly in England. What Shakespeare, and innumerable gardeners of his time, called the pansy was probably a variety of Johnny-jump-up (*Viola tricolor hortensis*), a European perennial with an erect stem, quite different from the nearly stemless modern pansy. The Johnny-jump-up is an easily grown perennial, which will persist in most gardens if the winters are not too severe, while the true pansy needs winter protection such as a hotbed or cool greenhouse. Neither will the pansy stand prolonged summer heat.

579. What was the yellow flag of Shakespeare's time? It was the yellow flag (*Iris pseudacorus*) that grows in the ditches along the Atlantic seaboard, and was introduced from Europe in colonial times. Shakespeare, and even the botanists of his time, called it a "lily," and some mistook it for the fleur-de-lis (see Question 570). The yellow flag, or water flag as it is often called, is an erect perennial, one to three feet high, its sword-shaped leaves bluish-green. The flowers are yellow, about two inches wide, the petals sometimes streaked with violet.

580. What flower was "the bright and perfect star" at the time of Shakespeare? The star-of-Bethlehem, which has since run wild in many lawns here, its star-like white flower very attractive in the lawn, but deplored by many. (See Question 229.)

581. What famous flower found in many gardens in Elizabethan times was ignored by Shakespeare? With all his love of flowers our greatest dramatist does not mention the tulip in any of his plays or sonnets. The tulip (*Tulipa*) had been brought from Turkey to Holland, was widely hybridized and became extremely popular. Speculation over rare varieties reached such a point that when one bulb sold for $10,000 in 1634 the Dutch government put a stop to such

sales. The tulip had reached Holland about 1572, and was common
in England by 1600. Ever since its introduction the Dutch have dominated the tulip world and have originated hundreds of varieties.

Today, for most amateurs the tulip can be divided into four classes,
although there are many more. The four most popular kinds are:

1. Breeder tulips: Tall-stemmed and May-flowering. The colors are
   mostly purple, bronze, copper and dull reds. The petals are
   slightly incurved at the tip.
2. Cottage tulips: Tall-stemmed and May-flowering. The colors are
   yellow, pale ivory, orange and pink. The petals are usually
   pointed.
3. Darwin tulips: Tall-stemmed and flowering later than Nos. 1 and
   2. The color range is infinite, even nearly black, and the flowers
   are more or less square-sided, the petals incurved at the tip.
4. Triumph tulips: Tall and late-flowering. The colors are white,
   pink, red, but few or no yellows.

It is impossible here to list the scores of varieties in each category;
the best guide is a catalog with colored illustrations from a reliable
dealer. All tulips should be planted five to seven inches deep, in good,
rich garden soil in late October or early November, always in full sun.
Since the bulbs need a winter chilling, tulips do not thrive where the
winters are too mild. No amount of frost hurts the bulbs so long as
they are in the ground.

582. What was the lily Conally of Shakespeare?   This was his
name for the lily-of-the-valley. (See Question 519.)

583. What is the bluebell of England?   Shakespeare called it the
crowflower or squill (*Scilla nonscripta*), but it is often called the wood
hyacinth, for it is common all over England in the woods and is widely
cultivated in gardens here and in Europe. It is a bulbous plant, six to
nine inches high, with narrow, almost grass-like leaves, and generally
blue, hyacinth-like, fragrant flowers arranged in a terminal cluster
that is more slender and less compact than the hyacinth. Plant bulbs
four to five inches deep, in masses, in October for late April bloom.

584. Did Shakespeare know the true hyacinth?   If he did, he
never mentioned it in any of his writing, although it was common in

English gardens at the time. (For description and culture of the hyacinth, see Question 523.)

585. Are the daffodil and narcissus the same? Yes, if we exclude the jonquil and poet's narcissus (see Questions 524 and 525). The daffodil or trumpet-narcissus (*Narcissus Pseudo-narcissus*) is a stout bulbous plant from Europe, its prevailingly yellow flower with a central crown or "trumpet." Many horticultural varieties have been developed since Shakespeare's time, mostly in paler shades of yellow or white. Plant bulbs in the fall, about five inches deep, in any ordinary garden soil, as these flowers are less demanding than tulips or hyacinths.

586. Were the jonquil and the poet's narcissus known to Shakespeare? Both were well known and there are frequent references to both of them in his plays. (See Questions 524 and 525.)

587. Why was the Annunciation lily called the Madonna lily? At the time of Queen Elizabeth there was a bitter religious quarrel between the Roman Catholics and Protestants, the latter not favoring the adoration of the Virgin. But the Madonna or Annunciation Lily (*Lilium candidum*) had come from Catholic France, and so it has been called ever since. It is a Eurasian bulbous plant, not over four feet high. The flowers are white, about three inches long, and not nodding. Plant the bulbs in spring or fall, at least six to seven inches deep, in good rich garden soil, preferably in a partially shady place.

588. What is the crow-flower? This was Shakespeare's name for the bluebell of England. (See Question 583.)

589. Was our common spring crocus known to Shakespeare? Very well and it was just as popular then as now, for what can be more pleasant than to see sheets of vari-colored crocus in April. The common spring crocus (*Crocus vernus*) came originally from Europe and is a bulbous, essentially stemless plant with rather thick but grass-like leaves. The flowers are stemless, borne practically at ground level very early in the spring. The colors vary from white to almost black and there are many varieties to choose from. Plant the bulbs three to four inches deep, and about that far apart, preferably by the dozen, by the score or even in hundreds, as few spring-flowering bulbs are so showy, and they persist for years.

590. Did the saffron crocus grow in Elizabethan gardens? Yes. Saffron Hill in London, and Saffron Walden in Essex were both named for the plant, much grown then for coloring and flavoring pies and cakes. (See Question 518.)

591. Who first brought the crown imperial to London? About 1590, Nicholas Leate, a wealthy merchant in London, where he kept a magnificent garden, had "an agent in Aleppo" from whom came the bulb of the crown imperial (*Fritillaria imperialis*), which ultimately became popular as a bulbous garden plant all over the world. It is a rather rank-smelling plant, a native of Persia, two to four feet high, with many leaves, some in a terminal cluster above the flowers which are lily-like, nodding and bell-shaped. The flowers are reddish-purple, but in some horticultural varieties red, orange, or yellow and very showy in May or June. Plant bulbs in the fall, six to eight inches deep, in sandy, well-drained loam, using a teaspoon of lime for each bulb, thoroughly mixed with the soil. They will persist for years. (For related plants all from the western United States, see Questions 374–376.)

592. What is the wood hyacinth? A rather common name for a low, hyacinth-like flower found in the woodlands of England and cultivated in many American gardens under its more usual name of bluebell of England. (See Question 583.)

Just after Question 548, it was noted that during the time of Queen Elizabeth and Shakespeare there was not only a great influx of garden flowers into England, but this era became the greatest period of garden-making. These were often very elaborate affairs, modelled after French and Italian gardens, but cottage gardens along the Thames were as beautiful then as now, and who can ever forget the entrancing cottage gardens scattered all over England today.

None of these palace gardens could have been made with herbaceous plants alone, and many flowering shrubs and trees were used to create unsurpassed garden pictures. Some of these shrubs and trees are treated in the next few questions. Many fine shrubs were wholly unknown to the English at that time, for the forsythia, camellia, weigela and dozens of others had yet to be discovered.

593. What fragrant flower did English rustics refuse to bring into their houses? The English hawthorn (*Crataegus Oxyacantha*), redolent of the Maypole and May Day, has flowers that no bees or butterflies will touch. Only certain kinds of carrion flies will carry pollen to it. At any rate English rustics thought that its peculiar odor was such that cut sprays of it brought into the house would be followed by a death in the family. Most moderns prefer to follow Keats who wrote:

> So I straitway went to pick a posy,
> Of luxurious May both white and rosy.

The English hawthorn, usually called the May in England, because it blooms in that month, is a very thorny shrub or small tree, with lobed leaves and white or pink flowers like miniature apple blossoms in rather showy clusters, followed by scarlet fruits. There are now forms with deep red flowers and one with weeping branches. The hawthorn is easy to grow and hardy nearly everywhere.

594. Is English boxwood really English? Perhaps the box (*Buxus sempervirens*) should not be included in a book devoted to flowers for the flowers of the box are so small and inconspicuous that most people think they have none. Commonly called English boxwood here, it is fairly sure that it was not native in England, but was brought there by the Romans. Without it few of the stately gardens of England or of Virginia, Maryland and Delaware would be possible, for it is the finest—although the most slow growing—of any of the broad-leaved evergreens. Usually six to ten feet high and as broad, after many years, it can be sheared to any shape desired, but most growers prefer its dense mass of foliage undisturbed by shearing. It will not stand severe, long winters or prolonged heat, and its finest development is in the states of Virginia, Maryland and Delaware.

595. What flower did Shakespeare mention only once? In *The Tempest* he speaks of "thy broom-groves, whose shadow the dismissed bachelor loves." The broom (*Cytisus scoparius*) was very common in Elizabethan gardens, grown for its profusion of yellow, pea-like flowers. Often called the Scotch broom, it is a European shrub, four to nine feet high, with green branches. The leaves are compound, its leaflets are about one-half of an inch long, sometimes with only a single leaflet. The flowers, one or two together at the leaf-joints, are showy in May or June. The broom is frequently grown here and is hardy nearly everywhere.

596. What did the English first call the lilac?   The Earl of Salisbury had as his gardener a noted Dutch horticulturist, John Tradescant, who in his own garden, is credited with first bringing the lilac to England. Tradescant called the lilac the blue pipe flower, a name that never survived, although the shrub has since gone all over the temperate world. The lilac (*Syringa vulgaris*) is a European shrub, six to twenty feet high, with opposite, ovalish leaves and a terminal truss of extremely fragrant, small, tubular flowers, originally of lilac color, but now to be found in shades of pink, white, blue and red. Some of them are double-flowered. Scarcely any of these hybrids is as fragrant as the old-fashioned lilac, which is May-blooming. The species is hardy everywhere.

597. What fragrant shrub was popular with ladies but not with men?   A cynical old English gardener once wrote, "Where rosemary grows best the mistress is master." Rosemary (*Rosmarinus officinalis*) has had legends clinging to it for centuries, perhaps because of the delicious lasting fragrance of its foliage. Shakespeare loved the plant and mentions it in several plays, the best remembered instance being Ophelia's handing a sprig of it, saying, "There's rosemary; that's for remembrance; pray you, love, remember." Rosemary is a shrub, two to six feet high, native to the Mediterranean region. Its small but very numerous leaves are grayish and extraordinarily and lastingly fragrant, the dried foliage retaining its odor for months. The flowers, which are blue and not very showy, appear in May. It is a densely-foliaged shrub, hardy in the East only from New York City southward, but grows best in coastal California.

598. What flowering shrub did Shakespeare place beneath Juliet's window?   The pomegranate (*Punica Granatim*), fabled in history and legend since the days of Homer. Its brilliantly scarlet flowers are assumed to reflect the fiery passion of Romeo and Juliet. It is an

"There's rosemary; that's for remembrance." Ophelia loved *Rosmarinus officinalis* for its lasting, haunting fragrance.

Asiatic tree, anciently called apple of Carthage because the Romans brought it from that city to Rome. It is often shrub-like, but grows ten to twenty feet high in its native country. It has a few spines, and its opposite, shining leaves are one and a half to three inches long. From them spring short twigs with one to five wrinkled flowers about one and a half inches wide and very handsome. The fruit is little known in this country, but the flowering shrub is not uncommon from Norfolk, Virginia, southward. It is not safely hardy north of this area.

599. What prickly evergreen shrub was early known to have separate male and female flowers? Observant gardeners in Shakespeare's time knew that the holly (*Ilex Aquifolium*) had male flowers on one plant and female on another, and that if you did not grow both reasonably near together, there would be no red berries at Christmas time. Here it is called English holly to distinguish it from our native sort. The English holly is a magnificent broad-leaved evergreen tree, ultimately up to fifty feet high, but only after many years of slow growth. The leaves are leathery and a brilliantly shining green; the margins with several spiny teeth, hence very prickly. The small, inconspicuous, yellowish green flowers bloom very early, and are often destroyed by late frosts in the East. It is essential to have male and female plants near each other so that the latter will produce the berries for which holly is most prized. The tree is not certainly hardy north of Philadelphia, Pennsylvania, and flourishes best in coastal Washington and Oregon.

600. What did Shakespeare's contemporaries call the oleander?
In his time the nearly universal name for the oleander was the rose-bay, a name we apply to quite different plants. (For the oleander, see Question 483. For two other plants called rose-bay in America, see Questions 183 and 424.)

601. Was the fragrant myrtle a rarity in Shakespeare's time? Yes, for it apparently had come fairly recently to England from the eastern Mediterranean and adjacent Asia. Because of its fragrant foliage Shakespeare has Venus and Adonis meeting under a shade of myrtle. This must be poetic license for myrtle (*Myrtus communis*) is an ever-green shrub only three to nine feet high! The leaves are somewhat oval, nearly stalkless, one to two inches long and a shining green. The flowers, which are not showy, are white, fragrant; about five-eighths of an inch wide and are borne singly at the leaf joints. The myrtle wreaths of the Romans were symbols of pleasure or victory in battle. The shrub is of easy culture, but only south of Charleston, South Carolina, in the East, and flourishes along the Pacific Coast from Santa Barbara northward to Vancouver, where it is often clipped for hedges.

602. What vine helped to shade lovers' bowers in Shakespeare's plays? Lovers' bowers are common in Shakespeare's plays, as a place for a pleasant chat or delightful flirtation, but sometimes for more animated antics. Quite often these bowers were shaded by the lady's-bower (*Clematis Viticella*), more often called the vine bower. It is a scrambling or climbing woody vine, with very slender stems. The leaves are opposite, compound, the leaflets with no marginal teeth but sometimes three-lobed. The flowers are few, rose-purple or violet, nearly two inches wide. This Eurasian vine is easily grown and hardy nearly everywhere in North America.

603. What flowers did Shakespeare mention most often? Although it is rather difficult to be precise, for old and new names of flowers often vary, from the best recent estimate Shakespeare seems to prefer the following eight flowers to the scores that a careful reading could unfold. Arranged in the order of his apparent preference, they are:

Carnation, but he often lumped it with closely related pinks (see Questions 497 and 556).

Marigold (see Question 553)

Primrose (see Question 573)

Columbine (see Question 560)

Anemone, although it is often impossible to tell whether he meant the anemone or the pasqueflower (for pasqueflower, see Question 563).

Pansy, his "pansy" was the Johnny-jump-up (see Question 578).

Daffodil. It is not always certain whether the true daffodil or related species of *Narcissus* were involved in some of the references (see Question 585).

Larkspur (see Question 558).

VI. CULTIVATED FLOWERS TODAY

604. Why separate the older cultivated flowers from those of today? The comparative meagerness of the plants known in Shakespeare's time makes us astonished at his knowledge and affection for them. Still more wonderful were the quite surpassing gardens that were constructed to grow them in—probably the most costly and elaborate in the world.

England, Holland and Spain were in a race to exploit the treasures of China and Japan, the Indies and the New World. Many of these expeditions involved commercial rivalry for the rich prizes of these far-off lands, but as a sideline they sent back to Europe hundreds of flowers never seen there before.

Many years later the Royal Horticultural Society backed exploration devoted only to the finding of new flowers. The Kew Gardens at London and the botanic garden at Leiden were equally active. The history of such exploration is studded with the names of the famous: Banks, Solander, Cook, Tradescant, Forsyth, Robert Brown, David Douglas, Hooker and, years later, Charles Darwin.

Many Europeans were sent to this country as botanical explorers, and, after the Lewis and Clark expedition, Americans began a systematic exploration of the West.

Today we are the inheritors of these far-flung explorations. Their spoils went mostly to England, Holland and Spain, and to a lesser degree to France, Austria and Russia. It is that huge legacy of new flowers that make our gardens incomparably richer in species of plants than those of Shakespeare's time. But there was one other feature of modern times that is so much in our favor that no flower lover can ignore it.

605. When did plant breeding really begin to create new flowers? It could not get a start until the discovery in Germany in 1694 of sexuality in flowers. And not until the Austrian monk Gregor Mendel made his epoch-making discoveries in 1866 did we understand the scientific basis of inheritance, crossing and hybridization. Ever since the German discovery of sexuality in flowers there had been more or less haphazard crossing of flowers, but the results were unpredictable, until Mendel gave us the guide to what has come to be called Mendelian inheritance.

For centuries before these discoveries careful growers had isolated desirable varieties of flowers, and we have profited by their skill in hundreds of cases. But the real breeding of flowers for predictable qualities did not come until the middle of the nineteenth century.

We are thus the fortunate inheritors of wide exploration, careful selection and scientific breeding. The combination of these has given us the profusion of flowers that make our gardens so much richer than those of three hundred years ago. Still more recently have come the technique of producing tetraploid flowers (see Question 446) and the realization that flowers are affected by the length of the day. (See Question 448.)

606. How can the garden amateur get to know and use these flowers? First of all must come some simple arrangement of them into easily recognized categories. Culturally, the easiest way is to sort them into groups based on their garden demands. There are perhaps five such groups and the next few questions will note them and give some simple directions for their culture.

The five main groups are:

> Annuals: Questions 612–659
> Tender Annuals: Questions 660–698
> Biennials: Questions 699–702
> Perennials: Questions 703–834
> Bulbous plants: Questions 835–870

607. What is an annual? A plant that completes its growth within a single growing season and then dies is called an annual. Germination of its seed is followed by the production of leaves, then it flowers and sets its seed upon which it absolutely depends for perpetuation, as it has no roots that winter over.

Annuals provide the gardeners with the quickest return for his time. The only expense is the purchase of seeds, which is almost negligible compared to the profusion of flowers that comes from a single packet of seed, given the proper care.

That care is quite simple. Most annuals are planted where they are to grow. Seed should be scattered or put in shallow trenches, and after the seed germinates the plants must be thinned out to prevent crowding, although some annuals flower more profusely when a bit crowded.

Prepare the seed bed carefully by seeing that all stones and rubbish are removed, and the ground is dug deeply (eight to ten inches) and the surface smoothed over with a fine steel rake. A fair general rule is to plant the seeds about as deep as two or three times their diameter. Most good seedsmen print specific directions for planting on the packet, and these should be followed.

After planting see that the seed bed *never dries out*. This does not mean soaking it in water, which may well rot the seeds before they sprout. It does mean a daily application of a light spray of water, preferably with a watering pot, usually not by a force of water from a hose. Such forceful watering often packs the soil and may retard or prevent germination.

If there is clay or silt in the soil, it often pays to shade it from the sun until the seedlings are growing. White cheesecloth is enough for shading.

Once the seedlings are growing, there is little that needs to be done except to keep down the weeds, and to water the seedlings if a drought is prolonged more than a week or two.

608. What is a tender annual?   This does not mean that the plant is really tender, likely to die if conditions are unfavorable. A tender annual almost invariably comes from a region with a longer growing season than ours, and hence needs more time to mature than our climate will permit.

Careful gardeners prepare for this emergency by planting the seeds indoors six to eight weeks before settled warm weather is expected in their locality. Perhaps when lilacs are blooming is fair indication of such a date.

Seeds are planted in boxes or flower pots filled to within a half inch of the top with fine garden soil and clean sand, mixed half and half. Follow the directions of seed planting and watering as for annuals (see Question 607). The boxes or flower pots should be put in a window—a gas-free kitchen window is fine—until the seedlings are two to three inches high.

These young seedlings must then be quickly transplanted to other boxes or flower pots, filled with good garden soil (no sand). Space the seedlings about three to four inches apart each way. If they get too crowded, repeat the transplanting and space them six by six inches.

They must not go outdoors until settled warm weather has arrived, for most of them will die if touched by a late frost. If all this seems a bit burdensome, remember that some of our finest garden flowers are tender annuals, and that dealers often offer seedlings of these for sale at the proper time.

609. What is a biennial?   This is a plant that lives for two years and then dies. Fortunately very few garden flowers are biennials, for they are frankly troublesome to maintain.

The typical biennial will produce some leaves, often a basal rosette of them, the first year, but no flowers. The second year it will send up its only flowering stalk, produce its crop of bloom, seed and then die.

Sometimes they will sow their own seed, which may germinate the next spring, but this is too hazardous to be counted upon. The only remedy is to plant seeds every spring exactly as though they were annuals, following the directions in Question 607. Ideally sowing seeds every other year should be sufficient, but most gardeners prefer to plant biennials every spring. The finest of the biennials is the foxglove.

610. What is a perennial?   This is a plant that lives from year to year, by dying down to the ground each autumn, but whose roots live underground over the winter, and send up new shoots, leaves and flowers the following spring, also producing seed. Theoretically such a protective habit should ensure annual growth forever. Some perennials do persist for many years, but there are short-lived perennials which have to be replaced every fourth or fifth year.

Raising perennials from seed is a simple matter, but it takes at least two years in some cases, although a few perennials will bloom from seed in a single season. Much the simplest method is to purchase dormant plants in spring or fall and plant them where wanted. Most of our garden flowers are perennials.

611. What is a bulbous plant?   One that is propagated by the planting of bulbs, such as the tulip, hyacinth and many others. Many are spring-blooming, and for such the bulbs are planted the autumn before. But some are fall-flowering; the bulbs are planted usually in mid-summer.

The bulbs of still other bulbous plants cannot be left in the ground over the winter. Directions for planting each of these different bulbous plants will be found under the appropriate questions.

ANNUAL FLOWERS
(See Question 607)

612. What is the pheasant's-eye? A useful Eurasian annual (*Adonis annua*) much grown because its flowers are fine for cutting. It grows about eighteen inches high, has dissected leaves and showy, solitary flowers about three-fourths of an inch wide, its petals red, but the center of the flower a darker red.

613. What is the Joseph's coat? A showy, tropical annual (*Amaranthus tricolor*) sometimes called the fountain-plant. The leaves are sometimes blotched and colored; the small, chaffy flowers in stalkless, head-like clusters at the leaf joints, or in spire-like, interrupted clusters which are red and showy. It is rather a weedy plant one to four feet high. (For a related species see Question 662.)

614. What is the winged everlasting? A stunning Australian annual (*Ammobium alatum grandiflorum*), grown as an everlasting because when dried the flower cluster will hold its color for months. It is a bushy, spreading plant one to three feet high, its twigs prominently winged. The flower heads are about one and a half inches wide, with tiny, silvery-white leaves (bracts) beneath.

615. Is there a cultivated prickly poppy? Yes, a stout Mexican annual of that group (*Argemone grandiflora*) is grown for its showy, summer-blooming flowers. It is two to three feet high, with lobed, white-veined leaves and yellow or white flowers that are three inches wide. The whole plant is somewhat prickly. (For a wild relative see Question 267.)

616. What blue-flowered annual was named for a bishop? The beautiful South American annual (*Browallia speciosa major*) was named for Bishop John Browall, who was also a Swedish botanist and who wrote an important botanical book in 1739. The browallia, which has no common name, is a very popular garden annual, eight to twelve inches high, with somewhat oval leaves pointed at the tip. The flowers are bright blue, tubular but expanded at the tip, the centers yellowish, about one and a half inches wide.

617. What is the basket-flower and why was it so called? The basket-flower (*Centaurea americana*) from the central United States and Mexico, is a popular garden annual, four to six feet high, its oblongish leaves usually without marginal teeth. The flower heads are four to five inches wide, pink, and look as though set in a shallow basket. The basket-flower is easily grown and flowers most freely when the plants are a bit crowded.

618. What is the national flower of Germany? The cornflower (*Centaurea Cyanus*). Probably the most widely cultivated annual in the country, it has a variety of other names like bachelor's-button, bluebottle, ragged sailor and blue buttons. It is inclined to sprawl,

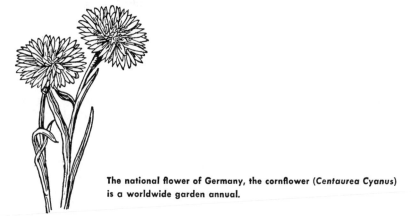

The national flower of Germany, the cornflower (*Centaurea Cyanus*) is a worldwide garden annual.

is one to two feet high, ultimately green, but woolly when young, its narrow leaves nearly five inches long. The flower heads are blue (but of other colors in some horticultural varieties) and about one and a half inches wide. If some flowers are left on the plant, it seeds freely and often maintains itself from self-sown seed. Its popularity for men's buttonholes is nearly world-wide, although the plant originated in southern Europe. (For a close relative see Question 507.)

619. What beautiful California annual has become a fine garden flower?   The usually purple or rose-colored *Clarkia elegans,* which has no common name, has several horticultural forms, like Salmon Queen (salmon) and Vesuvius (red). (For a description of *Clarkia,* see Question 389.)

620. What is the spiderflower?   A popular annual from tropical America (*Cleome spinosa*), four to five feet high, with strong-smelling foliage. Its leaves are compound, the five to seven leaflets oblong and long-stalked. The flowers, which have an irregular appearance, because of the long-clawed petals and the protruding stamens (see Question 3), are very showy, rose-purple or white and about three inches wide. The plant is vigorous and should be thinned out to allow two to three feet between each plant. (For a Rocky Mountain relative see Question 294.)

621. What western *Coreopsis* is best grown as an annual?   The perennial *Coreopsis atkinsoniana* is apt to be a short-lived perennial in cultivation, and is best grown as a hardy annual. It is two to three feet high, with twice- or thrice-compound leaves, the ultimate leaflets very narrow. The flower heads are long-stalked, yellow, the centers brownish-purple. The flower head is about one and a half inches wide and autumn-blooming. (For a related plant see Question 410.)

622. What is the most popular garden annual originating in Mexico?   Without much doubt it is the tall, slender and profusely flowering plants derived originally from *Cosmos bipinnatus,* which grows six to ten feet high and is inclined to have a weak stem, that is greenish. The leaves are cut into five thread-thin segments. The flower heads are one to two inches wide, the rays white, pink or red, the center of the head yellow. The plant is easily grown as a hardy annual and will bloom from summer to frost. Those who want to save time often treat it as a tender annual (see Question 608). It has no common name but cosmos.

623. What is the Chinese forget-me-not?   This is an Asiatic biennial (*Cynoglossum amabile*), closely related to the true forget-me-nots, but best grown as an annual, as it will flower from seed in a single growing season. It grows eighteen to twenty-four inches high and has rough, somewhat oblong or narrower leaves, two to three inches long. The flowers are small, blue, but in a relatively showy, arching, one-sided cluster that blooms from July to October. *Cynoglossum* is from the Greek for "hound" and "tongue," in allusion to the rough leaves.

624. Is the bluebottle another name for the cornflower? Yes; see Question 618.

625. What is the rocket larkspur? An annual relative of the perennial larkspurs of our gardens (see Question 558), the rocket larkspur (*Delphinium Ajacis*) is an annual from southern Europe and does not grow higher than twenty-four inches. It has an erect stem, its finely-divided leaves more or less bunched at the joints. The flowers are typically blue, but in its many horticultural forms, violet, pink, rose or white. Unlike the perennial larkspurs, the rocket larkspur is easy to grow even in warm or hot regions.

626. What is the China pink? A Eurasian biennial or perennial pink (*Dianthus chinensis*), that is apt to die out and hence is best treated as an annual. Often called the Indian pink, it is a green-foliaged plant, twelve to eighteen inches high, with erect and rather stiff stems. The flowers, one to two inches wide, are solitary or in meagre clusters; red, white or lilac and only faintly fragrant. It is one of the best of the annual pinks. (For related plants see Questions 497–499.)

627. Are there color forms of the California poppy? This widely grown garden flower (*Eschscholtzia californica*), mostly grown as an annual, has many horticultural forms with white, pink, rose or reddish flowers. The original wildflower is orange-yellow. (See Question 354 for a description of the plant and its culture.)

628. What is the ragged sailor? Another name for the cornflower. (see Question 618.)

629. What is the Mexican fire-plant? This is the annual relative, *Euphorbia heterophylla*, of the tropical poinsettia, grows wild from the Mississippi Valley to Peru and sometimes escapes from gardens elsewhere. It is one to three feet high, the leaves lobed or angled, gradually reduced in size towards the top of the plant, and then red or mottled with white. They are so showy that they are often mistaken for the flowers, which are small, yellowish and relatively inconspicuous. The plant often persists from self-sown seeds. (For related plants see Questions 219, 261 and 962.)

630. Is snow-on-the-mountain a garden annual? Yes, and a very popular and showy one native on our prairies. (For its description and culture see Question 261.)

631. Is there an annual gaillardia worth growing? Yes, and it is often called Indian blanket, or annual blanket-flower. *Gaillardia pulchella* grows naturally on our prairies, but has been much improved in cultivation. It grows twelve to twenty inches high, with oblongish leaves three to four inches long and softly hairy. The showy flower heads are two to three inches wide, the rays yellow but the head rose-purple at the center. In some forms the rays are all red, yellow or white. The plant is easily grown anywhere. (For the perennial gaillardia see Question 798.)

632. Is there an annual baby's-breath? *Gypsophila elegans grandiflora* is an annual widely grown for its small, beautifully scattered flowers. Originally from the Caucasus, it is an upright, forking plant ten to eighteen inches high, its leaves small, pointed and a little fleshy. The flowers are small, but so profuse that from a distance the plant looks as though flecked with snow. Normally the flowers are white, but in some forms they may be pink or rose-colored. It is of the easiest culture as an annual. (For the perennial baby's-breath see Question 740.)

633. Where did the sunflower come from? This huge annual (*Helianthus annuus*), is a native from Minnesota to the Pacific Coast, and is considered by many to be too coarse for culture. Its generic name is from the Greek for "sun" and "flower," and the second implies that it is an annual. A strong plant, eight to twelve feet high, it has ovalish, hairy leaves nearly a foot wide. The flower heads are usually solitary, yellow and about one foot across. The seeds are full of oil, and for this thousands of acres of sunflowers are grown in the Argentine and in Russia. The plant is too large for ordinary gardens. A dwarf variety with much smaller flower heads, which are more plentiful when cut, is known as cut-and-come-again.

634. What are "blue buttons"?   The flower heads of the cornflower. (See Question 618.)

635. Do the flowers of flower-of-an-hour last only that long?   Not quite, but the flowers of this central African annual are apt to be fleeting. Flower-of-an-hour (*Hibiscus Trionum*) is eighteen to twenty-four inches high, with three- to five-parted leaves, the middle lobe larger than the others. The flowers are pale-yellow or yellowish-white with a purplish center, about one and a half inches wide, very fleeting in the original form, but persisting most of the day in modern varieties. It should be sown where wanted, and is easy to grow.

636. What is the Mexican tulip-poppy?   A perennial (*Hunnemannia fumariaefolia*) from Mexico, but usually grown in the United States as an annual. Often called the golden cup, it is a woody-based plant with bluish-green and much-dissected foliage, the stem twelve to twenty inches high. The flowers are solitary, about three inches wide, yellow but its numerous stamens orange, and hence very showy; in bloom from July to October. The plant can be grown as an annual, but to speed up bloom is often grown as a tender annual. (See Question 608.)

637. What garden flower was named for Spain?   The old name for Spain was Iberia, and when some of the candytufts were found in that country, the plant name *Iberis* was coined. The annual candy-tuft (*Iberis umbellata*), sometimes called the globe candytuft, is an erect annual, eight to fifteen inches high, with narrow thin leaves two to three and a half inches long. The small but numerous flowers grow in tight clusters, the four petals lilac, pink, red or violet, according to which variety is grown. It is of very easy culture as an annual, and there are many horticultural varieties. (For the perennial sort, see Question 766.)

638. Where did the morning-glory come from?   This ever-popular annual vine (*Ipomoea purpurea*) originated in tropical America, most probably in Mexico. It will stand no frost but can climb ten to fifteen feet in a single season, producing many showy trumpet-shaped flowers. The leaves, ovalish or heart-shaped, are four to five inches long, and the flowers nearly three inches long. Originally bluish-purple, it is now found in white, pink and purple as well as in a very fine pale blue form known as Heavenly Blue. The seeds are very hard and, if untreated, are slow to germinate. It is better to nick the seeds with a file or, alternatively, to soak them in tepid water eight to twelve hours before planting. Plant them one-half of an inch deep, in full sunshine.

639. Is the sweet pea hard to grow?   Not if you live in the right climate and can give it the care it demands; otherwise it is difficult or impossible. The sweet pea (*Lathyrus odoratus*) is an annual from the mountains of Sicily and will not tolerate summer heat. It is a

The modern sweet pea (*Lathyrus odoratus*) has lost much of the fragrance of its wild ancestor from the mountains of Sicily.

weak-stemmed plant four to six feet high; brush or wire netting must be provided for support. The leaves are compound, their leaflets tipped with a soft prickle. The flowers are pea-like, very fragrant in the original form, but less so in most of the much finer modern varieties. The seeds are slow to germinate, and should be soaked in tepid water for twenty-four hours before planting. All that do not swell should be nicked with a file. Plant two inches deep in rich garden soil in

February or early March, as the plants will stop blooming when really hot weather arrives. Some growers even plant seeds in November in order to get them established as quickly as possible. (For related plants see Questions 211 and 349.)

640. What is the tree mallow? It is no tree but an extremely showy annual (*Lavatera trimestris splendens*) from the Mediterranean region, much grown for its red or rose-pink flowers that may be four inches wide. It grows two to three feet high, and has irregularly round-toothed leaves. The flower is solitary and summer-blooming. A fine and easily grown annual. (For a related plant see Question 405.)

641. Does the common flax have only blue flowers? Mostly, but occasionally there will be some white flowers. Flax (*Linum usitatissimum*) is a European annual of very simple culture, and grows three to four feet high. From its stems comes the fiber that goes into linen. The leaves are small and narrow. The flowers are about one-half inch wide, followed by a fruit containing a seed which is the source of linseed oil. The plant sometimes escapes from gardens to roadsides in the eastern states.

642. What is the flowering flax? A much finer garden plant than the common flax (see Question 641) and a North African annual (*Linum grandiflorum*), one to two feet high. The leaves are small and narrow. The flowers, about one and a half inches wide, are red, pink or scarlet, depending on the variety; they are borne in slender clusters and quite showy. The plant has a weak stem and needs staking if the site is windy.

643. Is there a showy annual lobelia? Yes, the edging lobelia (*Lobelia Erinus compacta*), an annual from South Africa, is one of the best edging plants for the garden. Scarcely five inches high, it is compact of habit and has narrow, small leaves. The flowers are typically blue, but among a dozen varieties there are several other colors. As an annual edging plant it has few superiors. It is easily grown as an annual, but those who want earlier flowers grow it as a tender annual (see Question 608). (For related plants see Questions 103 and 457.)

644. What is the sweet Alison?   Merely another name for the sweet alyssum. (For its description and culture see Question 510.)

645. What annual has better fruits than flowers?   Honesty (*Lunaria annua*) is never grown for its flowers, although they are fragrant and purple. The plant, a Eurasian biennial but grown mostly as an annual, is eighteen to thirty inches high, its leaves coarsely toothed. Its most attractive feature is the silvery, satiny pods, which are flat, thin and nearly one and a half inches wide. Because of their sheen, honesty is also called satin-pod, moonwort and satin-flower. The circular pods make fine, long-keeping winter decorations.

646. What is the Rose-of-Heaven?   A rather pretentiously named annual catchfly (*Lychnis Coeli-rosea*), a native of the Mediterranean region and a rather widely planted garden annual. It is twelve to eighteen inches high, and has very narrow leaves. The flowers are solitary, about one inch wide, and rose-pink in the original form, but some of its varieties are of different colors. It is well to thin the plants to five inches apart. (For related plants, see Questions 502 and 568.)

647. Is there an annual forget-me-not?   Yes. A Eurasian annual plant (*Myosotis sylvatica*) makes a fine carpet between other garden flowers, since it is nearly prostrate and never over eight inches high. The leaves are narrowly oblong, about three-fourths of an inch in length. The flowers are blue and have a yellow center, which is also true of white or pink horticultural forms. They bloom most freely when the plants are a bit crowded. (For a perennial relative see Question 712.)

648. What is the best blue-flowered annual from California?   Without much doubt it is the baby blue-eyes, for which see Question 388. (For other species of *Nemophila* see Questions 386 and 387.)

649. Is there a night-fragrant flower that is first cousin to tobacco?   Yes, it is the beautiful jasmine tobacco. (See Question 504.)

650. What is the other name for love-in-a-mist?   In Europe and often in the United States, many people also call it devil-in-the-bush —both names in allusion to the way the fine double flowers are nestled in a mass of thread-like foliage. It is a European annual (*Nigella damascena*), eight to ten inches high, its bluish-green leaves cut into thread-thin segments. The flowers are blue (rarely white), about one and a half inches wide, nearly stalkless among the foliage and summer-blooming.

651. What is the moonwort?   Another name for honesty. (See Question 645.)

652. Where did the Shirley poppy come from?   The Reverend W. Wilks of Shirley, England, originated this variety from the corn poppy (*Papaver Rhoeas*), which was immortalized in Flanders fields during World War I. Often called the field poppy or corn rose, it is a European annual with a wiry, branching stem one to three feet high. The leaves may be lobed or unlobed; the flowers about two inches wide and typically red, but some forms are purple or white. The Shirley poppy has white-edged petals and exists in most colors except yellow. It is a finer garden annual than the corn poppy. Both are easily grown, but neither likes transplanting and should be thinned to nine inches apart. (For related plants see Questions 354 and 484.)

653. Is there an annual phlox?   Yes. The annual phlox, originally from Texas, has gone all over the world because of its ease of culture and long blooming period, and the variety of color in its flowers. (For a description and culture, see Question 276.)

654. What showy annual flower is closely related to a pernicious weed?   The pussley is one of our most obnoxious weeds, but its near relative is the garden portulaca (*Portulaca grandiflora*), an annual from Brazil suited to dry, poor soil. It has various common names such as the rose moss, sun moss and wax pink—all of them inappropriate, for it is neither a pink nor a moss. It is a low prostrate annual with a much-branched and fleshy stem and foliage. The flowers are very profuse and showy, about one inch wide, of nearly all colors but yellow. A useful plant for edging or any other place, in full sun.

655. Is the satin-pod the same as the satin-flower?   Yes, both names apply to honesty (see Question 645).

656. What Egyptian annual was called little darling? When the mignonette (*Reseda odorata*) first reached Paris in the mid-eighteenth century, it was speedily called mignonette (little darling) because of its ravishing odor. It is an easily grown annual, eight to fifteen inches high and apt to sprawl. The leaves are clustered. The flowers are rather inconspicuous, typically greenish-yellow but red in some forms and of such fragrance that many pick the flowers for the house—only to learn that they quickly lose their fragrance when picked. Two varieties, Red Monarch and Red Goliath, keep their odor a little longer when picked.

657. Is there an annual coneflower? The Erfurt coneflower (*Rudbeckia bicolor superba*) is an annual developed from a coneflower of the southern United States, and unlike its relatives it is only one to two feet high. The leaves are lance-shaped, about two inches long. The flower heads are yellow, about two inches wide, the center of the head brown-purple. This is a good annual for dry places and relatively poor soil. (For related plants see Questions 256 and 359.)

658. Is there a dwarf nasturtium? Yes, and many prefer it to the tall climbing kind. It blooms faster and a little more profusely than its much taller relative. (See Question 550.)

659. What is the wax pink? A completely inappropriate name for the garden portulaca. (See Question 654.)

TENDER ANNUALS
(For the significance of the term and the culture of tender annuals, see Question 608.)

660. What is the garden ageratum? A low tender annual from tropical America, named *Ageratum houstonianum,* and one of the most widely used of all plants for edging or for carpet bedding. In its original form it was eight to fourteen inches high, but modern, compact forms are lower and ideal for edging. The leaves are sticky and the flower heads are a misty blue, about one-fourth of an inch thick, borne in small clusters. Some modern forms are pink or white, but the blue-flowered plants are unique for their stature and color.

661. Can the hollyhock be grown as a tender annual? Yes, and some growers prefer this method, as it ensures earlier bloom. (For description and culture see Question 557.)

662. What is love-lies-bleeding? A rather coarse, tender annual from the tropics, very variable and often called the tassel-flower (*Amaranthus caudatus*). It grows one to three feet high, with spreading branches, and has oval or oblong leaves pointed at both ends and

Love-lies-bleeding (*Amaranthus caudatus*) thrives best in poor, sandy soils, where its color is striking.

may be green or blood-red, especially near the flower cluster. The flowers are minute and chaffy, crowded in a dense, finger-thick, red, drooping spike, which *en masse* are very striking. Another form has similarly chaffy flowers in a tight head. The plant must be grown in poor, sandy sites, for if the soil is too rich the leaves, although larger, lose most of their showy color. (For a related plan see Question 613.)

663. Can the snapdragon be grown by the amateur? Yes, if conditions can be controlled. The snapdragon (*Antirrhinum*) is really a perennial in its own region along the Mediterranean, but is grown outdoors in the United States as a specially-demanding tender annual. It is twelve to twenty inches high and has somewhat sticky, narrow leaves two to three inches long. The flowers are pouch-like and irregular, crowded in a dense, showy terminal cluster; they are of all colors but blue and do not last well in the house. Sow seeds very shallowly, six to eight weeks before the plants can go outdoors; but the room where grown should not be over 55° F. At the latitude of New York move the seedlings to a cold frame about April 15, and try to get them in permanent sites around May 8–15. They do not like intense heat and should bloom before it arrives. An easier method, of course, is to buy properly grown seedlings from a professional.

664. What is the African daisy? There are four quite different plants so called, all tender annuals and all from South Africa. Perhaps the best known is *Arctotis stoechadifolia,* which is thirty to forty-eight inches high and taller than the other three. It has ovalish, white-woolly leaves and a long-stalked, showy, solitary flower head which is nearly three inches wide and nearly every color. The center of the head is usually darker than the rays. (Other African daisies are described in Questions 665, 666, and 667.)

665. What is a Gazania? A beautiful, South African tender annual (*Gazania longiscapa*) also called the African daisy, but only eight to twelve inches high and with slender, narrow leaves quite unlike those of *Arctotis.* The flower heads are solitary, short-stalked, two to three inches wide and close at night. They are prevailingly yellow, but some modern forms are white, reddish-brown or orange-red. It is grown less than some of the other African daisies, but is an extremely handsome, summer-blooming plant.

666. What is the Transvaal daisy? Still another tender annual (*Gerbera jamesoni*) is called the African daisy and is by far the best of all the plants so named. It is the most difficult to grow without a greenhouse. It is also called the Barberton daisy, and grows twelve to twenty-four inches high, its leaves nearly eight inches long, deeply cut and white-woolly beneath. The flower heads are three and a half to four and a half inches wide; their pointed rays more spreading than in the other African daisies, and usually orange, but in some forms scarlet, yellow, white, pink or salmon. Seeds sown in January or February should produce seedlings ready to pot by March 15. These need a cool greenhouse to harden before outdoor planting is safe; *i.e.,* not before settled warm weather. Buying properly grown seedlings avoids the preliminaries. The plants will stand no frost and can be wintered over in a cool greenhouse, if lifted and re-potted.

667. Is the Cape marigold also called the African daisy?   Yes, and it is the one perhaps least entitled to the name. The Cape marigold (*Dimorphotheca aurantiaca*) is a South African perennial, but since it blooms from seed in a single season, it is best grown as a tender annual. It is twelve to eighteen inches high and its mostly basal, narrowly oblong leaves are somewhat rough. The flower heads, closing at night, are three to four inches wide and usually yellow, but other colors are to be found in seedsmen's catalogs. Its rays are blunt, and the plant thrives in hot, dryish places.

668. What is the Swan River daisy?   An Australian tender annual (*Brachycome iberidifolia*), growing six to fifteen inches high and a useful plant for edging a path. The leaves are small and much divided, the final segments very narrow. The flower heads are about one inch wide, of all colors but yellow; the center of the head is lighter in color than the rays, which are rather blunt. If treated as an annual, it will thrive but the bloom will be delayed.

669. Is the pot marigold the same as the African marigold?   No; the African marigold has highly scented foliage, while the pot marigold is practically scentless. (For description and culture of the pot marigold see Question 553.)

670. In Question 192 there was brief mention of the China or annual aster. Is this a true aster?   No, it is a tender annual (*Callistephus*) from China and Japan and to most gardeners it is *the* aster; it has nothing to do with the group properly named *Aster,* which includes fine perennials, the Michaelmas daisies among them. The China aster or, as it is often called, the garden aster, is a branching plant nine to twenty-four inches high with hairy, oval-shaped leaves that are deeply toothed. The flower heads are solitary borne at the end of a long stalk, and are of all colors but yellow. The plant is easily grown, and now comes in many varieties so that bloom may stretch from July to frost. Some of the scores of varieties have quilled or incurved rays and are very handsome.

671. Is the canna a tender annual?   No; but it is grown as an annual and is so tender that it is killed by frost. Perhaps our finest summer bedding plant, it originated somewhere in the tropics, but has been so much hybridized that the real origin and parentage of modern cannas is conjectural. They have fleshy stems and very large, often colored leaves. The stems are three to five feet high, crowned by a gorgeous cluster of red, orange, crimson, yellow or pink, very irregular flowers in large trusses. Cannas are best grown by purchasing young potted plants, which should be set in rich garden soil, at least three feet apart each way. The roots cannot be left in the ground except in the mildest climates. Store them in a frost-free, gas-free, cool cellar until spring planting, which cannot come until the weather is really warm.

672. What is the cockscomb?   A fantastically grotesque tender annual (*Celosia argentea cristata*) from the tropics, widely grown for its brilliant summer color which will last for weeks after being cut. It grows twelve to twenty-four inches high, and its brightly colored, chaffy, minute flowers are tightly packed in crested or rolled clusters, others like a cock's comb, some fan-shaped, others spire-like and still others in an open feathery cluster. All are gorgeously colored—red, scarlet, pink, white, etc. They are easily grown in any garden soil, but should not be planted until warm weather arrives.

673. Is the wallflower difficult to grow in the East?   Yes; the wallflower (*Cheiranthus Cheiri*) does far better in England and in the Pacific Northwest than it ever does in the East. It is actually a European perennial, but can be grown here, either as a biennial (see Question 609) or as a tender annual. The plant is ten to fifteen inches high and has a profusion of orange-brown or yellow flowers in May or June. The plants must be started in the house early in March and put outdoors as soon as frost is no longer a hazard. It will not stand bitter cold or summer heat, and it resents slushy winters. Everyone who has seen millions of wallflowers in English cottage gardens wants to grow it, but it is really not suited to the eastern climate.

674. What is the golden wave?   A Texas annual (*Coreopsis drummondi*) which can also be grown as a tender annual if early bloom is desired. It is twelve to fourteen inches high, with leaves much divided into narrow segments. The flower heads are long-stalked, about two inches wide, the yellow rays notched at the tip, but darker colored toward the center of the head.

The wallflower (*Cheiranthus Cheiri*), a favorite in English gardens, is not happy in the East, but thrives in the Pacific Northwest.

675. Does the golden coreopsis have a flower head with a dark center? Yes, noticeably so; the flower rays of the golden coreopsis (*Coreopsis tinctoria*) are pure yellow but the center is red. The plant is native in the central United States, grows twenty to thirty-six inches high and stays in bloom from early July to October. It can be grown as either an annual or a tender annual.

676. Where did the dahlia come from? Along country roads in the uplands of Guatemala and Mexico, one can still see growing wild the ancestor of our modern dahlia. It is a tuberous-rooted plant two to five feet high, with somewhat divided leaves and a simple flower head about two inches wide, resembling a somewhat large colored daisy. Since its discovery early in the eighteenth century, the dahlia has been vastly improved, so that today there are at least fourteen different classes of these most popular summer-blooming plants. Of these perhaps five are the most preferred:

1. Single: open-centered flower heads, usually two to three inches wide, with a single set of rays.
2. Peony: open-centered flower heads with not more than four

rows of rays, as well as twisted, smaller rays at the center;
usually two to three inches wide.

3. Cactus: double-flowered, the center of the head hidden, the rays
partly or wholly recurved, often bent downward; mostly three to
four inches wide.

4. Decorative: a collective term for the fully double, large-headed
dahlia, its rays so numerous and some of them incurved so
that the head is tight and ball-like, and usually four to five
inches in diameter or even wider.

5. Pompon: a lower plant with double flower heads not over two
inches in diameter.

There are literally hundreds of varieties in each of these classes,
and many more in classes too specialized to be included here. All of
them must be grown the same way. Plant tuberous roots three to five
inches deep in a rich garden soil, but do not let any manure touch
the roots. The tall varieties need staking if the site is windy. In the
fall, just before the first frost, dig up the roots and store them in a
cool, frost-free cellar. In the spring divide the tuberous roots and
plant only one of the divisions in each hole, spacing the plants two to
three feet apart. *Dahlia* was named for Andreas Dahl, a Swedish
pupil of Linnaeus.

677. Are there several varieties of farewell-to-spring?   This beautiful wildflower from the Pacific Coast has at least four horticultural
forms that are better as garden plants than the typical species. They
are double-flowered; pink, lilac-crimson, rose-purple and of several
variations of these colors. (For a description of the plant and its culture see Question 393.)

678. What is the globe amaranth?   A chaffy-flowered tender annual (*Gomphrena globosa*) from the tropics of the Old World, grown
for its brightly-colored, almost clover-like small heads of minute,
chaffy flowers. It grows twelve to twenty inches high and has opposite, oblongish leaves, two to four inches long. The flower heads are
about three-fourths of an inch thick and red, or sometimes white, pink
or orange, very persistent, holding their color so long after picking that
the globe amaranth is a valuable everlasting.

679. Where did the strawflower come from?   The ever-popular strawflower (*Halichrysum bracteatum*) is an Australian tender annual, and one of the most valuable everlastings as its flower heads are attractive while fresh and, when dried, hold their color for months. It is a slender plant, twelve to thirty inches high, with very narrow, alternate leaves. The flower heads are terminal, solitary and chaffy, of nearly all colors but blue; the head is one to two inches wide.

680. Is the garden balsam related to our common jewelweed?
Yes, but they don't look very much alike, except for the structure of the flowers. Jewelweed is a glistening native plant of moist places (see Question 115), but the garden balsam (*Impatiens balsamina*) is a

Related to our native jewelweed is the tropical garden balsam (*Impatiens balsamina*) which will stand no frost.

tender annual from tropical Asia, twenty-four to thirty inches high with rather stiff, brittle stems. The leaves are lance-shaped and smooth, alternate, and one to two inches long. The flowers are very variable; always irregular and spurred. They are about one and a half inches long, of nearly all colors except blue, but prevailingly red, borne in a leafy terminal cluster in midsummer. This is a fine garden plant but it will not stand frost. The flowers are often called lady's-slippers.

681. What is summer cypress?   A tender annual of Eurasian origin (*Kochia scoparia trichophila*) that should perhaps be excluded from a book about flowers, for all its beauty resides in its leaves. Often called the standing cypress or Belvedere cypress, it is a stiffish plant, very bushy, and grows twenty to thirty-six inches high. The leaves are very numerous, round in cross-section, thin, and green, red or yellow, but turning purple-red in autumn. The leaves are so numerous and the plant is so striking that it is also called the burning bush. The flowers are inconspicuous and negligible. To preserve the color of the leaves, as for winter decorations, cut the colored leaves in August and dry them quickly.

682. Is the yellow sage a tender annual?   Technically, it is not, but it is grown as an annual and is extremely tender. Actually the red sage, as it is also called, is a tropical American shrub (*Lantana Camara*), widely used as a summer bedding plant. It is eighteen to thirty inches high, with opposite leaves, oval, rough and three to six inches long. The flowers are small, in a flat-topped cluster that may be yellow, red, or orange, or quite often two or more colors in the same cluster. They are summer-blooming, but lasting to frost. Without a greenhouse to start them, *Lantana* plants can be purchased from dealers, ready to plant when warm weather arrives. They will not stand frost.

683. Can the ten-weeks stock be grown outdoors?   This tender annual from southern Europe is grown by the millions by the florists, and it can be grown in the garden by giving it the care it demands. In its own country it may be a biennial or perennial, but as grown for the garden it must be started from seed, planted indoors eight to ten weeks before outdoor planting is safe (see Question 608). Known botanically as *Mathiola incana annua,* the ten-weeks stock is one to two feet high, or less than this in the dwarf varieties. The leaves are alternate, oblong-shaped, two and a half to four inches long. The flowers are faintly fragrant, of practically all colors, crowded in an extremely showy, terminal spire-like or thicker terminal cluster. The plant does not like summer heat, and should go outdoors as soon as frosts are no longer a hazard. (For the beautiful night-scented stock see Question 505.)

684. What is Nemesia?   A genus of very beautiful tropical African tender annuals, grown much more in England than here, although they present no cultural difficulties for American flower lovers. The one most likely to be grown here is *Nemesia strumosa suttoni,* which has no common name. It is a slender plant eight to twenty inches high, with alternate narrow leaves two to three inches long. The flowers are pouch-like and irregular, with two lips and a small spur and crowded in terminal clusters of almost all colors, and in some varieties the flower is spotted. In spite of their African origin they do not thrive in summer heat.

685. Is the balcony petunia different from the one commonly grown in flower beds? Yes. The garden petunia, a tender annual from the Argentine, has been much hybridized, and as to habit is of two types; a weak-stemmed sort apt to sprawl, used for window boxes and called the balcony petunia, and an erect form used for bedding. Both are extremely shy of frost and do better along the seashore than elsewhere. The ordinary garden petunia is seven to fifteen inches high, its leaves sticky and a little flabby. The flowers are funnel-shaped; now, however, some varieties are double-flowered, fringed, ruffled or crisped and extremely handsome. They may be of any color but yellow. Some of the modern varieties are tetraploids. (See Question 446.) Petunias do better in good garden soil, in full sun, and they need a long growing season.

686. What is Belvedere cypress? Another name for the summer cypress. (See Question 681.)

687. What is the painted-tongue? A quite stunning, Chilean tender annual (*Salpiglossis sinuata*) with petunia-like flowers. Sometimes called the poor-man's-orchid, because of its showy flowers, it is eighteen to thirty inches high, and its leaves are lance-shaped, blunt-toothed, alternate and about one and a half to two inches long. The flowers are trumpet-shaped, about two inches long and nearly as broad, always with golden markings on the throat of the flower which may be of any color but blue. From plants set out as soon as warm weather arrives, bloom may be expected by July, and continue until September.

688. What is the most popular salvia in this country? Unquestionably it is the scarlet sage (*Salvia splendens*), which is a Brazilian shrub always grown here as a tender annual, as it blooms brilliantly from seed in a single growing season. It is so widely grown that it is anathema to many, and one expert has called it "the first resort of the inexperienced gardener." Such maligning will never stop its popularity. It grows fifteen to thirty inches high, and its leaves are oval-shaped, toothed, opposite and two and a half to three and a half inches long. The flowers are a dazzling scarlet, prominently two-lipped, about one inch long, and profusely borne in a fiery, terminal cluster. No other bedding plant can set a garden aflame as will the scarlet sage used freely. (For related plants see Questions 319 and 545.)

689. Do some flower lovers call the sweet scabious the pincushion? Yes; and it is not an inappropriate name for the globe-shaped flower heads of the sweet scabious. (See Question 513.)

690. Is the burning bush the same as summer cypress?   Yes. (See Question 681.)

691. What is the butterfly-flower?   A very fine tender annual, derived by hybridization from Chilean plants and often called the fringe-flower. Still another name is the poor-man's-orchid because of its showy flowers, which keep well after cutting. Named *Schizanthus wisetonensis,* the plant is two to four feet high, loosely branched and brittle, its leaves cut into fine segments. The flowers are highly irregular, two-lipped and about one and a half inches wide, in loose, lax ter-

Aptly called poor-man's-orchid, the beautiful flowers of *Schizanthus wisetonensis* are usually called butterfly-flowers.

minal clusters. The color range includes white, pink, blue and brownish and the upper lip of the flower is yellow-streaked. The plants are so brittle that they must be handled carefully.

692. Are there two kinds of marigolds? Yes, and the term is a little confusing, for both are tender annuals—one native to Europe, the other to Mexico. The European species has been known for centuries and is usually called the pot marigold. Its foliage is scentless. (See Question 553.) The African marigold (*Tagetes erecta*), a tender annual from Mexico, often called the Aztec marigold and the big marigold, was long but erroneously thought to be African, hence its misleading but universal name. It is eight to twenty-four inches high, and its bushy foliage is made up of finely divided leaves which have a strong odor when crushed. The flower heads are two to four inches wide and solitary; the flower stalk is swollen immediately below the head, which is prevailingly yellow or orange. However, there are many modern varieties, some double-flowered, others colored red or cerise, and some with quilled rays. The plant is not difficult to grow as a tender annual, or as an annual; in the latter case bloom will be delayed. There are tetraploid marigolds. (See Question 446.)

693. What flower is sold by your florist as *Didiscus*? The beautiful Australian tender annual, better called the blue-lace flower (*Trachymene caerulea*), is sometimes incorrectly known as *Didiscus*. It is a rather weak-stemmed plant, eighteen to thirty inches high, its compound leaves having the ultimate leaflets cut into narrow segments. The flowers are very small and pale blue, crowded in a flat-topped cluster two to three inches wide and strongly suggesting a blue version of Queen Anne's lace. The blue-lace flower blooms more freely if the plants are a bit crowded. It is not difficult to grow as a tender annual.

694. Is the garden verbena a native plant? No; it was originated by crossing two unknown South American species of *Verbena*. The result is the garden verbena (*Verbena hortensis*), which has gone all over the temperate world. It is really a perennial in mild climates, but is usually grown as a tender annual, eight to twelve inches high, but often in dwarf forms, five to eight inches. It is a somewhat weak-stemmed plant, apt to sprawl, and its opposite leaves are lance-shaped and two to four inches long. The flowers are fragrant, small, and pink, red, yellow or white, with the central "eye" always of some contrasting color. The plant should be grown as a tender annual and not put outdoors until settled warm weather has arrived.

695. What is the Madagascar periwinkle?   A very different plant from, although closely related to, the common periwinkle, is the tender annual known as the Madagascar periwinkle (*Vinca rosea*) which came from that island. It is a rather stiff, erect plant, ten to twenty inches high, with prominently veined, lance-shaped, opposite leaves. The flowers are slightly twisted, about one and a half inches wide and pink or white, usually with a dark central "eye"; they are borne at the leaf joints and bloom most of the summer if the plant is treated as a tender annual.

696. Is the pansy related to the violets?   Yes, although in the evolution of *Viola tricolor hortensis* the typically spurred flower of the violet has been replaced by the overlapping petals and relatively flat flower of the modern pansy. Shakespeare called the Johnny-jump-up a pansy, but it is very doubtful whether he ever saw any flower like our modern pansy. This is treated as a tender annual, but for most amateurs it is far easier to buy properly grown young plants from a dealer, who has wintered them in a cold frame or hotbed. The pansy does not tolerate summer heat or severe winter cold, but few bedding plants are so satisfactory from mid-April to mid-June. Pansies are now to be had in almost all colors, even a velvety black. The plants are practically stemless and the flowers are almost scentless.

697. Where did the zinnia come from and when?   The tall, showy zinnias of our gardens are derived from a Mexican tender annual (probably *Zinnia elegans*), but were never of much garden importance until 1886, although the dwarf forms were developed a little earlier. Zinnias are bristly-stemmed plants with opposite, somewhat oval leaves that are almost stem-clasping. The flower heads are dense and solitary, up to four and a half inches wide, very showy and of a wide range of colors, including purple, reddish-lilac, pink, red, yellow and many other shades, but not blue.

These flowers are so popular that there are at least five different groups of them, each having many varieties. They are:

1. Giants: flower heads four to five inches wide.
2. Dahlia-flowered: double-flowered heads nearly five inches wide.
3. Cactus-flowered: double-flowered, some of the rays quilled; up to five inches wide.
4. Lilliput, including dwarfs, miniature, pompon and baby zinnias: lower plants with smaller heads.
5. Cut-and-come-again: heads about two and a half inches across, profusely flowering if cut often.

698. What is the big marigold?   The African marigold. (See Question 692.)

BIENNIALS
(For definition of the term and directions for culture, see Question 609.)

699. What is the most important biennial garden flower?   Without any doubt it is the foxglove. (For its description and culture, see Question 474.)

700. What are Canterbury bells?   The blue flowers of a European biennial (*Campanula Medium*) which are of two varieties. In one variety there is apparently a flower within a flower, both bell-shaped and usually called hose-in-hose. The other has a bell-shaped inner flower, apparently set in a saucer, called cup-and-saucer type. Both are prevailingly blue, but white, pink and purple varieties are offered. The plant is one to two feet high and blooms in May or June. (For related plants, see Questions 721 and 741.)

701. What showy prairie biennial has become a fine garden flower?
The prairie lily. (See Question 265.)

702. Is the night-fragrant dame's rocket really a perennial?   Yes, but it is apt to die out rather quickly and is therefore best grown as a biennial. (See Question 503.)

PERENNIALS
(For definition of the term and how to start with perennial flowers, see Question 610.)

By far the larger number of garden flowers are perennials. They are grown not only for their beauty but because they are the only things beside trees and shrubs that suggest the idea of permanence in the garden. Once established they relieve us of the annual chore of seed-sewing for annuals and tender annuals, and the summer or fall planting of bulbs. In other words, few things are so satisfactory as a garden of perennials. They give us variety of color, a succession of bloom and relative permanence.

The number of perennials is so much greater than that for any other category that, for the garden-minded, it seems best to sort them into groups. This cannot be done by the color of the flowers, for many species come in various colors. Neither can they be safely sorted into different categories of stature, for many species have dwarf varieties.

Biologically and from the garden standpoint, the best arrangement is by the succession of bloom, from winter to early spring and late spring, and so on to the waning fall and the next winter. It should be understood that only perennials are here considered, and that many early-blooming bulbs will be found in another part of the book, devoted to bulbous plants.

It should also be understood that the dates given below are approximate only, and apply to the latitude of New York City and to about the 40th parallel westward. High mountains and proximity to the sea will change the dates, and it should also be understood that when a flower is in a category like "June" it may begin flowering then and go on blooming until frost. In other words, the dates indicate the approximate time when the flower first blooms and are not a precise floral timetable.

The seasonal categories are:

Winter to March

703. What hellebore has flowers that peep out through the snow?
The Christmas rose. (See Question 481.)

704. What is the Lenten rose?   A relative of the Christmas rose,
blooming any time in February or March. Named *Helleborus orientalis,* it is not well known here but is much prized in Europe. It has
very large, mostly basal leaves that are evergreen, the five to eleven
segments with coarse marginal teeth. The flowers are in clusters of two
to six; the individual flower basin-shaped, two to two and a half inches
wide and cream white at first, ultimately brownish-green. The juice
of the root of this perennial, originally from Asia Minor and Greece,
is dangerously poisonous.

705. What is the "New Year's gift"?   A Eurasian perennial whose
yellow flowers may peep out between snow patches any time in
December or January. It is also called the winter aconite (*Eranthis
hyemalis*), and some call it wolfsbane. Its leaves are finely divided, but

Peeping through the snow during Christmas week are the yellow
flowers of New Year's gift (*Eranthis hyemalis*).

will not be found until it begins growth in October, as in the summer
it is resting and nothing will show above ground. The flowers are
solitary, not showy, and are about one and a half inches wide. To start
it, plant purchased tubers about three inches deep in late August,
preferably in partial shade. The plant may persist for years.

706. What is the Siberian tea?   A very stout, fleshy-leaved Asiatic
perennial (*Bergenia crassifolia*), often grown for its flowers, which
bloom in March or early April. It is twelve to eighteen inches high,

and its thick fleshy leaves are pitted, somewhat colored and not quite round, the blade merging into the leaf stalk and measuring six to eight inches wide. The flowers are rose-pink or lilac, in a dense, branched, showy cluster, on a thick and fleshy stalk.

April Flowers

707. What is the May-blob, and is it the same as "gools"? Both of these common names are applied to the marsh marigold (*Caltha palustris*), which is common and brilliantly yellow in April or early May. (See Question 90.)

708. What is the purple rock cress? A tiny perennial from Italy and Greece (*Aubrieta deltoidea*), quite useful in the rock garden or in the open border, but it can often be smothered there for it is only three to six inches high. It is a fine edging plant as it forms dense mats. The leaves are scarcely one inch wide, hairy and with one or two marginal teeth. The flower is about one-half of an inch wide, its four petals purple and narrowed to a stalk-like base. The flowers are borne in a small terminal cluster.

709. Is the trailing arbutus difficult to grow in the garden? It is impossible to grow this most fragrant of April-blooming wild flowers without following the directions for it at Question 137.

710. What is the earliest native iris to flower? The crested iris (*Iris cristata*), which is found wild from Maryland to Oklahoma and Georgia, grows in dense patches because of its creeping underground rootstocks. It is scarcely five inches high, is practically stemless, and its pale blue flowers are crested. It is a fine garden plant, especially for edging a border, and is often called the dwarf iris.

711. What is the leopard's-bane? A rather showy European perennial (*Doronicum plantagineum*), often planted for its early, yellow flowers. It is a branching plant, eighteen to thirty inches high, with mostly basal leaves their stalks winged and stem-clasping at the base. The flower heads are about three inches wide, long-stalked and solitary, the yellow rays very numerous. This is a fine plant to grow among spring bulbs, and its foliage dies down during its summer resting period.

712. Is there an early flowering forget-me-not? Yes, the almost prostrate Eurasian perennial (*Myosotis scorpioides*) blooms in April or early May, and is a fine plant as a ground cover among taller plants. It hugs the ground, and has small, narrow alternate leaves. The flowers are small, blue or pale blue in terminal more or less one-sided clusters. (For an annual forget-me-not, see Question 647.)

713. Why was the Bethlehem sage called Pulmonaria? It was once thought this European perennial was good for pulmonary troubles, but the Bethlehem sage (*Pulmonaria saccharata*), which neither came from Bethlehem nor is a sage, is now useful only as a spring-flowering plant that blooms in April or early May. It has mottled, mostly lance-shaped and usually basal leaves, grows twelve to eighteen inches high, and has coiled, one-sided clusters of flowers, the cluster straightening out as the flowers bloom. The flowers are small and white or reddish-purple.

Flowers of May

714. Is the German iris the same as the tall bearded iris? Yes, and the change from "German" to "tall bearded" came after World War I, when all things German were anathema to some. The tall bearded irises are an extraordinarily complex group, the result of many years' hybridization and now comprising thousands of named forms with a kaleidoscopic color range. All are assumed to be derived from *Iris germanica* which is itself a hybrid.

Modern tall bearded irises comprise plants ten to thirty inches high with thick, shallowly buried rootstocks and sword-shaped leaves. The flowers are gorgeous, often three to five inches wide, comprising three nearly erect petals (the standards), which are beautifully bearded, and three petals that are bent downwards (the falls).

Among the nineteen or twenty color classes of tall bearded iris, by far the greatest number are blue-flowered varieties. Next come varieties that range in color from pink, red and orchid-pink to purple. Then there is a large group that are in the yellow-orange class, and finally the whites and a few other smaller groups. The varieties are so legion that the iris-lover would do well to visit an iris nursery at flowering time to make a selection, or failing that to get a catalog with good colored illustrations from a reliable dealer.

715. What is the gold-dust?   One of the most useful of all plants for pavement planting or to fill in cracks on steps or a wall. Often called madwort or basket-of-gold, *Alyssum saxatile compactum* is a

One of the best plants for pavement planting is the yellow-flowered gold-dust (*Alyssum saxatile compactum*).

low European perennial, six to eight inches high, its dense, compact foliage gray-dusty. Its profusion of yellow flowers bloom in compact clusters in May, and sometimes last into June. It prefers sandy loam in the garden, but tolerates the heat of a pavement very well and has few peers for pavement planting.

716. Can the prairie pointer be grown in the garden?   Yes, but only in partial shade in a moist site, preferably in the wild garden. (For a description see Question 268.)

717. Is there a red-flowered yarrow?   The common yarrow or milfoil is a weedy perennial with white flowers that few would pick or plant. But a red-flowered variety (*Achillea Millefolium roseum*) is a garden form well worth growing for May bloom. It is a perennial found in the north temperate zone, grows about eighteen inches high and has much-dissected, strong-smelling foliage. The flower heads are small, pink or red in flat-topped clusters about three inches wide. The plant was named for Achilles, who is supposed to have used it to heal his wounds, although today there is no scientific evidence of its value. (For a related plant, see Question 750.)

718. Is there a form of the bugleweed worth growing? Yes, in spite of the fact that the bugle or bugleweed (*Ajuga reptans*) is a European weed that most gardeners like to destroy. But a horticultural variety of the bugleweed with metallic, crisp leaves and blue flowers is a useful, summer ground cover. The plant roots at the joints, and its opposite leaves are coppery. The flowers are borne in interrupted clusters and bloom in May. The plant is leafless all winter.

719. What bleeding-heart has the most showy flowers? There is a wild bleeding-heart (see Question 161) native in America, but it does not compare with the perennial from Japan, which is the best one for bloom and easy culture. It was christened *Dicentra spectabilis,* and it is a spectacular garden plant in May. It grows twelve to twenty-four inches high and its handsome rose-colored or red spurred flowers are borne in an unbranched one-sided cluster that may be four to five inches long. Its culture is easy in partial shade. (For related plants, see Questions 162, 406 and 407.)

720. What is *Astilbe davidi*? In the middle of the last century Abbé David, a French priest, travelled extensively in China, and for him was named a stunning, spirea-like Chinese perennial, *Astilbe davidi,* now much grown in gardens. It was no common name, and is a bushy plant four to six feet high, with compound leaves, its elm-like leaflets coarsely toothed. The flowers are small, pink, crowded in a long, showy spirea-like cluster, starting to bloom in mid-May and often continuing into August.

721. Is there a bellflower with leaves like the peach? Yes, the Eurasian perennial known as peachbells (*Campanula persicifolia*) is a bellflower, although it does not have the bell-like flowers of the usual campanulas. It grows two to three feet high, and its peach-like leaves are finely toothed, alternate, and six to eight inches long. The flowers are more like a deep saucer than a bell, blue (rarely white), about one and a half inches wide and borne in a showy, terminal cluster. The plant prefers a gritty soil, or even a sandy one.

722. Does the basket-of-gold bloom in May?   Yes, and its best known name is gold-dust. (See Question 715.)

723. What is Brunnera macrophylla? An Asiatic perennial without a common name, but worth one as it has a showy terminal cluster of blue flowers, that is very handsome. It grows twelve to eighteen inches high; the stem hairy. Basal leaves are heart-shaped, the upper ones narrower and tapering. The flowers are irregular, not much more than one-quarter of an inch long, but densely crowded in the cluster. The plant was named for Samuel Brunner, a Swiss botanist, but by some mischance it is often incorrectly known as *Anchusa myosotidiflora*.

724. What wall cress was named for Arabia?   A white-foliaged perennial from the Caucasus is known as the wall cress (*Arabis albida*) as it is a fine white-flowered plant for planting in crevices in a wall. Because some of its relatives came from Arabia, Linnaeus called all of the group *Arabis,* although very few of the one hundred species actually come from Arabia. It is generally less than twelve inches high, and its coarsely toothed leaves, which are widest at the tip are one and a half to three inches long. The flowers are white, fragrant, and are borne in loose clusters. It prefers sandy or gritty soil and does well in pockets in a masonry wall.

725. What is the wall pepper?   A delightful little prostrate, Eurasian perennial, also called mossy stonecrop (*Sedum acre*), but frequently called golden moss or love-entangle; some call it gold-dust. It is so

As a ground-cover the mossy stonecrop (*Sedum acre*) carpets gardens with ground-hugging foliage and yellow star-like flowers.

commonly cultivated in gardens that it often escapes in the eastern states. The plant is prostrate, composed of slender stems covered with a multitude of tiny fleshy leaves scarcely one-eighth of an inch long. The flowers are yellow, star-like, and in terminal clusters. It makes a fine ground cover in summer, but loses its leaves in winter.

726. What blue flower is called Jacob's-ladder? A European perennial also called Greek valerian (*Polemonium caeruleum*) which is also, but rarely, called charity. It is a fine garden plant, two to three feet high, its compound leaves with many leaflets arranged a little like a ladder. The flowers are blue, nodding, and about one inch long, arranged in a large, branching cluster. A handsome May-flowering garden plant, which does well in moist, partly shady places. (For related plants see Question 302.)

727. Are the maiden pink and the meadow pink the same? Yes; both names apply to a Eurasian, mat-forming perennial, also known as spink (*Diathus deltoides*), its very small leaves carpeting the ground. From this prostrate mass of foliage springs a forked flower stalk, four to nine inches high, crowned with pink but red-centered flowers, about one-fourth of an inch wide; it is May-blooming. Once established, it carpets the ground, dotted with its profusion of dainty flowers.

728. Can the beautiful wax-like flowers of Shortia be produced in a garden? Only if you have a shady wind-free wild garden, with good woodsy soil. (See Question 131.)

729. What flower was named for the old German word for "round"? That German word was *trol,* and because it meant "round" Linnaeus used it to name the European globeflower, *Trollius europaeus.* It is the best of the globeflowers, growing eighteen to twenty-four inches high, having handsome leaves cut into five lobes, and an almost perfectly globe-shaped yellow flower at the ends of the branches, the individual flower being about two inches in diameter.

730. Is there a finer cranesbill than our native one? Yes; much finer. The Asiatic perennial, also called a cranesbill (*Geranium grandiflorum*), is eight to fifteen inches high, has handsome five-parted leaves and produces a profusion of blue flowers in May that are streaked with purple veins, the center of the flower being yellowish. It is much easier to grow than our native species, for which see Question 141.

731. What is golden moss?   Another name for the wall pepper. (See Question 725.)

732. Is charity just another name for the Greek valerian?   Both these common names apply to Jacob's-ladder. (See Question 726.)

733. Is there a flower called the spink?   Yes; but most people call it the maiden pink. (See Question 727.)

734. Is the polyanthus a primrose?   It is a hybrid plant derived by crossing the English primrose, the oxlip and the cowslip. The polyanthus (*Primula polyantha*) is much easier to grow than any of its forbears, and is an essentially stemless perennial with a basal rosette of leaves having winged leafstalks. In the center of the leaf cluster the almost stalkless flowers also appear in a dense cluster, the colors ranging from maroon through pink, orange, yellow, blue and white. Once the May flowering period is over, some plants tend to die out and must be renewed, but generally the plant will grow in moist (but not wet) soil. It prefers the filtered sunlight beneath not too shady trees. (For related plants see Question 573.)

735. What is the globe daisy?   A blue-flowered perennial from Asia Minor, which, in spite of its name, is not a true daisy. The globe daisy (*Globularia trichosantha*), is a low, somewhat woody plant, with mostly basal, fine-toothed leaves about one inch long. The flower heads are pale blue, nearly globular, about one-half of an inch thick, on a stalk six to eight inches high. It prefers partial shade.

736. What perennial is called the barrenwort?   A nearly perfect groundcover from Persia and the Caucasus, with half-evergreen foliage is known as barrenwort (*Epimedium pinnatum colchicum*), and if left alone makes a good ground cover in a few years. Its leaves are compound, the ultimate leaflets finely toothed. The flowers are yellow, May-blooming, spurred, in rather sparse terminal clusters. *Epi-*

medium is from the Greek, named for a plant assumed to grow in Media, *i.e.* the old name for the country of the Medes, which is Persia.

737. Are there two flowers known as gold-dust? Yes; one of them is the wall pepper (see Question 725) and the other is often called madwort and will be found in Question 715.

738. What besides catnip will attract cats? The fragrant flowers of a perennial from the Caucasus and Persia, a relative of the weedy catnip, has a strong attraction for cats and is a far more handsome plant. It has no common name and was called *Nepeta mussini,* in honor of Grafen A. A. Mussin-Puschkin, a chemist who studied the plants of the Caucasus. It grows about one foot high, has opposite, stalked ovalish leaves and beautiful pale blue, irregular and dark-spotted flowers arranged in a terminal, leafy cluster. It is so popular as a garden flower that there are several hybrid forms with a longer flowering period, and with lavender flowers. (For the catnip see Question 542.)

June Flowers

739. What makes so many perennials come into flower in June and early July? During that period there is the longest exposure to sunlight, usually ample rainfall and coolish nights. Of these factors the most important is almost certainly the length of the day, and this plays an important part in forcing into bloom a profusion of June flowers. (For a discussion of the length of the day see Question 448.)

740. Is there a perennial baby's-breath? Yes; the usual florist's flower for trimming bouquets is a Eurasian perennial (*Gypsophila paniculata*), called also gypsum pink and mist. It is a delicate, forked plant eighteen to thirty inches high, with many branched stems and tiny leaves. It has such a profusion of minute white flowers that the name "mist" seems singularly appropriate, especially when they are grown in masses, for then the plants look like a faint patch of fog or mist. The plant is easily grown in any ordinary garden soil. (For the annual baby's-breath see Question 632.)

741. What is the bluebell of Scotland?   It *is* a bluebell, but why
the Scotch should appropriate it as *their* bluebell no one knows, for
it is really the harebell, and is wild in eastern North America as well
as over most of the north temperate zone. It is a delicate little perennial, six to nine inches high, but weak-stemmed and apt to sprawl.
The leaves are mostly basal, rounded and soon withering, leaving a
few narrow stem leaves. The flowers are blue, about three-fourths of
an inch long, in a lax, sparse cluster. (For related plants see Questions
700 and 721.)

**742. Is the showy flower head of the pyrethrum the same as that
going into the manufacture of Flit?**   No, the insecticide that goes into
Flit is made from the small flower heads of a plant nothing like so attractive as the garden pyrethrum (*Chrysanthemum coccineum*) which

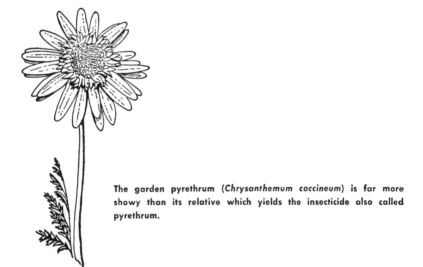

The garden pyrethrum (*Chrysanthemum coccineum*) is far more
showy than its relative which yields the insecticide also called
pyrethrum.

is a perennial from the Caucasus and Persia. It grows one to two feet
high, is scarcely at all branched, and its aromatic leaves much dissected. The flower heads are about one and a half inches wide, often
crimson, but also white or lilac, and are sometimes double-flowered.
It is closely related to the common chrysanthemum, but is June-flowering. It is often called the painted lady or painted daisy.

743. Is there a blue-flowered everlasting?   Yes, the blue succory (*Catananche caerulea*) is one of the few blue-flowered everlastings, and is a perennial from Europe often called Cupid's-dart or cupidone. It grows twelve to eighteen inches high, its mostly basal leaves oblongish, densely hairy but not ashy-gray, as so many everlastings are. The flower heads are about two inches wide, pale blue, with rays notched at the tip; they are June-flowering.

744. What is the alkanet?   A splendid, blue-flowered perennial from Southern Europe, often called bugloss (*Anchusa azurea*) and sometimes called sea bugloss. It is a stout, very hairy plant, two to three feet high, its oblong shaped leaves three to five inches long, almost or quite stem-clasping. The flowers are irregular, bright blue, and arranged in a one-sided, very showy cluster. It is such a popular garden flower that there are several hybrid forms, all of which are in shades of blue.

745. Is there a yellow-flowered columbine?   A superb columbine (*Aquilegia chrysantha*) from the Rocky Mountains is often cultivated for its very showy yellow flowers. It is a perennial, two to four feet high, with divided leaves and immense yellow, spurred flowers, the spurs arched. Unlike some native columbines, this one is of the easiest culture in any reasonably good garden soil; it is June-flowering. (For related plants see Questions 144, 290 and 560.)

746. Do the artemisias have showy flowers?   Scarcely ever, but some of them are as fragrant as their foliage, especially the wormwood (see Question 538), the mugwort (see Question 537) and the sagebrush (see Question 291).

747. What relative of the candytuft has longer-keeping flowers? The stone cress (*Aethionema grandiflorum*) is a Persian perennial whose terminal clusters of pink flowers keep much better than those of the candytuft. It is essentially unbranched and has bluish-gray foliage. The flowers are very small, but rather showy in the erect, stiff, terminal cluster, which is not over six to nine inches high. The plant does well in gritty soil in the rock garden, but it needs a spoonful of lime for each plant, which has a bad habit of dying off in a year or two. It is June-flowering.

748. Is Jupiter's-beard a valerian? Not technically, but many people call it, quite correctly, the red valerian. This is very different from the garden heliotrope (*Valeriana*). For Jupiter's beard or red valerian see Question 495.

749. Is the Shasta daisy a chrysanthemum? Yes; but it does not come from Mount Shasta, but was drived from *Chrysanthemum maximum*, a daisy-like perennial from the Pyrenees. Luther Burbank, who much improved it, gave it the name of "Shasta" daisy, and so it has been called ever since. It is a thrifty plant, twelve to twenty inches high, with long narrow leaves that are not deeply cut. The flower heads are daisy-like, white, two to four inches wide and very showy. Unfortunately the plant is apt to die out in a couple of years and must be constantly renewed.

750. Is the sneezewort related to the yarrow? Yes, but the sneezewort (*Achillea Ptarmica*) is a far more showy plant and has become a garden favorite, largely because the parent plants have been greatly improved. Originally a perennial of European origin, it is now a stout, somewhat stiff plant, one to two feet high, with toothed, lance-shaped leaves. The flower heads white, not large, but so numerous that the plant is very showy in June, especially in some of its horticultural forms. (For a related plant see Question 717.)

751. Is the musk rose a mallow? Yes, and it is better called the musk mallow from its musky odor. (See Question 494.)

752. Is there a flower called "mist"? Yes, "mist" is a fanciful name for the tiny white flowers of the baby's-breath, seen *en masse*. (See Question 740.)

753. Are there both annual and perennial delphiniums? Yes; for the annual sort, see Question 625. For the much finer sorts, usually called larkspur, and always perennial, see Question 558.

754. What is the harebell? Another name for what most people call the bluebell of Scotland. (See Question 741.)

755. Is the thrift an everlasting? Yes, and one of the best because its flowers keep for weeks when picked. Often called sea pink (*Ar-*

The long-keeping flowers of the thrift (*Armeria maritima*) have made this perennial everlasting a favorite garden plant.

meria maritima), it grows on shingle beaches in southern Europe and thrives here in sandy or gritty soil. It has a dense basal rosette of tiny, evergreen leaves, and from this springs a flowering stalk eight to twelve inches high, crowned with a small head of chaffy flowers that are pink, white or purple. It will not tolerate wet, heavy soils.

756. What makes Sweet William a tricky garden plant?   This perennial from southern Europe (*Dianthus barbatus*), often called the bunch pink, has been popular as a garden favorite, in spite of its erratic behavior. While a true perennial in its native habitat, it hardly ever is so in the garden, except in mild climates. Sometimes it is best treated as a biennial (see Question 609), and many prefer to grow it as a tender annual (see Question 608). Without one or the other of these methods it is apt to die out, unless, as sometimes happens, it persists from self-sown seeds. It grows twelve to twenty inches high, and can now be had in various shades of dark red, scarlet, pink, bronzy-red and white—usually with a darker center. Its quite fragrant flowers bloom from late June to frost. (For related plants see Questions 497, 498, 499, 626 and 727.)

757. What is the painted lady?   This is a fanciful name for the flower of the garden pyrethrum. (See Question 742.)

758. Do all daylilies bloom in June?   No, although a good many do; and by a careful selection from the scores of varieties now available

it is possible to have daylily bloom from June to frost. The daylily
(*Hemerocallis*) comprises hundreds of forms of lily-like flowers, all
originally derived from perennial plants, native from Europe to Japan.
They have narrow, mostly basal, sword-shaped leaves. The flowers are
in branched clusters, higher than the leaves. A selection of varieties
might include:

Early: Gold Dust (bronzy-yellow), Brocade (amber rose and night
blooming), Tangerine (deep orange)

Intermediate and midseason: Baronet (red), Black Prince (dark
yellow), North Star (pale yellow or cream), Bold Courtier (red
and yellow), Tasmania (gold and coral)

Late: August Pioneer (chrome-yellow), Galatea (pink), Jean
(terra-cotta and yellow), Rajah (red and orange), Windsor Tan
(tan and buff)

759. What is the lemon lily?   A wild species of the daylily (*Hemerocallis flava*), a perennial from eastern Asia, and one of the ancestors of modern daylilies (see Question 758). It has lemon-yellow,
lily-like flowers and is easily grown in any ordinary garden soil. It
looks like many of the modern varieties and is hence often called the
lemon daylily.

760. Are there two different flowers known as standing cypress?
Yes, and they are completely different. One plant, called the standing
cypress, is described at Question 681. The other, better known as
tree cypress (*Gilia rubra*), is a perennial native in the southeastern
states. It is a showy, slender plant three to five feet high, with finely
dissected leaves, the segments thread-thin, and brilliantly scarlet,
tubular flowers, the inside of which is red-dotted. (For related plants
see Questions 401 and 421.)

761. What flower is called the cupidone?   The blue succory (see
Question 743).

762. What is the cushion spurge?   Like some of its close relatives,
the cushion spurge (*Euphorbia epithymoides*) relies more on its
colored foliage than its flowers for real attraction. It grows about one
foot high, its many stems making a mound-like clump. It is a European

perennial, its lower leaves oblongish and green, but the upper leaves, near the rather indifferent yellow flower, becoming also yellow, the mass of them quite handsome. (For related plants see Questions 219, 261, 629, 762 and 962.)

763. Is the Japanese iris mostly June-flowering? Yes, and it normally follows the tall bearded or German iris by about one month. The Japanese iris (*Iris kaempferi*) is a perennial, cultivated for centuries in that country and now in a bewildering number of Japanese-named forms. It is doubtful that any amateur ever sees the true *Iris kaempferi,* but everyone knows the derivative Japanese irises. Far taller than other kinds, they have long, sword-shaped leaves with a prominent midrib, and immense flattened flowers, frequently five to six inches wide and not bearded. The varieties are in such confusion that it is impossible to suggest reliable sorts. The only remedy is a color catalog from a reliable dealer. The Japanese iris is the aristocrat of all irises and prefers a reasonably moist site. (For the tall bearded iris see Question 714. For other species of iris, see Questions 123, 570, 579 and 710.)

764. Is the sea bugloss the same as the bugloss? Yes; both names apply to the alkanet (see Question 744).

765. What is the plume poppy? A bold, striking perennial from China and Japan (*Macleaya cordata*) the flowers of which have no petals but are still showy. It is a spreading plant four to six feet high; its large, lobed leaves nearly eight inches wide and white beneath. The flowers are small, consisting mostly of the twenty-four to thirty stamens (see Question 3) which are cream-colored. A very handsome garden flower, the cluster frequently twelve to fourteen inches long and with many blooms. It is also called tree celandine.

766. Is there a perennial candytuft? Yes, and it is a far more satisfactory plant than the annual candytuft for which see Question 637. The perennial candytuft (*Iberis sempervirens*) is a low plant, rather bushy but not over eight to ten inches high, with evergreen foliage in reasonably mild regions. The flowers are small, white, in somewhat long, finger-thick clusters. Because of its wide use for edging, this Eurasian perennial is often called edging candytuft.

767. Do peonies ever have a woody stem?   No; the ordinary garden peony is a true perennial that dies down to the ground each winter and sends up a new crop of leaves and flowers each spring. (For this peony see Question 565.)

768. What is the tree peony?   A Chinese perennial or woody sub-shrub, whose stems persist over the winter and put forth leaves and flowers from the persistent stem and not from the ground. It is considered by the experts as the finest of all the peonies and now comes in many named forms. Its woody stem is four to six feet high, sometimes less, with large twice-compound leaves, the ultimate segments lobed and pale beneath. The flowers are immense, nearly twelve inches wide; they are white, pink or red, or in varying shades of these. The tree peony is safe to grow as far north as New York but a little hazardous north of this, except along the coast. They are very expensive.

769. Does the garden poppy yield opium?   No, and for the opium poppy see Question 484. The garden poppy (*Papaver orientale*) is a strong-growing perennial from the Mediterranean region, with very large, showy flowers that last only a brief time when picked. It grows three to four feet high, its sharply-toothed leaves up to eighteen inches long and covered with stiffish hairs. The flowers are nearly six inches wide, the petals scarlet, but the flower purplish-black at the center. There are over 140 horticultural forms, varying from pink, lilac and white to apricot in color. (For related plants, see Questions 354, 652 and 770.)

770. Do flowers of the Iceland poppy keep better than the large garden poppy?   Yes, and for this reason the Iceland poppy (*Papaver nudicaule*) has always been a popular garden flower, although its flowers, which are faintly fragrant, are much less showy than those of the common garden poppy. The Iceland poppy is a perennial from the Arctic regions, scarcely one foot high, its leaves lobed. The flowers are solitary, the stalk hairy, the flower one to two inches wide and orange, yellow, red or white. It is not suited to regions of hot nights and high humidity.

771. What is the Texas plume?   In Texas they call tree cypress Texas plume. It has gorgeous scarlet flowers. (See Question 760.)

The cut flowers of the Iceland poppy (*Papaver nudicaule*) keep far better than the more showy garden poppy.

772. Why do people get killed collecting edelweiss? The plants grow on high summits in the Alps, usually in such dangerous places that mountaineers are in much peril in attempting to collect it. To anyone who has seen the flower the wonder is that so much is risked for so little. Edelweiss (*Leontopodium alpinum*) is a woolly-leaved perennial, scarcely six inches high, its small, button-like flower heads with a row of silvery bracts (see Question 163) beneath them, neither showy nor striking. But the plant is the best publicized one in Austria, Switzerland and alpine Italy. It does not take kindly to cultivation in hot, humid regions.

773. Is there a passion-flower worth cultivating in the garden? Not in the North, for most passion-flowers are tropical, and while some of them have gorgeous flowers they cannot be grown outside a greenhouse. (For the only native passion-flower, which is seldom cultivated, see Question 193.)

774. Is there a native phlox called the wild Sweet William? Two native species of phlox are so called, but neither of them very correctly, for the true Sweet William is a pink. One of these is *Phlox divaricata,* for which see Question 166. The other is *Phlox maculata,* a perennial native in eastern North America, two to three feet high, the stems purple-spotted, and the narrow leaves three to five inches long. The flowers are pink or purple, about one-half of an inch wide and borne in loose clusters. (For related plants, see Questions 202 and 276.)

775. What is the sandwort?   A delightful little mountain plant, scarcely four inches high, named *Arenaria verna caespitosa*, the first term means "growing in sandy places," and the last means "forming dense tufted mats." Both statements are true of this perennial found both in the Rockies and in European mountains. The leaves are very small, flat and narrow. The flowers are solitary on thread-thin stalks, not over one-half of an inch wide, the five petals white. The plant needs rock garden culture in gritty or sandy soil.

776. Is there a beard-tongue worth growing in the garden?   Of the scores of beard-tongues found in the West—some of them very showy as wild flowers—only a comparatively small number are widely cultivated. Of these *Pentstemon barbatus* is perhaps the most popular in eastern gardens. It is a perennial, four to six feet high with smooth stems, its narrow leaves opposite or clustered. The flowers are irregular, the corolla with two lips and red, the lower lip bearded like a miniature hairy tongue. The flowers are borne in rather showy, branched clusters; they appear in June and often last several weeks. (For related wild plants, see Questions 327 and 328.)

777. What scarlet-flowered plant is called trailing fire?   The tree cypress, for which see Question 760.

778. In the East we have a beautiful wild flower called the alum-root. Is there a finer one in the West?   Yes, the coral bells (*Heuchera sanguinea*) is a far finer plant, that came originally from New Mexico, Arizona and Mexico, and is now cultivated throughout the temperate world. It grows one to two feet high, its basal leaves short-stalked. The flowers are bell-shaped, red, about one-third of an inch long, but profuse in a terminal, more or less one-sided cluster. A very valuable garden perennial; and June-flowering.

779. Who was George Russell and what flower did he improve?   He was a dedicated English breeder of lupines in Yorkshire, where, after many years of selection and hybridization, he produced what have come to be called Russell lupines. Starting with *Lupinus polyphyllus* from western North America, he ultimately produced many color forms, but the most important of his lupines have a terminal truss of pea-like flowers, far more showy than any wild species. The

(Department of Botany, University of Arizona)

A low, clump-forming desert plant is the strawberry-cactus (*Echinocereus engelmanni*) with purplish flowers. (Question 334)

(Department of Botany, University of Arizona)

A fearfully spiny cactus (*Mammillaria microcarpa*) from our southwestern deserts is often called the fish-hook cactus because some of its spines are hooked. (Question 340)

(Roehrs)

One of the chollas is the Teddy bear. (*Opuntia bigelovi*) which is

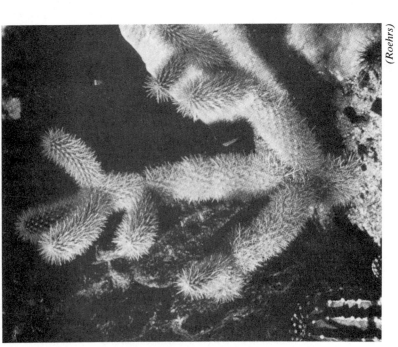

(Roehrs)

An almost spineless cactus is the beavertail (*Opuntia basilaris*)

An American lupine was used in England to develop the Russell lupines, the finest of all garden lupines.

Russell lupines are the standard garden lupines of today, their stems often four to five feet high, and the flowering truss often two and a half to three feet long.

780. What white flower was named for a Jesuit professor of natural history? The whitecup (*Nierembergia rivularis*), a perennial from the Argentine, was given that name to honor J. E. Nieremberg, a Spanish professor of natural history. It creeps over the ground, forming mats of foliage, which is made up of oblongish leaves about one inch long. The flowers are bell-shaped, one to two inches wide, mostly borne at the ends of the twigs; they are white (rarely pinkish or bluish tinged), the throat yellow. It is best suited to the rock garden.

781. What is the London pride? A rather fleshy European perennial, in Ireland often called St. Patrick's cabbage (*Saxifraga umbrosa*), the second name meaning "shade enduring," which it partly is, as it does not like hot dry places. Never over one foot high, and often considerably less, it is used as an edging plant. The leaves are in basal rosettes, somewhat oval, thick, one to two and a half inches long, sometimes reddish beneath, the margins tough. The flowers are small, white but red-spotted, the stalk of the cluster red. (For another plant called London pride, see Question 230.)

782. What is betony?   An extremely handsome perennial (*Stachys grandiflora*) from Asia Minor, growing two to three feet high. The leaves are opposite, stalkless and almost stem-clasping. The flowers are conspicuously irregular and two-lipped, about one inch long, violet, arranged in a dense, terminal, showy cluster. As it tends to die out after about three years, the plant must be renewed from time to time.

783. Is there a meadow rue with male and female flowers on separate plants?   One meadow rue (*Thalictrum aquilegifolium*), a stout Eurasian perennial, has its sexes on different plants, and the male flowers are much more showy than the rather drab females. The leaves are compound, the ultimate leaflets nearly round and sparsely toothed. The flowers have no petals, and the small sepals are white but not very conspicuous. The showy feature is the great number of stamens (see Question 3) that are crowded in each male flower. The stamens are pinkish-purple and quite showy. The plant is two to three feet high and its flower cluster is terminal and branched.

784. What flower was named for the saint who is reputed to have wiped the face of Christ on His way to Calvary?   Saint Veronica was much later memorialized by Linnaeus when he named the speedwells *Veronica* and the germander speedwell *Veronica latifolia*. This is a curious dedication, considering that Linnaeus was rather violently anti-Catholic. The germander speedwell is a fine garden perennial, native to most of Europe and Asia. It grows twelve to eighteen inches high, and has opposite, oblongish, coarsely-toothed leaves, and a terminal spike of brilliantly blue flowers. It is easily grown in any ordinary garden soil, and is June-flowering. (For the germander, see Question 829.)

785. Is the periwinkle the same as the Madagascar periwinkle?   Not at all. The Madagascar periwinkle is a tender annual, for which see Question 695. But the true periwinkle (*Vinca minor*) is an evergreen ground cover, with a woody, vine-like, prostrate stem. Often called creeping myrtle, it has opposite, evergreen leaves that are about two inches long, and solitary blue flowers about three-fourths of an inch wide, borne at the leaf joints. Originally European, the periwinkle has escaped from cultivation in the eastern states and is one of the best ground covers in shady or partly shady places.

786. What is Aaron's-rod? A native perennial (*Thermopsis caroliniana*) with a fine terminal cluster of lupine-like yellow flowers. It is a stiffly erect plant, three to five feet high, with compound leaves, the leaflets silky on the underside. The flower cluster may be eight to twelve inches long and is showy in June and often into July. As a garden plant it is not safely hardy north of New York City.

Midsummer Flowers

We enter now into the full splendor of midsummer bloom. No season is more prolific, and garden and roadside may be a riot of color. But, also, especially in August, there are hints of approaching autumn. This is no effusion of the poets, but the result of the waning length of the day. So pronounced is this that there is a dearth of mid-summer-flowering shrubs and trees, which is fortunately compensated for by a wealth of flowers from non-woody plants.

Those described below are all perennials, most of them of easy culture in any ordinary garden soil, preferably in full sunshine. A few questions relate to flowers that need special conditions for satisfactory growth, and these are noted especially wherever they occur.

787. What is Morden's pink? A very superior form of the purple loosestrife, developed in Canada and now grown in many gardens. (See Question 243.)

788. Has the black-eyed Susan a tall relative? Conspicuously so, and so common in cultivation that many sniff at the goldenglow (*Rudbeckia laciniata hortensis*), which was derived from an American plant with single flowers. The goldenglow, in spite of its critics is a sturdy perennial, five to eight feet high, its leaves divided into three to five lobes. The flower heads are always double, and cabbagy according to the cognoscenti, yellow, about three inches thick, profuse and never-failing. A useful, if some think too common perennial, needing room and apt to be invasive. (For related plants see Questions 256, 359 and 657.)

789. Is there a rampant garden coreopsis? Yes, one of the tick-seeds (*Coreopsis grandiflora*) from the central and southern states is perhaps the finest and easiest grown coreopsis, but it is so rampant and invasive that some gardeners fear it. It is a profusely flowering perennial, twelve to twenty inches high, with leaves cut into many segments. The flower heads are solitary, long-stalked, yellow, with the tips of the rays eroded or fringed, and the whole flower head thus appearing "ragged," but extremely showy. For related plants, see Questions 410, 621, 674 and 675.

790. Is the mountain bluet closely related to the cornflower? Yes, but the cornflower (see Question 618) is an annual, while the closely related mountain bluet (*Centaurea montana*) is a European perennial. It grows one to two feet high, its oblongish leaves silvery at first, but ultimately green. The flower heads are very showy, nearly three inches wide, and blue. Beneath the usually solitary flower head is a row of miniature, black-fringed leaves (bracts). (For related plants see Questions 507, 617, 618 and 791.)

791. What garden flower is grown as much for its foliage as for its bloom? One of the plants called "dusty miller" (*Centaurea Cineraria*) has such handsome, ashy-white foliage that some gardeners pinch off the flower heads to promote a greater growth of foliage. It is an Italian perennial (not to be confused with the florists' cineraria), growing twelve to eighteen inches high, with leaves cut into blunt segments and densely covered with white-felty hairs. The flower heads are small, yellow or purple. The plant does not like slushy winters and is not reliably hardy north of New York City. (For the florists' cineraria see Question 988.)

792. Are there other plants called "dusty miller"? There are quite a good many, and the name has thus come to be a little confusing. Originally it was applied to several plants whose ashy-white foliage suggested a flour-dusted miller. Some of these plants had the specific name *cineraria* applied to them (see Question 791) because that name is derived from the Latin *cineria,* which means "covered with ash." But the florists' cineraria is quite different from the plants called "dusty miller," and will be described in Question 988. The other plants called "dusty miller" belong in such groups as *Artemisia, Senecio,* or *Lychnis,* but are little known as flowers and not much cultivated.

793. Has the yellow star a finer relative from the Old World? The perennial *Inula glandulosa laciniata* from the Caucasus is a much more showy flower than the yellow star for which see Question 247. The latter is the familiar elecampane, but the plant from the Caucasus is only two to four feet high, and has oblongish, hairy leaves without marginal teeth. The flower heads are solitary, yellow, the heads three to four inches wide, the rays cut, fringed and drooping, and hence very showy. The flower has no common name.

794. Is there a blazing star worth growing in the garden? There are several plants called blazing star, but the finest and most showy is *Liatris squarrosa,* a perennial from the United States, often called rattlesnake master or colicroot. It grows one to two feet high, and its very narrow leaves are nearly six inches long and numerous. The flower heads are button-like, nearly one and a half inches thick, rose-purple, and borne in interrupted clusters on the wand-like stem. This is a fine plant for hot, dry places. (For a closely related plant see Question 216.)

795. What gorgeous flowers came from hybridizing our native rose mallow? The rose mallow of our salt marshes (see Question 84) was used as one of the forbears of modern mallows, derived by crossing it with several foreign species. The resulting hybrids are four to six feet high, with hollyhock-like flowers that may be four to five inches wide and come in a variety of colors, including pink, white with a red center, crimson with a red center and pure white. There are no yellows. All bloom in midsummer, and belong to the group known as *Hibiscus.*

796. Is there a garden flower related to the prairie smoke? A Chilean relative of prairie smoke (see Question 264) is a very showy perennial (*Geum chiloense*) widely cultivated for its brilliantly scarlet flowers. It grows twelve to twenty inches high, and its leaves are divided into lobes of which the terminal one is much larger. Its scarlet flowers are about one and a half inches wide, borne in small clusters and followed by silky, plume-like fruit. Its only common name is avens; and it is summer-blooming.

797. What is the Rose-of-Sharon?   A Eurasian, evergreen perennial (*Hypericum calycinum*), related to a common Saint Johns-wort of roadsides, for which see Question 245. This evergreen variety is not over one foot high, somewhat woody, and its opposite, resinous-dotted, oblong leaves are three to four inches long and pale beneath. The flowers about two inches wide, the five petals yellow. It prefers a sandy soil and some shade, and is often called Aaron's-beard.

798. Is there a perennial gaillardia?   Yes, the blanket-flower (*Gaillardia aristata*) is a rough-hairy perennial from the western United States, growing two to three feet high and is a fine garden plant. The leaves are narrow, and nearly five inches long. The flower heads are very showy, three to four inches wide, and yellow, but the center of the head is much darker and prevailingly red. (For the annual gaillardia see Question 631.)

799. What is the feverfew?   In the olden days it was thought that an infusion of the foliage and flower heads of feverfew (*Chrysanthemum Parthenium*) would abort an attack of fever, but today the plant is cultivated only for ornament. It is a European perennial, two to three feet high, and its divided leaves have the odor of camomile when crushed. The flower heads are button-like, white, scarcely over one-fourth of an inch thick, but profuse; they are summer-blooming. (For related plants see Questions 232, 536, 742 and 749.)

800. Where did the modern chrysanthemum come from?   For three thousand years the Chinese and then the Japanese have been selecting and hybridizing the chrysanthemum, so that its exact parentage may never be known. It is the national flower of Japan, where scores and perhaps hundreds of varieties are known and much venerated. They must have originated from a Chinese perennial, or perhaps from several of them, all having scented foliage, and at first having flower heads that were single and probably daisy-like, since really double-flowered heads, such as those found in modern chrysanthemums, are all but unknown in wild plants.

Today there are two main types of chrysanthemums. The first is the kind familiar to everyone from the displays in florists' windows, comprising a single flower head to each stalk, either naturally or by pinching off unwanted blooms. These are immense globe-shaped heads, five to six inches in diameter, much doubled and with the rays incurved or quilled or otherwise modified.

It was long supposed that this type of chrysanthemum was fit only for greenhouse culture, as it still largely is. But hardy varieties have been developed that can be grown outdoors, with proper attention to culture and a regular program of pinching off unwanted shoots and so allowing only a single flower to develop to maturity. All varieties of this type under outdoor culture will begin flowering towards mid-September and, in at least some varieties, will last up to severe frosts. Few or none flower in midsummer, as this type of chrysanthemum is a short-day plant (see Question 448).

The other type of hardy chrysanthemum is much more free-flowering, but the heads are considerably smaller. So profusely do they bloom that the foliage is almost obscured when they are in full flower. Blooming may begin as early as August first and, according to variety, last well into October.

Because of their habit of growing in cushion-shaped mounds, these free-flowering plants are usually called cushion chrysanthemums. They are of two types. The first is rarely over two feet high. The second may be three to four feet high and correspondingly wide, almost perfectly mound-like. For these, the dealers have coined the singularly inappropriate name of azaleamum—the absurdity of which is obvious, for they have nothing to do with any azalea.

Nevertheless, these tall cushion chrysanthemums are extremely handsome and striking plants. One modification, much in favor in Japan, requires a good deal of pinching and training to vastly increase the size of the mound-like shape of the flowering plant. Such plants, which are uncommon here, are called cascade chrysanthemums. They require much care and training, sometimes over wire frames, but plants five to six feet in diameter are not unusual.

A good many of the hardy chrysanthemums, both early and late-flowering, have flower heads anywhere from one-fifth or one-fourth the size of the usual varieties. These are the pompon chrysanthemums, which, like the larger-flowered varieties, come in a variety of colors, mostly yellow, cream, white, bronze, copper, orange, lavender, pink or red, but no blues.

801. What is *Campanula carpatica*? A beautiful bellflower from eastern Europe, without any specific common name, as bellflower applies to many other species. It is a perennial, nine to fifteen inches high, its ovalish leaves toothed and only one inch long. The flowers are erect, solitary, nearly two inches wide and a brilliant blue. The plant is suited mostly to the rock garden, and there are white or pale blue varieties.

802. What are Coventry bells? The almost perfectly bell-shaped bluish-purple flowers of a Eurasian perennial (*Campanula Trachelium*). It is a fine garden plant, two to three feet high, its coarsely-toothed leaves narrowly oval and two to three inches long. The flowers are about one inch long, nodding, and are borne in a loose cluster. The plant is vigorous and inclined to be invasive. For related plants see Questions 700, 721, 741 and 801.

803. The leaf of what flower was used by the Greeks as the chief motif in designing the capital of the Corinthian columns? The bear's-breech (*Acanthus mollis*) is a perennial from southern Europe,

The acanthus-like leaves of the bear's-breech (*Acanthus mollis*) were used by the Greeks in designing the capital of the Corinthian columns.

and its thistle-like leaves were the chief design at the top of Corinthian columns. Today we grow it for its striking, terminal cluster of showy flowers that are essentially stalkless and interspersed with tiny, spiny leaves (bracts). The flowers are white, lilac or rose, decidedly irregular and two-lipped, about two inches long. It is not safely hardy north of New York City, and is usually fifteen to thirty inches high.

804. Is the asphodel of the poets a true *Asphodeline*?   Almost certainly not, as the Greek asphodel may have been a narcissus, and the asphodel of Milton was probably a daffodil. The asphodel of today, *Asphodeline lutea,* is a European perennial occasionally cultivated here. It grows two to three feet high, with innumerable, very narrow leaves and a finger-shaped cluster of yellow flowers that are funnel-shaped or tubular. The flower cluster may be seven to fifteen inches long.

805. Is snow-in-summer well named?   So many vernacular names are meaningless or actually misleading that the amateur should be thankful for the singular appropriateness of snow-in-summer (*Cerastium tomentosum*). It is a prostrate European perennial, mat-forming and a fine ground cover. Its many tiny leaves are ashy-gray, and from this mass of foliage spring the pure white flowers in considerable profusion. It prefers sandy soil and full sunlight, in which it looks like snow on an ashy carpet.

806. What flower has the most meaningless common name?   That distinction should certainly go to the Jerusalem artichoke, which is not an artichoke and does not come from Jerusalem. When the French landed in Canada they called it *girasole,* their name for a sunflower, which ultimately became corrupted into *Jerusalem.* Because it bears edible tubers the plant was quite incorrectly called also an artichoke. Actually it is a sunflower (*Helianthus tuberosus*), found wild over much of the United States and Canada, and, not inappropriately called the Canada potato. Its tubers were a favorite food of the Indians and are still favored by some. It is a tall, coarse sunflower, six to twelve feet high, with leaves nearly eight inches long and hairy. The flower heads are yellow, and about three and a half inches wide. This was one of the few plants cultivated by the Indians.

807. What is *Boltonia asteroides*?   A native perennial often found in gardens, but without a commonly used vernacular name. When first discovered here it was named in honor of James B. Bolton, an English botanist who died in 1799. It is an aster-like perennial, hence, for its profuse bloom, sometimes called thousand-flowered aster. It grows three to five feet high, has lance-shaped leaves three to five inches long, and a profusion of white (rarely purplish) flower heads that are about three-fourths of an inch wide. It is of the easiest culture in any ordinary garden soil.

808. What is Stokes' aster?   This is a very showy, midsummer-blooming perennial (*Stokesia laevis*) found wild in the southeastern states, but hardy as a garden plant as far north as Boston. It was

This showy, native perennial, Stokes' aster (*Stokesia laevis*) thrives in gardens and has handsome lavender-blue flowers.

named in honor of an English botanist, Jonathan Stokes, who died in 1831. Growing twelve to thirty inches high, its purplish stems are covered with white hairs. The leaves are lance-shaped, seven to ten inches long, and the flower heads two to four inches wide, born in a showy, branching cluster, with rays very numerous and lavender-blue. A fine garden plant.

809. Is the houseleek appropriately named?   Only partly so, for, of course, it is not a leek, but its scientific name of *Sempervivum tectorum* emphasizes that the plant does grow on the thatched roofs of Eurasian cottages. *Tectorum* is Latin for "house roof." The plant is a perennial, growing also in the ground and often called the roof houseleek, hen-and-chickens and old-man-and-old-woman. The leaves are fleshy, often fifty to sixty in a basal rosette, from which springs a fleshy flowering stem eight to twelve inches high, crowned with a curved, one-sided cluster of red flowers. As a garden plant it prefers full sun and a fairly sandy loam.

810. What is the globe thistle?   A thistle-like, steely-blue, Eurasian perennial (*Echinops Ritro*), two to five feet high, its stems white-felty. The leaves are alternate, two to five inches long, cut into narrow, spiny segments. The flower heads are globe-shaped, about two and a half inches thick and spiny, steely blue and very handsome. The plant is easily cultivated, but apt to die out after three to four years, so that it must be renewed from time to time.

811. What is the sea holly?   It is not a holly, but a handsome, bluish-green European perennial (*Eryngium amethystinum*), growing one to two feet high, its leaves deeply lobed, the margins spiny. The flowers are crowded in a cone-like mass, beneath which is a row of steely-blue miniature leaves (bracts), which give the flower its chief and very attractive color. If grown in the garden, add a pinch of lime to the soil of each plant, but only if the soil is acid.

812. How does the heliotrope differ from the garden heliotrope?   The easiest way to distinguish between them is that the garden helio-trope (see Question 486) has finely dissected leaves, while the helio-trope (*Heliotropium arborescens*) has undivided, oblongish, alternate leaves. The latter is a Peruvian perennial, two to four feet high, with rather small, vanilla-scented flowers, borne in one-sided, forked clus-ters, purple or violet and showy. Because it blooms from seed in a single season, it is best grown as a tender annual (see Question 608), as it may die out if treated as a perennial.

813. Question 758 mentions several flowers known as daylily. Are there any others so called?   Yes, a whole group are often called daylily, but they are better called plantain-lily and were named *Hosta* (sometimes incorrectly as *Funkia*). Of several sorts the most showy is *Hosta plantaginea,* a thrifty Asiatic perennial, ten to eighteen inches high, with rather oval, prominently-ribbed leaves that are long-stalked, the blade of the leaf often eight inches long. The flowers are white, tubular, four to five inches long, and fragrant. Another plantain-lily is *Hosta caerulea,* with pointed, sometimes vaiegated leaves, and smaller, blue or lavender flowers. It is a good edging plant.

814. Is the leadwort a shrub or a perennial? This beautiful, blue-flowered plant from China might be called either, for it is a bit woody and yet resembles an herbaceous plant; it is not over one foot high. It was named *Ceratostigma plumbaginoides* and has leaves broadest at the middle and tapering towards the base. The flowers are about one-half of an inch wide, tubular but flaring at the tip; borne in loose, head-like clusters and quite showy. The plant blooms from August through September.

815. What red-flowered plant is called the hen-and-chickens? The houseleek. (See Question 809.)

816. Are the red-hot-poker and the torch lily the same? Yes, and this African perennial, called also flame flower and pokerplant (*Kniphofia Uvaria*), has flaming flowers throughout the summer. It is a stout plant, two to four feet high, its mostly basal leaves narrow and maybe two to three feet long. The flowers are tubular, about one and a half inches long, nodding or downward pointing, and gathered in a thickish spike that may be ten inches long and is spectacular. The flowers in the upper part of the spike are brilliant scarlet, the lower ones yellow. It is not quite hardy in the north without a winter mulch of salt hay or straw.

817. What garden flowers, from a distance, look like a faint blue haze? The beautiful sea lavender (*Limonium latifolium*), found in Europe and Asia, resembles our native sea lavender of the salt marshes in having tiny bluish-lavender flowers in a thin, airy, branching, dome-like cluster. The flowers are so numerous that from a little distance one sees only a faint blue haze. The Eurasian plant, which can be grown in the garden, has rather leathery leaves that taper towards the base—all arising at ground level, the leaves in a loose rosette. The tiny flowers are faintly fragrant.

818. What roof-top plant with red flowers is called old-man-and-old-woman? The houseleek. (See Question 809.)

819. Why is the balloon-flower so called? This eastern Asiatic perennial (*Platycodon grandiflorum*) is first cousin to the true bell-flowers (see Questions 700, 721, 741 and 801), but instead of bell-shaped flowers, these are flaring. The plant is eighteen to thirty inches high and has alternate, somewhat oval leaves two to three inches long. The flowers are blue, nearly saucer-shaped, two to three inches wide, and showy. The plant is inclined to be weak-stemmed and needs staking in windy sites.

820. What coneflower is called Black Sampson? The hedgehog coneflower (*Echinacea purpurea*) is so called because the central cone of the flower head, when old, resembles a black head. It is a rather coarse, native perennial, three to four feet high, its broadly oval leaves five to seven inches long, tapering to a winged base. The flower heads are purple, two to three inches wide, and the rays few and drooping. The central cone of the flower head nearly one inch long.

821. Are the flame flower and the poker-plant the same? Yes, both are alternative names for the red-hot-poker. (See Question 816.)

Autumn Flowers

822. What makes flowers much more scarce after the beginning of September? Many midsummer flowers, and even some that started blooming in June, will prolong their flowering well into the autumn, and a few will still be in bloom until cut off by frost.

But in spite of this hold-over profusion the number of plants that initiate their blooming in the fall is comparatively very limited. The few that do so are hence all the more welcome to the gardener who often ignores the basic cause of the scarcity of fall flowers. This, almost certainly, is not the cooler nights as fall matures, except that a premature frost will, usually, end all flowering.

Much more certainly we can ascribe the waning of flowers with the daily decrease in the hours of sunshine. By September 21, for instance, we definitely enter a period when there is only about twelve hours of sunshine, even on a clear day. That means that we are already in a short-day period, which gets shorter by about two minutes per day up until about December 21. By that time most perennials have entered the period of winter dormancy, and length of the day is no longer of significance.

But the period from about the first of September until the first frost is quite critical and it is, in all probability, the basic factor in the reduction of fall flowers. (For a discussion of the effect of this length of the day on plants in general, see Question 448.)

The greatest show of fall bloom, of course, comes from chrysanthemums. But because certain types of them begin to bloom in August, they are described among midsummer flowers (see Question 800). The rather meager list of the perennials that start their blooming in the fall will be found in the next few questions.

823. What is the most popular of all garden anemones?   Without question the Japanese anemone (*Anemone japonica*) is not only that, but perhaps the most widely grown of all fall flowers. It originated somewhere in eastern Asia, and is a several-stemmed perennial about two and a half feet high, its leaves compound, but having only three leaflets. The flowers are extremely showy, about two and a half inches wide, and of practically all colors except blue and yellow. It has been so long in cultivation that there are now many varieties, mostly differing in the color of the flower, some of which are double. (For related plants see Questions 263, 356 and 563.)

824. Is there a hardy cyclamen?   Most cyclamens are florists' flowers, but there is one (*Cyclamen neapolitanum*) which can be grown in any garden in California, but is difficult to grow in the East unless it can be kept from alternate freezing and thawing; it does not like slush at its roots. It is about eight inches high, has black-skinned tubers, and wavy-margined, rounded leaves that may be eared at the base. The flowers are solitary on each stalk, about two inches wide, the tips of the corolla lobes contorted and recurved. This is a handsome plant but not easy to grow in the East.

825. Is there a hardy ageratum?   A native perennial is often so called, but it has nothing to do with the real ageratum, for which see Question 660. Our native plant is better called mist flower or blue boneset (*Eupatorium coelestinum*), a stout plant eighteen to thirty inches high, usually branched, its opposite leaves ovalish, but pointed, two to four inches long. The flower heads are about one-third of an inch in diameter, blue, and quite numerous in forked clusters. The flower heads are definitely ageratum-like. The plant is easily grown anywhere, especially in reasonably moist places. (For related plants see Questions 120 and 460.)

826. What American asters acquired an English name? Strangely enough, two well-known native asters were taken to England many years ago, and after much selection and a huge amount of hybridization came to be called Michaelmas daisies. In the autumn they give a great profusion of color to almost every garden in England. Unfortunately, in the United States they do not do so well as in England, the only exception being in the Pacific Northwest, where their performance as garden plants is better than in the East.

The two plants from which the Michaelmas daisies were developed are the New York aster and the New England aster (see Question 192), and it was assumed that their derivatives would thrive as well here as their parents. There are perhaps 150 varieties of Michaelmas daisies in England, but only a handful are available here. Of these a selection might include:

Derived from the New England aster:
   Arizona Sunset (four to five feet, salmon-pink)
   Jessie Curtis (four to five feet, red-purple)
   Survivor (four feet, deep pink)
Derived from the New York aster:
   Blue Skies (three to four feet, light blue)
   Peace (two and a half to three feet, rosy-mauve)
   Violetta (three feet, deep blue)
   Winston Churchill (two and a half to three feet, almost red)

In addition there are so-called Oregon-Pacific hybrids, which are dwarf or semi-dwarf (eight to twenty inches) and come in a variety of colors (all but yellow and orange), and of which there are many more varieties than are available among the true Michaelmas daisies.

827. What is *Aster frikati*? A hybrid aster, one of its parents Italian, the other Himalayan, and in many ways an acceptable substitute for areas where the Michaelmas daisy does not thrive. It is two to three feet high and has a profusion of lavender-blue flower heads, two to three inches wide, that are mildly fragrant. A good variety of it is Wonder of Stafa which is available at most good nurseries.

828. Is the true mandrake fall-flowering? Yes, and it never needs to be confused with the plant often called mandrake here, which is spring-flowering and is better called the Mayapple (see Question 454).

The true mandrake *Mandragora officinarum*) is often called the devil's-apple, perhaps because of its poisonous properties and its ancient history, much of which is unprintable. It is a deep-rooted European perennial, the roots often forked man-like and hence once thought to promote conception! The leaves are ovalish, nearly twelve inches long. The flowers are bluish, cup-shaped, and about one inch long. It is fall blooming. Centuries before ether was discovered, a decoction of mandrake was used as an anesthetic in surgery, which is certainly one of its more respectable uses.

829. Is the germander the same as the germander speedwell?   No; the latter is a *Veronica,* for which see Question 784. The germander is a European perennial (*Teucrium Chamaedrys*) which is almost shrubby and has evergreen foliage. The leaves are ovalish, toothed, and about three-fourths of an inch long. The flowers are rose-purple, about three-fourths of an inch long, in dense clusters, these arranged in a terminal spike. The plant is not over eight inches high, and makes a good ground cover, but is not safely hardy north of Norfolk, Virginia.

830. Is there any fall-flowering gentian easy to grow?   Yes; the easiest of all the gentians to grow is the beautifully blue-flowered closed gentian (*Gentiana andrewsi*), for a description of which see Question 101. It is best to grow it in partial shade, a moist site and in woods soil.

831. Is there a better garden aconite than the medicinal one?   Yes, and its juice is just as dangerous (see Question 562). The garden aconite (*Aconitum fischeri*), usually called monkshood, is a stunning Asiatic perennial, four to five feet high, its leaves divided. The flowers are highly irregular and unsymmetrical, blue, and are arranged in a close, terminal, very showy spike that does not begin to flower much before mid-September. It is easier to grow than the closely related larkspurs.

832. What color are the flowers of the lavender cotton?   Its flowers are borne in a close, button-like, yellow head, which is solitary and stands above the ashy-gray, evergreen foliage. The plant has a rather formidable scientific name for it was christened *Santolina Chamaecyparissus.* The first name means "holy flax," which it is not, and the second is Greek for "dwarf cypress," perhaps because of its evergreen, dissected leaves. It is a European perennial, one to two feet high and not reliably hardy north of Boston.

833. Does the live-forever really do so?   Not quite, but it is a very persistent, Eurasian perennial, also called the orpine (*Sedum Telephium*). It grows twelve to eighteen inches high, and has ovalish, thick, toothed leaves, two to three inches long. The flowers are very numerous in a large, showy, reddish-purple cluster, and are fall blooming. Best suited to open sandy places.

834. What stonecrop has the most showy flowers?   Without much doubt this distinction would rest on *Sedum spectabile,* a stout Asiatic perennial, twelve to twenty inches high, with a thick, fleshy stem and equally fleshy leaves that are arranged in clusters of three. The leaves are grayish-green, ovalish, with only the upper part of the leaf toothed. The flowers are small, pink, arranged in a dense, terminal, pyramidal cluster. They are fall blooming and very showy.

FLOWERS DERIVED FROM BULBOUS PLANTS
(See Question 611)

835. What is the major difference between bulbous plants and all annuals, biennials and perennials?   Flowers derived from bulbous plants are among the finest we have, for they include such old favorites as crocus, hyacinth, narcissus, tulip and many others. But they differ from all annuals, biennials or perennials in one fundamental characteristic. All annuals, biennials or perennials have fibrous or slender roots, some of them may have tuberous roots, but practically none of them has a bulb. Many of them, however, have an underground stem, usually called a rhizome. (See Question 85.)

The bulb is a highly specialized underground stem, from the base of which spring the true roots. The bulb not only stores food over the dormant season, but contains within it, in miniature, the potentiality of producing leaves and flowers.

836. Do all bulbous plants bloom in the spring?   So many do, like the tulip and hyacinth, that many people think all of them do. Nothing could be more incorrect, for most lilies are summer-blooming, as are the gladioli. Others bloom only in the fall, like the Autumn crocus or the amazingly fragrant tuberose.

The flower lover, whether he grows these plants or not, would often like to know when to expect them to bloom, and if he does grow them, when they must be planted. Arranged in the approximate period of blooming they may be divided thus:

Spring-blooming: Questions 837–852
Summer-blooming: Questions 853–866
Autumn-blooming: Questions 867–870

Spring-blooming Bulbous Plants

837. Is the flower of the most popular of all bulbous plants fragrant? Most of the Darwin tulips are scentless, but Cherry Blossom, Joan of Arc and Pride of Haarlem are fragrant if brought into a warm room. Among Cottage tulips several are fragrant, notably Dido, Rosabella and Arethusa. For culture and classes of tulips, see Question 581.

838. What is the most fragrant flower among bulbous plants? Nearly everyone would give his vote to the hyacinth, but some think the fall-blooming tuberose far exceeds it. (For description and culture of the hyacinth, see Question 523.)

839. What is the guinea-hen flower? The curiously checkered flower of a bulbous plant (*Fritillaria Meleagris*) from Eurasia, often called the checkered lily and by some known as the toad lily or snake's head. It has very narrow leaves and purplish or violet, bell-shaped, nodding flowers that are three to four inches wide and bloom in mid-May or early June. Plant bulbs in the fall, three to four inches deep and six to eight inches apart. For related plants see Questions 374, 375, 376 and 591.

840. What is glory-of-the-snow? An Asiatic bulbous plant that blooms here just as the snow leaves, or even a little before. It is known as *Chionodoxa luciliae,* the first name being from the Greek for "glory of the snow." It is only about three inches high with grass-like leaves. The flowers are blue, with a white center, very small but in profuse clusters. Plant bulbs in autumn, three inches deep and as far apart, preferably by the dozens or hundreds, as they make sheets of bloom when once established.

841. What is the snowflake? An early-blooming bulbous plant (*Leucojum vernum*) from southern Europe, with solitary, nodding flowers, the flower stalk hollow. The leaves are a little broader than

The white-flowered, early-blooming snowflake (*Leucojum vernum*) gives sheets of white bloom if planted in masses.

grass-like. The flowers are bell-shaped, white, but green-tipped, about three-fourths of an inch long and fragrant. While it blooms very early, it is not so early as the snowdrop. Plant bulbs in the fall, four to five inches deep and the same distance apart, preferably in a partly shady place.

842. How does the snowdrop differ from the snowflake? They are somewhat similar and both are early bloomers—especially the snowdrop, which may be in flower any time after February, and where they are together always before the snowflake. The snowflake has nodding, solitary flowers, but so does the snowdrop, but the latter has more open, less bell-shaped flowers. The snowdrop (*Galanthus nivalis*) is a Eurasian bulbous plant, apparently indifferent to cold, about seven to twelve inches high, its narrow leaves six to eight inches long. The flowers are white, but the inner petals partly green. Plant bulbs three inches deep in August or September for early bloom, often among snow patches.

843. What is the Siberian squill? An Asiatic bulbous plant (*Scilla sibirica*) and one of the few bulbs that thrives under the shade of evergreen trees. Closely related to the bluebell of England (see Question 583), but its leaves are not grass-like but are nearly one-half of an inch wide. The flowers are nodding, blue, less bell-like than in the bluebell of England, and also found in a white-flowered form. They are never more and usually less than six inches high, and usually in bloom in April. Plant bulbs three to four inches deep and as far apart, in October.

844. What flower should be called a narcissus? This is a rather confusing term, for the technical name *Narcissus* applies to plants called by everyone narcissus, but also to some others like the jonquil, which few would class as a narcissus. The generic name *Narcissus* was given these plants because the boy of that name was so beautiful and addicted to looking in a pool that he mistook his likeness for an enchanting nymph, with whom he fell in love. Centuries later, such was the fame of these flowers that Mahomet wrote: "Bread is the food of the body, but narcissus is the food of the soul."

The identity of the flowers that belong to the technical genus *Narcissus* and their culture are described as follows:

Narcissus Jonguilla = jonquil (see Question 524)
Narcissus poeticus = poet's narcissus (see Question 525)
Narcissus Pseudo-narcissus = daffodil, or as it is often called, the trumpet narcissus (see Question 585)
Narcissus Tazetta orientalis = Chinese sacred lily (see Question 526)

845. What is the triplet lily? One of the few Californian bulbous plants of the group known as *Brodiaea* that takes kindly to culture in the East. The triplet lily (*Brodiaea laxa*) is twelve to eighteen inches high, with grass-like leaves that soon wither after the plant blooms, usually in May or June. The flowers are blue, purple or white, crowded in a dense, terminal cluster, the individual flowers about one inch long. Plant bulbs three to four inches deep in the autumn, and when the leaves wither after next season's bloom, lift the bulbs, store them in a dry place, and replant in the fall. This species is not reliably hardy north of Washington, D.C. (For related plants see Questions 362, 363 and 364.)

846. What is the toad lily? Another name for the guinea-hen flower. (See Question 839.)

847. Is the lily-of-the-valley a bulbous plant? Yes, and a very fragrant one, blooming in May. (For its description and culture see Question 519.)

848. Are any of the western dog-tooth violets even moderately easy to grow in the East? Yes; the best of them is the chamise lily (*Erythronium grandiflorum*), for culture and description of which see Question 372. (For other flowers in this group see Questions 156, 370 and 371.)

849. Can the quamash be grown in the East? Yes, by following the directions at Question 366. Its bulbs were once a valuable Indian food and are readily available from the garden dealers.

850. What is the grape hyacinth? A name for several, mostly blue-flowered bulbous plants, one of the best of which is also known as bluebell (*Muscari botryoides*) and by some called the starch hyacinth. It is of European origin, is scarcely six inches high, and has narrow, grass-like leaves. The whole plant resembles a miniature hyacinth. The flowers are small, urn-shaped, drooping in a relatively dense terminal cluster; they are typically blue, but white and pink forms are offered. Plant bulbs, in quantities, three inches deep in October. Planted thus, they make sheets of spring bloom.

851. Does the spring meadow saffron look like a crocus? Very much so, for its purple, crocus-like flowers are stemless and arise at ground level. It is a European bulbous plant (*Bulbocodium vernum*), not over five inches high, its grass-like leaves not appearing until after the plants bloom. The flowers are stemless, naked, about two inches long, blooming in April. Plant bulbs three inches deep in October in a gritty soil. If the foliage is allowed to wither, *i.e.* is not mown, the plant will persist for years. (For the ordinary spring crocus see Question 589.)

852. Is the snake's head the same as the checkered lily? Yes, both are names for the guinea-hen flower. (See Question 839.)

Summer-flowering Bulbous Plants

853. How do the summer-flowering bulbous plants differ from those that bloom in the spring?   The spring-bloomers usually are planted in the fall for the flowers that will mature the following spring. They definitely need a winter chilling. But the summer-flowering bulbs are often not quite hardy in the North, and a few of them are so averse to winter cold that their bulbs must be lifted in the fall, and stored in a cool, frost-free and preferably dark place. A cellar with a furnace in it is usually too warm.

Of the summer-blooming bulbous plants whose bulbs must be dug up each fall the following are the most important: zephyr lily (see Question 854), montbretia (see Question 855), the summer hyacinth (see Question 856) and, most important of all, the gladiolus (see Question 857).

854. Why was the zephyr lily named *Zephyranthes*?   This generic name is from the Greek for the west-wind flower, in allusion to the fact that all of them are American. The commonest of them is *Zephyranthes grandiflora*, much cultivated for its beautiful, but rather

The summer-blooming zephyr lily (*Zephyranthes grandiflora*) must be stored in a frost-free place in the East.

fragile, lily-like, pink flowers. It has very narrow, almost grass-like leaves. Originally coming from tropical America, it is a summer bloomer, its flowers about two inches long and solitary. North of Washington its bulbs must be dug up in the fall and stored. South of this and in California, it can stay in the ground all winter.

855. What is the garden montbretia? A very showy, summer-blooming bulbous plant derived from the crossing, in 1880, of two South African bulbous plants, one of them a *Tritonia* and the other a *Crocosmia*. The result is the common garden montbretia (*Tritonia crocosmaeflora*), a tall, branching plant, closely related to the gladiolus, and which must be grown the same way. It is three to four feet high, with sword-shaped leaves. The flowers are in a loose, terminal cluster, and are typically orange-red, but there are now many color forms. Unlike gladiolus, its flowers are nearly regular and not unsymmetrical.

856. Is the summer hyacinth like the spring one? Not in the least, although both belong to the lily family. The summer hyacinth (*Galtonia candicans*) is a tall, branching plant from South Africa, named in honor of Sir Francis Galton, a noted British scientist. It grows two to three and a half feet high, has basal, strap-shaped leaves and a tall, branching flower cluster. The flowers are bell-shaped, nodding, about one inch long, white and fragrant. Plant bulbs five to six inches deep, after settled warm weather, and lift the bulbs for winter storage before the first frost.

857. Where did the gladiolus come from? The modern gladiolus, now found in hundreds of varieties, is the result of crossing several South African wild species of *Gladiolus,* a tender bulbous plant belonging to the iris family. It has sword-shaped, mostly basal leaves, although some leaves are borne on the stem. Flowers, of nearly all colors, are borne between minature leaves (bracts) in a tall, terminal spike that blooms from the bottom upwards. These flowers are slightly irregular and unsymmetrical, about two inches long and extremely showy. Plant bulbs (corms) four to five inches deep only after settled warm weather, and lift in the fall for winter storage. South of Norfolk, Virginia, they may be left in the ground throughout the year. The taller kinds may have to be staked if the site is windy.

Scarcely any of the modern plants are fragrant, but a highly fragrant species is *Gladiolus tristis,* for which see Question 516. For the disputed pronunciation of gladiolus, see Question 517.

858. Are there summer-blooming bulbous plants that can be left in the ground all winter? There are several, all of which save the trouble of annually planting and lifting the bulbs, as is true of those in Questions 854–857. These hardy, summer-blooming bulbous plants include some of our showiest flowers. Among them are the hardy amaryllis (see Question 859), the foxtail lily (see Question 860) and the true lilies (which begin at Question 861).

859. What flower was named for the mistress of Mark Anthony? A beautiful and famous Roman actress was also his mistress and the hardy amaryllis (*Lycoris squamigera*) was named in her honor. It is a Japanese bulbous plant, two to three feet high, with leaves

The only hardy amaryllis (*Lycoris squamigera*) is a stunning, summer-blooming bulbous plant, hardy up to Philadelphia with a little protection.

about one inch wide, twelve inches long and strap-shaped. The flowers are fragrant, nearly three inches wide and rose-lilac, borne in a tight, terminal cluster, on a solid, thick stalk. Plant bulbs in mid-summer, six to eight inches deep. South of Washington, D.C., they can be left in the ground; northward to about Philadelphia they need a winter mulch of straw or salt hay but are not reliably hardy north of this. The plant needs a good, rich soil.

860. What is the aristocrat of all flowers?   Without much question it is the foxtail lily (*Eremurus elwesi*) of unknown, but probably of hybrid origin; most of its relatives are from the Himalayan region. It is a magnificent plant, its flowering stalk ten to twelve feet high, the upper third of it covered with hundreds of tiny pink, bell-shaped flowers. Its culture is frankly difficult as instead of a bulb it has extremely fragile roots that must be handled very carefully. Dig out all poor soil and fill in two feet deep with rich, well-manured soil. Spread the roots out, six to eight inches deep, in October, and cover with soil and a mulch of straw or salt hay. In the spring put on a top-dressing of manure, as the foxtail lily is a voracious feeder. In windy places it needs staking. The roots are expensive and must be handled gingerly.

861. What are the true lilies?   Hundreds of flowers have had the name *lily* attached to them, such as foxtail lily, torch lily, lily-of-the-valley, toad lily, triplet lily, etc., not one of which is a true lily, although some of them have lily-like flowers.

The true lilies all belong to the genus *Lilium,* which was the original Latin name for all the lilies known at that time. Since then over eighty different species of *Lilium* have been found, and many of these are cultivated in gardens for their showy flowers. Some are native in the United States, but the finest wild lilies are Asiatic. Still finer as garden flowers are the hybrid lilies; some of these were developed abroad but many of the most superb varieties have been produced on the Pacific Coast.

Besides those in Questions 862–866, there are some that have already been noted; *e.g. Lilium columbianum* and *Lilium rubescens* at Questions 378 and 379, and the Madonna lily at Question 587. There is room here for only five more species of lily.

862. What is the Turk's-cap lily?   A native American lily (*Lilium superbum*) found in moist places in the eastern states. It grows five to eight feet high and has orange-red, dark-spotted flowers that are about four inches wide. It is best grown in moist places, especially in the bog garden.

863. Is there another Turk's-cap lily besides the native one?   Yes; the Martagon lily (*Lilium Martagon*) of Eurasia is also called the

Turk's-cap lily. But it is not usually over five feet high, and has rose-purple, dark-spotted, drooping flowers that are only about two inches wide. As in our native Turk's-cap lily, the tips of the petals are strongly recurved.

864. What is the Easter lily?   A Japanese lily (*Lilium longiflorum eximium*), widely forced by the florists for the Easter festival, mostly in the form known as the Croft lily, which was developed on the Pacific Coast. But the Easter lily is also a garden plant in mild regions, variously called the Bermuda lily and the white-trumpet lily. It is not over three feet high and has horizontal, fragrant, trumpet-shaped, white flowers that may be six to seven inches long.

865. What is the royal lily?   A beautiful Chinese lily (*Lilium regale*) growing four to five feet high, with horizontal, fragrant flowers nearly six inches long, lilac-purple outside, white inside and yellow at the base. It is widely cultivated for its showy bloom.

866. Is the tiger lily native?   Most people think so, for it has run wild in many places in the eastern states, but actually it is an Asiatic plant (*Lilium tigrinum*) which has long been in cultivation and perhaps got its name of tiger lily from its salmon-orange or reddish flowers that are irregularly black-spotted. The plant grows four to six feet high and its drooping flowers are nearly five inches wide with the tips of the petals recurved.

Fall-flowering Bulbous Plants

867. Is the autumn crocus a real Crocus?   No; it got its name from its fall-blooming, crocus-like flowers that are quite unrelated to the true *Crocus*. (For the plant called the autumn crocus, see Question 475.)

868. Is there a true Crocus that blooms in the fall?   Quite a few do, unlike the usual spring crocus, for which see Question 589. Of true *Crocus* species, one that blooms in the fall is the saffron crocus, which has yellow flowers and is described in Question 518. Another fall-blooming species is *Crocus speciosus,* which has no common name. It has lilac or purple-tinged flowers that are scarcely two inches long; hence much smaller than the common crocus of spring. Plant the bulbs three to four inches deep, in midsummer for bloom that fall. They will persist for years, and make a fine show in autumn if planted in quantity.

869. Is there another crocus-like, fall-blooming flower? Yes, the winter daffodil is a yellow-flowered bulbous plant that blooms in the fall. (See Question 521.)

870. What is the most sweet-smelling of all fall flowers? Of all the bulbous plants that bloom in the fall, the most fragrant is the tuberose. (See Question 522.)

VII. FLOWERS FROM TREES
AND SHRUBS

871. What is the difference between a shrub and a tree? In Question 174 it was noted that some trees and shrubs have such small or inconspicuous flowers, usually wind-pollinated, that many people think they have no flowers at all. This, of course, is completely erroneous, for all trees and shrubs *must* bear flowers and seeds or they would perish. But in a few trees and shrubs the flowers are so conspicuous and often so very showy that they are generally cultivated under the name of flowering trees and shrubs. A tree usually has a single woody stem (the trunk) that is mostly rather tall (anywhere from fifteen to two hundred feet). A shrub usually has several woody stems and is generally lower (one to twenty feet high). But Nature appears to delight in producing exceptions from any definition so that there are tree-like shrubs, such as the mountain laurel in the Carolina mountains, and shrub-like trees such as the redbud often is.

The only safe rule is one of judgment, and this usually results in sorting woody plants into the two categories of trees (usually with a single trunk) and shrubs (usually with several stems). In the questions below they are so arranged, and the exceptions are noted if they are significant.

872. How do the flowers of trees and shrubs differ from those produced on herbaceous plants? All herbaceous plants, like a peony or the Shasta daisy, die down to the ground each winter, and in the spring send up a stem that bears leaves and flowers. Such leaves and flowers are never the result of buds that have persisted over the winter on twigs that are exposed above ground. In all shrubs and trees, leaf buds and flower buds must survive the winter, for they are completely exposed to the weather on twigs and branches that persist above ground from year to year.

Flowering Trees

873. Are the tulip-tree and the tulip poplar the same? Yes; the tulip-tree (*Liriodendron Tulipifera*) is so popular that it has many other common names such as tulip poplar, whitewood and yellow poplar. It is not related to the poplar, but is a magnificent forest tree of eastern North America, with a single, very straight trunk from 80 to 150 feet high if in the forest, but lower and usually branched if in the open. The leaves are ovalish, alternate, the tip very blunt and deeply notched. The flowers are solitary, but rather profuse, tulip-like, about two and a half inches wide, greenish-white but with an orange base and very handsome; they are June-flowering.

874. Does the locust have white flowers? The locust (*Robinia Pseudo-acacia*) has pea-like, white, fragrant flowers in a handsome, hanging cluster, mostly in June. It is a tree seventy to eighty feet high, its compound leaves with seven to nineteen oval shaped leaflets that are one to two inches long. At the base of each leaf there is a pair of spines. Its smooth pods are three to four inches long. A native tree, it is often a nuisance in gardens from its invasive habit.

875. Does the honey locust also have white flowers? No; its flowers are greenish and not pea-like, and they have three to five nearly equal petals. It is a native tree often called black locust or three-thorned acacia and named *Gleditsia triacanthos*. It may be 100 to 150 feet high, its trunk and branches usually armed with branched thorns. The leaves are compound, the twenty to thirty leaflets oblongish and one to one and a half inches long. The pods are twisted, about fifteen inches long, and persistent for months.

876. What is the pride-of-India? An extremely handsome Asiatic tree (*Koelreuteria paniculata*), often called the China-tree or varnish-tree and usually not over thirty feet high, often less. The leaves are compound, the seven to fifteen leaflets oblongish and deeply eroded or cut, especially near the base. The flowers are small, yellow, but numerous in an erect cluster twelve to eighteen inches long, in mid-summer, followed by papery pods. This is a fine but short-lived lawn tree.

877. What is the chaste tree?   A beautiful, midsummer-blooming shrub-like tree or tree-like shrub, eight to twenty feet high, often called the hemp tree (*Vitex Agnus-castus*) and called by some the monk's pepper-tree. A native of southern Europe, it has compound leaves with five to seven narrow, grayish leaflets that are pleasantly odorous when crushed. The flowers are very small, pale lilac-blue, in dense, terminal, showy spikes. It is not quite hardy north of Wilmington, Delaware.

878. What is the Chinese scholar tree?   Probably the correct name for *Sophora japonica,* famous in ancient China, its native home, as a tree under which students gathered to hear lectures. Introduced into Japan, it is also called pagoda tree and Japanese pagoda tree. It is forty to sixty feet high in nature but much less as cultivated, with compound leaves, composed of seven to seventeen oval shaped leaflets, one to two inches long. The flowers are pea-like, about one-half of an inch long, gathered in extremely showy, loose clusters that are twelve to fifteen inches long, blooming from July to September. This is a beautiful but slow-growing flowering tree.

879. What is the flowering tree called "mimosa" in the South? The correct name for it is silk tree and will be found in Question 6.

880. Does the flowering dogwood have white flowers?   No; the true flowers are greenish, but the floral leaves (bracts) beneath them are white. (See Question 181.)

881. What is the cornelian cherry?   A relative of the flowering dogwood but looking nothing like it. The cornelian cherry (*Cornus Mas*) is a small Eurasian tree or large shrub, its naked twigs in March or April covered with a multitude of tiny yellow flowers, followed in August by scarlet, acid, edible fruit. This is a good flowering tree for inhospitable places, and it will stand city air.

882. Are the greenish flowers of the whitewood the same as those of the yellow poplar?   Yes, both names apply to the tulip-tree. (See Question 873.)

883. Are there two flowering trees known as black locust?   This confusing term is applied to two quite different trees. One is the locust, for which see Question 874. The other is the honey locust described at Question 875.

884. Is there a finer redbud than our native species? Many gardeners think that the Asiatic redbud (*Cercis chinensis*) is a finer flowering tree or small tree than the native *Cercis canadensis,* because the Asiatic species has more numerous, rosy-purple flowers on its bare twigs in early spring. As usually grown the Asiatic sort is apt to be more shrub-like than tree-like. (For the native redbud see Question 180.)

885. What flowering tree that is not a chestnut is called chestnut in Europe? In Paris and London they call the horse-chestnut (*Aesculus Hippocastanum*) the chestnut, ignoring the fact that the true chestnut of Europe is an entirely different tree. The horse-chestnut is a splendid flowering tree from southern Europe, often one hundred feet high and with a dense dome-shaped canopy, casting so dense a shade that little will grow beneath it. The leaves are compound, the five to seven leaflets five to nine inches long, broad at the tip but wedge-shaped at the base and stalkless. The flowers are white, but red tinged, about three-fourths of an inch wide, and gathered in extremely showy, erect clusters that may be eight to fifteen inches long; they bloom in May and June. (For a related American tree see Question 426.)

886. What is the false acacia? The true locust. (See Question 874.)

887. Is there an ash tree with showy flowers? Most ash trees have greenish, rather inconspicuous flowers, but the flowering ash (*Fraxinus Ornus*) of Eurasia bears dense, fragrant clusters of whitish flowers that bloom just as the leaves unfold. It is a round-headed tree, not usually over fifty feet high, its compound leaves with seven leaflets, the terminal one larger than the others. From its trunk a sweetish exudate is collected, known as manna, and the tree is often called the manna ash. It is the showiest of all the ash trees.

888. From the root of what flowering tree did the pioneers make a lasting yellow dye? In Kentucky and Tennessee the pioneer women found that the roots of the yellow-wood (*Cladrastis lutea*) when boiled yielded a fine long-lasting yellow dye. But in addition it is a showy-flowered tree thirty to fifty feet high, its white, fragrant, pea-like flowers borne in long, drooping clusters that may be ten to twenty inches long; it is spring-blooming. Often called Kentucky yellow-wood or gopherwood, the tree has compound leaves with seven to eight ovalish leaflets about three and a half inches long.

889. What is the golden chain?   A rather fanciful but reasonably accurate name for one of the showiest trees in cultivation. For the golden chain (*Laburnum anagyroides*) produces splendid hanging clusters of pea-like flowers in June, yellow or golden yellow. The tree, a native of southern Europe is scarcely over twenty feet high, and has compound leaves with only three downy leaflets. The flower clusters may be four to twelve inches long, suggesting a yellow wisteria. Its narrow pods are bean-like, and the tree is often called the bean-tree.

890. What white-flowered tree blooms in late April or early May? The woods in the southeastern United States are especially beautiful at such times with the white, bell-shaped flowers of the silver-bell (*Halesia carolina*) which is a medium-sized tree of the under-canopy of the forest. It is perfectly hardy as far north as New England and is much planted as a lawn specimen. Its alternate leaves are ovalish, three to four inches long, pointed at the tip, and have remote, shallow marginal teeth. The flowers are about one-half of an inch long, nodding and so much suggesting a snowdrop that the tree is also known as snowdrop-tree; they are followed by a winged fruit.

891. In classical Rome what flowering tree produced strawberries? None; but the fruit of the strawberry-tree (*Arbutus Unedo*) is much like a strawberry and Virgil and other Latin writers often mentioned it. Never much over ten feet high it has alternate, oblong, evergreen leaves that are about three inches long and toothed. The flowers are urn-shaped, about one-half of an inch long, white or pinkish, and are borne in hanging clusters that are about two inches long. The fruit is orange-red, strawberry-like, edible but flavorless. Its close relative is the Pacific Coast madroña (see Question 431). The strawberry-tree is European and not safely hardy above Norfolk, Virginia. It has, of course, nothing to do with the trailing arbutus, for which see Question 137.

892. Do the Japanese flowering cherries bear any fruit?   Yes, but they are not juicy like a cherry and no one would think of growing

Better than our native bleeding-heart is this one from Japan, *Dicentra spectabilis*, a very popular garden flower. (Question 719)

Perhaps the best of the African daisies is the Transvaal daisy (*Gerbera jamesoni*) but its culture needs a greenhouse. (Question 666)

(J. Horace McFarland Company)

Improved forms of the Shasta daisy (*Chrysanthemum maximum*) have larger and more showy flower heads than this

(J. Horace McFarland Company)

The Japanese anemone (*Anemone japonica*) now comes in many horticultural forms that are more showy than the original

them for anything but their gorgeous mass of spring flowers. The Japanese flowering cherries all belong to the group known as *Prunus* and have been hybridized by the Japanese for centuries. Today Japan is a mass of dazzling color in mid-April, for there are thousands of trees scattered along roadsides and in gardens. Here the many named sorts are medium-sized trees with narrow, toothed leaves and an enormous production of white or pinkish flowers, mostly blooming a little before the leaves unfold or with their unfolding. The flowers typically have five strap-shaped petals, but often much doubled in some of the finest varieties. There is a magnificent collection of these trees around the Tidal Basin in Washington, D.C., presented by the City of Tokyo in 1912. They bloom here about mid-April.

893. What flowering tree was named for a Russian princess? When the gorgeous Empress tree (*Paulownia tomentosa*) was first discovered in China the botanist who named it did so in honor of the daughter of Tsar Paul I, whose name was Anna Paulowna and who ultimately became a princess of Holland. It is a quick-growing tree, thirty to fifty feet high, its large, ovalish, alternate leaves six to ten inches wide, and much wider on young shoots. The flowers bloom before the leaves unfold, are pale violet, about two inches long, borne in large, pyramidal clusters that are about eight inches long and very showy.

894. Do we have a flowering tree here that is related to the English hawthorn? We have several scores of them, commonly called thorn or hawthorn, and badly confused as to identity. One of the best is the cockspur thorn (*Crataegus crus-galli*), the latter name signifying that the tree bears thorns like a cock's spur. It is a wild tree of the eastern states, not over thirty feet high, often less and shrub-like. It has numerous slender thorns three to four inches long, and wedge-shaped leaves that are two to three inches long. The flowers are about one-half of an inch wide, in small, dense, very profuse clusters in May. The fruit is like a miniature apple, drooping, red and almost as showy as the flowers. For the English hawthorn see Question 593.

895. Do the flowering crabapples bear real apples? No, but the small apple-like, acidulous fruits look like apples and are closely related to them. The flowering crabapples all belong to the group known as *Malus,* a name given them by the Romans. The flowering trees are medium-sized and as now grown in gardens are the result of much hybridizing. Almost as showy as the Japanese flowering cherries, they have alternate, apple-like leaves and a profusion of white or pink flowers blooming in early spring, sometimes before the leaves unfold. The flowers typically with five rounded petals (strap-shaped in the Japanese flowering cherries), but often much doubled. The trees are completely thornless, unlike the thorny hawthorns.

896. What flowering tree yields a pleasant-tasting mucilage?   All country boys and girls know of the pleasantly flavored, aromatic, mucilaginous twigs of the sassafras (*Sassafras albidum*), a usually medium-sized tree of the eastern states with green twigs and extremely variable leaves. These may be ovalish, lobed only on one side or often three-lobed, all on the same tree. The flowers are small, greenish-yellow, faintly fragrant, and are borne in small clusters before the leaves unfold. The bark of the root yields a drug once widely used, but dangerous if too much is taken. The tree is not much grown but its autumnal color is a more brilliant scarlet than any other native tree.

897. What showy flowering tree is even more showy in fruit?   The mountain ash (*Sorbus Aucuparia*) of Eurasia is covered in spring with showy clusters of white flowers, but from summer to late fall its profusion of berry-like, red fruits is even more showy and long lasting. It is not over fifty feet high and has compound leaves with nine to fifteen rather oblong leaflets that are one to two inches long. The small flowers are borne in a branched cluster that may be four to six inches wide. It is much cultivated for ornament, often under its English name of rowan tree.

898. What flowering tree is especially favored by bees?   The small-leaved European linden (*Tilia cordata*) is alive with bees in mid-June, and the honey from these flowers is much favored by connoisseurs. It is a magnificent shade tree, universally called the lime in Europe, grows 90 to 120 feet high and casts a dense shade. The leaves are alternate, ovalish but pointed, three to four inches long. The flowers are yellowish-green, extremely fragrant, borne in small clusters from the middle of a strap-shaped, leaf-like organ, and are so profuse that the tree is a fragrant delight when in bloom. There are native relatives usually called basswood, but not so fine as this European tree.

899. What native maple has the most gorgeous autumnal color? Of the many native maples in the United States the most brilliant fall color is certainly found in the sugar maple (*Acer saccharum*) which is wild in the eastern states. It grows from 80 to 120 feet high and has alternate, three-to-five-lobed leaves that turn first yellow and ultimately scarlet. The flowers are small, greenish-yellow, opening before the leaves expand, not particularly showy. The tree has shaggy bark, and from its early spring sap maple sugar is made.

900. What other maple has yellow flowers? Perhaps the most widely planted tree in the United States is the Norway maple (*Acer platanoides*), a European tree, not over one hundred feet high and usually with a dome-like canopy and smooth bark. The leaves are alternate, five-lobed, four to seven inches long, the lobes toothed and turning yellow in the fall. The flowers are yellow or greenish-yellow, in erect, stalked clusters, appearing just before the leaves expand. It has few equals as a lawn or street tree.

901. Is there a native maple with red flowers? In March or early April there is often a great profusion of tiny red flowers that litter the lawn or pavement, long before most flowers indicate that spring is on its way. They all come from the red maple (*Acer rubrum*) which is very common in moist places throughout the eastern states. It grows 80 to 120 feet high, its alternate leaves three to five lobed, green above, distinctly paler beneath and sometimes even gray; yellow or scarlet in the fall. The flowers are very small, red, and extremely profuse, weeks before the leaves unfold.

FLOWERING SHRUBS

For landscape effects it is impossible to avoid the use of shrubs. Almost universally shorter than trees, their use is imperative in gardens too small for trees. For the difference between a shrub and a tree see Question 871.

Shrubs provide most of the color in a permanent garden, and the variety of color and size of the plants makes it comparatively easy to get almost any effect one desires. But an important consideration in planning any garden is *when* the shrubs will be in flower. For the convenience of gardeners who want a floral timetable, and for those interested only in the identification of shrubs, the questions that have arisen about flowering shrubs have been arranged thus:

Shrubs that are winter-blooming, or that bloom on practically bare twigs very early in the spring, (Questions 902–909)

Shrubs that bloom as the leaves unfold, or soon after, mostly in late April or May, (Questions 910–926)

June– and early summer–flowering shrubs, (Questions 927–944)

Midsummer– and fall–flowering shrubs, (Questions 945–960)

902. What is the most popular of all winter-blooming shrubs? To judge by the hundreds of varieties that are grown in the South, the camellia (*Camellia japonica*) is surely the favorite winter shrub. It is an evergreen shrub, five to twenty feet high, closely related to tea, and originally from China, although the Japanese have produced many varieties. The leaves are alternate, ovalish, three to four inches long, dark green and leathery. The flowers originally had roundish petals but are now much doubled, waxy, of nearly all colors but blue, and are always solitary, practically stalkless and without much or any odor. The plants need a rich, somewhat acid soil and partial shade, and are not reliably hardy north of Norfolk, Virginia. Camellia was named for George J. Kamel or Camellus, a Moravian Jesuit who travelled in Asia late in the seventeenth century. Nearly all camellias are winter-blooming, but a few flower in October–November, and still fewer in April.

903. What yellow-flowered shrub blooms in zero weather? A Japanese relative of our witch-hazel, often called the winter hazel (*Corylopsis pauciflora*) habitually blooms from any time in late January to early March. It is a shrub five to six feet high, with alternate, somewhat oval, toothed leaves two to three inches long. Weeks after they have fallen the yellow flowers appear on the bare twigs, sometimes during a snow storm but are uninjured by it. The flowers are fragrant, yellow, about three-fourths of an inch long, and are borne in rather sparse but most welcome clusters.

904. What fragrant Chinese shrub blooms all the winter in the South?   A shrub without a common name but known as *Chimonanthus praecox* is very popular throughout the South for its winter bloom. It has opposite, sometimes evergreen, long-pointed leaves four to six inches long, and the shrub itself may be nine to ten feet high. The flowers are about one inch wide, yellow, but the inner segments with brown-purple stripes. It is not reliably hardy much above Norfolk, Virginia.

905. About what American shrub did Emerson write a poem?
Ralph Waldo Emerson wrote an exquisite little poem on the beauty of the rhodora (*Rhodora canadensis*) which is a native azalea-like shrub that blooms before the leaves unfold, usually in early April. It is scarcely three feet high and has alternate leaves without marginal teeth. The flowers are irregular, two-lipped, rose-purple, nearly two inches wide and very showy. It needs the same cultural care as its close relative, the azalea. (See Question 176.)

906. What is the best of all the shrubby magnolias that bloom before the leaves unfold?   Many would vote for the star magnolia (*Magnolia stellata*), a beautiful Japanese shrub, five to fifteen feet high, with rather oblong leaves that do not appear until the flowers are withered. All the young twigs and especially the buds are densely soft-hairy. The flowers are white, fragrant, star-like, about three to four inches wide, the many petals narrow and strap-shaped. It blooms in late March or early April, and in the north the flowers are sometimes blasted by a late frost. This is an extremely handsome shrub, but like all magnolias must be planted carefully and the brittle roots never exposed to the sun and wind. For related plants see Questions 18 and 175.

907. Why was the golden bell named Forsythia?   About the time that the different kinds of golden bell were being discovered in China and Japan, William Forsyth was perhaps the most noted horticulturist in London. To honor him these outstanding shrubs were named *Forsythia* and many gardeners prefer that name to golden bell. They are shrubs six to eight feet high, with opposite, lance-shaped leaves that are three to five inches long. Just before the leaves expand the twigs are covered with a profusion of yellow flowers that have four strap-shaped petals. Of the many kinds of forsythia now available, by far the best is a hybrid known as *Forsythia intermedia spectabilis.* Its flowers are larger and more profuse than those of any other.

908. What is the Japanese flowering quince? It is not related to the tree that bears the fruit, as this is an ornamental shrub (*Chaenomeles lagenaria*), originally a native of China, but widely grown in Japan and here for ornament. It is a somewhat spiny shrub, four to six feet high with alternate, oblongish leaves, two to three inches long and finely toothed. Before the leaves expand, usually in March or April, the twigs bear rather showy, scarlet flowers about one and a half inches wide, which are solitary or in small clusters. The fruit is yellowish, about two inches long and is used by some in preserves. Its early flowering and ability to stand considerable clipping make it fine for informal hedges.

909. What native shrub bears yellow flowers long before the leaves expand? The very aromatic spicebush (*Lindera Benzoin*), often called spicewood or Benjamin-bush, is covered with tiny yellow flowers, borne on naked twigs weeks before the leaves expand. It is found in moist thickets in the eastern United States and grows eight to fifteen feet high. The leaves are alternate, wedge-shaped at the base, three to five inches long. The flowers are small, yellow, crowded on the bare twigs in close, essentially stalkless clusters. This native shrub is not related to the East Indian tree that yields the drug known as benzoin, although it is almost as aromatic.

Flowering Shrubs That Bloom with the Expansion of the Leaves, or after This, Usually in May or June (Arranged in the Approximate Order of Blooming)

910. Does the shadbush bloom about the time that shad come up the rivers? Not exactly, but the bloom of this shrub so nearly coincides with the appearance of shad that the names shadbush and shadblow seem perfectly appropriate. There are several kinds, all belonging to the group known as *Amelanchier,* and there are one or two which are small trees. Mostly, however, they are medium-sized shrubs, the white flowers of which bloom just as the leaves expand, usually in mid-April. There are five rather narrow petals. The fruit is like a tiny red apple.

911. What is the red chokeberry?   A small native shrub with a superficial resemblance to the shadblow but with a distinctive difference to the sharp-eyed. The shadblow has narrow petals while the red chokeberry (*Aronia arbutifolia*) has rounded petals and black anthers, the prolongation of the stamen. (See Question 3.) The flowers hence look like apple blossoms, and flower just as the leaves expand. The fruit is small, pear-shaped, red, and quite acid. The shrub is common in thickets throughout the eastern states.

912. What flowering shrub was thought to be the "laurel" of the ancient Greeks?   It is a disputed point among the experts as to what was the "laurel" used by the Greeks as a symbol of victory in war or the athletic games. Many think it was the spurge laurel (*Daphne Laureola*), and Linnaeus must have thought so or he would not have named it *Laureola,* which means laurel. It is a low, evergreen shrub from southern Europe, never over thirty inches high, with alternate oblongish leaves, two to three inches long, and narrowed at the base. The flowers are greenish-yellow, in close, stalkless clusters; blooming in April and practically scentless. The other candidate as the "laurel" of the ancients is *Laurus nobilis,* a much larger shrub or small tree with larger, evergreen leaves.

913. What is the beauty-bush?   A charming little flowering shrub (*Kolkwitzia amabilis*) from China, much cultivated for its profusion of spring bloom. It was named for a German professor of botany, and *amabilis* means lovable or pleasing which it certainly is. The shrub is four to six feet high, and has opposite, ovalish leaves two to three inches long. The flowers are bell-shaped, about one half of an inch long, crowded in a flat-topped cluster nearly three inches wide, and hence very showy. The flowers are pink, but with a yellow throat. They bloom in May and June.

914. Is the bridal wreath a *Spiraea*?   Yes; there are at least two different species of *Spiraea* to which the name bridal wreath has been applied. The most widely planted is *Spiraea prunifolia plena,* which is perhaps the most popular white-flowered shrub in America, blooming in early May. It came originally from eastern Asia, is four to six feet high and has elliptic leaves one to two inches long. The flowers are very small, white, double, and so numerous as practically to smother the bush. Each flower cluster contains three to six flowers and the cluster is stalkless. For related plants, see Question 97.

915. Some American gardeners still cling to the name pipe-tree for a very fragrant shrub. What is it? In rural Virginia and some other areas you will hear a shrub called the pipe-tree. Such a term is surely a local holdover, slightly garbled, from the name first applied to the lilac when it reached England and was called the blue pipe-flower. For the lilac see Question 596.

916. Are there any other kalmias besides the mountain laurel? Yes; besides the superlative, May-blooming mountain laurel (see Question 185) there is the sheep laurel that blooms a little later. For the sheep laurel see Question 98.

917. Are azaleas and rhododendrons the same? Technically they are regarded by the experts as all belonging to the genus *Rhododendron,* but few amateur gardeners are inclined so to group them. For most azaleas are not evergreen and generally bloom before the predominantly evergreen rhododendrons. For the differences between the two groups, see the next two questions.

918. What is an azalea? One of a group of shrubs that usually drop their leaves (there are a few evergreen exceptions), and often have minute hairs on the leaf margins. The leaves are alternate. There are scores of species, mostly natives of North America or eastern Asia, and these have been extensively hybridized by Dutch and Belgian growers so that there are now hundreds of named forms, usually divided into several classes.

The flowers are always irregular, very showy, and mostly bloom in May, sometimes before the leaves expand. In some forms the stamens protrude beyond the tip of the corolla.

It is impossible here to list named varieties or to assign them to the different classes. For those interested in such a study the best book is *The Azalea Book,* by Frederick P. Lee, sponsored by the American

Horticultural Society, Washington, D.C. (For two native azaleas, see Questions 176 and 177.)

919. What is a rhododendron?   Overwhelmingly evergreen shrubs and trees belonging to the genus *Rhododendron,* mostly blooming later than the azaleas, and the flowers much larger and more showy. The leaves are alternate, practically never with marginal hairs, and in many species the underside is brown and scurfy. The flowers are always slightly irregular, usually crowded in dense trusses and hence about as showy as in any flowering shrub. There are scores of wild species both in North America and in Asia, especially in the Himalayas and in China. For several centuries these have been hybridized so that today there are several hundred horticultural varieties, comprising the finest evergreen shrubs in the world. To list even a fraction of them here is quite impossible; those who want to really study the rhododendron should consult *Rhododendrons and Azaleas* by Clement G. Bowers, issued by The Macmillan Company. (For two native rhododendrons, see Questions 183 and 424.)

920. What shrub has brownish-purple flowers that are spicily fragrant?   (See the Carolina allspice at Question 178.)

921. Is there a native wisteria?   Yes; in the southeastern states there are two wild wisterias, but they do not compare with the Asiatic species. Of the latter, *Wistaria sinensis* is one of the finest. It is a high-climbing woody vine, often reaching the tops of trees or houses. It originated in China, and has compound leaves with usually eleven leaflets, rarely with seven or thirteen. The leaflets are oval or oblong, two and a half to four inches long. The flowers are typically bluish-violet, and pea-like, in drooping clusters that may be eight to twelve inches long. A variety of the closely related Japanese wisteria may have clusters of flowers nearly three feet long. Both sorts have, also, a white variety.

922. Is there a flowering barberry that is an evergreen?   In the exploration of China forty years ago, a great many species of barberry were discovered, some of them evergreen and a good many of them doubtfully hardy in the United States. One of the finest is the wintergreen barberry (*Berberis julianae*), a rather spiny evergreen

shrub four to six feet high, with lustrous green leaves that are also
spiny. The flowers are yellow, in rather close clusters and May-
blooming. The plant is perfectly hardy as far north as New York
City, but not safe inland or north of that. (For a related plant see
Question 17.)

**923. What popular flowering shrub in America lacks a common
name?** After the exploration of eastern Asia in the eighteenth century many handsome shrubs reached Europe and were given the
name *Deutzia,* because Johan van der Deutz, a Dutch patron of
botany had backed the expedition that found them. Ever since they
have been called *Deutzia* and some of them are among the most
popular of flowering shrubs. They may be anywhere from two to fifteen feet high, have opposite leaves and (usually) shreddy bark, and
their small twigs are hollow. The flowers are more or less bell-shaped
and typically white, but pinkish forms are known. They owe their
popularity to their profuse bloom and their ease of culture. They
grow readily in any ordinary garden soil. Most of the fifty species are
Asiatic, but two grow in Mexico.

924. Are two different, white-flowered shrubs known as snowballs?
Yes, and although they are apt to be confused, they need not be.
Both have large globe-like clusters of flowers, hence the name snowball. In both sorts the flowers are completely sterile, and, of course,
produce no seed. The most common snowball is *Viburnum Opulus
sterile,* a Eurasian shrub eight to twelve feet high, with maple-like
leaves that are three to five lobed. It is often called the guelder rose.
The other snowball, usually called the Japanese snowball, is *Viburnum
tomentosum sterile.* It is native to China and Japan and is seven to
ten feet high. Its leaves are entirely unlobed, oval, three to four inches
long and hairy on the underside, and with marginal teeth. Both kinds
bloom in late May or early June.

925. What flower "molests the head in a strange manner"? John
Gerard, in 1597, noted the heavy, almost disturbing odor of the
flower many people call the syringa. Its penetrating, almost cloying
sweetness is anathema to many, but the mock orange (*Philadelphus*)
is grown in thousands of gardens, often under the quite inappropriate
name of syringa, and in spite of the fact that *Syringa* is the correct

Latin name of the lilac. The mock oranges, of which there are several different sorts, are medium-sized shrubs, often with shreddy bark, opposite leaves, and white, waxy, very fragrant flowers suggesting in odor and texture the orange blossom. They are of easy culture in any ordinary garden soil.

926. Has the Japanese rose any relation to a rose?   Nothing whatever, and how this delightful, double-flowered shrub acquired the absurd name of Japanese rose (*Kerria japonica pleniflora*) is a mystery, for it is not native in Japan and is not a rose. Sometimes called Jews' mallow, it is a green-twigged shrub, four to six feet high, called also, and, incorrectly, the Guelder rose, the leaves are alternate, oval and one and a half to four inches long. The flowers are yellow, always much doubled, and bloom in late May or early June. An attractive and easily grown shrub.

Shrubs That Bloom in June and Early Summer

927. What June-flowering shrub is a scrambling vine and a superb ground cover?   The bearberry is a prostrate woody vine with evergreen leaves and small white flowers. It is our finest native ground cover, but difficult to grow. (For notes on its culture see Question 212.)

928. What color are the flowers of the lingon-berry?   This prostrate evergreen shrub, often called the cowberry (*Vaccinium Vitis-Idaea*) is found wild over much of the cooler regions of the north temperate zone. Also called the red whortleberry, joyberry and mountain cranberry, it has tiny oval-shaped leaves and many small pink, urn-shaped flowers that bloom in June, followed by the lingon-berry, which is red, tart, and much used in preserves. The plant is difficult to cultivate, although common in the far North. (For a related plant, see Question 94.)

929. Are the beautyberry and French mulberry the same?   Yes; both these common names apply to a native shrub (*Callicarpa americana*), otherwise called sour-bush or Bermuda mulberry. The latter name as well as French mulberry are merely illustrations of the singularly inappropriate names that get attached to native shrubs, for the plant is not a mulberry and does not come from Bermuda or France. It is four to five feet high, has opposite leaves that are rusty beneath and small flowers that may be bluish, lilac, white, purple or (rarely) red. No one would grow it for its bloom, but in late summer it has beautiful, violet, polished and very showy, berry-like fruits. It is a native of the southeastern states and not reliably hardy above Norfolk, Virginia.

930. What is the state flower of Georgia?   A Chinese rose (*Rosa laevigata*), much naturalized in the South and so commonly (and erroneously) thought to be a native that it is called the Cherokee rose. It is a tall-climbing rose, ten to fifteen feet high, with compound, evergreen leaves that have only three (rarely five) leaflets. The flowers are white, solitary and fragrant. The Cherokee rose is one of the parents of the much finer rose known as Silver Moon.

931. Where did the rose originate?   There are perhaps several hundred species of *Rosa,* which is the Latin name for all the roses. Ever since debauched Romans strewed their banquet halls with rose petals, the flower has been perhaps the most widely cultivated shrub on earth, for its color and especially for the haunting fragrance of its flowers.

The common cultivated roses of today have been derived from centuries of selection and hybridizing, a notable example of which are the varieties which produce attar-of-roses in southern France.

It is almost impossible to describe a "typical" rose, for there *is* none, so great is the variation in the hundreds of wild species and the thousands of horticultural forms, which are those best loved by the gardener. Generally roses are prickly shrubs, always with compound leaves, the leaflets of infinite variation, but often with three to nine leaflets, always with an odd one at the tip. In some species the leaves are evergreen. In the wild species there are nearly always five petals and the flower is followed by the usually red, berry-like fruit, which is the familiar rose hip. Such a skeleton outline of a rose is a vast oversimplification of the real facts and structure of the genus *Rosa.*

There are, for instance only twenty species of wild roses in the eastern United States and a few more in the West. But Europe and especially Asia are far more prolific in wild species of rose than is the New World. Of over seventy-five species of rose known to be in cultivation in this country, more than fifty-two originated in Europe and

Asia. Only fifteen cultivated species are of American origin. The rest have been derived by hybridization.

932. What are the main classes of garden roses?   All of these, instead of having the five petals that are usual in wild roses, have much-doubled and often sterile flowers due to the supression of normal sexual organs. Some enthusiasts claim that there are over four thousand named horticultural forms of the rose. While this may have a tinge of salesmanship, there is certainly a huge number of garden roses, all double-flowered, of all colors but blue and, in some cases these much hybridized forms have lost much of the fragrance of their wild ancestors.

For the convenience of the gardener most cultivated roses have been divided into twelve to fifteen classes. Of these the most important are:

Damask roses: five to eight feet high, mostly pink
Gallica roses: six to eight feet high, pink, red or blush
Bourbon roses: four to five feet high, mostly pink, often blooming again in late summer
Tea roses: three to four feet high, pink or white
China roses: four to five feet high, red or pink
Floribunda roses: scrambling and valuable as an impentrable hedge; small, numerous, red, white, pink or yellow flowers

It must be understood that there are anywhere from dozens to hundreds of roses in each class, so that the gardener had better visit a well-labelled nursery before attempting a selection. In most of the classes there are many climbing roses, some of them superb like Silver Moon or Paul's Scarlet Climber.

933. What is the showiest flowering vine in June?   The very slender woody vine known as *Clematis jackmani,* which is of hybrid origin, has spectacular bloom in late June and may extend even into July. It was derived by crossing two Asiatic species of *Clematis* and is itself the source of several hybrids, some of which have very large flowers that may be purple, red, blue, gray or lavender. It is five to eight feet high, its compound leaves with ovalish leaflets. The flowers are usually in threes, four to six inches wide and very showy. The plants prefer a somewhat alkaline or neutral soil and freedom from wind.

934. What is the nandin?   An attractive Asiatic shrub (*Nandina domestica*) sometimes called sacred or heavenly bamboo, although it has nothing to do with any bamboo. It grows six to eight feet high and has graceful compound leaves, the narrow leaflets extremely handsome in their brilliant red, fall color. The flowers are small, white, the hanging cluster nearly one foot long. The fruit is a red, showy berry. The shrub is not certainly hardy north of Norfolk, Virginia.

935. What summer-flowering shrub is dangerously poisonous?
The juice of the oleander and its seeds are poisonous if eaten. (See Question 483.)

936. Is the mountain cranberry the same as the cranberry?   No, although they are closely related. The mountain cranberry is merely another name for the cowberry, for which see Question 928. For the true cranberry see Question 94.

937. Is the sour-bush the same as the beautyberry?   Yes; the sour-bush is an alternative name for the shrub described in Question 929.

938. Are furze and gorse the same?   Yes; both are widely used common names for a spiny, yellow-flowered European shrub (*Ulex europaeus*), often called the whin in Scotland. It is a twiggy shrub, two to three feet high, its leaves scale-like or reduced to spines. The flowers are pea-like, yellow, fragrant, blooming all year in California, but mostly from June to July in the East. It is difficult to grow except in acid, sandy places.

939. Is there a currant grown for its flowers rather than its fruit?
The golden or flowering currant (*Ribes aureum*) is never grown for its fruit which is indifferent, but is widely grown as an ornamental shrub, four to six feet high. It is native in the western part of North America, has alternate, lobed leaves and a showy cluster of yellow flowers that turn reddish before withering. It is hardy everywhere and is easily grown.

940. What Asiatic shrub is popular in the South for its extremely fragrant flowers?   The tea olive (*Osmanthus fragrans*) is an evergreen shrub, rarely tree-like, and usually not over eight to ten feet high, but in favorable climates sometimes as high as twenty-five feet. The leaves are opposite, somewhat oblong, two to four inches long, without marginal teeth or with only a few. The flowers are small, white, never showy but of entrancing fragrance. The shrub cannot be safely grown in the East, north of Norfolk, Virginia. Because of its fragrance, it is often called sweet olive. It is not related to the true olive.

941. The fruit of what native white-flowered shrub is used to make wine? The dark, purplish-black berries of the elder or elderberry (*Sambucus canadensis*) were once widely used to make a wine for those who had none better. The shrub is native in North America, scarcely over ten feet high and thrives in moist places. The leaves are opposite, compound, the seven short-stalked leaflets two and a half to six inches long. The flowers are very small, white, and crowded in a flat-topped cluster that is nearly four inches wide. The fruit is about one-sixth of an inch thick, but very numerous.

942. What beautiful Chinese flowering shrub has no common name? In June most gardens have a great show of the usually pink flowers of *Weigela florida,* a shrub seven to ten feet high, with opposite, oblong-shaped leaves that are three to four and a half inches long and toothed. The flowers are mostly in clusters of one to three, the corolla slightly irregular but generally funnel-shaped, about two inches long, typically pink, although dark red and white forms also common. It was named in honor of C. E. Weigel, a German physician.

943. What is the Bermuda mulberry? An attractive flowering shrub that does not come from Bermuda and is not a mulberry. It is the beautyberry and is referred to in Question 929.

944. Are the foxberry and red whortleberry the same? Yes; both are common names for the cowberry. (see Question 928.)

Midsummer and Fall-flowering Shrubs

945. What is the difference between a flowering shrub and a flowering woody vine? Technically there is none; the experts agree that a woody vine is a shrub that climbs. Many gardeners take little notice of such a definition as they well know that vines like the Dutchman's-pipe (see Question 10) or *Clematis jackmani* (see Question 933) and many others have uses for covering porches that no shrub can supply.

Gardeners also know, or should, the difference between a woody vine and annual ones like the morning-glory (see Question 638) or nasturtium (see Question 550), for these annual vines die down to the ground each winter, while woody vines have persistent woody stems above the ground like any other shrub, which they technically are.

There are three woody vines that bloom in midsummer or later and these are noted at the next three questions.

946. What is the traveler's-joy?   A high-climbing, European woody vine, often reaching a height of twenty-five feet, also called the withy-wind (*Clematis Vitalba*). Its compound leaf has usually five ovalish leaflets that are one and a half to four inches long and coarsely toothed or even three-lobed. The flowers are only slightly fragrant, white, about one inch wide, in rather showy clusters, followed by long, plumely fruit, hence its other name of old man's-beard.

947. Is there a native clematis also called old man's-beard?   Yes; our native woodbine (*Clematis virginiana*) is common in the eastern states and scrambles over shrubs or climbs trees, but not usually over fifteen feet high. Often called virgin's-bower or love-vine, it has compound leaves, comprising three ovalish leaflets that are two and a half to four inches long and coarsely toothed. The flowers are white, about one inch wide, in showy clusters, the male and female flowers on separate plants. The fruit is plumey. It flowers in late summer and early fall.

948. What is the silver-lace vine?   An extraordinarily showy late-blooming Chinese vine, called also Chinese fleece-vine (*Polygonum auberti*) and sometimes simply lace-vine. It grows twenty-five to forty feet high, has alternate, lance-shaped leaves, and a mass of tiny white or greenish-white flowers in erect or hanging clusters. It is extremely showy after nearly all vines are through flowering. It was named in honor of Pere G. Aubert, a French missionary in China.

949. Is the heather really Scotch?   Years ago Sir Harry Lauder made the "bonny, bonny heather" so popular that many of his millions of admirers thought that the heather was confined to Scotland. Actually heather (*Calluna vulgaris*), often called ling, stretches from England, all through northern Europe and into higher elevations in Asia Minor. It is a low, evergreen shrub, apparently leafless, but its tiny leaves actually hug the twigs. The flowers are typically purple or pink, very small, and drooping in terminal clusters. The corolla may not be more than one-fifth of an inch long, and is persistent after being in full bloom. It requires an acid, sandy soil and does better in the North than southward. The plant is rarely over one foot high.

950. What blue-flowered shrub can be trained against a wall? The blue blossom is often so trained in England and California and may be south of Norfolk, Virginia. (See Question 432.)

951. Can the fragrant gardenia of the florists be grown outdoors? It is commonly so grown from Norfolk, Virginia, throughout the South. It was originally thought to come from South Africa and was called the Cape jasmine, from its spicy, heavy fragrance. It was named *Gardenia jasminoides,* in honor of Dr. Alexander Garden of Charleston, South Carolina, a friend of Linnaeus; and the *jasminoides* was certainly appropriate on account of its jasmine-like fragrance. It is a Chinese evergreen shrub, two to five feet high with opposite, lance-shaped leaves that are three to four inches long, thick and leathery. The flowers are white, waxy, solitary, two and a half to three inches wide and very fragrant. The only variety of it safe for cultivation outdoors is the variety *fortuniana,* which is more hardy than the typical florists gardenia.

952. Can the jasmine of Cleopatra and the poets be grown outdoors? Cleopatra drenched the sails of her ship with the perfume of the jasmine so that the very "winds were lovesick." That was in Egypt and the jasmine (*Jasminum officinale*) which is native from Persia to southern China, is now much grown in our South, where it is often called jessamine. It is probably the most fragrant shrub on earth, with weak stems that are almost vine-like and need support, as they may reach forty feet in height. It has compound, opposite leaves, the five to seven ovalish leaflets about one and a half to two and a half inches long. The flowers are small, white, and of such alluring fragrance that a Persian poet wrote:

Art thou, then, musk or ambergris, I said
That by thy scent my soul is ravished.

The jasmine cannot be safely grown outdoors north of Norfolk,
Virginia.

953. What is Abelia grandiflora?   An extremely valuable flowering
shrub of hybrid origin, its parents certainly Asiatic, that stays in
bloom from July to frost. It is half-evergreen, grows three to five feet
high and has opposite, nearly stalkless, oval leaves that are about
one inch long. Flowers very numerous, bell-shaped, about three-
fourths of an inch long. In the South it is practically evergreen and
is perfectly hardy up to coastal Massachusetts. It was named in honor
of Dr. Clarke Abel, physician at the British Embassy in China in 1817.

954. Which is the best butterfly-bush for the amateur gardener?
The orange-eye butterfly-bush (*Buddleia davidi*) from China is the
hardiest and most easily grown of these showy shrubs. It grows four
to ten feet high and has opposite, lance-shaped leaves, six to nine
inches long, finely toothed and white-felty beneath. The flowers are
small, fragrant, lilac, but orange at the throat in very showy, nodding
clusters five to twelve inches long; it blooms from July to frost. It is
sometimes called summer lilac. It is hardy as far north as Philadelphia,
and in sheltered places somewhat north of it. If it winter-kills, next
season's growth will usually provide adequate bloom.

955. Are there two flowers known as old man's beard?   Yes; one
is the traveler's-joy (see Question 946); the other is our native woodbine for which see Question 947.

956. What is the finest of all summer-blooming shrubs?   It is
fairly sure that anyone south of Wilmington, Delaware, would vote
for the crape myrtle (*Lagerstroemia indica*), a magnificent Chinese
shrub two to thirty feet high. It usually has opposite, nearly stalkless,
oblongish leaves, one to two inches long, without marginal teeth.
The flowers are normally pink (red or white in some varieties), about
one and a half inches wide, in immense, showy trusses, so profuse
that they practically hide most of the foliage. It frequently winter-kills
in exposed places, but new shoots bloom the following season. It is

not reliably hardy much north of Wilmington, Delaware. It was named by Linnaeus in honor of his friend Magnus Lagerstroem of Gothenberg, Sweden.

957. What native, white-flowered shrub provides midsummer fragrance? The sweet pepperbush (*Clethra alnifolia*) is certainly one of the most fragrant of all summer-blooming shrubs in the East. Called also summer-sweet and spiked alder, it does not grow higher than nine feet, and is often half this. The leaves are alternate, oblongish, two and a half to five inches long, toothed and short-stalked. The flowers are small, white, very fragrant, in erect, terminal clusters that are nearly five inches long. It prefers a moist, somewhat acid soil and is hardy everywhere.

958. What *Hibiscus* is a summer-blooming shrub? Most species of *Hibiscus* are annual or perennial plants (see Questions 84 and 635) but a showy Chinese plant called rose-of-Sharon (*Hibiscus syriacus*) is a summer-blooming shrub, five to fifteen feet high. The leaves are alternate, ovalish, two to five inches long, sharply toothed and sometimes three-lobed or unlobed, often with both sorts of leaves on the same bush. The flowers are broadly bell-shaped, three to five inches long, solitary, red, purple, violet or white. It is hardy everywhere and there are fine white, double-flowered varieties. It is sometimes called shrubby althaea, a singularly inappropriate name, for *Althaea* is the correct name of the hollyhock. For another rose-of-Sharon, quite unrelated to this one, see Question 797.

959. What is hydrangea P.G. or pee gee? The last two designations are florists' slang, and appear in many nursery catalogs standing for *Hydrangea paniculata grandiflora,* which is perhaps the most widely cultivated shrub in the country. So common that it is anathema to some, it is an extremely hardy Asiatic shrub, often tree-like and eight to twenty-five feet high. The leaves are opposite, ovalish, three to five inches long and wedge-shaped at the base. The flowers are almost all sterile, white at first, but ultimately pink or purple and long persistent. They are borne in a stout, very floriferous, pyramidal truss, eight to twelve inches long, and these are numerous enough to make the shrub very showy from late summer well into the fall. It is hardy everywhere and thrives vigorously, even under considerable abuse.

960. What blue-flowered shrub is called blue spirea?   A beautiful Asiatic, September-blooming shrub was unfortunately called blue spirea, although it has nothing to do with the true *Spiraea,* for which see Questions 97 and 914. The fall-flowering blue spirea (*Caryopteris incana*) is three to five feet high and is a grayish-hairy shrub with opposite, ovalish, coarsely-toothed leaves, two to three inches long. The flowers are small, blue, in dense, showy clusters at the leaf-joints. From its conspicuously protruding stamens the plant is sometimes known as bluebeard. It is not entirely hardy north of Wilmington, Delaware, but is often grown northward where it winter-kills, but sends up flowering shoots the following season.

VIII. SOME TROPICAL AND
SUBTROPICAL FLOWERS

961. Do tropical flowers differ from those found in the temperate zones? Technically they do not, for the fundamental structure of flowers, as outlined in Questions 1–4, does not change with increased and continuous heat, heavy rainfall and high humidity.

What changes enormously, especially in the rain-forests of South America, Africa, Malaya and Java, is the tremendous diversity of species, the high incidence of trees and shrubs and the huge amount of tree-perching plants, known technically as epiphytes. Such dense jungles have far more species of plants than similar areas in the temperate zones, and, incidentally, make sensational writers talk about such places as being a "green hell." From considerable familiarity with such rain-forests, I prefer W. H. Hudson's *Green Mansions*.

In a book like this it is obviously impossible to give an adequate idea of such conditions or to make a significant selection from among the thousands of different flowers that grow in these forests.

Perhaps the best alternative is to select some of them that are familiar to nearly everyone, for the plants that bear them are rather common in cultivation, mostly in greenhouses or, on a gigantic scale, on tropical plantations. Such, for instance, is the pineapple in Hawaii.

Tropical flowers that it is possible to mention here can be roughly divided into those that grow on shrubs and trees (see Questions 962–982) and the flowers found on herbaceous plants (see Questions 983–1001).

TROPICAL FLOWERS THAT GROW ON TREES, SHRUBS AND WOODY VINES

962. What tropical flower did our ambassador to Mexico bring to the United States? Somewhere in tropical America, and quite possibly from lowland Mexico, there grows a shrub now known throughout the world as a Christmas plant. In 1828 Dr. J. R. Poinsett, our ambassador there, brought a few plants here, and appropriately enough its common name is now poinsettia (*Euphorbia pulcherrima*).

No Christmas plant is so popular as the poinsettia (*Euphorbia pulcherrima*), but few survive in the average living room.

Today it is mostly grown as a greenhouse pot plant, which usually languishes in the average home a few days or weeks after Christmas, for it needs continuous heat and moisture. Normally it is a shrub eight to twelve feet high, but as trained for the florists trade, mostly two to three feet. Its ovalish leaves are three to six inches long, shallowly lobed, and towards the top of the plant, gorgeously colored, vermilion or scarlet. It is for these upper leaves (bracts) that the plant is grown as the true flowers are greenish-yellow and negligible. It is almost impossible to grow poinsettias in the average living room, and one expert writes of gift plants that "you'll be smart to discard them." For related plants see Questions 219, 261, 629 and 762.

963. What is the queen-of-the-night?   When the Spaniards conquered Mexico they took there and ultimately to southern California a West Indian shrub since called night jasmine or queen-of-the-night (*Cestrum nocturnum*). It is a rather inconspicuous shrub, six to nine feet high, and no one would grow it for the beauty of its small, greenish-white flowers, which have little or no odor by day. But at night, especially if it is damp and windless, it has such an enticing fragrance that the Mexicans call it *dama de noche*.

964. What Brazilian tree has flowers nearly a foot long?   The angel's-trumpet (*Datura suaveolens*) is a medium-sized Brazilian shrub ten to fifteen feet high, with alternate, very large leaves that are unpleasantly scented when crushed. The leaves are nearly twelve inches long. The flowers are solitary, nodding, trumpet-shaped, white and nearly one foot long. This is an extremely handsome shrub locally called floripondio.

965. What color are the flowers of the orchid tree?   The common name is a misnomer for there are no trees that bear orchids. But the name is perhaps permissable, for the flowers are highly irregular, very showy, lavender or purple and clustered at the leaf-joints. It is a tree, ten to twenty-five feet high, a native of Indo-China, usually and more correctly called mountain ebony (*Bauhinia variegata*), and commonly planted in Florida. It has either simple leaves with two oblique lobes, or compound leaves with two oblique leaflets. *Bauhinia* was named for the brothers John and Caspar Bauhin, noted European botanists, the twin leaflets suggesting the two brothers.

966. What is the "blue spiral" of the florists?   The young, leafy twigs of an Australian gum tree (*Eucalyptus pulverulenta*) which are bluish-green or bluish-gray, the opposite, essentially stalkless leaves roundish and about two and a half inches wide. The twigs are slightly twisted, hence the spiral appearance. It is a tree not over thirty feet high, much cultivated in California for the production of the young twigs which are shipped East in great numbers for the florist trade. The flowers are white, and are borne in clusters of three at the leaf joints.

967. What color are the flowers of the gold-dust tree?   This familiar greenhouse shrub (*Aucuba japonica variegata*) is also grown outdoors in the south, and called by some the Japanese laurel, although it grows wild in Eastern Asia. It is an evergreen shrub, four to fifteen feet high, its opposite leaves longish-oval, pointed, four to eight inches long, and peppered with yellow spots. The plant is grown for its handsome foliage. The flowers grow with the male on one plant and the female on another, pinkish-red and rather small. Only if male and female plants are in close proximity will the female flower produce the brilliant scarlet berries.

968. Where does the florists' fuchsia come from?   All the shrubby species of *Fuchsia* come from South America or Central America, but the plant known to everyone from its frequency as a pot plant in florists' windows is a hybrid. One of its parents is Mexican, the other is wild from Peru southward. As usually grown, it is a pot plant, two to three feet high, its opposite leaves ovalish and two to two and a half inches long. The flowers are always nodding, very showy, red, blue, purple or white and somewhat tubular. It was named in honor of Dr. Leonhard Fuchs, a German physician, who published a book of woodcuts of plants.

969. What is the bottle-brush?   A splended Australian tree, but usually a shrub in California where it is much cultivated; somewhat less so along the Gulf Coast, where it thrives on beach fronts. As

Only for subtropical or tropical regions is the gorgeous Australian bottle-brush (*Callistemon lanceolatus*) with its scarlet flowers in clusters like a bottle brush.

cultivated it is ten to twenty feet high, shrubby, and christened *Callistemon lanceolatus*. The first name is particularly appropriate, for it means beautiful stamens. It is for these that the plant is so popular as the small, scarlet flowers are crowded in a dense spike suggesting a bottle-brush, from which protrude the numerous stamens, for all the world like scarlet bristles of a brush.

970. Where does the silver tree come from?   This common plant in greenhouses does not thrive well in California where it was brought from Table Mountain, South Africa. There it is extremely limited in distribution, but has since gone all over the subtropical world. Both its Latin names describe it, for *Leucodendron argenteum* mean quite literally a silvery tree, which it is. In the wild it is never over thirty feet high, often less and short-lived in cultivation. Its foliage and young twigs are covered with silky, white or silvery hairs and one expert writes that it is "the whitest of all trees." Its alternate leaves are lance-shaped and about three to five inches long. The male and female flowers grow on separate trees and are generally negligible.

971. Is the silk oak really an oak tree?   No one would think so if he saw it in a florist's shop in the only form that most people ever see this large Australian forest tree. The silk oak (*Grevillea robusta*) grows one hundred to one hundred and fifty feet high in its native home, but here it is practically always a greenhouse pot plant two to four feet high. Only in California and along the Gulf Coast is it used as a valuable street tree. In northern greenhouses it is grown for its extremely handsome foliage. The leaves are twice divided into graceful, feathery, fern-like segments. The flowers (rarely produced in the greenhouse) are orange, borne in one-sided, rather showy clusters. In Australia, because the wood suggests oak, it is called silk oak but is not related to real oaks. The under side of the leaf segments are a little silky. It is widely grown in greenhouses for its very fine foliage.

972. What blue-flowered shrub was supposed to be a remedy for lead poisoning?   The Romans thought that certain plants had this medicinal property and christened them *Plumbago,* from the Latin *plumbum* or lead. One of the finest is the leadwort (*Plumbago capensis*) from South Africa, much grown in greenhouses and popular outdoors in California, where it is remarkably resistant to drought. It is a sprawling shrub, five to eight feet high, with alternate, thin, lance-shaped leaves, two to three inches long. The flowers are pale azure blue, tubular, about one and a half inches long, borne in terminal clusters.

973. What is the frangipani?   A beautiful tropical American shrubby tree (*Plumeria rubra*) with a milky juice and stunning red

The Romans thought *Plumbago capensis* was useful against lead poisoning, but it is grown in California for its pale blue flowers.

or pink flowers. It grows ten to fifteen feet high, has a stout stem or trunk and oblong, leathery leaves twelve to sixteen inches long. The flowers are tubular, the corolla slightly twisted, very fragrant (hence its other name of red jasmine), red or pink, borne in a terminal, showy cluster. It is much grown in southern Florida and is widely planted in India where it is called the temple tree. It was named in honor of Charles Plumier, a French botanist.

974. What Asiatic flowering shrub is much used for hedges in California?   The tobira is a Japanese name for *Pittosporum Tobira,* a tender shrub from the subtropical parts of China and Japan. It grows six to fifteen feet high and has thick, evergreen, alternate, leaves that are broader at the tip, three to four inches long. The flowers are white, fragrant, about one-half of an inch long, and are borne in erect terminal clusters. There is also a form with white-splotched leaves. It is easily sheared and a popular hedge and lawn shrub in California.

975. What New Zealand shrubs have all but dominated California gardens?   In the South Island of New Zealand there are perhaps one hundred species of gorgeously flowered trees and shrubs belonging to the group known as *Veronica* of which we have a few low herbs in the eastern states. But the New Zealand species, of which at least a dozen have reached California, are far more showy than any native sort. Those in Pacific Coast gardens are mostly shrubs three to eight feet high, with opposite leaves below but alternate towards the top of the plant. The flowers are prevailingly blue (white or red ones are known), not large but in extremely showy, profuse terminal clusters. For a related native *Veronica,* see Question 784.

976. What Mexican flowering vine has gone all over the tropical world? To judge by its many common names, the coral vine or corallita (*Antigonon leptopus*) must be the most popular of all tropical vines. It is also called mountain rose, pink vine and Confederate vine in the deep South where it is widely grown. It climbs up to thirty feet high, is rampant and bears hundreds of small flowers in drooping clusters borne at the leaf joints. The flowers are prevailingly pink, rarely white. The vine covers porches and fences with astonishing speed, but cannot be grown in any frosty region.

977. What universally grown tropical vine has no common name? Louis Antoine de Bougainville, who fought in our American Revolution and was the first French navigator to sail around the world, was honored by having named for him a Brazilian woody vine ever since known as *Bougainvillaea.* It has completely captured the tropical and subtropical world, and festoons many California houses. It is a high-climbing vine, often reaching fifty feet by virtue of its many recurved prickles. The leaves are alternate and ovalish. The flower clusters very showy, but most of the color comes from the leaf-like bracts that are beneath the real flowers. These bracts are pink or red and quite persistent, so that the vine is a glorious sight for weeks or even months in the tropics.

978. What is the "wooden rose"? Of course there is none, but the name is florists' jargon for the woody pod of a morning-glory from Ceylon (*Ipomoea tuberosa*). It is a perennial vine, its leaves nearly eight inches wide and divided into five to seven narrow segments. The flowers are funnel-shaped and yellow. The fruit is a woody pod, ultimately splitting and with its adjacent parts forming a "wooden rose," two and a half to four inches wide. It is cultivated in most tropi-

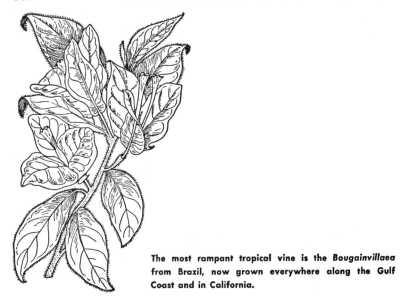

The most rampant tropical vine is the *Bougainvillaea* from Brazil, now grown everywhere along the Gulf Coast and in California.

cal countries, but is virtually unknown here except for imported "wooden roses," often from Hawaii.

979. What beautiful flowering vine from Chile was named for the daughter of a French artillery officer in Martinique?   Marie Josephe Tascher de la Pagerie, who ultimately married Napoleon and became the Empress Josephine, was so honored by having the Chilean bell-flower christened *Lapageria rosea.* It is grown outdoors along the Pacific Coast and is a high-climbing vine with alternate leathery, three-veined leaves. The flowers are trumpet-shaped, three to four inches long, solitary or in clusters of three to four, rose-pink and showy.

980. What fragrant tropical vine is best suited to house culture? The waxplant (*Hoya carnosa*) which grows wild from tropical Asia to northern Australia does rather well if the room is kept reasonably warm and moist. It is a milky-juiced vine, six to ten feet high, with very thick, opposite leaves, two to four inches long, toothless and fleshy. The flowers are fragrant, white with a pink center, wax-like, about one-half of an inch wide, in nearly stalkless clusters at the leaf joints. It is grown outdoors in warm regions along the Gulf Coast and California.

981. What is the showiest yellow-flowered tropical vine? It is probably the golden trumpet (*Allamanda cathartica hendersoni*) a Brazilian woody vine often climbing as high as forty feet. The leaves are opposite, ovalish, glossy green, at about six inches long. The flowers are yellow, numerous, nearly five inches wide, and slightly twisted. The milky juice of this vine is poisonous. It can only be grown in very warm regions.

982. Are the pink vine and the Confederate vine the same? Yes; both are alternative names for the coral vine. (See Question 976.)

Tropical Flowers from Herbaceous Plants

983. How do tropical herbaceous plants differ from tropical trees and shrubs and from herbaceous plants of temperate regions? From all tropical trees and shrubs, the herbaceous plants differ in having fleshy, not woody stems. They are thus like the herbaceous plants of the temperate zone, but with one fundamental difference. Temperate zone plants die down to the ground during winter and produce a new crop of leaves and flowers the following spring. Tropical herbaceous plants never have to do this and are thus in more or less continuous growth, which means that they may be in flower in the middle of our winter.

984. Does the century plant bloom only after one hundred years? No, and there is no authentic record that any century plant even lives that long. The common century plant (*Agave americana*) is a huge stemless, succulent plant; its basal rosette of fleshy leaves may at maturity be six to eight feet wide. The leaves are very thick, five to six feet long, with stout, recurved marginal spines and a sharp-pointed tip. The plant flowers only once, any time after ten to fifteen years, and then dies, but before doing so produces several young plants to perpetuate itself. The flowering stalk is slender, twenty-five to forty feet high, and at and near the summit bears a cluster of greenish-yellow flowers. It has over 250 relatives, all from tropical America; and the common century plant is often, incorrectly, called American aloe.

985. What is the sensitive plant? Visitors to southern Florida and even more so to tropical America are often astounded to find a low plant so sensitive that it appears to collapse if touched even gently. This is the famous sensitive plant (*Mimosa pudica*) which is often

The highly sensitive leaves of the sensitive plant (*Mimosa pudica*) are more interesting than its rather small, rose-purple flowers.

called humble plant because of its propensity to collapse if touched. It is a low, woody perennial with twice compound leaves and many leaflets. It is these that almost instantaneously react by closing up when touched, a purely physiological response, for the plant has no "nerves" as many have implied. The flowers are rose-purple in small, ball-like clusters.

986. Does the rex begonia bear any flowers? This, one of the most popular house plants, and in nearly every greenhouse, is a weak-stemmed herb, originally from Assam, but now found in many horticultural varieties. It is grown mostly for the unique colored markings on its rather large leaves at the end of a long, shaggy leaf stalk. The leaves are blotched, marbled with metallic markings on the upper surface, nearly always red beneath. If the greenhouse is fairly warm and the air moist, it produces rose-pink flowers that are about one and a half inches wide. It is sometimes, but incorrectly, called beefsteak geranium.

987. Does the night-blooming cereus ever bloom in the daytime?
No. Many tropical cacti are night blooming, but one of the most
famous is a scrambling, spiny, leafless Mexican cactus (*Selenicereus
pteranthus*), its four-to-six-angled stems about one and a half inches

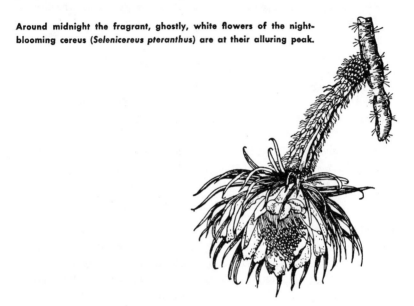

Around midnight the fragrant, ghostly, white flowers of the night-
blooming cereus (*Selenicereus pteranthus*) are at their alluring peak.

thick, the spines solitary or in clusters of two to four. The flowers are
very fragrant, trumpet-shaped, nearly twelve inches long and ghostly
white. It starts opening around 10 P.M., is fully opened about midnight and gradually withers about dawn. Watching it is a nocturnal
delight. The plant can only be grown in the greenhouse, except in the
far South.

988. Where did the florist's cineraria come from?   On the wild,
rocky mountains of the Canary Islands, less than a hundred miles
from the coast of Africa, there are over two hundred flowers known
nowhere else. One of them gave rise to the florist's cineraria (*Senecio
cruentus*), a perennial herb now found in several varieties. It has oval-
shaped, large and long-stalked leaves, sometimes covered with white-
woolly hairs, the margins wavy and toothed. The flowers are daisy-like,
prevailingly blue (but of nearly all colors but yellow in some varieties),

borne in a showy truss standing well above the foliage. It is a relative of one of the dusty millers, for which see Question 792.

989. Why was the shrimp plant so called?   Perhaps this relatively inappropriate name was rather recently coined to suggest the flowering cluster of a Mexican perennial (*Beloperone guttata*). It grows twelve to eighteen inches high and has opposite, somewhat oval leaves one and a half to two and a half inches long. The terminal flower cluster is beset with a series of reddish-brown miniature leaves (bracts) between which are borne the tubular, white but purple-spotted flowers that are about one and a half inches long. The whole cluster is rather showy and its color is shrimp-like.

990. Can the florist's cyclamen be grown outdoors?   Only in the South and in California. There is a relatively hardy cyclamen, for which see Question 824. The florist's cyclamen is a tuberous-rooted perennial growing wild from Greece to Syria and, in the North, must be grown in a cool greenhouse. It was named *Cyclamen indicum* from the mistaken notion that it was native in India. It is a stemless herb, with roundish or heart-shaped leaves about two and a half inches wide, the marginal teeth blunt. The flower is about two and a half inches wide, its segments contorted and with recurved tips; usually white or rose-pink, but dark purple at the mouth. The flowers are solitary at the ends of stalks six to eight inches high.

991. Why did the Dutch suggest the name baboon-flower for a South African plant?   When the Dutch controlled South Africa, they found the bulbs of a beautiful, iris-like flower were eaten by baboons and so they called it baboon-root or baboon-flower. From the Dutch word for baboon came the Latin *Babiana stricta*. It has basal, sword-shaped leaves. Over-topping these and about eight to twelve inches high, are the spiky clusters of usually red flowers (lilac, blue or yellow in some horticultural varieties). The plant can only be grown in the cool greenhouse.

992. What is the most fragrant flower to come from South Africa?
The christener of *Freesia refracta*, which has no common name, wished to honor one of his pupils, F. H. T. Freese, in naming this most fragrant bulbous plant to come out of South Africa. It can be grown

only in the greenhouse and is a familiar sight in any florist shop in winter. The plant has a zigzag stem eighteen to twenty inches high and long, narrow sword-shaped or even grass-like leaves. The flowers are tubular yellow (rarely white) about two inches long and borne in rather sparse clusters but of highly enticing fragrance.

993. South Africa has furnished us with many tropical or subtropical flowers; what is the most widely grown? The common garden geranium which is second cousin to some of our native wild flowers (see Questions 141 and 730) but belongs to the group known as *Pelargonium,* of which there are over 250 kinds in South Africa. It is a tender, fleshy plant two to four feet high, never surviving outdoors over a northern winter. The leaves are roundish, two to four inches wide, somewhat lobed and toothed. The flowers (in the modern varieties) come in a dense showy cluster, three to four inches wide, are prevailingly pink, red or white. Some householders winter the stems by hanging them upside down in a cool cellar, and replanting these in the spring after all danger of frost is over. For the rose geranium see Question 531.

994. Is the bird-of-paradise flower from South Africa? Yes; from the warmer parts of it came the exotic, very beautiful flower often seen in florist shops and always rather expensive. It was named *Strelitzia reginae* in honor of Queen Charlotte Sophia of the Mecklenburg-Strelitz family and wife of King George III. It is like a miniature banana plant, to which it is closely related, and does not grow over three feet high, with banana-like leaves about one and a half feet long and about six inches wide. The flowers are orange-yellow and very showy, having a blue tongue and borne between handsome boat-shaped, purple bracts. It is an extremely striking flower, often five to seven inches wide, the bracts often eight inches long. It can only be grown in a moist, warm greenhouse.

995. What is the most popular house plant ever to come from tropical Africa? The African violet (*Saintpaulia ionantha*) is, of course, not a violet, but that name is almost as common as the cultivation of the plant. It is a stemless perennial, found years ago near Zanzibar by a German, Baron Walter von Saint Paul. It has a basal rosette of nearly round leaves with shallow teeth and is covered with soft hairs.

The bird-of-paradise flower (*Strelitzia reginae*) from South Africa, is a showy and expensive flower in good florist shops.

The flowers are two to eight in a cluster, the corolla about one inch wide, and typically violet. The plant has become so popular that there are scores (some think hundreds) of varieties that may be white, red, or salmon, and some of them with fringed flowers. It is of comparatively easy culture in the house and is sometimes called Usambara violet.

996. Is the calla lily the same as the water arum?   No; but they are first or second cousins and their names are apt to be confusing. Our water arum is technically called *Calla palustris,* and is described at Question 76. But the calla lily (*Zantedeschia aethiopica*) comes from Africa and is common in the florist shops. It is a stout herb, eighteen to thirty inches high, with arrowhead shaped leaves that may be fifteen inches long and half as wide. The flower is solitary, brilliantly white, six to nine inches long, its tip prolonged into a sharp point. The plant needs greenhouse culture except in mild climates.

997. Is there a leopard lily from Africa that is a first class house plant?   Scarcely any plant will stand so much neglect and abuse as one of the bowstring hemps from Africa, called by the florists snake plant (*Sansevieria thyrsiflora*), more properly called leopard lily. It is a stiff-leaved perennial, the fiber from its leaves used by the native for making bow-strings. The leaves are about eighteen inches long, three and a half inches wide, flat, thick, banded with pale green, the margins yellow. The flowers are greenish-yellow, in a cluster ten to twelve inches high, often wanting in house plants, but with care it often blooms in the house in August. It will stand no frost.

998. What florist's flower is called slipperwort?   A beautiful yellow-flowered Chilean herb (*Calceolaria crenatiflora*) is much grown by florists for its winter bloom. It grows one to two feet high, its leaves opposite, the lower ones four to seven inches long, the upper much smaller and stalkless. The flowers are slipper-shaped, nearly one inch long, yellow but with orange-brown spots. They are borne in an irregular cluster that may be a little one-sided and is very handsome. They are best grown in a cool greenhouse that is kept between 45° and 50°F.

999. What tropical flower was named for Queen Victoria?   In the hot steaming valley of the Amazon River are many quiet lagoons in

The royal water lily (*Victoria regia*) has floating leaves that will
support a child and the largest aquatic flower on earth.

which grows the largest water lily in the world. Named *Victoria regia,* its immense floating leaves are round, three to six feet wide, the rims or upturned margins two to four inches high, so that the leaf looks like a huge floating dish; hence its other name of water platter. It is also called the royal water lily, perhaps because its large white, floating flower may be seven to ten inches wide. It turns a dull red the second day after opening, and then withers. It is difficult to grow unless a heated pool can be kept between 75° and 85°F throughout the growing season, and the roots must be in a greenhouse over the winter. Even with this attention it is difficult to force it into flower in the North.

1000. Where does the flamingo flower grow wild?   This showy florist's flower (*Anthurium scherzerianum*) grows in the humid forests of Central America. It is apt to sprawl and has thick, leathery, oblong-ish leaves, six to eight inches long and about two inches wide. What is usually called the flower is like a gorgeously colored replica of our Jack-in-the-pulpit. The central "Jack" is coiled and yellow, surrounded by a brilliantly scarlet "pulpit" about three inches long. Some varieties have white or variously colored "pulpits." It can be grown only in a warm, moist greenhouse.

1001. Do we ever eat a tropical flower?   Not quite, but we find the abortive flower cluster of the pineapple (*Ananas comosus*) rather delicious. Its original home was almost certainly in the Amazon Valley, although its wild ancestor is unknown, as the Indians had developed several varieties long before the Conquest. The structure of a pineapple is one of the most interesting in the world of tropical plants. What we call the "fruit" is the thickened, fleshy stalk of the flower cluster, the core of which passes through the fruit and bears at the summit the familar tuft of scaly leaves. The petals are completely abortive and the sterile ovaries of the flower are embedded in the angular segments that we cut off as rind. If these ovaries were functional they would produce berries. The flowers, if ever produced, as they may be in some semi-wild reversions of the modern pineapple, are violet or red, followed by a more or less open cluster of berries. Such a plant is useless, but the abortive and coalesced flower cluster forms one of the most fragrant and delicious "fruits" of the tropics.

INDEX

A CATALOG OF SELECTED

DOVER BOOKS

IN ALL FIELDS OF INTEREST

A CATALOG OF SELECTED DOVER
BOOKS IN ALL FIELDS OF INTEREST

CONCERNING THE SPIRITUAL IN ART, Wassily Kandinsky. Pioneering work by father of abstract art. Thoughts on color theory, nature of art. Analysis of earlier masters. 12 illustrations. 80pp. of text. 5⅜ × 8½.   23411-8 Pa. $3.95

ANIMALS: 1,419 Copyright-Free Illustrations of Mammals, Birds, Fish, Insects, etc., Jim Harter (ed.). Clear wood engravings present, in extremely lifelike poses, over 1,000 species of animals. One of the most extensive pictorial sourcebooks of its kind. Captions. Index. 284pp. 9 × 12.   23766-4 Pa. $12.95

CELTIC ART: The Methods of Construction, George Bain. Simple geometric techniques for making Celtic interlacements, spirals, Kells-type initials, animals, humans, etc. Over 500 illustrations. 160pp. 9 × 12. (USO)   22923-8 Pa. $9.95

AN ATLAS OF ANATOMY FOR ARTISTS, Fritz Schider. Most thorough reference work on art anatomy in the world. Hundreds of illustrations, including selections from works by Vesalius, Leonardo, Goya, Ingres, Michelangelo, others. 593 illustrations. 192pp. 7⅛ × 10¼.   20241-0 Pa. $9.95

CELTIC HAND STROKE-BY-STROKE (Irish Half-Uncial from "The Book of Kells"): An Arthur Baker Calligraphy Manual, Arthur Baker. Complete guide to creating each letter of the alphabet in distinctive Celtic manner. Covers hand position, strokes, pens, inks, paper, more. Illustrated. 48pp. 8¼ × 11.
24336-2 Pa. $3.95

EASY ORIGAMI, John Montroll. Charming collection of 32 projects (hat, cup, pelican, piano, swan, many more) specially designed for the novice origami hobbyist. Clearly illustrated easy-to-follow instructions insure that even beginning papercrafters will achieve successful results. 48pp. 8¼ × 11.   27298-2 Pa. $2.95

THE COMPLETE BOOK OF BIRDHOUSE CONSTRUCTION FOR WOOD-WORKERS, Scott D. Campbell. Detailed instructions, illustrations, tables. Also data on bird habitat and instinct patterns. Bibliography. 3 tables. 63 illustrations in 15 figures. 48pp. 5¼ × 8½.   24407-5 Pa. $1.95

BLOOMINGDALE'S ILLUSTRATED 1886 CATALOG: Fashions, Dry Goods and Housewares, Bloomingdale Brothers. Famed merchants' extremely rare catalog depicting about 1,700 products: clothing, housewares, firearms, dry goods, jewelry, more. Invaluable for dating, identifying vintage items. Also, copyright-free graphics for artists, designers. Co-published with Henry Ford Museum & Green-field Village. 160pp. 8¼ × 11.   25780-0 Pa. $9.95

HISTORIC COSTUME IN PICTURES, Braun & Schneider. Over 1,450 costumed figures in clearly detailed engravings—from dawn of civilization to end of 19th century. Captions. Many folk costumes. 256pp. 8⅜ × 11¼.   23150-X Pa. $11.95

STICKLEY CRAFTSMAN FURNITURE CATALOGS, Gustav Stickley and L. & J. G. Stickley. Beautiful, functional furniture in two authentic catalogs from 1910. 594 illustrations, including 277 photos, show settles, rockers, armchairs, reclining chairs, bookcases, desks, tables. 183pp. 6½ × 9¼. 23838-5 Pa. $9.95

AMERICAN LOCOMOTIVES IN HISTORIC PHOTOGRAPHS: 1858 to 1949, Ron Ziel (ed.). A rare collection of 126 meticulously detailed official photographs, called "builder portraits," of American locomotives that majestically chronicle the rise of steam locomotive power in America. Introduction. Detailed captions. xi + 129pp. 9 × 12. 27393-8 Pa. $12.95

AMERICA'S LIGHTHOUSES: An Illustrated History, Francis Ross Holland, Jr. Delightfully written, profusely illustrated fact-filled survey of over 200 American lighthouses since 1716. History, anecdotes, technological advances, more. 240pp. 8 × 10¾. 25576-X Pa. $11.95

TOWARDS A NEW ARCHITECTURE, Le Corbusier. Pioneering manifesto by founder of "International School." Technical and aesthetic theories, views of industry, economics, relation of form to function, "mass-production split" and much more. Profusely illustrated. 320pp. 6⅛ × 9¼. (USO) 25023-7 Pa. $9.95

HOW THE OTHER HALF LIVES, Jacob Riis. Famous journalistic record, exposing poverty and degradation of New York slums around 1900, by major social reformer. 100 striking and influential photographs. 233pp. 10 × 7⅞. 22012-5 Pa $10.95

FRUIT KEY AND TWIG KEY TO TREES AND SHRUBS, William M. Harlow. One of the handiest and most widely used identification aids. Fruit key covers 120 deciduous and evergreen species; twig key 160 deciduous species. Easily used. Over 300 photographs. 126pp. 5⅜ × 8½. 20511-8 Pa. $3.95

COMMON BIRD SONGS, Dr. Donald J. Borror. Songs of 60 most common U.S. birds: robins, sparrows, cardinals, bluejays, finches, more—arranged in order of increasing complexity. Up to 9 variations of songs of each species. Cassette and manual 99911-4 $8.95

ORCHIDS AS HOUSE PLANTS, Rebecca Tyson Northen. Grow cattleyas and many other kinds of orchids—in a window, in a case, or under artificial light. 63 illustrations. 148pp. 5⅜ × 8½. 23261-1 Pa. $4.95

MONSTER MAZES, Dave Phillips. Masterful mazes at four levels of difficulty. Avoid deadly perils and evil creatures to find magical treasures. Solutions for all 32 exciting illustrated puzzles. 48pp. 8¼ × 11. 26005-4 Pa. $2.95

MOZART'S DON GIOVANNI (DOVER OPERA LIBRETTO SERIES), Wolfgang Amadeus Mozart. Introduced and translated by Ellen H. Bleiler. Standard Italian libretto, with complete English translation. Convenient and thoroughly portable—an ideal companion for reading along with a recording or the performance itself. Introduction. List of characters. Plot summary. 121pp. 5¼ × 8½. 24944-1 Pa. $2.95

TECHNICAL MANUAL AND DICTIONARY OF CLASSICAL BALLET, Gail Grant. Defines, explains, comments on steps, movements, poses and concepts. 15-page pictorial section. Basic book for student, viewer. 127pp. 5⅜ × 8½. 21843-0 Pa. $4.95

BRASS INSTRUMENTS: Their History and Development, Anthony Baines. Authoritative, updated survey of the evolution of trumpets, trombones, bugles, cornets, French horns, tubas and other brass wind instruments. Over 140 illustrations and 48 music examples. Corrected and updated by author. New preface. Bibliography. 320pp. 5⅜ × 8½. 27574-4 Pa. $9.95

HOLLYWOOD GLAMOR PORTRAITS, John Kobal (ed.). 145 photos from 1926-49. Harlow, Gable, Bogart, Bacall; 94 stars in all. Full background on photographers, technical aspects. 160pp. 8⅜ × 11¼. 23352-9 Pa. $11.95

MAX AND MORITZ, Wilhelm Busch. Great humor classic in both German and English. Also 10 other works: "Cat and Mouse," "Plisch and Plumm," etc. 216pp. 5⅜ × 8½. 20181-3 Pa. $5.95

THE RAVEN AND OTHER FAVORITE POEMS, Edgar Allan Poe. Over 40 of the author's most memorable poems: "The Bells," "Ulalume," "Israfel," "To Helen," "The Conqueror Worm," "Eldorado," "Annabel Lee," many more. Alphabetic lists of titles and first lines. 64pp. 5³⁄₁₆ × 8¼. 26685-0 Pa. $1.00

SEVEN SCIENCE FICTION NOVELS, H. G. Wells. The standard collection of the great novels. Complete, unabridged. First Men in the Moon, Island of Dr. Moreau, War of the Worlds, Food of the Gods, Invisible Man, Time Machine, In the Days of the Comet. Total of 1,015pp. 5⅜ × 8½. (USO) 20264-X Clothbd. $29.95

AMULETS AND SUPERSTITIONS, E. A. Wallis Budge. Comprehensive discourse on origin, powers of amulets in many ancient cultures: Arab, Persian, Babylonian, Assyrian, Egyptian, Gnostic, Hebrew, Phoenician, Syriac, etc. Covers cross, swastika, crucifix, seals, rings, stones, etc. 584pp. 5⅜ × 8½. 23573-4 Pa. $12.95

RUSSIAN STORIES/PYCCKNE PACCKA3bl: A Dual-Language Book, edited by Gleb Struve. Twelve tales by such masters as Chekhov, Tolstoy, Dostoevsky, Pushkin, others. Excellent word-for-word English translations on facing pages, plus teaching and study aids, Russian/English vocabulary, biographical/critical introductions, more. 416pp. 5⅜ × 8½. 26244-8 Pa. $8.95

PHILADELPHIA THEN AND NOW: 60 Sites Photographed in the Past and Present, Kenneth Finkel and Susan Oyama. Rare photographs of City Hall, Logan Square, Independence Hall, Betsy Ross House, other landmarks juxtaposed with contemporary views. Captures changing face of historic city. Introduction. Captions. 128pp. 8¼ × 11. 25790-8 Pa. $9.95

AIA ARCHITECTURAL GUIDE TO NASSAU AND SUFFOLK COUNTIES, LONG ISLAND, The American Institute of Architects, Long Island Chapter, and the Society for the Preservation of Long Island Antiquities. Comprehensive, well-researched and generously illustrated volume brings to life over three centuries of Long Island's great architectural heritage. More than 240 photographs with authoritative, extensively detailed captions. 176pp. 8¼ × 11. 26946-9 Pa. $14.95

NORTH AMERICAN INDIAN LIFE: Customs and Traditions of 23 Tribes, Elsie Clews Parsons (ed.). 27 fictionalized essays by noted anthropologists examine religion, customs, government, additional facets of life among the Winnebago, Crow, Zuni, Eskimo, other tribes. 480pp. 6⅛ × 9¼. 27377-6 Pa. $10.95

FRANK LLOYD WRIGHT'S HOLLYHOCK HOUSE, Donald Hoffmann. Lavishly illustrated, carefully documented study of one of Wright's most controversial residential designs. Over 120 photographs, floor plans, elevations, etc. Detailed perceptive text by noted Wright scholar. Index. 128pp. 9¼ × 10¾. 27133-1 Pa. $11.95

THE MALE AND FEMALE FIGURE IN MOTION: 60 Classic Photographic Sequences, Eadweard Muybridge. 60 true-action photographs of men and women walking, running, climbing, bending, turning, etc., reproduced from rare 19th-century masterpiece. vi + 121pp. 9 × 12. 24745-7 Pa. $10.95

1001 QUESTIONS ANSWERED ABOUT THE SEASHORE, N. J. Berrill and Jacquelyn Berrill. Queries answered about dolphins, sea snails, sponges, starfish, fishes, shore birds, many others. Covers appearance, breeding, growth, feeding, much more. 305pp. 5¼ × 8¼. 23366-9 Pa. $7.95

GUIDE TO OWL WATCHING IN NORTH AMERICA, Donald S. Heintzelman. Superb guide offers complete data and descriptions of 19 species: barn owl, screech owl, snowy owl, many more. Expert coverage of owl-watching equipment, conservation, migrations and invasions, etc. Guide to observing sites. 84 illustrations. xiii + 193pp. 5⅜ × 8½. 27344-X Pa. $8.95

MEDICINAL AND OTHER USES OF NORTH AMERICAN PLANTS: A Historical Survey with Special Reference to the Eastern Indian Tribes, Charlotte Erichsen-Brown. Chronological historical citations document 500 years of usage of plants, trees, shrubs native to eastern Canada, northeastern U.S. Also complete identifying information. 343 illustrations. 544pp. 6½ × 9¼. 25951-X Pa. $12.95

STORYBOOK MAZES, Dave Phillips. 23 stories and mazes on two-page spreads: Wizard of Oz, Treasure Island, Robin Hood, etc. Solutions. 64pp. 8¼ × 11. 23628-5 Pa. $2.95

NEGRO FOLK MUSIC, U.S.A., Harold Courlander. Noted folklorist's scholarly yet readable analysis of rich and varied musical tradition. Includes authentic versions of over 40 folk songs. Valuable bibliography and discography. xi + 324pp. 5⅜ × 8½. 27350-4 Pa. $7.95

MOVIE-STAR PORTRAITS OF THE FORTIES, John Kobal (ed.). 163 glamor, studio photos of 106 stars of the 1940s: Rita Hayworth, Ava Gardner, Marlon Brando, Clark Gable, many more. 176pp. 8⅜ × 11¼. 23546-7 Pa. $11.95

BENCHLEY LOST AND FOUND, Robert Benchley. Finest humor from early 30s, about pet peeves, child psychologists, post office and others. Mostly unavailable elsewhere. 73 illustrations by Peter Arno and others. 183pp. 5⅜ × 8½. 22410-4 Pa. $5.95

YEKL and THE IMPORTED BRIDEGROOM AND OTHER STORIES OF YIDDISH NEW YORK, Abraham Cahan. Film Hester Street based on Yekl (1896). Novel, other stories among first about Jewish immigrants on N.Y.'s East Side. 240pp. 5⅜ × 8½. 22427-9 Pa. $6.95

SELECTED POEMS, Walt Whitman. Generous sampling from *Leaves of Grass*. Twenty-four poems include "I Hear America Singing," "Song of the Open Road," "I Sing the Body Electric," "When Lilacs Last in the Dooryard Bloom'd," "O Captain! My Captain!"—all reprinted from an authoritative edition. Lists of titles and first lines. 128pp. 5³⁄₁₆ × 8¼. 26878-0 Pa. $1.00

THE BEST TALES OF HOFFMANN, E. T. A. Hoffmann. 10 of Hoffmann's most important stories: "Nutcracker and the King of Mice," "The Golden Flowerpot," etc. 458pp. 5⅜ × 8½. 21793-0 Pa. $8.95

FROM FETISH TO GOD IN ANCIENT EGYPT, E. A. Wallis Budge. Rich detailed survey of Egyptian conception of "God" and gods, magic, cult of animals, Osiris, more. Also, superb English translations of hymns and legends. 240 illustrations. 545pp. 5⅜ × 8½. 25803-3 Pa. $11.95

FRENCH STORIES/CONTES FRANÇAIS: A Dual-Language Book, Wallace Fowlie. Ten stories by French masters, Voltaire to Camus: "Micromegas" by Voltaire; "The Atheist's Mass" by Balzac; "Minuet" by de Maupassant; "The Guest" by Camus, six more. Excellent English translations on facing pages. Also French-English vocabulary list, exercises, more. 352pp. 5⅜ × 8½. 26443-2 Pa. $8.95

CHICAGO AT THE TURN OF THE CENTURY IN PHOTOGRAPHS: 122 Historic Views from the Collections of the Chicago Historical Society, Larry A. Viskochil. Rare large-format prints offer detailed views of City Hall, State Street, the Loop, Hull House, Union Station, many other landmarks, circa 1904–1913. Introduction. Captions. Maps. 144pp. 9⅜ × 12¼. 24656-6 Pa. $12.95

OLD BROOKLYN IN EARLY PHOTOGRAPHS, 1865–1929, William Lee Younger. Luna Park, Gravesend race track, construction of Grand Army Plaza, moving of Hotel Brighton, etc. 157 previously unpublished photographs. 165pp. 8⅞ × 11¾. 23587-4 Pa. $13.95

THE MYTHS OF THE NORTH AMERICAN INDIANS, Lewis Spence. Rich anthology of the myths and legends of the Algonquins, Iroquois, Pawnees and Sioux, prefaced by an extensive historical and ethnological commentary. 36 illustrations. 480pp. 5⅜ × 8½. 25967-6 Pa. $8.95

AN ENCYCLOPEDIA OF BATTLES: Accounts of Over 1,560 Battles from 1479 B.C. to the Present, David Eggenberger. Essential details of every major battle in recorded history from the first battle of Megiddo in 1479 B.C. to Grenada in 1984. List of Battle Maps. New Appendix covering the years 1967–1984. Index. 99 illustrations. 544pp. 6½ × 9¼. 24913-1 Pa. $14.95

SAILING ALONE AROUND THE WORLD, Captain Joshua Slocum. First man to sail around the world, alone, in small boat. One of great feats of seamanship told in delightful manner. 67 illustrations. 294pp. 5⅜ × 8½. 20326-3 Pa. $5.95

ANARCHISM AND OTHER ESSAYS, Emma Goldman. Powerful, penetrating, prophetic essays on direct action, role of minorities, prison reform, puritan hypocrisy, violence, etc. 271pp. 5⅜ × 8½. 22484-8 Pa. $5.95

MYTHS OF THE HINDUS AND BUDDHISTS, Ananda K. Coomaraswamy and Sister Nivedita. Great stories of the epics; deeds of Krishna, Shiva, taken from puranas, Vedas, folk tales; etc. 32 illustrations. 400pp. 5⅜ × 8½. 21759-0 Pa. $9.95

BEYOND PSYCHOLOGY, Otto Rank. Fear of death, desire of immortality, nature of sexuality, social organization, creativity, according to Rankian system. 291pp. 5⅜ × 8½. 20485-5 Pa. $8.95

A THEOLOGICO-POLITICAL TREATISE, Benedict Spinoza. Also contains unfinished Political Treatise. Great classic on religious liberty, theory of government on common consent. R. Elwes translation. Total of 421pp. 5⅜ × 8½. 20249-6 Pa. $8.95

MY BONDAGE AND MY FREEDOM, Frederick Douglass. Born a slave, Douglass became outspoken force in antislavery movement. The best of Douglass' autobiographies. Graphic description of slave life. 464pp. 5⅜ × 8½. 22457-0 Pa. **$8.95**

FOLLOWING THE EQUATOR: A Journey Around the World, Mark Twain. Fascinating humorous account of 1897 voyage to Hawaii, Australia, India, New Zealand, etc. Ironic, bemused reports on peoples, customs, climate, flora and fauna, politics, much more. 197 illustrations. 720pp. 5⅜ × 8½. 26113-1 Pa. **$15.95**

THE PEOPLE CALLED SHAKERS, Edward D. Andrews. Definitive study of Shakers: origins, beliefs, practices, dances, social organization, furniture and crafts, etc. 33 illustrations. 351pp. 5⅜ × 8½. 21081-2 Pa. **$8.95**

THE MYTHS OF GREECE AND ROME, H. A. Guerber. A classic of mythology, generously illustrated, long prized for its simple, graphic, accurate retelling of the principal myths of Greece and Rome, and for its commentary on their origins and significance. With 64 illustrations by Michelangelo, Raphael, Titian, Rubens, Canova, Bernini and others. 480pp. 5⅜ × 8½. 27584-1 Pa. **$9.95**

PSYCHOLOGY OF MUSIC, Carl E. Seashore. Classic work discusses music as a medium from psychological viewpoint. Clear treatment of physical acoustics, auditory apparatus, sound perception, development of musical skills, nature of musical feeling, host of other topics. 88 figures. 408pp. 5⅜ × 8½. 21851-1 Pa. **$9.95**

THE PHILOSOPHY OF HISTORY, Georg W. Hegel. Great classic of Western thought develops concept that history is not chance but rational process, the evolution of freedom. 457pp. 5⅜ × 8½. 20112-0 Pa. **$9.95**

THE BOOK OF TEA, Kakuzo Okakura. Minor classic of the Orient: entertaining, charming explanation, interpretation of traditional Japanese culture in terms of tea ceremony. 94pp. 5⅜ × 8½. 20070-1 Pa. **$3.95**

LIFE IN ANCIENT EGYPT, Adolf Erman. Fullest, most thorough, detailed older account with much not in more recent books, domestic life, religion, magic, medicine, commerce, much more. Many illustrations reproduce tomb paintings, carvings, hieroglyphs, etc. 597pp. 5⅜ × 8½. 22632-8 Pa. **$10.95**

SUNDIALS, Their Theory and Construction, Albert Waugh. Far and away the best, most thorough coverage of ideas, mathematics concerned, types, construction, adjusting anywhere. Simple, nontechnical treatment allows even children to build several of these dials. Over 100 illustrations. 230pp. 5⅜ × 8½. 22947-5 Pa. **$7.95**

DYNAMICS OF FLUIDS IN POROUS MEDIA, Jacob Bear. For advanced students of ground water hydrology, soil mechanics and physics, drainage and irrigation engineering, and more. 335 illustrations. Exercises, with answers. 784pp. 6⅛ × 9¼. 65675-6 Pa. **$19.95**

SONGS OF EXPERIENCE: Facsimile Reproduction with 26 Plates in Full Color, William Blake. 26 full-color plates from a rare 1826 edition. Includes "The Tyger," "London," "Holy Thursday," and other poems. Printed text of poems. 48pp. 5¼ × 7. 24636-1 Pa. **$4.95**

OLD-TIME VIGNETTES IN FULL COLOR, Carol Belanger Grafton (ed.). Over 390 charming, often sentimental illustrations, selected from archives of Victorian graphics—pretty women posing, children playing, food, flowers, kittens and puppies, smiling cherubs, birds and butterflies, much more. All copyright-free. 48pp. 9¼ × 12¼. 27269-9 Pa. **$5.95**

PERSPECTIVE FOR ARTISTS, Rex Vicat Cole. Depth, perspective of sky and sea, shadows, much more, not usually covered. 391 diagrams, 81 reproductions of drawings and paintings. 279pp. 5⅜ × 8½. 22487-2 Pa. $6.95

DRAWING THE LIVING FIGURE, Joseph Sheppard. Innovative approach to artistic anatomy focuses on specifics of surface anatomy, rather than muscles and bones. Over 170 drawings of live models in front, back and side views, and in widely varying poses. Accompanying diagrams. 177 illustrations. Introduction. Index. 144pp. 8⅜ × 11¼. 26723-7 Pa. $8.95

GOTHIC AND OLD ENGLISH ALPHABETS: 100 Complete Fonts, Dan X. Solo. Add power, elegance to posters, signs, other graphics with 100 stunning copyright-free alphabets: Blackstone, Dolbey, Germania, 97 more—including many lower-case, numerals, punctuation marks. 104pp. 8⅛ × 11. 24695-7 Pa. $8.95

HOW TO DO BEADWORK, Mary White. Fundamental book on craft from simple projects to five-bead chains and woven works. 106 illustrations. 142pp. 5⅜ × 8. 20697-1 Pa. $4.95

THE BOOK OF WOOD CARVING, Charles Marshall Sayers. Finest book for beginners discusses fundamentals and offers 34 designs. "Absolutely first rate . . . well thought out and well executed."—E. J. Tangerman. 118pp. 7¾ × 10⅝. 23654-4 Pa. $5.95

ILLUSTRATED CATALOG OF CIVIL WAR MILITARY GOODS: Union Army Weapons, Insignia, Uniform Accessories, and Other Equipment, Schuyler, Hartley, and Graham. Rare, profusely illustrated 1846 catalog includes Union Army uniform and dress regulations, arms and ammunition, coats, insignia, flags, swords, rifles, etc. 226 illustrations. 160pp. 9 × 12. 24939-5 Pa. $10.95

WOMEN'S FASHIONS OF THE EARLY 1900s: An Unabridged Republication of "New York Fashions, 1909," National Cloak & Suit Co. Rare catalog of mail-order fashions documents women's and children's clothing styles shortly after the turn of the century. Captions offer full descriptions, prices. Invaluable resource for fashion, costume historians. Approximately 725 illustrations. 128pp. 8⅜ × 11¼. 27276-1 Pa. $11.95

THE 1912 AND 1915 GUSTAV STICKLEY FURNITURE CATALOGS, Gustav Stickley. With over 200 detailed illustrations and descriptions, these two catalogs are essential reading and reference materials and identification guides for Stickley furniture. Captions cite materials, dimensions and prices. 112pp. 6½ × 9¼. 26676-1 Pa. $9.95

EARLY AMERICAN LOCOMOTIVES, John H. White, Jr. Finest locomotive engravings from early 19th century: historical (1804–74), main-line (after 1870), special, foreign, etc. 147 plates. 142pp. 11⅜ × 8¼. 22772-3 Pa. $10.95

THE TALL SHIPS OF TODAY IN PHOTOGRAPHS, Frank O. Braynard. Lavishly illustrated tribute to nearly 100 majestic contemporary sailing vessels: Amerigo Vespucci, Clearwater, Constitution, Eagle, Mayflower, Sea Cloud, Victory, many more. Authoritative captions provide statistics, background on each ship. 190 black-and-white photographs and illustrations. Introduction. 128pp. 8⅞ × 11¾. 27163-3 Pa. $13.95

EARLY NINETEENTH-CENTURY CRAFTS AND TRADES, Peter Stockham (ed.). Extremely rare 1807 volume describes to youngsters the crafts and trades of the day: brickmaker, weaver, dressmaker, bookbinder, ropemaker, saddler, many more. Quaint prose, charming illustrations for each craft. 20 black-and-white line illustrations. 192pp. 4⅜ × 6. 27293-1 Pa. $4.95

VICTORIAN FASHIONS AND COSTUMES FROM HARPER'S BAZAR, 1867–1898, Stella Blum (ed.). Day costumes, evening wear, sports clothes, shoes, hats, other accessories in over 1,000 detailed engravings. 320pp. 9⅜ × 12¼. 22990-4 Pa. $13.95

GUSTAV STICKLEY, THE CRAFTSMAN, Mary Ann Smith. Superb study surveys broad scope of Stickley's achievement, especially in architecture. Design philosophy, rise and fall of the Craftsman empire, descriptions and floor plans for many Craftsman houses, more. 86 black-and-white halftones. 31 line illustrations. Introduction. 208pp. 6½ × 9¼. 27210-9 Pa. $9.95

THE LONG ISLAND RAIL ROAD IN EARLY PHOTOGRAPHS, Ron Ziel. Over 220 rare photos, informative text document origin (1844) and development of rail service on Long Island. Vintage views of early trains, locomotives, stations, passengers, crews, much more. Captions. 8⅞ × 11¾. 26301-0 Pa. $13.95

THE BOOK OF OLD SHIPS: From Egyptian Galleys to Clipper Ships, Henry B. Culver. Superb, authoritative history of sailing vessels, with 80 magnificent line illustrations. Galley, bark, caravel, longship, whaler, many more. Detailed, informative text on each vessel by noted naval historian. Introduction. 256pp. 5⅜ × 8½. 27332-6 Pa. $6.95

TEN BOOKS ON ARCHITECTURE, Vitruvius. The most important book ever written on architecture. Early Roman aesthetics, technology, classical orders, site selection, all other aspects. Morgan translation. 331pp. 5⅜ × 8½. 20645-9 Pa. $8.95

THE HUMAN FIGURE IN MOTION, Eadweard Muybridge. More than 4,500 stopped-action photos, in action series, showing undraped men, women, children jumping, lying down, throwing, sitting, wrestling, carrying, etc. 390pp. 7⅞ × 10⅝. 20204-6 Clothbd. $24.95

TREES OF THE EASTERN AND CENTRAL UNITED STATES AND CANADA, William M. Harlow. Best one-volume guide to 140 trees. Full descriptions, woodlore, range, etc. Over 600 illustrations. Handy size. 288pp. 4½ × 6⅜. 20395-6 Pa. $5.95

SONGS OF WESTERN BIRDS, Dr. Donald J. Borror. Complete song and call repertoire of 60 western species, including flycatchers, juncoes, cactus wrens, many more—includes fully illustrated booklet. Cassette and manual 99913-0 $8.95

GROWING AND USING HERBS AND SPICES, Milo Miloradovich. Versatile handbook provides all the information needed for cultivation and use of all the herbs and spices available in North America. 4 illustrations. Index. Glossary. 236pp. 5⅜ × 8½. 25058-X Pa. $6.95

BIG BOOK OF MAZES AND LABYRINTHS, Walter Shepherd. 50 mazes and labyrinths in all—classical, solid, ripple, and more—in one great volume. Perfect inexpensive puzzler for clever youngsters. Full solutions. 112pp. 8⅛ × 11. 22951-3 Pa. $4.95

CATALOG OF DOVER BOOKS

PIANO TUNING, J. Cree Fischer. Clearest, best book for beginner, amateur. Simple repairs, raising dropped notes, tuning by easy method of flattened fifths. No previous skills needed. 4 illustrations. 201pp. 5⅜ × 8½.   23267-0 Pa. $5.95

A SOURCE BOOK IN THEATRICAL HISTORY, A. M. Nagler. Contemporary observers on acting, directing, make-up, costuming, stage props, machinery, scene design, from Ancient Greece to Chekhov. 611pp. 5⅜ × 8½.   20515-0 Pa. $11.95

THE COMPLETE NONSENSE OF EDWARD LEAR, Edward Lear. All nonsense limericks, zany alphabets, Owl and Pussycat, songs, nonsense botany, etc., illustrated by Lear. Total of 320pp. 5⅜ × 8½. (USO)   20167-8 Pa. $6.95

VICTORIAN PARLOUR POETRY: An Annotated Anthology, Michael R. Turner. 117 gems by Longfellow, Tennyson, Browning, many lesser-known poets. "The Village Blacksmith," "Curfew Must Not Ring Tonight," "Only a Baby Small," dozens more, often difficult to find elsewhere. Index of poets, titles, first lines. xxiii + 325pp. 5⅜ × 8¼.   27044-0 Pa. $8.95

DUBLINERS, James Joyce. Fifteen stories offer vivid, tightly focused observations of the lives of Dublin's poorer classes. At least one, "The Dead," is considered a masterpiece. Reprinted complete and unabridged from standard edition. 160pp. 5³⁄₁₆ × 8¼.   26870-5 Pa. $1.00

THE HAUNTED MONASTERY and THE CHINESE MAZE MURDERS, Robert van Gulik. Two full novels by van Gulik, set in 7th-century China, continue adventures of Judge Dee and his companions. An evil Taoist monastery, seemingly supernatural events; overgrown topiary maze hides strange crimes. 27 illustrations. 328pp. 5⅜ × 8½.   23502-5 Pa. $7.95

THE BOOK OF THE SACRED MAGIC OF ABRAMELIN THE MAGE, translated by S. MacGregor Mathers. Medieval manuscript of ceremonial magic. Basic document in Aleister Crowley, Golden Dawn groups. 268pp. 5⅜ × 8½.   23211-5 Pa. $8.95

NEW RUSSIAN-ENGLISH AND ENGLISH-RUSSIAN DICTIONARY, M. A. O'Brien. This is a remarkably handy Russian dictionary, containing a surprising amount of information, including over 70,000 entries. 366pp. 4½ × 6⅛.   20208-9 Pa. $9.95

HISTORIC HOMES OF THE AMERICAN PRESIDENTS, Second, Revised Edition, Irvin Haas. A traveler's guide to American Presidential homes, most open to the public, depicting and describing homes occupied by every American President from George Washington to George Bush. With visiting hours, admission charges, travel routes. 175 photographs. Index. 160pp. 8¼ × 11.   26751-2 Pa. $10.95

NEW YORK IN THE FORTIES, Andreas Feininger. 162 brilliant photographs by the well-known photographer, formerly with *Life* magazine. Commuters, shoppers, Times Square at night, much else from city at its peak. Captions by John von Hartz. 181pp. 9¼ × 10¾.   23585-8 Pa. $12.95

INDIAN SIGN LANGUAGE, William Tomkins. Over 525 signs developed by Sioux and other tribes. Written instructions and diagrams. Also 290 pictographs. 111pp. 6⅛ × 9¼.   22029-X Pa. $3.50

ANATOMY: A Complete Guide for Artists, Joseph Sheppard. A master of figure drawing shows artists how to render human anatomy convincingly. Over 460 illustrations. 224pp. 8⅜ × 11¼.   27279-6 Pa. $10.95

MEDIEVAL CALLIGRAPHY: Its History and Technique, Marc Drogin. Spirited history, comprehensive instruction manual covers 13 styles (ca. 4th century thru 15th). Excellent photographs; directions for duplicating medieval techniques with modern tools. 224pp. 8⅜ × 11¼.   26142-5 Pa. $11.95

DRIED FLOWERS: How to Prepare Them, Sarah Whitlock and Martha Rankin. Complete instructions on how to use silica gel, meal and borax, perlite aggregate, sand and borax, glycerine and water to create attractive permanent flower arrangements. 12 illustrations. 32pp. 5⅜ × 8½.   21802-3 Pa. $1.00

EASY-TO-MAKE BIRD FEEDERS FOR WOODWORKERS, Scott D. Campbell. Detailed, simple-to-use guide for designing, constructing, caring for and using feeders. Text, illustrations for 12 classic and contemporary designs. 96pp. 5⅜ × 8½.
25847-5 Pa. $2.95

OLD-TIME CRAFTS AND TRADES, Peter Stockham. An 1807 book created to teach children about crafts and trades open to them as future careers. It describes in detailed, nontechnical terms 24 different occupations, among them coachmaker, gardener, hairdresser, lacemaker, shoemaker, wheelwright, copper-plate printer, milliner, trunkmaker, merchant and brewer. Finely detailed engravings illustrate each occupation. 192pp. 4⅝ × 6.   27398-9 Pa. $4.95

THE HISTORY OF UNDERCLOTHES, C. Willett Cunnington and Phyllis Cunnington. Fascinating, well-documented survey covering six centuries of English undergarments, enhanced with over 100 illustrations: 12th-century laced-up bodice, footed long drawers (1795), 19th-century bustles, 19th-century corsets for men, Victorian "bust improvers," much more. 272pp. 5⅜ × 8¼. 27124-2 Pa. $9.95

ARTS AND CRAFTS FURNITURE: The Complete Brooks Catalog of 1912, Brooks Manufacturing Co. Photos and detailed descriptions of more than 150 now very collectible furniture designs from the Arts and Crafts movement depict davenports, settees, buffets, desks, tables, chairs, bedsteads, dressers and more, all built of solid, quarter-sawed oak. Invaluable for students and enthusiasts of antiques, Americana and the decorative arts. 80pp. 6½ × 9¼.   27471-3 Pa. $7.95

HOW WE INVENTED THE AIRPLANE: An Illustrated History, Orville Wright. Fascinating firsthand account covers early experiments, construction of planes and motors, first flights, much more. Introduction and commentary by Fred C. Kelly. 76 photographs. 96pp. 8¼ × 11.   25662-6 Pa. $8.95

THE ARTS OF THE SAILOR: Knotting, Splicing and Ropework, Hervey Garrett Smith. Indispensable shipboard reference covers tools, basic knots and useful hitches; handsewing and canvas work, more. Over 100 illustrations. Delightful reading for sea lovers. 256pp. 5⅜ × 8½.   26440-8 Pa. $7.95

FRANK LLOYD WRIGHT'S FALLINGWATER: The House and Its History, Second, Revised Edition, Donald Hoffmann. A total revision—both in text and illustrations—of the standard document on Fallingwater, the boldest, most personal architectural statement of Wright's mature years, updated with valuable new material from the recently opened Frank Lloyd Wright Archives. "Fascinating"—*The New York Times.* 116 illustrations. 128pp. 9¼ × 10¾.
27430-6 Pa. $10.95

CATALOG OF DOVER BOOKS

PHOTOGRAPHIC SKETCHBOOK OF THE CIVIL WAR, Alexander Gardner. 100 photos taken on field during the Civil War. Famous shots of Manassas, Harper's Ferry, Lincoln, Richmond, slave pens, etc. 244pp. 10⅝ × 8¼.
22731-6 Pa. $9.95

FIVE ACRES AND INDEPENDENCE, Maurice G. Kains. Great back-to-the-land classic explains basics of self-sufficient farming. The one book to get. 95 illustrations. 397pp. 5⅜ × 8½. 20974-1 Pa. $7.95

SONGS OF EASTERN BIRDS, Dr. Donald J. Borror. Songs and calls of 60 species most common to eastern U.S.: warblers, woodpeckers, flycatchers, thrushes, larks, many more in high-quality recording. Cassette and manual 99912-2 $8.95

A MODERN HERBAL, Margaret Grieve. Much the fullest, most exact, most useful compilation of herbal material. Gigantic alphabetical encyclopedia, from aconite to zedoary, gives botanical information, medical properties, folklore, economic uses, much else. Indispensable to serious reader. 161 illustrations. 888pp. 6½ × 9¼. 2-vol. set. (USO) Vol. I: 22798-7 Pa. $9.95
Vol. II: 22799-5 Pa. $9.95

HIDDEN TREASURE MAZE BOOK, Dave Phillips. Solve 34 challenging mazes accompanied by heroic tales of adventure. Evil dragons, people-eating plants, bloodthirsty giants, many more dangerous adversaries lurk at every twist and turn. 34 mazes, stories, solutions. 48pp. 8¼ × 11. 24566-7 Pa. $2.95

LETTERS OF W. A. MOZART, Wolfgang A. Mozart. Remarkable letters show bawdy wit, humor, imagination, musical insights, contemporary musical world; includes some letters from Leopold Mozart. 276pp. 5⅜ × 8½. 22859-2 Pa. $7.95

BASIC PRINCIPLES OF CLASSICAL BALLET, Agrippina Vaganova. Great Russian theoretician, teacher explains methods for teaching classical ballet. 118 illustrations. 175pp. 5⅜ × 8½. 22036-2 Pa. $4.95

THE JUMPING FROG, Mark Twain. Revenge edition. The original story of The Celebrated Jumping Frog of Calaveras County, a hapless French translation, and Twain's hilarious "retranslation" from the French. 12 illustrations. 66pp. 5⅜ × 8½. 22686-7 Pa. $3.95

BEST REMEMBERED POEMS, Martin Gardner (ed.). The 126 poems in this superb collection of 19th- and 20th-century British and American verse range from Shelley's "To a Skylark" to the impassioned "Renascence" of Edna St. Vincent Millay and to Edward Lear's whimsical "The Owl and the Pussycat." 224pp. 5⅜ × 8½.
27165-X Pa. $4.95

COMPLETE SONNETS, William Shakespeare. Over 150 exquisite poems deal with love, friendship, the tyranny of time, beauty's evanescence, death and other themes in language of remarkable power, precision and beauty. Glossary of archaic terms. 80pp. 5³⁄₁₆ × 8¼. 26686-9 Pa. $1.00

BODIES IN A BOOKSHOP, R. T. Campbell. Challenging mystery of blackmail and murder with ingenious plot and superbly drawn characters. In the best tradition of British suspense fiction. 192pp. 5⅜ × 8½. 24720-1 Pa. $5.95

THE WIT AND HUMOR OF OSCAR WILDE, Alvin Redman (ed.). More than 1,000 ripostes, paradoxes, wisecracks: Work is the curse of the drinking classes; I can resist everything except temptation; etc. 258pp. 5⅜ × 8½. 20602-5 Pa. $5.95

SHAKESPEARE LEXICON AND QUOTATION DICTIONARY, Alexander Schmidt. Full definitions, locations, shades of meaning in every word in plays and poems. More than 50,000 exact quotations. 1,485pp. 6½ × 9¼. 2-vol. set.
Vol. I: 22726-X Pa. $16.95
Vol. 2: 22727-8 Pa. $15.95

SELECTED POEMS, Emily Dickinson. Over 100 best-known, best-loved poems by one of America's foremost poets, reprinted from authoritative early editions. No comparable edition at this price. Index of first lines. 64pp. 5$\frac{3}{16}$ × 8¼.
26466-1 Pa. $1.00

CELEBRATED CASES OF JUDGE DEE (DEE GOONG AN), translated by Robert van Gulik. Authentic 18th-century Chinese detective novel; Dee and associates solve three interlocked cases. Led to van Gulik's own stories with same characters. Extensive introduction. 9 illustrations. 237pp. 5⅜ × 8½.
23337-5 Pa. $6.95

THE MALLEUS MALEFICARUM OF KRAMER AND SPRENGER, translated by Montague Summers. Full text of most important witchhunter's "bible," used by both Catholics and Protestants. 278pp. 6⅝ × 10. 22802-9 Pa. $11.95

SPANISH STORIES/CUENTOS ESPAÑOLES: A Dual-Language Book, Angel Flores (ed.). Unique format offers 13 great stories in Spanish by Cervantes, Borges, others. Faithful English translations on facing pages. 352pp. 5⅜ × 8½.
25399-6 Pa. $8.95

THE CHICAGO WORLD'S FAIR OF 1893: A Photographic Record, Stanley Appelbaum (ed.). 128 rare photos show 200 buildings, Beaux-Arts architecture, Midway, original Ferris Wheel, Edison's kinetoscope, more. Architectural emphasis; full text. 116pp. 8¼ × 11. 23990-X Pa. $9.95

OLD QUEENS, N.Y., IN EARLY PHOTOGRAPHS, Vincent F. Seyfried and William Asadorian. Over 160 rare photographs of Maspeth, Jamaica, Jackson Heights, and other areas. Vintage views of DeWitt Clinton mansion, 1939 World's Fair and more. Captions. 192pp. 8⅞ × 11. 26358-4 Pa. $12.95

CAPTURED BY THE INDIANS: 15 Firsthand Accounts, 1750–1870, Frederick Drimmer. Astounding true historical accounts of grisly torture, bloody conflicts, relentless pursuits, miraculous escapes and more, by people who lived to tell the tale. 384pp. 5⅜ × 8½. 24901-8 Pa. $8.95

THE WORLD'S GREAT SPEECHES, Lewis Copeland and Lawrence W. Lamm (eds.). Vast collection of 278 speeches of Greeks to 1970. Powerful and effective models; unique look at history. 842pp. 5⅜ × 8½. 20468-5 Pa. $14.95

THE BOOK OF THE SWORD, Sir Richard F. Burton. Great Victorian scholar/adventurer's eloquent, erudite history of the "queen of weapons"—from prehistory to early Roman Empire. Evolution and development of early swords, variations (sabre, broadsword, cutlass, scimitar, etc.), much more. 336pp. 6⅛ × 9¼. 25434-8 Pa. $8.95

AUTOBIOGRAPHY: The Story of My Experiments with Truth, Mohandas K. Gandhi. Boyhood, legal studies, purification, the growth of the Satyagraha (nonviolent protest) movement. Critical, inspiring work of the man responsible for the freedom of India. 480pp. 5⅜ × 8½. (USO)   24593-4 Pa. **$8.95**

CELTIC MYTHS AND LEGENDS, T. W. Rolleston. Masterful retelling of Irish and Welsh stories and tales. Cuchulain, King Arthur, Deirdre, the Grail, many more. First paperback edition. 58 full-page illustrations. 512pp. 5⅜ × 8½.
26507-2 Pa. **$9.95**

THE PRINCIPLES OF PSYCHOLOGY, William James. Famous long course complete, unabridged. Stream of thought, time perception, memory, experimental methods; great work decades ahead of its time. 94 figures. 1,391pp. 5⅜ × 8½. 2-vol. set.
Vol. I: 20381-6 Pa. **$12.95**
Vol. II: 20382-4 Pa. **$12.95**

THE WORLD AS WILL AND REPRESENTATION, Arthur Schopenhauer. Definitive English translation of Schopenhauer's life work, correcting more than 1,000 errors, omissions in earlier translations. Translated by E. F. J. Payne. Total of 1,269pp. 5⅜ × 8½. 2-vol. set.   Vol. 1: 21761-2 Pa. **$11.95**
Vol. 2: 21762-0 Pa. **$11.95**

MAGIC AND MYSTERY IN TIBET, Madame Alexandra David-Neel. Experiences among lamas, magicians, sages, sorcerers, Bonpa wizards. A true psychic discovery. 32 illustrations. 321pp. 5⅜ × 8½. (USO)   22682-4 Pa. **$8.95**

THE EGYPTIAN BOOK OF THE DEAD, E. A. Wallis Budge. Complete reproduction of Ani's papyrus, finest ever found. Full hieroglyphic text, interlinear transliteration, word-for-word translation, smooth translation. 533pp. 6½ × 9¼.
21866-X Pa. **$9.95**

MATHEMATICS FOR THE NONMATHEMATICIAN, Morris Kline. Detailed, college-level treatment of mathematics in cultural and historical context, with numerous exercises. Recommended Reading Lists. Tables. Numerous figures. 641pp. 5⅜ × 8½.   24823-2 Pa. **$11.95**

THEORY OF WING SECTIONS: Including a Summary of Airfoil Data, Ira H. Abbott and A. E. von Doenhoff. Concise compilation of subsonic aerodynamic characteristics of NACA wing sections, plus description of theory. 350pp. of tables. 693pp. 5⅜ × 8½.   60586-8 Pa. **$14.95**

THE RIME OF THE ANCIENT MARINER, Gustave Doré, S. T. Coleridge. Doré's finest work; 34 plates capture moods, subtleties of poem. Flawless full-size reproductions printed on facing pages with authoritative text of poem. "Beautiful. Simply beautiful."—*Publisher's Weekly.* 77pp. 9¼ × 12.   22305-1 Pa. **$6.95**

NORTH AMERICAN INDIAN DESIGNS FOR ARTISTS AND CRAFTS-PEOPLE, Eva Wilson. Over 360 authentic copyright-free designs adapted from Navajo blankets, Hopi pottery, Sioux buffalo hides, more. Geometrics, symbolic figures, plant and animal motifs, etc. 128pp. 8⅜ × 11. (EUK)   25341-4 Pa. **$7.95**

SCULPTURE: Principles and Practice, Louis Slobodkin. Step-by-step approach to clay, plaster, metals, stone; classical and modern. 253 drawings, photos. 255pp. 8⅛ × 11.   22960-2 Pa. **$10.95**

THE INFLUENCE OF SEA POWER UPON HISTORY, 1660–1783, A. T. Mahan. Influential classic of naval history and tactics still used as text in war colleges. First paperback edition. 4 maps. 24 battle plans. 640pp. 5⅜ × 8½.
25509-3 Pa. $12.95

THE STORY OF THE TITANIC AS TOLD BY ITS SURVIVORS, Jack Winocour (ed.). What it was really like. Panic, despair, shocking inefficiency, and a little heroism. More thrilling than any fictional account. 26 illustrations. 320pp. 5⅜ × 8½.
20610-6 Pa. $8.95

FAIRY AND FOLK TALES OF THE IRISH PEASANTRY, William Butler Yeats (ed.). Treasury of 64 tales from the twilight world of Celtic myth and legend: "The Soul Cages," "The Kildare Pooka," "King O'Toole and his Goose," many more. Introduction and Notes by W. B. Yeats. 352pp. 5⅜ × 8½.
26941-8 Pa. $8.95

BUDDHIST MAHAYANA TEXTS, E. B. Cowell and Others (eds.). Superb, accurate translations of basic documents in Mahayana Buddhism, highly important in history of religions. The Buddha-karita of Asvaghosha, Larger Sukhavativyuha, more. 448pp. 5⅜ × 8½. ,
25552-2 Pa. $9.95

ONE TWO THREE . . . INFINITY: Facts and Speculations of Science, George Gamow. Great physicist's fascinating, readable overview of contemporary science: number theory, relativity, fourth dimension, entropy, genes, atomic structure, much more. 128 illustrations. Index. 352pp. 5⅜ × 8½.
25664-2 Pa. $8.95

ENGINEERING IN HISTORY, Richard Shelton Kirby, et al. Broad, nontechnical survey of history's major technological advances: birth of Greek science, industrial revolution, electricity and applied science, 20th-century automation, much more. 181 illustrations. ". . . excellent . . ."—Isis. Bibliography. vii + 530pp. 5⅜ × 8¼.
26412-2 Pa. $14.95